The Land
of Lost
Content

Ian Smillie

THE LAND OF LOST CONTENT

A History of CUSO

Deneau Publishers and Company Ltd.
608 Markham St.,
Toronto, Canada   M6G 2L8

ISBN 0-88879-125-9

Contents

vi

Foreword

I knew, when I was arrested late one sultry, mosquito-filled night in the small West African nation of Sierra Leone, and held for questioning as a suspected missionary, that it would make a good anecdote — if I survived. It was 1967, a time of considerable political tension in Sierra Leone: senior police and army officers had been jailed, and the two lance corporals who apprehended me had misunderstood the President's radio broadcast, warning against an attack by *mercenaries*. They were dutifully rounding up all foreigners who tallied with their image of a missionary — in my case, a twenty-two year old white male who had groggily answered the door in his underwear. I argued that I was neither mercenary nor missionary, but I found, under the circumstances, that Canadian University Service Overseas and CUSO volunteers defied both explanation and comprehension.

What I didn't realize, that bizarre night under the hot yellow lights and the rotating ceiling fan, was that my work in Sierra Leone would lead to many more postings in Asia and Africa, and that my unsatisfactory attempt to explain CUSO would eventually lead to a book on the subject. After leaving Sierra Leone, I worked as a CUSO Field Staff Officer in Nigeria for three years, during the Biafran War. I spent a year in CUSO's Ottawa office before joining CARE in 1972 and taking a job in newly independent Bangladesh. After various peregrinations in internationalism, I returned to CUSO in 1979 as Executive Director, a post I held for four years. Obviously, therefore, I was an active participant in some of the events described in this book, and worked closely with many of the individuals who meander, trot, gallop and occasionally slither through these pages.

Although my portrayal of CUSO is coloured by my own experience of it, I have attempted to let people speak for themselves wherever possible. The only major conceit is that I have removed myself from the action. While this may be slightly dishonest, the book is not a memoir, and in any event, CUSO's achievements have been the work of many people, only a few of whom have been mentioned here. The reader may assume, however, that the chapters on Nigeria, Bangladesh, various aspects of bureaucratic life in Ottawa, and many of the events between 1979 and 1983 contain a good deal of firsthand knowledge and direct experience.

This is not a Pollyanna version of CUSO. The volunteers are here, but I have chosen to tell the story through the events in which CUSO has participated over the past quarter-century. The book is therefore more than a history of CUSO; it is the story of Canada coming of age in the Third World. CUSO remains the only major Canadian presence in many countries of Asia, Africa, the Pacific and the Americas, giving it a unique and sometimes spectacular vantage point from which to view and participate in the beginning of the Third World's modern era.

A note on semantics is perhaps in order, although I have made what I consider a valiant effort to keep the use of 'development set' argot to a minimum. The word 'volunteer' has afforded CUSO many diverting hours of debate through the years and deserves special attention. When some people — perhaps incorrectly equating their own early perceptions of work in the Third World with the idea of self-denial — assumed that 'volunteer' was synonymous with 'sacrifice', the word began to fall from grace, and the search for a new one, devoid of negative connotation, began. 'Cooperant', a typically androgynous Canadian compromise, unknown to Webster and Larousse alike, seemed to do the trick. Even if it wasn't in the dictionary, it had an agreeably collegial ring, one that conveniently avoided any sense of mission, or duty, or burden. 'To cooperate' was, in every sense, reasonable. 'To volunteer' smacked of priggish self-righteousness.

Applying the 'cooperant' label to people who joined CUSO before the word was invented seems like revisionism, however, and in any case, 'cooperant' was never universally accepted. In fact when CUSO began investigations into program possibilities in French-speaking Togo in 1983, the Field Staff Officer was told that 'coopérant' had developed such negative connotations there, thanks to the universally disliked experts from France, that 'voluntaire' should be adopted. CUSO neologists notwithstanding, 'volunteer' still retains its original meaning for most English speakers; namely, someone who undertakes an activity willingly and without promise of recompense. This term has been used throughout the text, and it is hoped that apologies will be accepted by those who have thought of themselves as cooperants and have been otherwise described.

The word 'development' is liberally, even indiscriminately scattered throughout the CUSO odyssey, but a simple explanation of the term, a clear, succinct definition of what it is all about, will not be so easy to find. There is a reason: despite the hundreds of interpretations churned out over the years, development writers seldom agree with one another on a definition; and on the few occasions when they do, the upshot is usually vague, banal and consequently meaningless. Chinua Achebe, in his classic novel about Africa's struggle with conflicting values and cultures, took his title, *Things Fall Apart*, from Yeats, who added, "The centre cannot hold." Development theory is a bit like that, an explosion of ideas, flying off in all directions at once, exploding under the pressures of increasing world poverty, international political awareness and demand for change.

John Spellman, a CUSO Field Staff Officer in the early 1980s, once took the trouble to look up the word 'development' in a dictionary, and discovered to his perverse, academic delight, that it had its origins in the medieval Italian word, 'velupare.' Its nineteenth century French equivalent, 'desvelopper' still meant to unwrap, to free from constraint. Spellman traced the meaning to modern times when it came to imply evolution from a lower to a higher order, a slant altogether different from its original meaning. He detected the transition in the nineteenth century, when colonists, missionaries and anthropologists swarmed over Africa, Asia and the Americas, subduing, uplifting and studying 'primitive' people. Before World War II, the concept had changed slightly, and 'primitive' societies had turned into 'backward' societies. "From primitive, they became backward," Spellman wrote. "From backward they became underdeveloped and from underdeveloped they became developing — that is where they remain today — as developing societies. Or, to put it in political terms, they became known as the Third World. Amazing in its arrogance, that term is basically accepted today to describe most of the people in the world.''*   At its most general level, development implies change, progress, improvement in the human condition. Post-colonial development efforts have been lumped together into what the United Nations has vaguely termed ''development decades,'' the first one of which, from 1960 to 1970, is generally conceded to have been a failure in terms of producing any real change in the lot of ordinary citizens of the Third World. So is the second. The third is not faring much better, partly because governments tend, generally speaking, to concentrate on the *economics* of development: roads, drinkable water, hospitals, electrification and irrigation projects. What has become apparent through three decades of 'development', is that while such activities are essential, the effects will be marginal unless the poor have the means to take real advantage of them through individual and collective action. And without complementary human values — justice, charity, cooperation and respect for nature — economic activity is unlikely to be enough.

Non-governmental agencies like CUSO, though somewhat self-righteous on this point, tend to view development in more holistic terms than governments. At a theoretical level, they are generally satisfied with a brief roundup and speedy execution of pre-1970 'growth models' and 'takeoff theories'. They slalom quickly around and sometimes straight through latter-day concepts of redistribution with growth, basic human needs, the new international economic order and participatory development, behind which, billowing like cumulus clouds of bureaucracies, lurk tens of thousands of experts, studies, reports, conferences and organizations. Non-governmental organizations — NGOs — are more down-to-earth, even slightly subterranean in their pursuit of 'grassroots' development, although as John Spellman caustically but not incorrectly pointed out, they too are occasionally ''as grass roots as a banyan tree.''CUSO's own evolving approach to development will emerge, insofar as it can, through the story of its work.

No single book can do real justice to CUSO; every one of the 8,000

Development Programming in India, by John Spellman, Dec. 24, 1982; CUSO files volunteers who have served could easily fill a chapter, if not a volume, with the drama, the adventure, the hard work and the humour of a two-year assignment. I have tried to capture some of it, and I have not drawn back from describing, as I see them, some of the debacles that the organization has occasionally inflicted on itself. I take full responsibility for the opinions and conclusions, despite the substantial assistance of many friends and colleagues in Canada, Asia, Africa and Britain, who gave me their time and their cooperation. They include Jeanna Baty, Dave Beer, Keith Bezanson, Frank Bogdasavich, Tim Brodhead, Chris Bryant, Sharon Capeling-Alakija, David Catmur, Raymond Clark, Raymond Cournoyer, Colin Freebury, Terry Glavin, John Gordon, Marlene Green, Father Romeo Guilbeault, Jennifer Harold, Diego Lanneuville, Ronald Leger, Barbara and Walter MacLean, Pierpoint Thomson, Jim McFetridge, Bill McNeill, Jack Pearpoint, Jean Pelletier, Wendy Quarry, Ed Ragan, Rieky Stuart, Tim and Sherry Thomson, Murray Thompson, Paul Turcot, Dan Turner and Robin Wilson.

I am grateful for the contributions of several people who assisted at CUSO's birth and who nursed the baby as it grew and matured. They include Geoff Andrew, one of CUSO's most undersung heroes, Guy Arnold, Duncan Edmonds, Francis Leddy, Lewis Perinbam, Fred Stinson and Keith Spicer.

Bill McWhinney assisted with his invaluable recollections of the first years and by preserving, with Dave Godfrey, the early flavour of CUSO in *Man Deserves Man*. I am extremely grateful to Barbara and Peter Hoffman for their reminiscences and for their work in gathering much of the original material for the 'New Jerusalem' and 'Rollercoaster' chapters. Among the scholars whose research shed light on various facets of CUSO were Glen Filson, Paul McGinnis, John Saxby, Roxanna Spicer and Steve Woolcombe.

Special thanks are due to Ron Beltz, Shirley Gordon and Brian Rowe who spent long hours attempting, sometimes successfully, to persuade me into reappraisals, rewrites and reconstructions, and to Margaret Rubin for a typing job of heroic proportions. I would also like to thank the many others who assisted with their time, their friendly criticism and additional material, including Faruque Ahmed, Grant Curtis, Herman Falke, Richard Harmston, Paul Hitschfield, Elizabeth Hutton, Barbara Malone, Boyd McBride, Greg Morely, Michael Oliver, Stan Percival,

Betty Plewes, Robin Sears, Carol Seguin, Robert Sterling and Susanne Wise, Ron and Diane Wensel, Darrell Martindale and Helena Zukowski. I am also grateful to the CUSO Board of Directors for making CUSO's vast, if somewhat disorganized files available to me, along with the photocopier on the tenth floor of the old Slaterbunker.

I am particularly grateful to my wife, Dorienne, whose patience and forbearance gave me the time and place to write the book and who, in bravely struggling through the first draft of most chapters, gave me the confidence to continue.

Ian Smillie,
London,
October, 1985

Chapter 1

Peter Hoffman — The Journey to Lundu

Peter Hoffman's eyes opened. It was dawn, and already he was sweating. Through the soft, diffuse light, he could make out the seams in the tattered mosquito net where rips had been mended. Below, in the streets, there was hawking and spitting; Chinese shopkeepers argued as they clanked open the folding metal shutters of their shops. In the distance, a muezzin intoned the Arabic words that called the Muslim faithful to prayer.

Hoffman watched the ceiling fans rotate. He smelled the fragrance of Asia, redolent of spice and fruit and fish, and a thousand cooking fires. And he wondered how in hell he had talked himself into leaving his comfortable job as a teacher at Ottawa Tech for a position in Sarawak.

Gradually he roused himself. He washed and shaved, and crammed his clothes into his suitcase. He recalled the orientation program that had ended in Canada only days before. Days? It seemed like years ago that they had been practising a few phrases of Malay and talking about their postings.

Sarawak, on the north coast of the Island of Borneo, 450 miles across the South China Sea from Singapore, had for a century been the private fiefdom of the White Rajas, the Brooke family. James Brooke, a model for Conrad's Lord Jim, had assisted the Sultan of Brunei in putting down a rebellion in 1841. Brooke was proclaimed Raja of Sarawak by the grateful Sultan, and under his family's rule, the principality gradually encroached on Brunei, until it was twenty-five times larger than the Sultanate. The land mass was the only large thing about Sarawak, however. Well into the twentieth century, its small population was matched by the small ideas and smaller budgets of the benevolent but permanently Victorian Rajas. There were few roads and few government services; there was little in the way of modern agriculture, and virtually no industry had come to Sarawak. The capital, Kuching, was about the size of Dartmouth, Nova Scotia. It had a small hospital, a small library, a small museum and a beautiful park where a band sometimes played. Everything, including the Astana where the Rajas lived, was Lilliputian. After the Japanese occupation, Charles Vyner Brooke ceded his family's ambition to history, and his country to Britain. Seventeen years later, in 1963, Sarawak became part of the independent Federation of Malaysia.

Four years after that, Peter Hoffman struggled with his suitcase down several flights of narrow stairs to the lobby of his hotel. The manager's son, who apparently lived in his undershirt and boxer shorts, found a taxi and piled Hoffman's bags into the back seat after him. On China Street, the metalsmiths and foundrymen were already at work, hammering out kettles and pots and utensils; in India Street the shutters had been rolled up on shop fronts displaying a profusion of brightly coloured cloth: cotton, bolt upon bolt of brilliant Thai silk, intricate batiks, Dutch Java prints, lace, brocade. The river front was warm with wooden sampans and people with live animals and fresh produce for market. Hoffman saw pineapples, oranges, limes and bananas, and there was strange-looking, exotic fruit that he could not recognize — pomelo, papaya, durian, mango, rambutan.

"At the bus station," Hoffman recalled, "I purchased my ticket by standing at the wicket and muttering one word: 'Lundu.' The agent motioned me to sit and wait."[1] No Lord Jim, he sat obediently and waited, wondering if he would be put on the right bus, or for that matter, any bus. People stared at him. Self-consciously, he recalled the ceremonious West Block dinner in Ottawa for outgoing CUSO volunteers, and he remembered being asked to stand and tell the assembled Members of Parliament where he would be going and what he would do. Their indulgent approval of the volunteers' noble gestures of self-sacrifice had seemed a little overdone at the time. Any lingering vainglory, however, was dispelled at the orientation soon afterwards, when the first real sacrifice was demanded: there it was announced that Malaysia had reduced volunteer salaries from M$300 a month, to M$230 or $900 Canadian *a year*. Recalling what happened next, Peter Hoffman laughed. "We were asked to vote! Would we go at M$230?" Barbara Geddes, a returned volunteer — an 'RV' — from Sarawak, said confidently that they would be able to manage. "It had been perfect for her," Hoffman said, "and it would be perfect for us." So with little more than the enthusiasm of Barbara Geddes to guide them, eight voted to stick with their assignments, while four chose Singapore and five opted for tiny Brunei where the now oil-rich Sultan, having the last laugh on the defunct, oil-less White Rajas, offered salaries of M$600 a month. Retrospectively, in the Kuching bus station, not knowing what might happen to him in the next year, the next day, the next hour, it all seemed painfully remote to Peter Hoffman.

At long last, he was pointed towards the oldest, most decrepit bus at the depot. His bags were heaved onto the roof and tied down. "I climbed aboard, stumbling over bags of rice and crates of baby chicks, and jammed my long legs into a narrow seat. Although no one seemed to be paying particular attention, I was sure everyone in the bus had taken account of every clumsy move I had made."

The bus rattled out of Kuching and was soon rolling down a narrow paved highway, over bridges and through villages, past neatly ordered rubber plantations and spice gardens. Sarawak's rainfall, one of the highest in the world, nourishes a dark, luxuriant jungle that presses in on farm and river and road alike. Foliage and branches brushed lightly against the sides and roof of the bus as it passed, teasing, perhaps testing the mettle of those who ventured through the forest. The pavement ended and the road narrowed. "Every mile or so," Hoffman recalled, "the bus bumped to a stop and another family disembarked to disappear down a jungle path."

Hours passed and the bus rolled on, and finally, he was the only passenger left. He was drenched, as much from apprehension as from the heat. Suddenly, the bus stopped. The driver unloaded his bags, and standing beside Hoffman at the side of the dirt road, he pointed at the jungle and said, "Lundu." Hoffman looked incredulously at the man, and then at the jungle. "I nearly cried," he said.

Wheezing and groaning, the bus turned around and lumbered off in the direction of Kuching, leaving Hoffman, sodden and forlorn, staring at a towering wall of greenery. Gradually, he discerned an opening, and pushing himself forward, discovered, that there was indeed a path, a highly provisional opening, already partially usurped by the encroaching undergrowth. Tentatively, he made his way into the jungle, labouring with the weighty impediments of his previous existence, and after a few hundred yards he staggered into a clearing on the bank of a river. Moored to a stump was a boat, painted in the same colours as the bus that had carried him to the end of the road and standing on the bank nearby, a group of men. "As if they had been waiting my arrival, everyone jumped aboard," Hoffman said. "I followed."

The engine coughed to a start, and the boat, laden with goods and lithe, golden-skinned people, and one fair-haired, red-faced former teacher from Ottawa Tech, eased out into the Kayan River, moving gently against the current. Watching the tangle of trees and vines that reached out above the swirling eddies of the murky water, Peter Hoffman contemplated his position. He wondered if he could fulfill even the least of the rapidly evaporating expectations he had set himself; if he would ever get out alive; if he could survive without going bananas.

The boat nosed its way around bend after never-ending bend. "I tried to relax," he said. But he had little success. "Then, at long last, we pulled up in front of a row of unpainted shophouses lining the bank." *Lundu*. Straining with baggage, he clambered up onto the jetty and was immediately surrounded by dozens of laughing, chattering children.

It was the ultimate moment of truth which came to all volunteers; the moment when at last and finally, they were on their own, when detailed directions, carefully memorized aeons ago in the safety of an orientation program, or an airport, or even a hotel room in Kuching, ran out; the point at which there was no more writing on the page, when the busy, ordered, peopled past opened irrevocably onto a faceless, voiceless future. For weeks, all Peter Hoffman's thoughts had focussed on Sarawak: the land of the White Rajas, of Lord Jim, of the jungle. The enterprise, although somewhat irresolute in purpose, had seemed bold, virtuous, meaningful, and at least had a tangible focus — Lundu.

Now, here he was at last, a wet, pallid fish out of water, his ideas, such as they were, gasping for meaning and direction miles up some muddy river in Borneo. Lundu meant only that he was unknown, friendless, alone, more alone than he had ever been in his life. Surrounded by two dozen laughing, pointing children, his dignity in tatters, Peter Hoffman had reached the nadir of his existence. Unable to go back, afraid to go forward, he summoned all the courage he could command, and blurted out almost every word of Malay he could remember from orientation.

"Saya baharu chegu," he said. "Di mana scholah?" The children giggled, and for a moment, Hoffman thought he was doomed. Then a young man broke through the throng and greeted him. "You new teacher bah. Headmaster will come here to fetch you after class. Come with me."

The suitcases didn't seem quite so heavy as Peter Hoffman struggled up the bank away from the river, away from Ottawa Tech, away from the other life.

Chapter 2

The New Jerusalem

Bring me my bow of burning gold!
Bring me my arrows of desire!
Bring me my spear! O clouds unfold!
Bring me my chariot of fire.

—Blake

C USO was neither the brainchild nor the accomplishment of any single person, though of the many individuals who would later alternate between proprietary assertations of paternity and energetic denials of responsibility for what the child had become, one of the most unusual and enduring was the Malayan-born, Scottish-educated Lewis Perinbam. The summer of 1953, eight years before the creation of CUSO, found him in the southwestern Indian State of Mysore, in the midst of a raucous, irreverant group of Canadians; students and professors who had signed up for a World University Service seminar, and who were now enthusiastically enjoying a skit night, lampooning the Maharaja of Mysore who had opened the seminar in princely style days before.

Perinbam, a kind of proctor for the group, had flown to Mysore from his home in London where he was a staff member of WUS, then a loose international federation of student committees dedicated to principles of peace and international understanding, in the service of which, study seminars were held each summer. International understanding plummetted, however, when agents reported to the Maharaja, much loved by his people, that his Canadian guests had mocked him. Perinbam, unfamiliar with Canadians and Maharajas alike, was summoned to the palace. "I was told that I should make plans to get the Canadians out of Mysore," Perinbam recalled. "I had to plead with the Maharaja, to apologize and explain that no disrespect had been intended. In North America, no one was safe from lampoon; not the Prime Minister, the Governor General, not even the Queen."[1]

The Maharaja relented, but the experience was a seminal one for the young Perinbam who emigrated to Canada later that year to take up a staff position with World University Service of Canada (WUSC). He would always believe that the development of cross-cultural understanding — and caution — were as important an ingredient in international programs as any other.

He found Canadians, particularly students, both inward-looking and narrow, and he discovered, to his surprise, that WUSC was one of the few organizations offering the university community any sort of international involvement. He began to regard the seminars, which WUS headquarters in Geneva saw as an increasingly irrelevant Canadian preoccupation, as an important first step in helping Canadians to make contact with other people. His Asian background added an element of the exotic to his international experience, and the articulate persuasion he brought to bear on the WUSC committees conveyed to the organization some of his own enthusiasm for international development. He travelled extensively across Canada, building and strengthening committees on each campus and initiating fund-raising drives to increase the organization's programming capacity. The arrival of the WUSC 'Treasure Van' for example, loaded with saleable Third World handicrafts, became a major annual event on Canadian campuses.

Through the 1950s, a WUSC scholarship fund grew and a 'Program of Action' was created to assist with projects in developing countries. The seminars continued as well, with students and professors selected on the basis of their intellectual ability, their maturity, and their general leadership qualities. It was a mark of WUSC's proficiency in attracting future Canadian leaders, that so many seminar participants went on to play key roles in public life. The 'alumni' include businessmen, journalists, civil servants, Canada's first Controller General, and seven members of the final Trudeau Cabinet, including the Prime Minister.

During the same period, Perinbam nursed an idea he had derived from the Australian WUS committee. The Australian delegation to the WUS General Assembly in Bombay, in 1950, aware of the negative image that the 'White Australia' policy had created throughout Asia, proposed that Australian volunteers might assist in the reconstruction of post-independence Indonesia. By 1953, the plan had been put into operation, with small groups of volunteers serving as teachers on Indonesian terms and conditions and living with Indonesian families. The Australian government provided the air fare, £50, and a bicycle; after that, the volunteers were on their own. Perinbam visited Indonesia in 1955, and, meeting with some of the Australians and their Indonesian counterparts, was profoundly impressed.

He was particularly touched by the remarks of the Indonesian Ambassador to Australia, regarding the volunteers:

> The fact that for the first time in our experience — and our experience includes many long years of European rule — white people have been ready and eager to live among us on our own standards of salary and living, to share family life with us, to become in truth real members of our community, is indeed striking. Such a contribution is worth immeasurably more to us than the rupiahs which it saves our treasury. It is a demonstration of goodwill and understanding which has moved our hearts greatly and which we feel can do more than all the speeches of people in high places to cement friendly relations between our two nations.[2]

Despite the indifference that he found towards the idea when he returned to Canada, Perinbam kept it in the back of his mind, reviving it again in 1957 at the WUS seminar in Ghana — the first international university meeting to be held in Africa. When Perinbam discussed his idea with the newly independent government's Director of Recruitment and Training, the response was enthusiastic. It was not until the spring of 1959, however, that Perinbam developed a full proposal for what he called a "Canadian Volunteer Program." Voluntary assignments would be arranged in Ghana initially, he proposed, then perhaps in Indonesia, Malaya and Nigeria. It was described as a technical assistance scheme, but Perinbam also saw it as an important tool in providing international experience for Canadians. "Canada's growing stature in international affairs constantly imposes fresh and increasing demands for Canadian leadership," he wrote, but he felt that Canada desperately lacked people with adequate experience to take up the call.   He submitted the proposal to the Canadian government, suggesting a budget of $1,800 per volunteer and a total administrative cost of $3,500, but once again, the idea fell on deaf ears. Perinbam might have pursued the idea further through WUSC, but by now, having spent six years with the organization, he was ready for new horizons, and not long afterwards he left WUSC to become Secretary General of the Canadian Commission for UNESCO.

His dedication to the idea of a volunteer program was soon to be rewarded, however; what emerged in 1961 bore a remarkable resemblance to his 1959 proposal.

At almost precisely the same time as Lewis Perinbam was writing up his volunteer proposal in the summer of 1959, Keith Spicer, a young PhD student at the University of Toronto, received a pre-doctoral Canada Council fellowship to study Canada's tiny aid program in Asia. In the literature, he found a book written the year before by a Canadian missionary in Asia, Dr. Donald Faris. *To Plow With Hope* presented a general overview of bilateral and multilateral aid programs, and gave a competent description of grass roots development from a practitioner's perspective.

Spicer's attention, however, was caught by an imaginative proposal, almost an afterthought, buried in the final pages of the book. "Our youth," Faris wrote, "possess a tremendous potential of energy, idealism and enthusiasm, just waiting to be tapped.

"The reagent needed is the challenge that life's fullest expression is found in serving others. To this end, visualize placing not just a few thousand balding experts in the field to cope with the advancing enemy, but a hundred thousand young people to supplement the other and more seasoned men and women . . . they would be available for loan to governments or private agencies to work with indigenous leaders in the world's needy villages . . . if, in addition to technical skills, these junior experts were equipped with humility and courage, with sincerity and wisdom, they would be able to transmit not only physical satisfaction to the needy, but also lasting values such as friendship, goodwill and understanding."[3]

"It galvanized me," Spicer said. "It absolutely captured me."[4] He began to think how Faris's words might be transformed into something practical, and tried out his ideas on professors and fellow students. Spicer, (who would go on to become Canada's first Commissioner of Official Languages and later, Editor of *The Ottawa Citizen*), wrote a first paper on the idea and decided that it was important enough for him to consult with the highest authority in the land; so he went to Ottawa to see Prime Minister Diefenbaker.

"I was so naive," he said, recalling his trip to the capital. "I just walked in off the street and told the Prime Minister's brother, Elmer, that I had a great idea to help Canada save the world." Perhaps the Prime Minister needed a few good ideas, or maybe it was just a quiet day in Ottawa. In any case, Elmer Diefenbaker ushered Spicer into the august presence of The Chief, where the lanky, brash young scholar spread out his papers and explained the idea. "I told him I was going to Asia and asked if he could do anything to help. I found out what he did when I arrived. He had telegrammed all the embassies, telling them to roll out the red carpet and to let me see anything I wanted."

"Ambassadors (Robert Ford In Egypt) and high commissioners (Herb Moran in Karachi and Chester Ronning in India) treated me as a VIP, having me to grand dinners with ministers and other ambassadors, and sending limousines around. As a 'starving student', I was staggered. Good old Dief . . . ."

Spicer spent the first six months of 1960 doing firsthand research on his thesis while travelling through Egypt, Pakistan, India, Ceylon and Malaya. In India he traced Donald Faris, and became even more inspired from discussion with the great man. And he asked everyone else he met what they thought of the idea. The response was positive enough; not that Spicer in his enthusiasm, would have heard anything discouraging. He returned to Canada more determined than ever to get a project underway. He wrote and revised several versions of the proposal, encouraging his professors — Nathan Keyfitz, James Eayrs, Alexander Brady — to tear it apart. When they did, he rewrote it, answering their doubts.

Spicer returned to Ottawa to see the Prime Minister, and spent his honeymoon with his wife, Thérèse, in "an appalling little hotel" on Metcalfe Street, where sheets were seventy-five cents extra. As soon as Thérèse had typed out the latest version of his proposal in their hotel room, Spicer returned to the Parliament buildings. Elmer Diefenbaker admitted him again; but this time Spicer was so nervous that he dropped all the papers on the floor and was further rattled when the Prime Minister helped him pick them up.

He had good reason to be nervous, for, despite his claim that the plan was virtually operational, it was not. "The fact is," he said, "I was bluffing everybody. I had no money, no organization, nothing except an idea that was getting better and better as I refined it."

Armed with the Prime Minister's moral support and a promise that the Department of External Affairs would help where it could, Spicer proceeded to the Canadian Institute of Public Affairs' Couchiching Conference that summer, where he buttonholed anyone who would listen to his idea. One who listened was Toronto Member of Parliament, Fred Stinson. Stinson was a member of the Parliamentary Standing Committee on External Affairs, and had himself recently returned from a trip to Asia. As he sat under the trees at Couchiching listening to the onrush of ideas and taking repeated pectoral jabs from the Spicer forefinger, Stinson began to see how the scheme might work. Stinson found Spicer abrasive, but tremendously vital and talented — even brilliant; and he was fascinated by the young man's quick grasp of concepts and facts. For his part, Spicer found Stinson's political instincts, and his solid, practical advice, invaluable. A team had been formed.

The two men began preparing the groundwork for forming an organization. Spicer inveigled friends and professors into the scheme and began to recruit final-year students who might become candidates for posting the following summer. He wrote to his contacts in Ceylon and India soliciting job requests and followed a lead in Sarawak for other job possibilities. Canadian Overseas Volunteers was the name adopted for the scheme and Fred Stinson had it officially incorporated. Professor Nathan Keyfitz, Paul Martin and other well-known Canadians were persuaded to lend their names to the venture, and Stinson began searching for funds. In an early draft of the proposal, Spicer had suggested incorporating similar activities at the University of Laval and the University of British Columbia. One version, submitted to the federal government, proposed twenty graduate volunteers for India, Ceylon and Sarawak at a total cost of $50,000. It was rejected.

Undaunted, Spicer and Stinson devised a sponsorship scheme in order to raise money. "It was a kind of slave market," said Spicer, "in which we would sell volunteers at two thousand bucks a head, on the condition that sponsors would get monthly reports from volunteers telling them how things were going." Stinson approached the Toronto newspapers, starting with John Bassett, publisher of *The Telegram*. Bassett was chary of the idea, and, like Spicer, wanted an opinion from the Prime Minister, whom he was able to roust on the telephone in a matter of moments. "Prime Minister," Stinson recalled Bassett saying, "there's a fellow here trying to get two thousand dollars out of me."

"Well, give it to him," Diefenbaker retorted when Stinson's name and idea were mentioned.[5]

The *Toronto Star* and the *Globe and Mail* followed suit, and then the United Church and the Anglican Church 'bought' three volunteers between them. With recruitment now well underway, Spicer told prospective volunteers that they would have to sell themselves if they wanted to go overseas, and he pointed them in the direction of other churches, businessmen and service clubs. "We thought we had to create an inexorable momentum," he said, "so that when the money came there would be volunteers, and if there were volunteers, we could use them to shame donors into giving money."

As a Member of Parliament, Stinson had free postal services and access to government telephone lines, which made up in part for the government's parsimony; and other organizations were persuaded to lend whatever assistance they could. When the funding situation seemed blackest, the little band was having some of its secretarial work done courtesy of World University Service. One day while the WUSC secretary was typing out fund-raising letters, Spicer noticed tears running down her face. She had been so touched by the idealism and the energy that was going into the endeavour that she stopped and wrote out a personal cheque for ten dollars. "When she gave us that cheque," Spicer said, "we knew it would fly."

Perhaps not surprisingly, they easily surpassed their target of $20,000, raising $36,000 within the space of two months; they were able to increase the ten volunteers proposed, to fifteen.

The Canadian initiatives benefitted immensely from the publicity and media flourishes heralding the American Peace Corps as it emerged with John F. Kennedy in his race to the White House. Although several congressmen, including Senator Hubert Humphrey, had been discussing a 'Peace Corps' since 1957, and had even presented legislation on it, the idea seemed to spring forth — like Excalibur, shining resplendently in the hand of the youthful, would-be President — during a speaking engagement at the University of Michigan in the autumn of 1960.

The idea had been put to him a few days before by some University of Wisconsin students, and now, at two in the morning, his distinctive Bostonian tones pealing out through campus loudspeakers, he asked: "How many of you are willing to spend ten years in Africa or Latin America or Asia, working for the United States and working for freedom? How many of you who are going to be doctors are willing to spend your days in Ghana; technicians or engineers, how many of you are willing to spend your lives travelling around the world?"[6]

The enthusiasm of the response must have cheered Kennedy in the darkness of that pre-dawn October morning. His voice weakening from the strain, he continued: "I think Americans *are* willing to contribute, but the effort must be far greater than we have made in the past." Despite charges from his opponent, Richard Nixon, that the Peace Corps would become a haven for draft dodgers,[7] Kennedy made the establishment of the Peace Corps one of his first Executive Orders, signing it into existence on March 1, 1961.

The British Voluntary Service Overseas (founded in 1957), the Peace Corps, the Australian scheme and the Canadian efforts all owe their basic philosophy to the post-World-War I European work camps, and to Service Civil International — an organization which mushroomed through the 1930s, with branches in Europe, Britain and North America. In 1931, SCI founder, Pierre Ceresole spent several days with Mahatma Gandhi who was returning to India from the London Round Table Conference on Indian Independence. He was profoundly affected by Gandhi's practical attempts to advance the sort of peaceful revolution that SCI advocated, and when, three years later, a terrible earthquake hit Bihar, Ceresole and three other workers went to India to work on the rebuilding of devastated villages. The four volunteers spent three years in Bihar — facing hardship, living and eating in the villages and working *with* rather than *for* the villagers. They were, in a real sense, the first western volunteers to work in the Third World — long before it was known by that name, long before 'technical assistance' and 'development aid' had been conceptualized, politicized and bureaucraticized.

The end of the Second World War heralded an era of technological advance which, on the one hand, seemed to hold promise for mankind, while on the other, it posed a new and fundamental threat to human survival, in the form of the atomic bomb. The 'Sixties Generation,' living in a world expanded by jet travel, computers and instant communication, and always with the fear of annihilation, violently rejected old values, conventions and prejudices. This new view of the world among youth took several divergent paths. Desegregation, the human rights movement and black militancy shook the American republic to its very foundation. In Canada, the anti-war movement, the environmentalist groups, the counter-culture and Quebec's Quiet Revolution were all manifestations of youthful awareness and its need for an outlet in action.

International volunteerism was often dismissed by homegrown activists because it seemed to smack of anachronistic righteousness and cloying missionary zeal; it deliberately and irritatingly avoided the short, sharp, political nostrums common to the domestic 'movement'. In the days of campus rage, the term 'volunteer' had a Sunday school ring to it, and domestic militants in both Canada and the United States argued that national problems — in their abundance — should be solved before anyone was sent off to save the Third World. It was a 'neat' rebuff, and it was ironically reminiscent of the most durable Conservative excuse for avoiding making a donation. American activist Tom Hayden summed it up succinctly when he disparaged the Peace Corps as a bunch of 4-H graduates. But to Paul Cowan, Freedom Rider, member of Students for a Democratic Society, self-styled 'unAmerican', Hayden's glib dismissal of the volunteers was too pat.

"I partly agreed," Cowan wrote, "but only partly. For the fact was that most of them stayed in their foreign villages for two years. And too many of the self-proclaimed radicals I knew . . . remained in their rural towns or urban ghettoes for only a few months, or never tried to work with poor people at all. Actions seemed to me to be more important than attitudes: salvation by works a far more sensible doctrine than salvation by grace."[8]

By the autumn of 1960, as the Canadian Overseas Volunteers began to take shape, parallel efforts were developing in other parts of Canada. Brian Marson and Michael Clague, two students at the University of British Columbia, nurtured the concept in Vancouver after a Toronto meeting with Keith Spicer. They asked the President of the University, Dr. Mackenzie, for support. His deputy, Dr. Geoffrey Andrew, helped to establish a President's Committee on Overseas Service; after obtaining local financial assistance, they selected two graduates in home economics for teaching assignments in Ghana in 1961.

In Quebec, Les Chantiers, Le Centre de Formation pour L'Envoi de Techniciens en Pays Sous-developpées, Laval Missionaires and Le Mouvement Universitaire National pour le Developpment Outre-Mer all mounted programs for voluntary service either in Quebec or overseas. And in Toronto, a young Englishman, Guy Arnold, was working on an idea which owed its origins to both the work camps of Europe and the emerging idea of longer international service. The idea behind his organization — Canadian Voluntary Commonwealth Service (CVCS) — was not only Canadian service overseas, but also shorter, cross-cultural opportunities in work camp settings in Canada, for youth from throughout the Commonwealth.

By early 1961, the need for coordination was becoming obvious, not least because of the cost implications of so many similar and potentially repetitive activities. Lewis Perinbam, now Secretary General of the Canadian Commission for UNESCO, but still nurturing his original idea and sensing at last the opportunity to implement it, approached the man who would become CUSO's midwife, Dr. Francis Leddy.

Leddy, Dean of Arts and Science at the University of Saskatchewan and President of the Canadian UNESCO Commission, had been a keen internationalist and an inveterate traveller since his days abroad as a Rhodes Scholar. He had led the 1958 WUSC seminar to Yugoslavia and, knowing the British and Australian volunteer schemes, he was surprised when a student approached him about volunteer possibilities in South America to discover that there was no Canadian equivalent. Unaware of the schemes that were percolating in Toronto, at UBC and elsewhere, and no doubt strongly influenced by Lewis Perinbam's zeal and by mounting Peace Corps publicity, he began to consider how the Canadian university community might be used to foster a Canadian volunteer program.

He consulted some of Canada's key university presidents for their advice and opinions. "A few looked on the project with little favour," Leddy said, "and warned me that it was utopian, likely to prove troublesome and expensive to manage. Several others shared my enthusiasm and strongly encouraged me to proceed."[9]

Privately, some assured Leddy that a detailed proposal with strong University backing would help to pry loose annual grants from university budgets. In order to provide greater justification, therefore, Leddy convened a consultative meeting in March, 1961, under the auspices of the UNESCO Commission; many university bodies were invited as well as representatives of government and other organizations. Leddy had no doubt about the plan's potential, and he and Lewis Perinbam began to formulate plans for an inaugural meeting of what was already being called "Canadian University Service Overseas."

Douglas Mayer, Lewis Perinbam's successor at WUSC, provided invaluable encouragement and support in the formative months. He and Perinbam composed a draft constitution for the organization and spent hours agonizing over its name. "We tried first to get something that would work in both languages," Perinbam said, "and then we wanted to get an exciting name like the Peace Corps." In the end, the name they chose was unimaginatively prosaic and also required translation.

"We had to settle on Canadian University Service Overseas for very practical reasons," Perinbam said. "We had to get the universities involved in it because we needed their support; we wanted it to be clearly Canadian; and we wanted it to be a service organization."

Francis Leddy now approached Geoff Andrew at UBC, a friend of twenty-five years since their days as Canadian students at Oxford. Andrew was essential to the plan, not only because of his part in the establishment of the UBC President's Committee, but because he had recently been appointed Executive Director of the National Conference of Canadian Universities and Colleges of Canada which would soon merge with the Canadian Universities Federation to form the influential Association of Universities and Colleges of Canada (AUCC). Leddy proposed that a special meeting of University Presidents be held either just before or just after the AUCC meeting in June, with the creation of CUSO as the only item on the agenda. Andrew agreed.

In the weeks leading up to June 6, Leddy invited the presidents of all

Canadian universities, and drew up a list of other organizations with interests which he ''presumed to be at least somewhat related to the basic ideals to be served by CUSO.'' Among them were the Quakers, the Student Christian Movement, WUSC, UNESCO and the two nascent volunteer organizations, COV and CVCS.

Leddy, however, regarded the COV effort as parochial and amateurish, despite the fact that it was about to dispatch fifteen volunteers while the university-based organization was still only an idea. It was not surprising, therefore, that the June meeting was a difficult one. To COV, operating on a shoestring and scrounging to find the funds to mount a first contingent — with people already recruited and ready to go — the CUSO idea was almost an insult. That it should have such prestigious university and UNESCO backing and be the subject of pompous deliberations at a lofty meeting which had all but ignored COV, was equally difficult to swallow.

Keith Spicer was galled by the idea that 'CUSO' should be seen as a necessary takeover from amateurs. ''We had thought through the idea,'' he said, ''convinced everybody who needed to be convinced, from the Prime Minister on down, raised the money, got the people. Then all of a sudden we had a lateral move by a couple of bureaucrats — there is no other word — who said that this thing had to be put on a solid footing.'' A purist, who would always feel that the very essence of COV was its reliance on unalloyed voluntary fervour, Spicer was particularly annoyed that the CUSO meeting should include so many university presidents. ''I still don't know what they were doing there,'' he recalled. ''They hadn't done anything significant when we needed them. They didn't give us money; they only gave us a pat on the head until we got it going.''

The initiative, however, was with Francis Leddy, who felt strongly that a national effort with firm central backing was the only route to a secure operation which could adequately address both overseas requests and the large human resources base in Canada.

And so, the meeting of June 6 was called to order in McGill University's Redpath Hall. It was packed with academics, university presidents and representatives of twenty-one different organizations, ranging from CVCS — represented by its founder, Guy Arnold — to the Royal Architectural Institute of Canada and the grandiloquently named World Foundation Against Hunger and Misery. With Lewis Perinbam close at hand, Francis Leddy assumed the chair, while Fred Stinson, Keith Spicer and the COV contingent glowered up at him. Leddy — who would go on to become President of the University of Windsor, with all the difficult committee work and student relations that such a position would entail; who throughout his career served as President or Chairman of more than 20 national organizations; who would be nominated for the Nobel Peace Prize in 1984 — recalled that two-hour meeting more vividly than any other in his career: "I believed with relief, that I was coming to the successful conclusion of several years of persistent preparation. I had also developed a conviction, in advance, that CUSO would prove to be the most important voluntary activity in which I had ever been involved. But particularly, I remember the session as the most challenging and arduous I ever sustained in the chair."

The meeting began calmly, with a statement of intent and some questions of clarification. Then Fred Stinson stood up and listed a series of strong objections. He was assisted by the intervention of some of those who had come with him from Toronto, and, employing his eloquence as a lawyer and parliamentarian, he made a formidable case against the proposed 'Canadian University Service Overseas'. He argued that such an organization would require a heavy bureaucracy, would impose a compulsory uniformity on the many different approaches that were possible, and would "squeeze the life out of the voluntary spirit" that had allowed COV and others to begin. If the universities wanted to do what COV or CVCS had done, let them do it on their own.

The debate continued. "Finally," recalled Leddy, "in a sudden surge of apparent anger or emotion, Stinson stood, waving a sheet of paper in the air and declaring, 'Here is our charter! Take it away from us if you will!' "

There was an anxious moment of silence. Then a young woman in the audience stood and spoke. She said that she had recently spent two years in Afghanistan and had arranged everything, including the costs, herself. She had often wondered what might have happened had she become ill away from home, without support; and she talked of the need for more of what COV was doing and of what CUSO proposed to do. She asked if it were realistic, however, for ten or twelve groups to work independently of each other — each making its own separate arrangements with the governments of India or Nigeria.

When she sat down, the President of the University of Alberta, Walter

Johns, quickly stood and moved that Canadian University Service Overseas be established. The motion was accepted, and the vote was called without further discussion. The resolution carried by a wide margin with only Fred Stinson and seven others dissenting.

As the assembly adjourned, Geoff Andrew convened a small nominating committee to propose a Board of Directors. Among those later elected to the Board were Monsignor H. J. Somers, the President of St. Francis Xavier University, Francis Leddy, and others who had been instrumental in winning the day. Lewis Perinbam agreed to become Secretary-Treasurer in addition to his UNESCO duties. CUSO was on its way.

Despite the sibling rivalry among the organizations, COV, CVCS and other groups were willing to take out membership in CUSO, so long as CUSO acted only as a general coordinating body and did not encroach on territory already staked out. Too much had been invested in COV simply to hand it over to 'bureaucrats', as Spicer called them. Besides, he and Stinson had to get back to Toronto to finalize departure plans for the first COV contingent.

On the evening of August 16, a month before the departure of the first Peace Corps volunteers, fifteen COV volunteers boarded BOAC Flight 610 to London, destined eventually for India, Ceylon and Sarawak. Fourteen were graduates of the University of Toronto, and one, Dr. Hughette Leger, was from Laval. Helen Zukowski and Clendon Wooldridge threw a spanner into the works by falling in love during the orientation program and getting married; last minute arrangements had to be made to change Clendon's posting from Ceylon to Sarawak so he could be with Helen. "I didn't really believe we had it made until I saw these people board the plane," Keith Spicer said. "It was certainly a wonderful sight when it took off — and a wonderful relief."[10]

In Britain, the young pioneers boarded a P&O liner, the SS Arcadia, and drifted leisurely through the Mediterranean and the Red Sea, contemplating the enormous commitment they had made. The contrast between this shipboard luxury and the austerity of their postings would soon make a vivid impression on them. Richard Hamilton wrote from the Ganhiniketan Ashram in India where he was working: "Yesterday I finally made the move to a village. I sleep in the schoolhouse with about twenty-five others. (I guess they find their mud-and-cow-dung huts cramped and stuffy.) I take breakfast and supper with the family of the leader of the youth club, and noon dinner at the Ashram where I am continuing my job of teaching English.''[11]

John Andrews, an engineer posted to Ceylon, wrote, "After one month in Colombo, I was able to move to Matara where I feel I am now giving my two cents worth . . . for three rupees a day I get full room and board, three rice and curry meals a day. The room has a bed, a chair and a table, and except for two nests of pigeons (I have to cover all my belongings with newspaper before I leave) I have the room to myself. The latrines are buckets,'' he added, "and the washing water is rain collected from the roof.''[12]

At six feet six inches, Bill McWhinney — the second of three posted to Ceylon and the volunteer 'bought' by the *Toronto Telegram* — towered above his Ceylonese hosts. And he tended to have a bigger appetite as well. Assigned to work with a six-month-old Ceylonese cooperative bank, McWhinney understood the value of money, and a quick calculation of his 280 rupee per month salary ($56) against the alarming cost of a single night at the Grand Oriental Hotel where they had been booked, convinced him to relocate quickly in a youth hostel where there would still be change from a single rupee — even after three nights.

He wrote to Toronto about the cost of living and discussed it with the Canadian High Commissioner, James George. George, who had helped with some of the early arrangements, had parsimoniously asked Keith Spicer months before not to involve the High Commission "more than you can help.''[13] Now he wrote privately to Fred Stinson about the financial plight of the volunteers.

"After a long talk with Bill McWhinney reviewing their situation, my own feeling is that you may have to give them a bit more to live on. I did not tell Bill that I was writing to you; I think they are going to try very hard to make the best of it under present conditions . . . but if they do appeal to you I want you to know in advance that I think they really are having a difficult time of it.''[14]

Back in Toronto COV was having a difficult time of it as well. Keith Spicer had bid the organization farewell and had taken a badly needed job in Ottawa, in order to begin repaying his student loan. Ozzie Schmidt, a fellow student at the University of Toronto, had taken over his recruitment and training work, but Fred Stinson, who had almost singlehandedly managed the fund raising, was unexpectedly sidelined with a broken hip in January 1962. By March, with Stinson still in hospital and the debts mounting, decisions had to be made. "We had to have an aggressive personality on the hustings to help us raise money," said Stinson. "So with a heavy heart, we decided to ask McWhinney, riding his bike somewhere in Ceylon, to come back and help us." As soon as he could wind up his affairs, McWhinney returned to Toronto, and somehow they managed to raise the funds and dispatch a second group of sixteen volunteers later that summer. But it was clear that the administration could no longer be handled on a voluntary basis; it was already far too complicated and experience had quickly shown that unexpected difficulties in the field were too urgent to be dealt with by an ad hoc approach.

CUSO, meanwhile, was having its own problems. Shortly after the founding meeting, Lewis Perinbam had set off on a two-month trip to Asia in search of both job opportunities for volunteers and a clear-cut rationale for the organization that had been established. He discovered, however, that while Asians generally understood that the motivation behind CUSO was well-meaning, it was also regarded as a manifestation "of the superiority of the west over the non-westernized world, and as a kind of 'witness for the democracy'. There was a strong feeling that young Canadian graduates were, in a sense, coming to 'civilize', " he wrote, "and that this was why many of them wanted to work in villages rather than in towns where life might be more sophisticated. This emphasis on poverty and technical backwardness is very much resented among Asians, but there is little doubt that it is uppermost in the mind of many westerners."[15]

In some places, especially those which were still colonies — such as Sarawak, Brunei and North Borneo — the idea of CUSO volunteers was welcomed. In other countries — India, Pakistan, Malaya — he found varying degrees of interest, usually more positive when he stressed the contribution that Asians could make to Canada by allowing young Canadians to come and learn from them while, at the same time, performing some sort of useful function. In other countries, he was barely given the time of day. In Vietnam, he ran unexpectedly into a war, still largely unreported in the west, that was already claiming some eight hundred victims a month. The Minister of Education, Dr. Nguyen Quang Trinh, was brutally straightforward regarding CUSO. "Dr. Trinh informed me that they have too many unemployed graduates," Perinbam reported, "and he felt our scheme could not be of much value in Vietnam."[16]

Perinbam's trip, rather than clarifying CUSO's role, only seemed to confuse matters. Some countries wanted highly-paid experts; others sought teachers who might be paid professional salaries. In some cases, volunteers would have to be paid by CUSO; in others, salaries would be paid by the employers, on local terms and conditions — the system CUSO originally envisaged. The trip, however, reinforced Perinbam's conviction that a volunteer would have to remain overseas for two years to make an effective contribution — rather than the twelve-month assignment proposed by COV. And he made it clear to the CUSO Board that "charity, patronage and pity" were unacceptable motivations for work overseas, just as "goodwill and lofty idealism," as he put it, "though always appreciated and respected, would not be sufficient, especially in situations of frustration and despair." He wanted tough, realistic individuals, capable of doing a real job of work.

In Canada, Perinbam moved quickly to establish committees on forty campuses across the country. Within a year, thirty committees were actively recruiting candidates, and by June, 1962, more than two hundred dossiers had been compiled. CUSO soon came to the same realization as COV: that there was a limit to what could be achieved with voluntary workers and to the amount of money that could be raised without full-time staff. Lewis Perinbam still had his UNESCO job, and CUSO was clearly going to require much more in the way of administrative support than anyone had imagined.

The solution came at the First Annual General Meeting in June, 1962. CUSO's allegiance would be shifted from the Canadian Commission for UNESCO to the Association of Universities and Colleges of Canada. Geoff Andrew, AUCC Executive Director, recognized CUSO's need for more administrative support as well as the logic of placing it more securely within the university milieu. And because Andrew was neutral in the debate that had simmered between CUSO and COV, he was able to play the role of honest broker. Without wasting time in consulting the Board, he approached Bill McWhinney and persuaded him to become CUSO's first full-time Executive Secretary. With McWhinney, one of COV's stellar alumni, at the helm of CUSO, the way was paved for a formal merger — which took place within a matter of months. By 1963, COV and CUSO had united, and nearly one hundred volunteers departed that summer for assignments in fifteen different countries — under the CUSO banner.

Chapter 3

The Caribbean: Strangers in Paradise

Because of impatience we were driven out of Eden;
Because of impatience we cannot return.

— Kafka

In October 1983, one of the dozens of American military aircraft evacuating foreigners from Grenada's unfinished, Cuban-built Point Salines airstrip carried six CUSO people. Five were volunteers and the sixth was Marlene Green, CUSO's Regional Coordinator for the Caribbean, leaving her home of the past four years. Shaken and dazed; angry; frightened after days pinned down in the CUSO office by gunfire between American Marines and Grenadian armed forces, she looked back through the window of the plane at the deceptively tranquil spice island that had been blown apart by political fratricide and invasion.

The journey, from its easy beginnings in the Caribbean to that emotional evacuation from Grenada, had been long and difficult for CUSO. There had once been over one hundred and sixty volunteers in the West Indies, working in fifteen different islands and territories from Barbados in the east, to Belize, two thousand miles to the west. But the islands, which had originally been the most desireable of CUSO destinations — the 'holiday postings' — turned out to be the most difficult. The change

24

was epitomized in the attitude of one of CUSO's earliest supporters: In 1964, the Jamaican Minister of Development and Welfare praised CUSO and encouraged its expansion;[1] seventeen years later, the same man, Edward Seaga, was Prime Minister, and he expressed very different views about the organization following a raid by armed police on the CUSO office. When asked by a visiting CUSO official what the press might be told about their discussions, Seaga said, "Tell them we met and you briefed me on the CUSO program."

His Security Minister, Winston Spaulding added: "You can also say we support CUSO in its work."

"No," the Prime Minister returned. "I wouldn't go that far."[2]

The turbulence and confusion of CUSO's first two decades in the region reflected the turmoil of the times; but in a sense, CUSO was also paying the price for a longstanding and convoluted Canadian presence in the region, a presence based on a vision of the Caribbean that was both romantic and dangerously naive.

The West Indies is as vast as it is diverse. Belize, the westernmost Commonwealth nation, is as far from Jamaica and the Bahamas as Victoria is from Saskatoon and Great Slave Lake. The topography of the Caribbean ranges from the mist-shrouded Blue Mountains of Jamaica, to the dense mangrove swamps and spectacular waterfalls of Guyana, to the palm-lined white sand beaches of the Leeward and Windward Islands. The Pitons of Saint Lucia seem to soar straight out of the sea, while tiny Anguilla is little more than a sandbar in the ocean.

The cultural and political mosaic is as varied as the geography. Historically, the economy of the region has been based on one commodity: sugar; everything else, including the people, was imported. The native Amerindians in most Caribbean islands were either exiled or wiped out by war and disease; for manpower, the planters relied exclusively on the slaving vessels that brought their unhappy cargoes of shackled humanity from the west cost of Africa. "It was the negro slaves," wrote Trinidadian historian and Prime Minister Eric Williams, "who made these sugar colonies the most precious colonies ever recorded in the whole annals of imperialism."[3]

It was the American Revolution that sparked the initial contact between the Canadian colonies and their West Indian counterparts. For four decades, the British attempted to isolate the newly independent American Republic, discouraging old trading links between the Caribbean and the southern mainland while fostering more northerly connections. It was an artificial and unenforceable quarantine, but it did establish important ties, and a number of interesting cultural links; the Atlantic schooners became major traders, and gave the Caribbean an enduring appetite for Canadian saltfish, and the Maritimes a hearty taste for rum.

Many black Canadians can count among their ancestors Jamaican slaves who revolted during that period. The bloody Maroon Rebellion of 1795, one of several uprisings, was quelled at great cost, and six hundred of the slaves were moved to a kind of freedom in the Maritimes. Many of these people, as well as emancipated slaves from the newly created United States, eventually returned to Africa: but some of them stayed in Canada and carved out a life on the unwelcoming rocky soil of Nova Scotia.

With the abolition of slavery throughout the British Empire in the 1830s, much of the black West Indian population left the sugar plantations to establish independent family holdings, and, for a few years, plantation owners turned to indentured labour from Asia. But as other sources of inexpensive sugar developed, and the Industrial Revolution and free trade invigorated the economy of Europe, the importance of the Caribbean colonies declined. And the colonial government's decision to support sugar production at the expense of agricultural diversification prevented small farmers from developing enough modern-sector export agriculture to bring prosperity to the islands.

It was only after the American Civil War that Canada began to take a more serious commercial interest in the Caribbean. The Sun Life Insurance Company established its first office there in 1879, opening up a lucrative market for other Canadian insurance companies. Banking, too, became a profitable enterprise: in 1882, the Merchants' Bank of Halifax, later the Royal Bank of Canada, chose Hamilton, Bermuda as the location for its first overseas branch; in 1889, the Bank of Nova Scotia opened a branch in Kingston, Jamaica — even before it had an office in Toronto; and, between 1916 and the Second World War, the Royal Bank of Canada was the *only* bank operating in the Bahamas.

Canadian commercial interests in the Caribbean grew rapidly during the last quarter of the nineteenth century; by the twentieth century Canada was a major investor in the region. The discovery of bauxite in British

Guiana (and later in Jamaica) spurred outside investment. In British Guiana, bauxite operations were owned and managed almost exclusively by the Demerara Bauxite Company — 'Demba' — a subsidiary of Alcoa's Canadian operation, Northern Aluminium. In 1951, American anti-trust laws freed the Canadian operation from its Pittsburgh head office, if not from American shareholders, and, in 1966, the Canadian complex became known as Alcan. CN Steamships ran regular passenger and freight schedules through and between the islands, and with the advent of cheap air travel, Canadian tourism, hitherto an activity reserved for the rich, began to expand. In the late 1950s and early 1960s, as larger jets came into regular use and the Cuban tourist mecca expired in the wake of the Castro revolution, more and more Canadians discovered the sun, sand and sea — and expanding hotel complexes — of the Bahamas, Barbados and the north coast of Jamaica. Canadians invested in the tourist industry as well: Commonwealth Holiday Inns of Canada and CN Realties were largely responsible for the introduction of Holiday Inns to Antigua, Saint Kitts, Saint Lucia, Grenada, Barbados and Trinidad. Air Canada opened new routes to island airports built with Canadian money, by Canadian companies. In 1968, the airline purchased forty percent of the stock of Air Jamaica in a complicated buy-back arrangement, and for several years provided management services, training airline staff and helping the company to turn a steady profit.

In 1958, Prime Minister Diefenbaker allocated $10 million in financial assistance to the Caribbean over a five-year period. It was the first such program set up by Canada independent of the Colombo Plan. The money was used to build a residence — Canada Hall — at the Trinidad campus of the University of the West Indies, and to provide two ships — the Federal Palm and the Federal Maple — to help improve inter-island communication and transport. In later years, the aid effort was substantially increased, and Canadian experts in assistance programs joined the throngs of Canadian businessmen and tourists filling the aircraft that plied the routes from Montreal and Toronto to Barbados, Kingston and Port of Spain.

By the mid-1960s, the Commonwealth Caribbean seemed to be a Canadian reserve. The names of familiar Canadian companies and banks dotted the streets of cities and towns; Canadian goods lined the shelves; Canadian currency was widely accepted, and Canadian beer and rye

whiskey were readily available. Canadian managers were often on hand
to deal with Canadian problems, and Canadian airlines catered to Canadian travel and hotel needs.

With all the other Canadian activity in the region, CUSO was a logical
adjunct, although the genesis of its Caribbean activity lay in the unlikely
setting of Pickering College, a private boys' school north of Toronto,
where one of the 'masters' was a young Englishman named Guy Arnold.
Arnold felt a special affinity for the Commonweath as an international
force for good: he had spent the first decade of his working life — after
graduation from Oxford — in as many Commonwealth countries as possible, and had already written a book about an archaeological expedition
he had led to Borneo. To the students of Pickering College, he was a
dashing, almost romantic figure.

His next expedition, planned for the summer of 1960, was a study of
the folk tales of the Wapishana Indians in the wild hinterland of British
Guiana's Rupununi region. He decided that the trip would be an invaluable
experience for two of the grade 13 boys — David Milne and David Beer,
the headmaster's son. In July, their aricraft set down at British Guiana's
Atkinson Airport.

It was a memorable study in contrasts for the two eighteen-year-olds,
exposed as they were to a broad cross-section of people and experiences.
They met the Communist Chief Minister, Cheddi Jagan, whose Indian
immigrant family raised him in the barracks of sugar estates; they received
funding from Bookers, the nearly feudal sugar conglomerate. They saw
racism between the evenly divided black and Asian populations; they
witnessed the segregation practised by Canadians at the Demba bauxite
operations. They tasted the food, the music, the poverty and the wealth;
they saw colonialism in its intense Guianese microcosm.

Beer was particularly struck by an incident at breakfast in a guest house
on one of the sugar estates. The servants were expected to cater to every
need, and one particularly deferential steward went to almost incredible
lengths to please the young Canadians.

"Every time I put my hand down to the coffee cup," Beer recalled,
"a little brown hand would whip in and move it so it would be directly
in place for my own hand. Milne and I were going nuts. I remember
saying, 'God, Guy, this is awful. Get this guy out of here!'"[4]

For some time, Guy Arnold had been thinking about a way to give young people in the Commonwealth the kind of cross-cultural experience in which Milne and Beer were now immersed, and, as they trekked across the Rupununi, the idea began to take shape.

"We were the litmus test," said Beer. "It was a sense of shock at the poverty. We didn't have any sophisticated idea of changing the world, but we thought something could be done."

Arnold, like Lewis Perinbam, had been struck by the parochialism of Canada, and saw a tremendous opportunity to expand the horizons of its youth: "It was a mixing up of young people at different levels, rather than filling gaps that was my starting point," he said.[5] He spent the rest of 1960 travelling, and returned to Canada in March of 1961, with the idea for Canadian Voluntary Commonwealth Service formulated in his mind.

That summer, the first CVCS short-term volunteers left for Jamaica; among them was Charles Beer, David's brother. In the following year, Arnold formed a board of directors, wrote endless fund-raising letters and made speeches to promote the CVCS idea. In the summer of 1962, the year of Jamaican independence, a group of sixteen volunteers prepared to leave: some would remain in the field for a full year, travelling to British Guiana, British Honduras and Trinidad, as well as Jamaica. Arnold had always seen the "mixing up of young people" as a two-way street, and that summer he invited a Jamaican university student to come to Canada and work as a counsellor at Camp Mazinaw in the Kawartha Lakes.

CVCS and the Canadian Overseas Volunteers began joint recruitment activities in Toronto, and it became clear that the national activities of CUSO in Ottawa would have some bearing on the future of the two smaller groups. As thirty-two CVCS volunteers prepared for their Caribbean assignments in the summer of 1963, negotiations were already underway for a merger, which would take place the following spring.

For Dave Beer, the impact of that first trip to British Guiana remained fresh, and, in 1963, he interrupted his university studies to return to the Caribbean for a year with CVCS. He could hardly know that this was only the beginning: he would devote more than twenty years, off and on, to overseas service, most of it in Africa. But as he arrived at Cobbla

Camp, ten miles north of Mandeville in central Jamaica, the future never seemed further than a week away.

Beer was replacing CVCS's first full-year volunteer, Terry Glavin, who was, recalled Guy Arnold, "one of the best people I ever selected." The job was challenging: working in a camp of more than seven hundred young men, who were part of the newly established Jamaica Youth Corps. Jamaica was eager to upgrade its under-educated and unemployed youth as quickly as possible; Cobbla Camp was one of the vehicles. It stressed the virtues of farming and the back-to-the-land policies the government espoused; and it provided training in such skills as mechanics, plumbing, tailoring, secretarial work and barbering. As Assistant Director and Recreation Officer, Beer's job was challenging and diverse. He worked on curriculum development, coached, taught civics, managed many camp activities, and helped solve general problems.

Because the camp was in the countryside, trips to Kingston were rare, and Beer had to find his friends in the nearby rum shops and at village dances; almost without realizing it, he was starting to bridge the tremendous cultural gap that faces all volunteers in their first months. The contrast struck him most especially when the Canadian High Commissioner invited him and a few other Canadian waifs to Christmas dinner. Beer worried about what to wear, finally borrowing an oversized sports jacket; but the High Commissioner's wife — "Mrs. High Commish," as Beer called her — made him feel at home and had little difficulty in talking him into three helpings of turkey dinner. He remarked that none of the nineteen guests was Jamaican. At the end of the evening, as he stepped out into the night, the High Commissioner, in a touchingly avuncular way, pressed a bottle of Canadian Club into his hand, presumably to help him over the difficult times ahead in the hinterland.

"The next night I was at a bush dance," Beer said, "aeons away, and much, much happier."

That same Christmas, twelve hundred miles to the southeast, in Trinidad, another volunteer was running into serious difficulties with one of his first projects. Gordon Cressy was working with the Trinidad YMCA; months before, he had hit on a unique idea for raising funds to buy new ping-pong tables: they would import and sell Canadian Christmas trees. At first the idea seemed too far-fetched for his Board of Directors, but gradually Cressy persuaded them that the scheme could work if the trees were bought and shipped by the YMCA in Saint John, New Brunswick. Eventually, the board agreed, and 1,600 trees were purchased in New Brunswick and loaded on a vessel, with a firm arrival date of 15 December.

Then things started to go wrong. For the first time in Trinidad's history, a commercial firm also decided to import Christmas trees, and when their shipment arrived on 15 December and there was no sign of the YMCA trees, Cressy began to worry. He phoned Saint John and was told that there had been a fire on the ship, but that the trees had been saved and transferred to another vessel that would arrive in Trinidad on 22 December.

"The YMCA Board members, who had been quite kind to me up to that point, and who had put out quite a lot of money for the trees, began to look at me in a different light," said Cressy.[6]

He telephoned Bermuda in an effort to chart the southward progress of the ship, and was appalled to learn that it had been delayed there by a dock strike, and now expected to arrive in Trinidad on 26 December.

"This laid to rest completely my image with the Board as a nice young Canadian boy, and there was serious discussion as to whether I should be terminated immediately, or after Christmas."

Cressy then managed to persuade BWIA, the Trinidad airline, to fly a mercy mission to Barbados, where the ship was now about to dock. Somehow he convinced them that it would make a good publicity story, and with the newspapers dubbing it "The Christmas Tree Airlift," Cressy and three others left for Barbados on Sunday, December 22, aboard a stripped BWIA aircraft. He had not counted on the Barbadian dockworkers' Sabbath, but fortunately a foresighted Board member accompanying him had brought the appropriate supplies: persuasive Trinidad rum. The trees were eventually trucked to the Barbados airport where they were crammed into the hold, and even the cabins, of the waiting aircraft. The Saint John YMCA, as it turned out, had been able to purchase more trees than expected, so Cressy left 300 behind for the Barbados YMCA. Finally, they embarked for Trinidad, with Cressey sitting amidst one of the most unlikely cargoes ever to fly down the Windward Islands.

That night, the first trucks loaded with trees pulled into Victoria Square in Port of Spain, to a musical fanfare and a throng of YMCA members and Trinidadian journalists. By Christmas Eve, all of the trees had been sold and the YMCA got its ping-pong tables. And the Barbados YMCA made $700 from its unexpected windfall. Shortly after New Year's Eve, however, to Cressy's chagrin and his prescient Board's undoubted gratification, the Government of Trinidad and Tobago officially banned any future imports of Canadian Christmas trees.

"This was my first major foray into private enterprise," Cressy recalled, "and my last."

Christmas was often the turning point for volunteers: a realization that they actually *were* a million miles from home, family, and friends; from Christmas customs, and the snow that had always been a familiar part of their holiday season. Christmas was often a time of great loneliness, but it was also then that many of them came to realize the seriousness of their commitment. By January, many of the accumulated doubts and fears began to dissipate, and volunteers could settle into their jobs as functioning members of their communities.

By 1964, CVCS had merged with CUSO, and all postings thereafter were two-year assignments. Bill McWhinney took the talented Terry Glavin onto the CUSO staff as Associate Executive Secretary, a grandiose title belying the fact that there were no other officers whatsoever. Glavin's job was to reorganize and develop the Caribbean program, a mammoth task, but one unhampered by official reluctance. Most of the governments of the region were already under local self-administration and in anticipation of their imminent independence, they were eager to have Canadian teachers, technicians, pharmacists and nurses. When Glavin flew to Jamaica in September, 1964, with the new group of volunteers, they were met at the airport by a welcoming committee of government representatives, reporters from *The Gleaner*, and the TV cameras of the Jamaican Broadcasting Corporation. The incoming volunteers stayed for a few days at the Mona Campus of the University of the West Indies, and were warmly received by Jamaican students, who organized tours, social functions and a reception for them.

Any problems seemed simple at first. The salary question for example, was a thorny one, not because wages were too low, but because at £780 a year, many thought they were too high; but the volunteers faced the issue directly by agreeing to a ten percent reduction. The Canadian High Commissioner had a private chat with Glavin about problems of social adaptation among the volunteers, reproving him over certain "inappropriate activities" in the social lives of some of the female volunteers.

Once the staff had left and the volunteers were on their own at their postings, they began to encounter more serious problems, though not unlike those faced by volunteers everywhere. Linda West found that Frankfield Comprehensive High School in Jamaica already had a commercial teacher, and she faced the prospect of two idle years in a school which was more than adquately staffed, and seemed to be overflowing with expatriate teachers. She and her husband Ron requested a transfer and were reassigned to the only rural secondary school in Saint Vincent. In their new postings, romantic notions of a tropical paradise were quickly dispelled by the hard work, the many extra-curricular activities and an island climate they had not expected.

"We live on the Windward coast," Linda wrote from Saint Vincent, "which is constantly being battered by huge breakers. This makes swimming or fishing impossible. To us here, the sea is no friend. The constant salt spray has rusted our clocks, the beds, all the metal fixtures in the house, the hinges on our luggage and even our typewriter."[7]

For some, there were problems in the classroom. Betty Adams, who joined CUSO in 1965 at the age of forty-four, recalled her first day on the job at Jamaica's Holmwood Technical High School. Overcoming her fears and self-doubt, she stood in front of the class and began by explaining the first steps of learning how to type.

"I'd explain something, then say, 'Does everyone understand?' "

" 'YES MISS!' in a chorus."

" 'Then please do it'. I'd walk around and not one single person had understood!"

" 'Do you understand what I say, class?' "

" 'YES MISS.' "

"I felt completely stymied, for they seemed only capable of replying 'Yes Miss' to everything. The first day that one of them said 'No Miss', I could have hugged her. I knew I was winning. "[8]

Six years later, Ray Clark had a similar experience while teaching English in a rural Jamaican school. "I'd like to go back and apologize to a few of my first classes," he later recalled. "I remember my first lesson was dictation. It was something we had done in school, and I thought it had to do with listening and writing and being able to spell. I remember walking around the room and discovering after five minutes that they weren't writing a thing I was saying, because they couldn't even hear it, let alone translate it, or put it into a sentence, or know where the periods and commas went . . . That was MY first lesson.''[9]

Marie Chiasson arrived in Barbados only two weeks after completing a three-year nursing course in Canada, and was assigned to a hospital under construction in the small fishing village of Speightstown. Her first task was to set up a dispensary and to sort out the trunks of drug samples donated by the American Navy.

"Sorting out those drugs, some of them half rotten, was a very tedious and futile job as far as I was concerned. How could we possibly run a hospital on samples? But I persevered, and after about eight weeks, a dispensary was taking shape. Unfortunately, I was the only one who knew where anything was, and for a long time I couldn't even go for a shower without telling somebody.''[10]

After eight months of exhausting work, the hospital was finally opened with great fanfare by the Queen and Prince Philip during their 1966 Royal Tour of the Caribbean. Chiasson expressed her sense of accomplishment: "The hospital is going full swing now," she wrote a few months after the opening. "The pharmacy has been transferred to another location and to another manager, and it is doing very well. There is talk about opening another surgical ward . . . but we just haven't the staff. I have been teaching another class as nursing aides, all of whom are now employed. We could still do with more. All in all, the hospital has come a long way since September, 1965. I have watched it struggling to its feet, and the reward has been satisfying.''[11]

By the late 1960s some of the sheen was wearing off the Caribbean's image as a desirable posting for volunteers. The early termination rate began to climb, and, by 1969, had reached almost 25%, more than triple the rate in any other region.

In some islands, the rate of attrition had to do with the expectations of volunteers and the proximity of Canada. Sharon Capeling had been a teacher in Saskatoon when she joined CUSO in 1967, and despite a six-week orientation in Nova Scotia, had remarkably naive expectations of her posting in Barbados. She somehow imagined living in a mud hut on the beach, and the news that they were to be flown to the island by the

RCAF conjured visions of sitting on the floor of a troop carrier and possibly even parachuting in. Instead a comfortable flight preceded a comfortable lifestyle.

"We received the CBC news every morning at nine on Redifusion; you could get the *Globe and Mail* only two days late; you could phone home. The place was full of Canadian tourists and many other Canadian expatriates. You simply weren't cut off. Being close to all those other Canadians, all making a lot more money and living a higher life style, being treated as an 'expat' or a tourist yourself, all led to a high level of frustration."[12]

There were special problems for the single women: it was not only sun, sand and sea that attracted Canadian women tourists to the Caribbean; and Barbadian beach boys, mistaking CUSO volunteers for the tourists they had come to know (and to love), often ruined the few excursions volunteers could afford to make to the beach.

If you went to Accra Beach by yourself," said Sharon Capeling, "you couldn't lie down for thirty seconds before some hunk would drape himself down beside you and tell you that you were the most beautiful woman in the world and that he wanted to marry you."

Canadian men travelling in the region posed a different problem for female volunteers. "The Canadian High Commissioner, who was resident in Trinidad, was a bit like a pimp," Capeling said. Canadian naval vessels arrived in Barbados every winter on manoeuvres, and the officers, unlike enlisted men, could not frequent the more raucous and conspicuous night-spots on shore. As an alternative, the High Commissioner supplied the captains with the names of the single Canadian females on the island, and, inevitably, all the eligible CUSO volunteers received regular invitations to 'cocktail parties' on the ships.

Some of the CUSO people, however, developed more serious relationships. Chris Bryant, who had been a volunteer in Grenada in 1965, joined the CUSO staff in Jamaica in 1969: one of his early problems was a volunteer who had unwisely dated the husband of the gossip columnist for *The Gleaner*, causing something of a public sensation. When he went to admonish her he met one of her Jamaican roommates, a UWI biochemistry student whom he eventually married. Their wedding was one of the biggest functions ever held at the CUSO office on Waterloo Avenue.

The Caribbean program grew rapidly in its first years; perhaps too rapidly. In 1964, thirty-one volunteers had travelled south; by 1968, there were more than one hundred and sixty people working in thirteen different Caribbean countries and territories, severely straining CUSO's Canadian recruitment and selection procedures. In the rush to develop programs, staff was not always able to check requests very closely, and some volunteers, like Linda and Ron West, found that there was little for them to do in their postings. Those who had rose-coloured expectations about their contributions were also disappointed. Sharon Capeling, who eventually extended her posting for a third year in Barbados, came to terms with the problem, though many others did not.

"I had an idea that I was bringing great amounts of Canadian expertise, but most of the teachers at Lodge School were as well qualified as me, or better. Compared with Moose Jaw, the quality of education at Lodge School was high. The level of analysis and the depth of their Shakespeare, if not the breadth, was as rigorous as a fourth-year honours course at a Canadian university. They knew what the problems were with their education. It opened my eyes to the fact that the answers to whatever was ailing the Caribbean weren't going to come from CUSO volunteers."

In some of the islands, local teachers were being trained at a rapid pace: in 1963, CUSO volunteers filled large gaps in country schools; but by 1970, the vacancies had decreased significantly or even disappeared. CUSO salaries were paid by the employer — in most cases the government — an effective check on the demand for volunteers, but it was not the same for the Peace Corps, whose salaries were paid by the American government, giving local employers little reason to reject free manpower and no incentive to ensure that a real job existed. As a result, there was acute dissatisfaction among American volunteers, particularly those assigned to community development work. Unlike the Canadians, and true to Richard Nixon's uncharitable early prediction, many of the Peace Corps men had volunteered in order to avoid the draft, and could not quit so easily. As dozens of Peace Corps jobs collapsed, the volunteers would go into what Sharon Capeling called their 'Ernest Hemingway phase' — walking along the beach, listening to the waves crash, writing poems, watching the sunset, reading books and growing a beard. "But you can only play Ernest Hemingway for so long when you're twenty-two and there's no one to watch you. So then they would go into their 'Surf City' phase. They would save up their Peace Corps allowance, buy surfer shorts and a board, go down to Accra Beach to surf all day and pick up Air Canada stewardesses. It was the Peace Corps who introduced the first frisbee to the Caribbean.''

In the waning years of the 1960s, a much more serious, far-reaching, and eventually explosive issue began to beleaguer the Caribbean-Canadian relationship: racial tension.

It was one thing for the volunteers to discover and come to terms with their own subconscious racial feelings; it was quite another to realize that some people did not like them, perhaps even hated them, for no other reason than the fact that they were white: most coped, but it wasn't easy. Sharon Capeling felt the overt resentment of a Barbadian colleague who repeatedly told her that the only reason she was teaching upper school was that she was white — he was better qualified, but held a less prestigious position. She went home in tears more than once when the quietly-spoken barbs and whispered insults became too much. ''I was carrying the burden and the guilt of the white race on my shoulders,'' she said. ''Somehow I felt responsible.''

By 1968, an immutable tide of resentment was rising against Canadians, and it would not recede until the waves had crashed noisily over Canadians' simplistic attitudes towards their Caribbean 'playground'. The catalyst was a seemingly innocuous event at Montreal's Sir George Williams University in April, 1968, when six West Indian students asked for a hearing against Biology Professor Perry Anderson, whom they accused of racism in his marking practices. The university procrastinated and the students fumed. It was a dangerous time for university administrations; anti-war riots in the United States and Europe had already demonstrated the violent alienation, as well as the power, of youth. Riots in France almost brought down the government; students in the streets of Prague fought Soviet tanks with stones; in Northern Ireland, bloody riots had broken out for the first time in a generation.

While Sir George officials delayed and student anger mounted, a major Black Writers' Conference was held in Montreal in October, followed in November by a large ''Hemisphere Conference to End the War in Vietnam.'' Suddenly, radicals and fringe groups appeared as if from nowhere, and prominent black activists were making their demands in Montreal as well as in Chicago and New York. Trinidad-born Stokely Carmichael came; so did Black Panther Bobby Seale. The writers' conference had less to do with writing than it did with black liberation, and sympathetic whites were shocked when conference leaders closed them out of one of the sessions. Halifax activist Rocky Jones, in an angry reaction to white benevolence, told delegates: "We must strive to build a sense of unity that will never allow them to help us again."[13]

In December, the Sir George students staged a sit-in to get satisfaction in the Anderson case; there followed days of negotiations, crossed wires and missed opportunities for communication. Then, in January, several dozen students — black and white — marched to the ninth-floor computer centre, occupied it, and barricaded the single entrance. The occupation lasted for almost two weeks, ending only when police moved in, as students smashed computers, set fire to the centre and showered the throng in the streets below with IBM cards. Eighty-seven students, thirty-eight of them black, were arrested, and the damage was estimated at $2 million — higher than any other student riot in North America.

Bail for some of the black students was three times higher than for any of the whites, adding fuel to a racial drama that had been played out in front of the television cameras and been given prominent coverage in the Caribbean. Many of those arrested came from prominent families, and while parents and top West Indian lawyers flew in to Montreal, defence funds were started in Antigua and Trinidad, and the Trinidad government called for a common front by all Caribbean countries against racial discrimination. February 20 was declared a "Day of Solidarity" on the Jamaica campus of UWI; a week later, in Trinidad, Canadian Governor-General Roland Michener, on his first official overseas trip, was met by anti-Canadian student demonstrators, waving placards and spitting on his car as he passed.

It was as though a coating of syrup had been washed off the Canadian image of the Caribbean. It was not only the attitude towards blacks in Canada that was a problem for West Indians; Canadian activities in the Caribbean were as much at issue. Radical periodicals, such as *Abeng* in Jamaica and *Moko* in Trinidad, charged Canadian companies and banks with discriminatory hiring policies and anti-development business practices. Deposits had for years far exceeded loans among Canadian banks, which used capital generated in the Caribbean for operations elswhere. The loans that were made were restricted largely to traders, at the expense of local farmers and entrepreneurs; and even when lending policies were liberalized in the 1950s and 1960s, consumer loans predominated, again at the expense of small business and agriculture.

The friction over hiring practices ran particularly high in Guyana, where Canadians and other expatriates had established a virtual white ghetto in Demba's company town of Mackenzie. In Jamaica, a total investment in bauxite of over $550 million was providing Jamaica with only $25 million annually by 1972 — roughly $2 for every ton mined.[14] Jamaican economists, alert to the disproportionate profits being made by the companies, began to advise the government to step in. And while Canadian exports to the Caribbean were growing, imports from the region fell, in part because Canada continued to accord preferential Commonwealth tariff rates to South African sugar, to the anger and disgust of West Indian governments.

Sometimes the problem of communication seemed insurmountable. In an infamous public welcome, Toronto Mayor William Dennison greeted the Prime Minister of newly independent Guyana, Forbes Burnham, as Prime Minister of *Ghana* — four times.

In 1967, Barbados opened a small High Commission in Ottawa; although Canada had major investments and other interests in Barbados, the Canadian government would not reciprocate for nearly seven years, adding strength to the West Indian feeling that Canada simply took the region for granted.

Neither had tourism and its golden hordes proven the money-spinners they had promised to be. Almost as much foreign exchange was required for the sun-seekers once they reached the Caribbean as the amounts they brought with them. Although tourism created jobs, there was virtually no multiplier effect on the local economy. And while Canadians were being encouraged to frolic on West Indian beaches and to invest in profitable business ventures, West Indians were blocked from emigrating to Canada. The only encouragement before 1962 — when the immigration laws were eased somewhat — was a scheme inaugurated in 1955 to bring West Indian domestics to Canada. Even with such liberalization, the cards were heavily stacked in favour of the more highly educated. In 1965, 24% of West Indians admitted were professionals, compared to just 2%

of Italians, and this amplified charges that Canada not only discriminated, but was simply looting the Caribbean of its most qualified and badly-needed people. There began in 1966, however, one form of unskilled immigration that would endure: thousands of West Indian fruit and to-bacco workers were given temporary permits each year to do the menial work that unemployed Canadians either could not, or would not do.

Concerned about the growing antagonism, the Canadian Senate, not al-ways known for penetrating insight, decided in October, 1969, to conduct a broad investigation into Canadian interests in the Caribbean. A great many witnesses from government and the private sector were called, and in February, 1970, CUSO Executive Director Frank Bogdasavich ap-peared before the committee with his Public Relations Officer, Bob Sal-lery, and Caribbean Director, Father 'Howie' Gardiner. They had already submitted a detailed brief on CUSO activities in the Caribbean, which also outlined some of the difficulties the organization had faced in its first decade. The second part of the brief, with which almost all the senators were preoccupied, discussed the growing anti-Canadianism in the region, and the racial tension that had exploded into the Canadian consciousness.

In the two-and-a-half-hour presentation, it was Bob Sallery who sounded the most prophetic note. "There are problems and situations developing," he said, "which, despite all intentions to the contrary by well-meaning Canadians, are producing a climate of hostility, mistrust and frustration in the West Indies. . . . We are concerned with the increasing possibility that these relationships will get worse and not better."[15]

He was well aware of the anger that had been mounting in the Caribbean ever since the first trials of the Sir George students had begun in Montreal a month before, but he could hardly have known that the worst anti-Canadian eruption was only twenty-four hours away.

It began with 200 students in Port of Spain, Trinidad, marching on the Canadian High Commission and the head office of the Royal Bank of Canada. Within days, crowds of a few hundred had swelled to thou-sands. The demonstrations turned violent, and in April, the Trinidad Regiment mutinied and a state of emergency was declared.

Some in Trinidad, like third-year volunteer Jeanna Baty, who worked in the government's Planning and Development Department, had seen the trouble coming. One of her department's responsibilities was seasonal employment, and at Christmas 1969, the usual jobs had not been available. The men lined up and waited; but there were no jobs, and the crowd of protestors swelled as frustrations increased. Whereas the government admitted to a 25% unemployment rate, Jeanna Baty had seen the statistics, and knew that among young people it was 45% or higher.

As well, her social life began to change dramatically. For more than two years, she had enjoyed a special sort of popularity: "Being a white, single, Canadian female, not to mention plump — which was popular at the time — and barraged by requests for dates, gave me quite an inflated feeling of myself."[16] Suddenly, however, she became part of a very visible, unpopular minority: "I had felt a part of the society and I suddenly realized that I was not."

Now there were roadblocks everywhere and the police had begun to carry firearms; Molotov cocktails were thrown into homes; there were reports of rapes and violent robberies against whites. Baty was told to stay home from work so as not to make the situation worse. Finally she bought a plane ticket to Barbados where the CUSO office was, and every day for two weeks, kept moving the reservation twenty-four hours ahead in hopes that the situation would calm down. Eventually it did, but not before CUSO had pulled her out and had begun to wind down the Trinidad program.

But it was in Jamaica that the CUSO volunteers suffered the most overt racial tension and violence, even though postings were now made more carefully, and there were fewer volunteers — the numbers were halved in 1971, from thirty to fifteen. One of the 1971 group, Ray Clark, was posted to a country school and immediately ran into problems.

"The street boys — both unemployed school leavers and uneducated — would sit on the roadside and spew out obscenities at me because I was white, none of which made any sense, because I couldn't understand the patois — 'ras claat', 'bumba claat', 'pussy claat' — I thought it was all a form of greeting, so I just waved and carried on."[17]

But after just four days on the job he was given a message that was unmistakeable; leaving for the school, he found his Jamaican landlord's two dogs hanging on the fence, their throats cut.

"I knew instinctively that it was against me, but my reaction was one of anger — the poor bloody dogs. So I took the dogs to the rum bar at the bottom of the hill where the street boys were hanging out, and I threw them on the floor, and I said, 'If you killed them, you bury them!' I didn't even think of the danger; I just took it as a symbol of them not wanting me there, and I thought, 'I'm here and I'm going to stay.'''

Such an incident would have sent almost anyone packing. Eight of the fifteen volunteers to Jamaica that year left early. Clark's predecessor had stayed only three months, and, in his own way, had escaped even before that — smoking ganja, worshipping the sun and walking naked through the town. For those, like Clark, who reacted by determining to stay, the problems were difficult, but not insoluble: having confronted the issue, he surmounted it, and found increasing job satisfaction in a setting where there were no other expatriates with whom to compete — or commiserate.

Field Staff Officer Chris Bryant, sought alternatives to the random postings and job frustration which, increasingly, were the lot of volunteers in Jamaica. He and officials in the Ministry of Education tried to develop more coherent programming ideas; one of the more successful projects was a five-year 'Remedial Reading Program' which began in 1971. It involved, altogether, about 60 volunteers — mature, experienced, competent teachers — many of whom found enough satisfaction to keep them in Jamaica for three or four years. They were posted at first to junior secondary schools, two in each, and using the pilot projects as a base, they fanned out to other schools in the region. They worked, as well, in the primary schools and teachers' colleges. CUSO provided professional backup; the Ministry assisted with seminars and workshops, and Jamaicans were sent to McGill University where special remedial reading courses had been set up. The Jamaica Reading Association developed out of this program, and when Chris Bryant attended one of its meetings in 1974, he was proud to see over 600 members present.

But when the Remedial Reading Program ended in 1976, no coherent plan for new programming arose to replace it. Between 1975, when Bryant returned to Canada to become CUSO's Human Resource Director, and 1979, the Caribbean Program was staffed by people with almost no programming experience, and in some cases, no personal knowledge of the Caribbean. Declining requests, continuing West Indian resentment of

Canadians, and a critical lack of direction at the top led to a rapid deterioration of what had once been CUSO's most promising program.

As in other parts of the world, CUSO began to offer support — mostly financial — to local development organizations, but this sort of project development was painfully slow and required special field staff skills which could only be developed over time. A vaguely enunciated program of job-creation projects was put forward in response to what had become the biggest problem in the Caribbean. Unemployment was estimated regionally at 40%, and among youth at 60% and higher. Speaking of the changing CUSO emphasis, Jamaican Field Staff Officer Carl Mackenzie said, "A maturing process has taken place. We have completed our work in the form of placing volunteers. I would like to retain the capacity for recruiting volunteers as developmental needs arise, but our major focus is now in employment generation."[18]

He was putting a brave face on what had in a few short years become a weak and costly effort. With fewer and fewer acceptable programs to put forward, the Caribbean's share of the CUSO budget slipped, and when the organization's overall budget shrank in 1979, it was decided that the Barbados office should be closed. In its place, CUSO fielded a temporary Projects Officer for the Eastern Caribbean, whose job was to maintain the few existing projects and provide liaison with the remaining volunteers in the region.

When Marlene Green was appointed Projects Officer for the Eastern Caribbean islands in 1979, she had in mind a return to her home in Dominica, but she had seen many Canadianized West Indians become disillusioned after a brief return to the islands. She viewed the CUSO assignment as a means of testing the water and gradually easing herself back into life in the Caribbean. Green had moved to Canada in 1960 to study at the University of Toronto. After doing graduate studies in Windsor, she spent five years with Toronto's Black Education Project as a social worker: dealing with children and parents; teenagers in trouble; the police — and generally mobilizing the black community around the issues of the day. This was followed by two years working in school-community relations for the Toronto Board of Education. She worked with ethnic communities and parent-teacher associations, attempting to involve parents in the schools and to bring minority groups into the mainstream of Toronto society.

As an experienced social worker and as a West Indian, Green began her CUSO career with several advantages: she didn't have to worry about being misunderstood; there were no major racial or cultural barriers to overcome, and she didn't have to go to great lengths to prove herself.

It had been the intention for Green to open a small CUSO office in centrally located Dominica, but two weeks before her departure from Canada, nature intervened when Hurricane David swept in from the sea. Dominica was devastated: the banana crop was destroyed; 75% of the citrus and 90% of the coconut trees were badly damaged; 80% of the island's fishing boats vanished; electricity was knocked out; telephones were gone, and much of the capital city, Roseau, was flattened. So Green continued on and established the CUSO office in Grenada.

But Grenada was not just another Island in the Windwards. Maurice Bishop, a dynamic young lawyer with revolutionary ideas, had seized power in March, 1979. His Marxist declamations and his eager social transformation programs had attracted an eclectic assortment of socialists and idealists from other Caribbean countries, the curiosity and support of many international development agencies, Cuba's help in building a world-class airplane runway, and the darkening wrath of a bellicose American President. It was a concoction that was bound to spell trouble, especially with the swing to the right in many of the other islands, most notably Jamaica, where pro-business, pro-Reagan Edward Seaga had toppled the government of Social Democrat Michael Manley; and in Dominica where Eugenia Charles, a tough, Toronto-trained lawyer, presided over a small but decidedly conservative legislature.

To conservative politicians, Maurice Bishop represented a twofold threat: he had established a dangerous precedent in seizing power by the gun in the Commonwealth Caribbean's first coup d'etat; and he had established the first Marxist regime in the islands. Regardless of his achievements and social programs, regardless of the obvious improvements of his government over the previous one, Bishop was anathema to many of his neighbours, and those whose support for his regime seemed obvious from their presence in Grenada — CUSO included — became suspect.

Hurricane David, which had been Marlene Green's actual impetus for locating the CUSO office in Grenada, changed other plans as well: for one thing, a number of Canadian organizations were interested in providing relief assistance, and having no staff in the region, several approached CUSO for ideas, contacts, and ultimately, as a conduit for funds. Some of the small local organizations that CUSO had supported after 1975 had matured, and with financial assistance from CUSO and other agencies, were better able than outsiders to organize relief efforts, as well as reconstruction and farm assistance programs in the wake of the hurricane. When Saint Vincent's volcano — La Soufrière — erupted and Hurricane Allan struck in 1980, the number of Canadian agencies wishing to help multiplied.

Green hired local people as 'host national' volunteers, treating them as part of the regular CUSO volunteer complement, an idea CUSO had developed several years earlier but had only put into limited practice. In Dominica, she contacted the Youth Division of the Ministry of Education and provided CUSO support for three reconstruction projects. A cousin, Ronald Green, who had once been a Peace Corps volunteer in Nigeria, was taken on as a host national volunteer, along with another recently returned Dominican, Joey Pelletier; together they formed an organization called Special Projects Assistance Team (SPAT) to act as a go-between for local and foreign agencies, by identifying projects, writing them up, providing information for donors, and doing evaluative work.

In Grenada she developed projects with women's groups, with a fledgling cooperative movement, and with the Food and Nutrition Council. And throughout the islands there were still a small number of volunteers: a haematology technician in Dominica, a technical teacher in Saint Lucia, a volunteer working on a sea-moss commercialization project in Saint Vincent. A Vancouver nutritionist, Robert Kripps, assisted in setting up the Grenada Nutrition Council; he undertook a nutritional survey of the island and assisted the government with training programs for community health aides, with family education, coordinated feeding programs for the island's undernourished children, and education for mothers on the advantages of breast feeding over the use of imported baby foods.

In Jamaica, too, CUSO seemed to have developed a new lease on life. Carl Mackenzie's slow, painstaking efforts in the job creation projects he had suggested years before, particularly those involving youth, were beginning to bear fruit. As a Jamaican and as a former teacher, he had a special knack with young people, and he used it to good advantage. One of his most successful projects was not far from his own home, high in the hills overlooking Kingston. A group of young men who called themselves the Salisbury Plain Young Farmers, bought a plot of land with CUSO's assistance, and established a small piggery, a 1,000 unit hatchery, twenty goats and three hundred rabbits. They cleared four-and-a-half acres of Salisbury Plain, which, since it is mainly steep slopes rather than a 'plain', was backbreaking work; and they planted two acres of coffee, half an acre of yams, 2,000 plantains and assorted vegetables.

CUSO assisted the South West St. Andrews Citizens' Association, in the depths of one of Kingston's lifeless industrial estates, to develop a farm and excavate a giant fish pond for the cultivation of a species of fast-growing fish. The emloyees of the government-owned Casa Monte Hotel, which had been used as a hotel training school and which was about to be closed, approached CUSO for a loan so that they could keep the hotel open and manage it as a cooperative. *Sistren*, a group of unemployed ghetto women, was assisted in the formation of what would become an internationally acclaimed theatre company. Backyard foundrymen in the Kingston slums were helped with materials, organization and technical skills in recycling scrap. And in the hills above Montego Bay, CUSO provided grants to help the Adelphi Youth Agricultural Project establish a farm which raised goats, chickens and food crops. Mackenzie worked with many of the projects personally, sitting on their management boards and providing advice in a way that a Canadian Field Staff Officer would never have been able to do.

Mackenzie also discovered that while there was a ceiling on CUSO funds, the projects were attractive to other organizations in Canada and in Europe. Since most of the Jamaican groups were too young and inexperienced to deal directly with foreign agencies, he hit on the idea of establishing a Jamaican organization that could act as a clearing house. With CUSO funding, he incorporated "Projects for People," and became its first project director on a part-time basis. Projects for People proved to be a canny, positive move as far as other organizations were concerned, and funding for the projects flowed easily, with Mackenzie, courtesy of a CUSO salary and the convoluted administrative arrangement, acting in essence as a Field Staff Officer for Oxfam, the Dutch organization NOVIB, the Overseas Book Centre and a variety of other organizations. It seemed as though CUSO's Caribbean program had at last come of age, that the niche it had sought for so many years had been found.

Canada's official aid agency CIDA, also began to take a renewed interest in CUSO's work in the region, and CUSO's Ottawa office was able to negotiate a special increase in the 1981 budget allocation for further Caribbean job creation projects. Staff and Board members wanted to visit. Several Ottawa staff members took a personal interest — perhaps slightly over-zealous in their fascination with the Grenadian revolution and its 'new democracy' — arranging trips for teachers, union representatives and other holidaying CUSO staff. It all seemed to add to the positive climate that had developed in Head Office towards a program that had almost closed only two years before. Phil Esmonde, CUSO's British Columbia Board member, travelled to Jamaica in November, 1981 on a photo assignment, while at the same time former Cabinet Minister Iona Campagnolo, recruited by the Ottawa office as a special fund raiser, flew in to visit projects before mounting a cross-Canada CUSO fund-raising tour.

But CUSO was in for a sobering shock. On 12 November, Iona Campagnolo and Carl Mackenzie had set off from the office on Waterloo Avenue to spend the day visiting projects. Phil Esmonde stayed behind in the office with the secretarial staff. Then, without warning, the door crashed open, and fifteen heavily armed men, some carrying machine guns, others with pistols at the ready, invaded the house. Esmonde and the others were slammed against the wall, while the attackers secured the premises.

Once the initial panic had subsided, Esmonde was informed that the office was the subject of a police action, and that the plain clothes officers were searching for weapons. Great interest was shown in two dozen tea chests in the breezeway outside, but when they were pried open, the police seemed almost disappointed to find that they were full of books from Ottawa's Overseas Book Centre. They questioned everybody at length, and rummaged through the filing cabinets, apparently searching for subversive literature. Then they left.

Iona Campagnolo was not nicknamed "the Iron Lady" for nothing. When she and Mackenzie returned to the office to find a distraught Esmonde and the severely shaken staff, she demanded action from the Canadian High Commissioner who immediately phoned Prime Minister Seaga.

Seaga promised to investigate the matter. The following day, however, one of the staff leaked the story to NDP Member of Parliament, Father Bob Ogle, who raised it in the House of Commons during Question Period. Within hours it was the lead item on Jamaica's evening news and the subject of banner headlines in the following morning's *Gleaner*.

Two weeks later, a polite letter of regret arrived from Jamaican Minister of Foreign Affairs, Hugh Shearer. In it he wrote, "I should like to set your mind at rest and inform you that the raid had nothing to do with your organization as such, nor with the staff of that organization." He went on to add, "The police have informed us that they found no illegal activity by CUSO on the premises, nor is there any allegation made against the staff."[19]

The soothing tones were somewhat misleading, however. Such statements as no illegal activities "on the premises" and no "allegations" against the staff, did not exactly clear the air, especially when Prime Minister Seaga hinted at something else to a group of Canadian Members of Parliament. Gerald Utting, writing in the *Toronto Star*, reported Jamaica's Prime Minister as saying that CUSO had become " 'politically infiltrated in Jamaica' during the regime of former Prime Minister Michael Manley . . . The meeting was closed to the press, but the *Star* learned of Seaga's remarks through reliable sources." Utting went on to recall how "the Jamaican police searched the building for weapons and explosives, but apparently found none."[20] 'Apparently' Utting believed that something — perhaps Kalishnikovs or M-16s — had been held back.

A lurid article followed in the *Kingston Star*. Sharing a page with a buxom nude was a story headlined, "TOO MUCH SECRECY IN CUSO".[21] It detailed a number of 'suspicious' activities. Although the CUSO garage had been a transit point for school books for fifteen years, "No one could know that there were books in the crates" — it had apparently not occurred to police or reporters that a simple query might have avoided the fuss. The article went on to reveal that the Chairman of the CUSO Board of Directors was a member of "the left-wing New Democratic Party of Canada" and that a man once "seen around" a CUSO goat-rearing project had been killed in a police shootout elsewhere on the island. Some of the self-help groups which CUSO assisted in Jamaica were not supporters of Prime Minister Seaga's conservative brand of politics, and they too came in for a barrage of criticism and innuendo.

Prime Minister Seaga was unable or unwilling to admit that a mistake had been made, perhaps sensing fire where he smelled smoke. Embarrassed by the continuing publicity, he lent his name to the muddle of half truths and sinister allegations, charging that criminal elements had been involved in some CUSO projects and suggesting that in a few cases CUSO had been used, perhaps unwittingly, by the Workers' Party of Jamaica — a tiny radical Marxist party — to fund projects for which the WPJ took the credit.

The agricultural project in West St. Andrew was in a PNP stronghold, Seaga said, and it was impossible for it to not have political implications. He too had poultry projects in his riding, he added, and knew that they were seen as political, so he had never made any effort to attract external funding for them. He suggested, in conclusion, that there were problems with three CUSO projects in particular. He charged that CUSO had been lax in its project approvals and suggested ominously that further 'difficulties' might occur if remedial action was not taken.

In an attempt to get at the truth, CUSO engaged two individuals with impeccable credibility in Jamaica — one a staff member of the Caribbean Conference of Churches, the other an employee of the government's own Small Business Development Centre — to undertake a $10,000 evaluation of the three projects that seemed to have caused the greatest concern, and to investigate charges of 'political infiltration'. While one of the projects, the Adelphi Goat Farm, was found to be in a state of financial disarray and was subsequently cancelled, the other two — the Salisbury Plain Young Farmers and the Casa Monte Hotel — were given a clean bill of health, and CUSO was exonerated of any formal or informal links with political groups or criminal elements.[22]

CUSO's work in the island had almost ground to a standstill for six months while the drama played itself out and a series of CUSO representatives travelled to Jamaica to meet with the Prime Minister, government officials, journalists and project holders. Although crack *Toronto Star* reporters never bothered to clear up the 'apparent' weapons mystery, the *Kingston Star* did allow CUSO space to explain its programs under the headline ''NO SECRETS IN CUSO,'' and to share a page once again with a well endowed woman, who was this time less scantily clad. She wore a necklace.

As the Jamaica drama unfolded, an equally disturbing event took place in Dominica. One of the few volunteers on the island, a Jamaican-born haematology technician, was deported immediately following a violent December, 1981 coup attempt that had bizarre connections with the Canadian underworld and the Ku Klux Klan. Prime Minister Eugenia Charles announced in the legislature that the volunteer could have done "untold harm to the country," and the regional media gave the incident sensational coverage. The Prime Minister was quoted as saying, "Investigations indicated that by her associations and her utterances, (the volunteer) made it clear that she was bent on obtaining information not allied to her field of work, and in any way possible assisting plans which might be for the detriment of the country."[23]

Charles also asked the Canadian Department of External Affairs to have CUSO removed entirely from the island.

First Jamaica and now Dominica; it had become like a suddenly mounting tennis score — 15; 30; 40; game — with nothing in between. Gordon Cressy, the Christmas tree entrepreneur of 1963, now senior Toronto Alderman and Chairman of the CUSO Board, went to Dominica, where he met with the Prime Minister and several of her cabinet ministers. He was alarmed by the shallowness of the circumstantial evidence presented in the case of the expelled volunteer: a supposed romantic liaison with an opposition politician allegedly made her a communist; a colleague's makeup had supposedly been poisoned; by seeking a blood donation of the same type as the Chief of Police only days before his wounding in the coup attempt, the volunteer had somehow implicated herself.

It was only after extensive discussions ranging over several months regarding CUSO's projects, reporting and administration that the air cleared somewhat. Prime Minister Charles eventually dropped the charges of poisoned makeup and political intrigue that had been levelled against the volunteer. "Let me assure you," she wrote, "that Dominica is willing and ready and very honoured to participate in CUSO programs. However we feel bound to inform you that where CUSO is not performing as it should locally, we will not hesitate to inform you."[24]

For Marlene Green, the events in Jamaica and Dominica were symptomatic of a larger ill; real social change seemed to pose a substantive threat to conservative governments. "If we are going to continue to work with groups of people who come from a level of society where things have been very difficult and they are trying to change that, we have to expect close scrutiny," she concluded. "If people are involved in some sort of cooperative or collective project that is going well, they tend to have a different view of themselves and the world around them . . . they are often very outspoken politically. It is almost inevitable that the people you find who are going to be involved in that kind of work, who have the confidence to try some innovative approaches or to initiate things, tend to be people who are critical of the way governments have traditionally dealt with grass roots development in certain sectors of the population. It's not as though we don't look elsewhere to see what there is in the way of people who have the commitment and vision and energy; they're really not there, or if they are, they're keeping themselves well hidden."[25]

A month after her October, 1983 evacuation from Grenada, when the military situation had stabilized and a new interim government was installed, Marlene Green returned and began the delicate task of trying to pick up the CUSO pieces again. "My concern is for the ordinary Grenadians who put a lot of effort, sweat, tears and love into trying to build their country," she had said.[26] But in Canada she had also criticized the American invasion vehemently, and the interim government, as intolerant of external criticism as the one it had replaced, quietly asked her to leave the island.

There were a number of lessons in the resolution of the crises: one was that much better relations should have been developed with some of the island governments. As well, the bruised and chastened CUSO field staff were forced to look more closely at their own project management, and the criteria they were using for project approval. CUSO's infatuation with Grenada's doomed revolution had distressed the authorities in some of the more conservative islands, and it was clear that the staff's own liberal attitudes did not accord with some of the political trends in the Caribbean.

In a sense, CUSO had fallen into the trap that Executive Director Frank Bogdasavich had warned of years before: "What is required on our part is not to become terribly concerned about ideology; this preoccupation has been a tragedy."

But perhaps the real root of CUSO's problems in the Caribbean lay in confusion and uncertainty about its role, a confusion that existed from the beginning. Was it a development agency, or an organization whose primary function was to offer Canadians — mainly young Canadians — an opportunity to experience another culture? Or could the two concepts be joined?

To Gandhi, the Europeans working in his ashram were important for cultural and political reasons; they represented an essential form of solidarity with India and with the ideals of peace and development that he was attempting to promote internationally. That they may have brought useful skills to the ashram was almost incidental. Many of the first Canadian volunteers were posted to Indian ashrams not unlike those in which Gandhi had worked only fifteen years before, and they would argue, as Gandhi had, that the personal experience, the demonstration of commitment, the learning that would accrue to Canada when they returned, were as important as anything else.

But the money to simply 'be there' didn't exist, and the enthusiastic early attempt to find meaningful jobs for young Canadians in the Caribbean fell foul of an economy and a social inheritance that could not sustain it. Longstanding Canadian paternalism and exploitation exacted a heavy personal price from the volunteers, and demanded a reassessment and a redirection in which errors would be made. Beguiled by deceptively simple issues of right and wrong, and guided more by conscience than experience, CUSO had sought to perform its works in an increasingly capricious political setting. Moving into more socially relevant areas of endeavour, it had collided with intractable elements as hostile to criticism as they were apprehensive of social change.

In a sense, to use a Jamaican Proverb, CUSO had swapped a black dog for a monkey. In exchange for its naive innocence, its Canadian lesson plans, its Christmas trees and its goodwill, it had chosen a path as fraught with problems and as demanding of its ingenuity as any it had ever faced.

Chapter 4

Judy Pullen

Judy Pullen applied for a short-term CVCS posting in the Caribbean in 1962. Guy Arnold, who had a reputation for being unpleasant in his interviews, threw her as many curves as he could think of. "She would smile and immediately have an answer," Arnold recalled. "She was extraordinarily good. She was so good in her answers that I almost turned her down; I thought, 'My God, at her age she can't be this good. Where's the catch?' "[1]

But she *was* good, and she spent four months of that summer in Jamaica — 'a star volunteer', in Guy Arnold's recollection. She then returned to the University of Toronto where she enrolled in a pre-med course and became engaged. Among the speakers on the campus circuit that year was the legendary humanitarian jungle doctor, Tom Dooley, and Judy Pullen, itching for adventure from her Caribbean experience, found the stimulus she needed, perhaps wanted, in his inspirational words. "I asked my fiance if I could go and work with the Tibetan refugees for a year," she recalled. "He said I could, but just for a year."[2]

Tibet had maintained a centuries-old nominal independence under the vague suzerainty of the Chinese emperors, suffering the occasional indignity of British penetration in the twilight years of empire. But after Indian independence and the communist victory in Peking, Tibet became something of an international question mark. India finally settled its own inherited but unsubstantiated Tibetan interests in favour of Peking in 1954, ensuring Tibet's imminent incorporation into metropolitan China and eclipsing the ancient Buddhist theocracy of the oft-reincarnated Dalai Lama.

Chinese-inspired public denunciation of the Dalai Lama in 1959 was the signal, and the man who had become the fourteenth reincarnation of Chenresi, the Buddha of Mercy and protector of All Living Things, began his long and painful walk through the towering Himalayas towards India.

Some eighty thousand Tibetans followed him, settling in or near the Indian hill towns of Darjeeling, Mussurie, Simla and Dharamsala. Having journeyed from a cold dry climate with little disease and less hunger, they now faced both, in quantity. At Kangra, fifteen miles below Dharamsala, where the Dalai Lama settled, a school and makeshift home had been established for Tibetan children, and somehow a request for a nurse had found its way to CUSO. One of the volunteers already in India visited Kangra and wrote to Ottawa of the snow-covered mountains, the beautiful green valley, and the ancient stone roads said to have been built by the army of Alexander the Great. But within the refugee settlement, pain and suffering were writ large. The children were badly undernourished and were susceptible to disease of all kinds. They suffered from malaria, boils, sores, skin infections, dysentery, scabies, weak hearts, asthma, conjunctivitis and simple childhood diseases such as measles, mumps and chicken pox, which spread like killer plagues among a community that had never know modern vaccination. "If I were you," the volunteer wrote to Ottawa, "I would give serious thought to the advisability of sending both a nurse and a teacher. There is plenty of work for both, and if one fell sick, the other could help out."[3]

And so, late in 1963, on her short leave of absence from her fiance in Toronto, July Pullen arrived in Kangra, with a CUSO nurse, Lois James. The following year, the camp was moved up to Dharamsala where Judy would instruct monks in the newly established teacher-training school, adding modern subjects to their traditional studies of scripture, logic and poetry.

"In addition to two English classes, I'm giving lectures in geography, general science, hygiene, current events, world history, etc.," she wrote from Dharamsala in July. "It all sounds very grand, but I'm just trying to give some grounding in each subject.''[4] When study of the solar system began, the monks became very excited, and in the evenings clustered around the school's small globe with flashlights and balls, attempting to understand sunrise, the phases of the moon and solar eclipses. They were fascinated by the idea of rockets and communication satellites.

Jean Carberry, wife of the CUSO Field Staff Officer in New Delhi, visited Dharamsala in those years and shared July Pullen's rude accommodation. ''Judy lived in one little room with two beds and nothing much else. There was another room almost as big next door with a concrete floor; this was her bathroom.''

''I watched her training the monks, some of whom were ten times reincarnated, and far and away her superior in the Tibetan social structure. But their Rinpoche*who ran the school, read the riot act and told them they were to carry her books and assist her . . . She had a keep-fit class in the morning and she had them all doing deep knee bends and jumping. It was quite beneath them, but they did it.''[5]

Both Judy and Lois James were often ill, Judy with infectious hepatitis and Lois with liver problems. Nevertheless, work continued. On one occasion, Judy wrote about the arrival of a new group of 120 Tibetan children. ''Those kids had camped four months on the border without shelter, food, or help. They buried two of their number there, and then permission came to enter India — on the grounds of compassion. Seventeen were left in a nearby hospital — nearly dead — and the others came on here on a nightmare of a train ride in the most blistering heat. You wouldn't believe it unless you saw it — they're still only shells and skeletons of children. Two more have died — one in Lois's arms . . . of worm convulsions. Lois had to cremate the body herself.''[6]

In 1965, Lois's health gave out and she was forced to return to Canada. Judy's year in India had become two, and she was now planning to extend for two more. ''After a year, it was clear to me that if I had really wanted to get married, I wouldn't have come out here in the first place'' she said. Now that the first group of thirty-five monks had graduated, how could she refuse a request from the Dalai Lama himself, that she remain and expand the school?

Towards the end of her second two-year assignment, Judy became

---

* The title 'Rinpoche' means blessed incarnation.

engaged to Tsweang Cheogyal 'T.C.' Tethong, a Tibetan appointed by the Dalai Lama to run one of the large settlement projects. The wedding was held in Judy's hometown, in the incongruous ambience of an Oakville Ontario summer. Family friends, returned volunteers who had gone to India with Judy years before, and Tibetan children, all gathered and strolled on the broad lawns of the family home, while Tibetan and Canadian flags fluttered from the second floor of the house.

Judy and T.C. returned to India and a new project, cutting a home for 300 refugees out of a jungle tract. Their own honeymoon dwelling was a one-room hut of bamboo and grass, and the work was hard. Gradually, the first 300 settlers grew in number, eventually totalling 7,000, living in seven separate villages. Judy worked on the establishment and equipping of a new fifty-bed hospital, and organized public health training programs in the villages. By 1975, the area was almost totally self-sufficient, with workshops, temples, schools, stores and monasteries. That year, the eighth since their marriage, Judy and T.C. asked the Dalai Lama for a leave of absence, returning to Canada where T.C. would work on a masters degree and teach at the Lester B. Pearson College of the Pacific. Soon after their arrival in Canada, their third child was born, increasing by fifty percent the world population of Tibetan-Canadians. There would be honours — Judy was awarded the Order of Canada in 1976 — and there would be time to reflect. But they would chafe and think wistfully of their work in India.

"I can't wait to get back to India," Judy said after two years in Victoria, B.C. "We had a more sane existence and I have become accustomed to the life. We don't have television, cars or entertainment. We work hard all day and devote the evening to the family. I find the rat race here terribly unrewarding."[7]

And so, in 1980, Judy, T.C. and their children began to think of packing their bags once again and returning to their work in the lee of the high Himalayas, beyond which lay the Tibetan homeland.

Chapter 5

Where's Biafra?

And a man's foes shall be they of his own household.
—Matthew 11:36

The Nigerian Civil War, which began in June, 1967, and ended in January, 1970, was the most monstrous and destructive man-made event to take place in post-colonial Africa. It cost the lives of hundreds of thousands of people, pitted African nations against one another, and set back the development of Africa's most populous country by a generation. For churches and relief agencies, it marked a political coming of age, an awakening to the harsh realities of Third World warfare. And for CUSO, it was a growing conflict between the idealism that had marked volunteer programs during the early 1960s, and the grim realities of post-colonial underdevelopment that emerged once the first optimism of independence had faded.

CUSO had hoped to start operations in Nigeria with an auspicious debut, in response to a 1961 request for fifty teachers. Ultimately, because of bureaucratic confusion in Nigeria and difficulties with new recruitment and selection procedures in Canada, only seven volunteers actually left for Nigeria the following summer.

Nigeria was a vast country with over sixty million people, a compli-

cated federal system of government and less than two years of independence behind it; it was clear from the outset that if CUSO was serious
about working there, and expected to be taken seriously, some sort of
resident Canadian staffing would be essential. The solution presented
itself in the persons of Walter and Barbara McLean.

Walter, whose father was a Presbyterian minister in Victoria, had been
impressed by visits from Dr. Ted Johnson, the church's secretary for
Overseas Missions, who, in 1954, had urged the Canadian Presbyterian
Church into partnership in Nigeria with the Church of Scotland. In 1957,
Johnson brought one of the Nigerian Presbyterians with him to Canada
for a speaking tour, and Dr. Francis Ibiam made a tremendous impact
on the young McLean when he met with a group of students at UBC. "I
am inviting you to come to Nigeria," Dr. Ibiam said, and it was as though
he was speaking directly to McLean. "We need your help."[1]

McLean accepted the challenge after completing his studies and becoming President of the National Federation of Canadian University Students, a position which briefly placed him on the CUSO Board in 1961.
In December, 1962, his divinity studies complete, he and Barbara arrived
in Enugu, the capital of the Eastern Region of Nigeria, eager to take up
the challenge, however vaguely defined at first. Back in Canada, within
a matter of weeks, Bill McWhinney approached Ted Johnson to ask if
McLean might be made available to do some part-time work for CUSO.
The response was positive, and though the McLeans' contribution was
voluntary and unpaid, it quickly encroached on everything else they were
doing. The need for teachers in newly independent Nigeria was tremendous, and McLean spent long hours with the Permanent Secretary in the
Ministry of Education, N. U. Akpan — discussing schools, educational
policy, development issues and politics. He travelled extensively, visiting
hospitals, clinics and mission schools, and at his home, he was besieged
by a "lineup of nuns every morning waiting for teachers." He ran an
office out of the McLean house at Queen's School in Enugu where Barbara
taught, and they converted the garage into a kind of hostel for new
volunteers. He and Barbara worked tirelessly, often long into the night;
Walter dictating lengthy letters to Bill McWhinney back in Ottawa, and
Barbara typing until one or two in the morning.

When McWhinney came to Nigeria for a visit, he and McLean would
make extensive tours of the south in the McLeans' rickety old Volkswa-

gen, known fondly by its license number, 'EE 90'. On Sundays, they would also stop at a number of the churches that McLean served. Between cramped, cross-country forays in EE 90, the six-foot six-inch McWhinney had to sit through four services one Sunday, and he vowed never again to travel on the Sabbath with McLean.

It was a stimulating time for the McLeans, but the CUSO work was not easy. They had to invent policy as they went along. After a series of unpleasant motorcycle accidents, McLean decreed that all volunteers would henceforth be required to wear helmets. He insisted on knowing when they were leaving the country and where they were going; he worried about orientation programs, the volunteers' health and what he would do if one of them died.

Some of the volunteers were uncertain of McLean. Most didn't want to wear helmets and a few resented and questioned his authority. Some felt that his church connections identified CUSO too closely with a missionary image, (although years later this concern for the conflict between religious and secular matters was not shared by Prime Minister Mulroney, who appointed McLean — a Member of Parliament since 1979 — Secretary of State).

As CUSO's numbers grew and McLean's church activity began to take him further and further afield to Ibadan and Lagos, there was also criticism of some of the postings. McLean was now moving in more rarified circles: N. U. Apkan was soon to be elevated to a much more senior position; Dr. Ibiam, now Sir Francis Ibiam, had become Governor of the Eastern Region; and one of McLean's Lagos parishioners was Dr. Okoi Arikpo, Foreign Minister of Nigeria. In Enugu, McLean was treated as a kind of unofficial honorary Canadian consul, both by the far-off Canadian High Commission in Lagos, and by the regional government. Thus, by 1965, the need for a full-time staff person to take over from him had become apparent.

Before the McLeans left Nigeria for an extended home leave in the summer of 1965, Walter proposed to McWhinney that he appoint one of the volunteers, Bill McNeill, to the staff position. McNeill was a little older than most of the volunteers — at twenty-six, he was older than McLean — and he stood out in McLean's mind because he was one of the few who had offered to help with the baggage when the group had arrived the previous summer. McNeill accepted the job, at $5,000 a year, bought the ancient 'EE 90' from McLean, loaded it up with the files and the dictaphone, and headed for Ibadan in the Western Region, where he intended to set up the office. "I'll never forgive Walter for unloading that goddamned car on us," McNeill recalled, only half jokingly. "It was a menace, and I didn't know how to drive anyway. It kept slipping out of gear, so the only way you could drive it was to hold your knee around the shift stick."[2]

By now, there were dozens of volunteers in the East and growing numbers in the Mid-West and Western Regions; and McNeill was charged with expanding the program into the vast Northern Region where the needs were even greater. Events, however, intervened.

The Nigerian Federation was a cumbersome hybrid, welded from the former British colonies and protectorates (once stretching) from Lagos and the Oil Rivers in the south, to the Sultanate of Sokoto and the walled cities of Kano, Katsina and Maiduguri in the north. Bonded only by the British colonial status and a succession of clumsy, Westminster-inspired constitutions in the 1940s and 1950s, Nigeria followed Ghana into independence in October, 1960. The Fedcration, a patchwork of vastly different historical realities, with dozens of culturally distinct ethnic groups, was, to say the least, fragile.

The predominant Northerners were the Hausa and the Fulani. Largely Muslim, their country had been occupied by the British for less than sixty years. They were a proud, culturally self-confident people living in a feudal economy that had accommodated itself only minimally to the political requirements of the colonial power. In the south, the Youba dominated the fractious Western Region, and the Ibo people predominated in the Eastern Region. Overcrowding and limited arable land, however, had pushed the Ibos outward; by the time of independence, hundreds of thousands had moved north. Ambitious, literate and predominantly Christian, they were prominent throughout the nation's commercial life, and they dominated the civil service in the Northern Region.

Nigeria's political parties developed almost exclusively along ethnic lines, and the first independent government was a shaky coalition between the North and the Ibo East. During the election of 1964-65, a new alliance between the West and the North emerged, and the Ibos were suddenly left out. Then, in a January 1966 coup engineered by five young Ibo majors, the army took over, and an Ibo, Major General Johnson Aguyi-Ironsi, became Head of State. During the coup, the deposed Prime Minister — a Northerner — and the Premier of the Northern Region were murdered. For the North, their deaths, along with the emergence of an Ibo Head of State, were intolerable. Friction between the regions grew. In an effort to hold the nation together and to defuse inter-regional animosity, General Ironsi abolished the federal form of government, declaring a unitary state. Almost universally unacceptable, the coup was as profoundly upsetting to the Nigerian Regions as the abolition of provincial governments might be to Alberta or Quebec. In the North, particularly, it was seen as a thinly disguised attempt to consolidate Ibo power.

Suddenly, a series of vicious pogroms broke out across the towns and cities of Northern Nigeria and hundreds of Ibos were killed. As the military government began to lose control of the country, a second coup was staged by rebellious Northern troops; Ironsi was murdered along with more than a hundred Ibo officers and men. The army Chief of Staff, a young Christian Northerner named Gowon, emerged as the new Head of State, but Lt. Col. Ojukwu, the Military Governor of the East, refused to accept his authority. A series of complicated constitutional conferences were organised in an attempt to resolve the issue, but in the midst of these developments a second and more murderous wave of anti-Ibo massacres broke out in the North. Official estimates placed the dead at thirty thousand, and within days, more than a million Ibos were pouring back into the East from all over Nigeria — refugees in their own country. Ojukwu, not lacking in personal political ambition, now found himself under enormous pressure from his advisors and his people to secede from the federation.

In a final attempt to break the deadlock, the Federal Government announced the creation of new states, or rather, the division of the existing four regions into twelve states, a move which would have effectively destroyed the East as a power block. As a result, four days later, on May 30, 1967, Ojukwu declared the secession of the Eastern Region. Thus began the short and violent life of the Republic of Biafra.

"Nigeria never was and never can be a united country," Ojukwu later wrote. "The very nature of Nigeria inevitably gave rise to political power groups, goaded by sectional rather than national interests . . . From the moment of independence, all forms of corruption in public life found a good thriving ground in Nigeria, as also the different forms of injustice, oppression, discrimination, rivalry, suspicion and hate.''[3]

An eloquent, strikingly charismatic man, Ojukwu inspired both his own people and much of the world with the ideals which he espoused for Biafra. ''You ask me,'' he said, ''are the Biafrans fighting for milk and butter? No. We are fighting for higher ideals . . . We are fighting because we feel we have the right to map out our course in life, to control our destiny, to enable our children to live free, to develop at our own pace, to contribute to the world the best of our abilities.''[4]

By that eventful spring of 1967, Bill McNeill had successfully weaned the CUSO program from its original, almost exclusive concentration in the East, and was planning his own departure from Nigeria. There were now dozens of volunteers teaching in schools and working in hospitals in the West and the Mid-West, and a few postings had been made in the North, with many more expected that summer. McNeill was succeeded by Dan Turner, a volunteer in his early twenties who had come out the previous year to teach journalism at the Nsukka Campus of the University of Nigeria in the East, and later, English at the Enugu campus. Something of a roustabout, he had not even expected to pass his volunteer selection interview.

''I was a bullshitter,'' he said. ''I didn't know anything about international affairs; I didn't know anything about journalism. I didn't know what I was up to; it was just an adventure.''[5] Having passed the interview and the selection panel, he unintentionally seemed to do everything wrong at the orientation program in Montreal. He was arrested at a frat house party and spent a night in jail along with a number of found-ins; in a good-natured scuffle with another volunteer, he was accidentally pushed through a plate glass window. For days he expected to be deselected. Somehow, though, he survived and made it to Nigeria, where he suddenly realized how ill-equipped he was for the responsible teaching position he had been given. So when McNeill approached him early in 1967 to offer him a CUSO staff position, it was more than a surprise.

''I was astounded, having gone through the window and having been thrown in jail and all that stuff. I had never thought of myself in any kind of administrative or authoritative capacity. My jaw just dropped open. But then I looked around me and I thought, 'I'm not much good at *this*', so I said, 'Sure. *Sure!*''

Underneath the jokes and the nonchalance, however, Turner cared deeply about what he was doing, and in a short space of time had developed an intense commitment to the people he was working with. And after the massacres in the North, he felt a passionate bias against Northerners. ''To us, the Hausas were racial bigots; they were tyrants, they were murderers, and they were butchering our people.'' It was a bias that was totally incompatible with the impartiality required in the CUSO position he had accepted, but somehow, as events unfolded more and more quickly, it didn't seem to matter.

In 1966, Walter McLean returned from home leave and continued to act as part-time CUSO coordinator in the East, becoming friendly with the new Military Governor, Ojukwu, and sometimes carrying political messages between Enugu and other regional governments, during the twilight period when reconciliation still seemed a remote possibility. Early in 1967, Bill McNeill visited Enugu and dined with McLean and N. U. Akpan, who was now Chief Secretary to the Military Government. McNeill was startled to hear Akpan say that if the Federal Government didn't ''start something soon'' — militarily — the East would be obliged to. McLean, however, understood the gravity of the situation. He had been at Akpan's house the day a cousin, Phillip Effiong, had arrived from the North. A high-ranking officer in the Nigerian Army, Effiong — who would later command the Biafran army — had been on a death list during the pogrom, and had only escaped by bolting through a window and walking much of the 500 miles back to the East. In Lagos, however, CUSO's reports of profound political danger were dismissed by the Canadian High Commission as alarmist, and until the war actually began, official dispatches to Ottawa stated consistently that there was little danger of armed conflict.

As one of Turner's first field staff tasks, McNeill sent him back to Enugu in May to keep a close watch on the situation. Turner spent much of his time at the Enugu Sports Club, playing pool, awaiting developments and sending the occasional message to McNeill through a circuitous but safe route — courtesy of the British Deputy High Commission in Enugu and the Canadian High Commission in Lagos. After the Biafran declaration of independence at the end of May, there was a tense standoff period, during which many of the seven thousand foreigners in the East began to leave. The American Peace Corps pulled out; commercial companies reduced their staff; and wives and children were quietly evacuated as a Federal troop buildup massed to the north of Nsukka. But CUSO tried to hang on, fearing that a premature pullout would jeopardize future work in the region in the increasingly unlikely event that the matter was settled peacefully. In the midst of the strain and anxiety, one of the Enugu volunteers, Susan Rogers, approached Dan Turner and told him she wanted to go home — for purely personal reasons that were unconnected with the political crisis.

She taught at the private girls' school where Akpan's wife was principal," Turner recalled. "I remember dressing her down and telling her that if she went home she could goddamned well walk and we weren't paying her way — because it was so delicate. We were so hopeful of staying in, we didn't want the house of cards to be brought down by someone in as dicey a position as Susan Rogers at Akpan's wife's school bailing out. If she bailed out, she would give the impression that CUSO was bailing out . . . Then two days later, we all bailed out."

One of the few people sent in to assist with the evacuation of Canadians was the Second Secretary from the Canadian High Commission, Robert Sterling. Initially, many evacuees departed on specially arranged unmarked aircraft brought in by the British High Commission. Sterling flew to Port Harcourt alone on the last of these flights, and, clutching a tightly-furled umbrella as women and children rushed past him across the airport to the aircraft, he remembered with mild annoyance that he hadn't brought his tennis racquet.[6] A Canadian-made Chevrolet station wagon and a High Commission driver awaited him, and, with appropriate diplomatic aplomb, Sterling proceeded to Enugu and set up an office in the Presidential Hotel, as the few remaining diplomats in the city burned their files and made hurried plans to leave.

By now, the only way out was either by canoe, across the River Niger at Onitsha, where the only bridge had been closed; or by ship, from Port Harcourt. The two dozen remaining volunteers were told that the Biafran authorities would allow them to take no luggage, not more than £200 ($560) and that they could expect to be searched, perhaps several times. At first, feeling like deserters, many refused to go and had to be cajoled, threatened and begged by Dan Turner, who was himself ambivalent about the evacuation. Most went by ship. Some owned motorcycles which had to be sold quickly, leaving sizeable amounts of cash and hastily packed boxes and trunks — either to be collected by Turner or to be hidden from the anticipated searchers in a variety of ingenious ways. One volunteer stayed up all night before boarding the ship in Port Harcourt, wrapping £5 and £10 notes into sanitary napkins; another hid dozens of bills in her haircurlers, which she wore all the way out to sea and into Lagos.

A lot of them cried.

Graham Smith, a volunteer in Port Harcourt, refused to leave "his people," and Turner, now driving a pickup truck he had borrowed from an Italian construction company, went to get Smith and the trunks left behind by the others. The distance from Onitsha was only 130 miles and the road was good, but the journey took hours because of the roadblocks. Some were manned by police and military, searching for unknown saboteurs and uncertain contraband, but the majority had been set up by vigilantes: "Ever Vigilant, Ever Militant." Turner arrived in Port Harcourt hours later; he had passed through forty-nine road blocks; he was tired, hungry, and angry at having to drag Smith out. On the return journey (no less harrowing) Smith complained incessantly about his own hunger. "It infuriated me that he was hungry all the way back," said Turner. "Why should he be hungry? He was used to being skinny."

They worked their way slowly back through the same roadblocks, often able to see the next one before they had left the last one behind. On the back of the pickup, there was a "Hail Biafra" sign, which Turner had hoped might ease the passage. In some cases it did — people laughed and patted them on the back; in other instances, it was obvious that a truck, driven by an expatriate and loaded with trunks and suitcases, meant only one thing: they were jumping ship. At last they arrived at the forty-ninth and last checkpoint, just outside the city of Onitsha, where they were to rendezvous with other volunteers. It was dusk, and Turner was exhausted and emotionally drained. Ordered out of the truck by a particularly eager young soldier, Turner's frayed temper finally got the better of him and he snapped back. The soldier calmly pointed his machine gun at Turner's growling stomach and said, "I am going to shoot you."

"Shoot me, you stupid bastard!" Turner yelled. "I don't care." He regretted it immediately, thinking of the trunks in the back of the pickup and the thousands of pounds he had hidden under the seat — undetected at forty-eight checkpoints. He thought ruefully that it would be stupid to get shot at the last roadblock; if he were going to be killed, it might as well have happened at the first. But the soldier didn't shoot. — "God knows why he didn't," Turner thought later — and somehow they were able to pass on into Onitsha. At the river, on both the Biafran and the Nigerian sides, the authorities were "never vigilant, never militant"; there were no checks of any kind as men hauled bags, boxes, and even automobiles onto makeshift craft lashed together for the uneasy voyage to the far shore, a mile away. Turner made Smith and some of the other 'troublemakers' load the CUSO trunks.

By now, most of the Canadians, including the McLeans, had gone. In Enugu, his own job nearly completed, Second Secretary Robert Sterling suddenly remembered that it was almost July 1, and that this was Canada's Centennial Year. With the help of Murray Ross, a Presbyterian-mission architect, he organized one of the only diplomatic receptions ever held in Biafra. Then, as the Nigerian army began its southward thrust, he and Ross drove to Onitsha, pushed the Chevrolet onto a lopsided 'canoe' and drifted uncertainly across the Niger to the Federal side.

In Ghana, only a few weeks later, Dan Turner's passion for the Biafran cause would become his undoing. McNeill having departed for Canada, Turner was now in charge of the program and had flown to Accra for a CUSO regional meeting. Being away from Nigeria and enjoying a sense of incredible freedom, he imprudently engaged in an emotional argument with a man he thought was Ghanaian — pouring out all his feelings about Biafra, Nigeria and the brutal Northerners. When he discovered, to his surprise, that the man was Nigerian, he recanted immediately — backtracking; saying that gentlemen could always agree to disagree, and still part friends. The Nigerian eventually concurred, and later asked a favour of Turner: since the war had disrupted the mails, would he kindly take a letter to a friend in the Lagos Foreign Ministry? Eager to make amends, Turner agreed. The letter, dutifully hand-carried, denounced him as a security risk, and two days later, he was deported.

"God, I hated that guy. I hated him with a fierce passion for months . . . But as the years go by, I think of him in better and better terms . . . What a champion!"

Frederick Forsyth, author of *Day of the Jackal* and *The Dogs of War*, began his writing career as a journalist. His first book was an impassioned, erroneous and oft-quoted Penguin 'Special' published in 1969, entitled *The Biafra Story*, in which Forsyth portrayed Biafra in superlatives:

"In potential, (Biafra) has been variously described as the Japan, the Israel, the Manchester and the Kuwait of this continent. Each appellation refers to one of the many facets that cause surprise to the visitor who thought that Africa was uniformly backward."[7]

The Ibos were characterized as industrious, hardworking, avid for education, mutually supportive in family, village and nation — "a society destined to succeed," — while the Nigerians were portrayed along the same lines as those used by Radio Biafra — Muslim 'vandals', bent on jihad (religious war) and genocide.

There was an element of the groupie in Forsyth; he trailed around for weeks like a camp follower with racist mercenaries 'Taffy' Williams and the neurotic German, Rolf Steiner, for whom he acted as translator. He disgusted Alexander Madiebo, the Commander of the Biafran Army, who accused him of being a spy and threatened him with summary execution.[8] In spite of his peculiarities, however, Forsyth, like many other visitors to Biafra, adopted its cause as a personal crusade. And he knew the use and effectiveness of the media. At the lowest ebb, during the early summer of 1968, while Ojukwu was losing the major cities of Biafra to the advancing Nigerians, Forsyth was busy persuading foreign journalists to come there. It was another British journalist, Micheal Leapman, of *The Sun*, who reported the first signs of starvation among Ibo children, and once the story had been splashed across the British tabloids for a few days, Biafra became a household word. "The translation of the Biafra affair from a forgotten bush war to an international issue," wrote Forsyth, "was basically caused by a typewriter and a strip of celluloid, used many times over. It showed the enormous power of the press to influence public opinion when its organs are used in concert."[9]

Among the Canadians to visit Biafra in the following months, often after lengthy discussions with CUSO RVs, were politicians Stephen Lewis, Andrew Brewin and David MacDonald, all of whom wrote extensively on the issue and raised Canadian awareness through the newspapers and in the House of Commons. In a highly publicized gesture, Stanley Burke, who read the CBC television news, resigned from his job in order to work full-time in support of the fledgling nation. But the war had only

begun to impinge on Canadian consciousness when starvation became an
issue, making it unclear to supporters of Biafra whether the struggling
country should be viewed as an object of pity, or as the bright new hope
for Africa's future. Clearly, international interests could be stirred more
easily by pictures of starvation than by political reasoning, and on this
distinction, a minor point in the early days of the war, the entire future
of Biafra would eventually pivot.

In October 1968, David MacDonald and Andrew Brewin returned to
Canada from their journey, and spoke of the six thousand deaths a day.
They hailed the Biafran people and nation, and said: "What action can
be taken to stop the war? The only possible action is international action
— through the United Nations."[10]

Their plea was contained in a jointly authored book, *Canada and the
Biafran Tragedy*, based on their thirty-two-hour stay in the country.

Charles Taylor, London correspondent for the *Globe and Mail*, spent
several weeks in Biafra; Stephen Lewis, who later became leader of the
Ontario New Democratic Party, and Canada's Ambassador to the United
Nations, had taught in Eastern Nigeria several years before, and visited
Biafra for a week as a correspondent for the *Toronto Star*. A series of
his articles was later expanded into an emotive booklet, *Journey to Biafra*,
in which he quoted a World Council of Churches estimate that the death
rate would soon reach twenty-five thousand per day, unless there were
an immediate cease-fire. His firsthand accounts of the horrors of starvation
and warfare gave both urgency and credibility to the growing international
fear that the death of millions — genocide — was at hand. Lewis also
expressed, as well as anyone, the contradictory emotions that faced many
CUSO RVs. Summarizing what he thought Canada could do to alleviate
the agony of Biafra, he said that the most important thing would be an
immediate call for a UN-supervised cease-fire; secondly, Canada should
persuade Britain to halt the sale of arms to Nigeria.

> But if both those failed and relief was, *as expected*, an inconclu-
> sive remedy, then a third alternative presents itself; it is the politi-
> cally difficult proposition of recognizing Biafra and supplying
> small arms and ammunition in sufficient quantity to create a mili-
> tary stalemate . . . I did not meet a single church relief worker,

Protestant or Catholic, who didn't feel that *guns were more important than food.*[11]

Ironically, while the rapid escalation of relief activities helped Biafra to survive the late summer and autumn of 1968, and probably sustained the war for another eighteen months, it basically robbed Ojukwu's regime of its early international credibility and made Biafra an object of pity. Biafra had become a humanitarian rather than a political problem, the emphasis on suffering ultimately ruining its chances for international recognition.

Among the relief agencies there were two broad groupings — those who assisted the International Committee of the Red Cross (ICRC) effort on both the Nigerian and the Biafran sides of the front, and those who comprised the loose consortium known as Joint Church Aid (JCA). The Presbyterian Church and Ted Johnson, supporting the latter through the Canadian operation, Canairelief, underlined the tremendous potential of individuals and small groups to motivate millions of people far from the event.

The churches were pre-conditioned in their view of the conflict by their own vision of what was good and desirable for Africa, and by their ready access to the Biafran leadership, which was educated, eloquent — and Christian. While they understood the Biafrans — often equating academic achievement with intellect and integrity — the Nigerian position seemed to them riddled with undesirable influences; even the Organization of African Unity, which supported the Nigerian position, seemed dominated by Arabs and, therefore, Muslim and anti-Christian forces.

Referring to Biafra, Ted Johnson said, "This country has a group in leadership which would be hard to match in any country in the world, and would certainly not be matched in any African country. This is one of the first expressions of a totally African country." Wrote one observer: "A characterization of Biafra as the first African country totally Westernized would have been more appropriate."[12]

"Could the small amount of relief food, spread so thinly, really have significantly buoyed the war effort," asked a long-time CARE field worker. "Almost certainly not," he concluded.[13]

This was the feeling of many — both at the time and subsequently. Others, however, disagreed: after the war, N. U. Akpan wrote, "The efforts of the relief agencies did in fact help prolong the war."[14] And during the war, a senior official of the World Council of Churches raised doubts about the JCA airlift, "because of its political side effects . . . which include exposing the churches to charges of prolonging the war and adding to the suffering of the people."[15]

In July and August of 1968, Biafra reached a low point which was not paralleled again until the final days of the war. The food situation was extremely poor, and the military situation was even more bleak; Onitsha, Calabar, Port Harcourt and the capital of Enugu had all fallen before rapidly advancing Nigerian forces; very little stood between Biafra and total defeat. In an explanation of how Biafra survived this darkest period of the war, Ojukwu cited three factors: the logistical advantage of the Biafran forces operating within a tiny enclave criss-crossed with good roads; the confusion and logistical problems faced by the advancing Nigerians; and the financial aid he was receiving from the churches and relief agencies.

"The only source of income available to Biafra was the hard currency spent by the churches for yams and garri. That's all. At this stage we had no loans or anything else. It wasn't much, but enough to sustain us."[16]

He referred to the massive doses of hard currency being made available to Biafra by the relief agencies through the purchase of large amounts of goods and services *in* Biafra, using Biafran pounds exchanged at an artifically low pre-war rate. By early 1969, when the war was in its second year, the price of garri and cassava flour, still produced in great quantity by Biafran farmers, had increased thirty-six fold, and the Biafran pound was virtually worthless. Nevertheless, the relief agencies needed Biafran pounds for such local expenditures. As long as they accepted the pre-war exchange rate, which never changed, the Biafran government coffers kept on swelling, and the arsenal kept on growing.

The WCC representative in Orlu, one of ten Biafran provinces, reported local purchases worth $140,000 per month in November, 1968.[17] A German agency reported expenditures of $1.25 million up to October, 1968.[18] In addition to local purchases, distribution costs were borne totally by the relief agencies. Nordchurchaid, in August 1969 alone, spent more than $50,000 renting trucks and cars.[19] The personal living expenses of 100 ICRC staff, about one hundred representatives of the Protestant churches, and the several hundred Catholic priests and nuns, added up to significant cost over a period of time. In addition to the relief support, the agencies were also funding projects to grow food or build clinics, hospitals and camps. Before September 1968, the British and Irish Catholic churches alone were estimated to have spent more than $400,000 on special projects.[20] These funds were all exchanged for local currency at the pre-war rate.

All relief flights to Biafra were obliged to pay landing fees amounting to several thousand dollars per day, despite the fact that the agencies had virtually built the Uli airstrip. Affectionately nicknamed 'Annabelle', and described as no more than a highway of improvised tarmac, Uli was handling fifteen or twenty flights a night by 1968. The relief agencies improved the airstrip with 30,000 square feet of aluminum planking, repairs to feeder roads, parking aprons, landing lights to replace the kerosene flares, radio equipment, a standby generator and a direction finder.[21] Uli became, after Johannesburg, the busiest airfield in Africa, with relief flights providing the cover for those bearing arms.

All told, the best estimate of the cost of the relief effort is $250 million.[22] If even a conservative fifteen percent of this were spent inside Biafra, it would have made as much foreign exchange available to the secessionist government as was spent by Nigeria on arms during the entire war.[23] This figure, moreover, does not take into account the vast amounts of foreign exchange and Nigerian currency with which Biafra started the war.

Mike Okwechime, Biafra's Chief of Military Planning recalls: "Financing the war was largely accomplished through private and humanitarian contributions. Much was diverted from funds raised abroad. Those who wished to make strictly humanitarian contributions could give to specific agencies but those giving to 'Biafra' often didn't ask any questions, and the money could be used to purchase arms on the black market. Often funds would be raised for a specific project and then someone comes along and donates the project outright — the Canadians gave a big hospital for example — freeing the funds already raised."[24]

The importance of Biafra to the churches was explained by the fact that 77% of its population was Christian, a higher proportion than anywhere else in Africa. And though the area was predominantly Protestant, nearly 70% of all Nigerian Catholics lived in the East. Despite the popular support for Biafra, however, official bilateral support was always limited. Only Tanzania, Zambia, the Ivory Coast, Gabon and Haiti gave official recognition and their support was largely moral. South Africa, Portugal and France all provided material assistance, mostly weapons trans-shipped through Rhodesia, Libreville and the Portugese colonies of Angola and Sao Tome. South Africa's interest in damaging a potentially strong African nation was obvious: Portugal's African empire, ripping apart at the seams, might have been even more vulnerable to a strong, anti-colonial Nigeria. French support was a curious combination of interest in the potential of Biafra's untapped oil fields; maintenance of the commercially lucrative francophone client state network surrounding Nigeria, and General De Gaulle's notoriously perverse attitude towards Britain's erstwhile colonial confederations.

The planned intake of sixty-five CUSO volunteers to Nigeria in 1967 was diverted to other countries, but the following year a second office was opened in Kaduna in the North, and by the end of 1968, there were 125 volunteers in the West and Northern States, unaffected by and sometimes oblivious to the war that raged a few hundred miles from their postings.

But to the former volunteers who were evacuated from the East and were back in Canada, the escalation of the war and the horrifying photographs and news reports coming out of Biafra were soul-wrenching; and for them the continuation of a CUSO program in Nigeria seemed almost a pact with the devil. A few thought that their place was actually in Biafra. Diane North, who had been a CUSO nurse in the East, arranged to return; she stayed throughout the war, treating the wounded and the growing numbers of malnourished children.

An impromptu American organization contacted CUSO in the summer of 1968 about the possibility of Canadian volunteers for Biafra. Dan Turner, working temporarily in the Ottawa office, was excited at the prospect, and with two other returned volunteers, offered to go himself. In mid-September, a dramatic tape recording arrived from Sao Tome — the jumping-off point for relief flights — outlining what the volunteers would do: "We need a volunteer for each of the stations where the aircraft at airstrip 'Annabelle' offload, plus two at large who will be at either end of the field with walkie-talkies . . . they should be males, they should know Biafra, they should know how to work with African labour, they should not be shrinking violets . . . they don't have to bring their own food because we can supply them from the airlift. What they need is air mattresses, mosquito netting, mosquito repellant and waterproof flashlights and batteries . . . "[26]

But Bill McNeill, now working in the Ottawa office as Director of the West African Program, objected strenuously, and insisted that the matter be discussed by the Board before action was taken. He feared that the move would be seen as a political gesture by the Nigerians, and that it would seriously affect CUSO's work in other parts of the country; and he privately threatened to resign if it went ahead. By October, the issue had reached crisis proportions within CUSO, and the Canadian High Commissioner to Nigeria had become involved. He sent a priority cable to External Affairs in Ottawa; "CUSO, plans to send three volunteers into rebel held area of Nigeria has disturbing implications for whole CUSO program and for Canadian image generally in this country . . . CUSO thus far has maintained a clear slate with Nigerians as body which has not meddled in local affairs. Standing of organization has been sufficiently high to weather recent press storm here reported Canadian Government intention to raise problem in UNGA (United Nations General Assembly) . . . however CUSO persons could have sticky time of it if word of CUSO aid to rebels were to be broached in local press . . . "[27]

Turner and the others assembled at Ottawa's Beacon Arms Hotel in preparation for the Board meeting. "But as much as we impressed them," Turner said, "they weren't about to be hooked into what might have been one of the stupidest moves CUSO ever made."

The idea was rejected and the three were disconsolate: "I guess we thought we could do something useful," Turner said, though for the life of me I can't remember what it was. Those Biafrans were three times stronger than us. What were we going to do? It was being there; it was the gesture. Diane North, the nurse, was still in there and we felt terrible that we weren't."

Other RVs saw that they could be more useful to the Biafran cause by speaking, lobbying and raising funds in Canada. As early as November, 1967, some of them were involved in forming a "Canadian Union for the Rights of Biafrans," which tried to publicize the political aspects of the war, through speaking tours, marches and non-violent sit-ins. They were incensed that the Canadian government, apparently nervous about any form of secession, was taking a very distant view of the war, and they made it a target of their anger.

"I used to writhe in bed at night, thinking of ways that somebody could make an impression on this goddamned government that seemed to have no sense of humanity," recalled Turner. They lobbied the media, attempting to shame the government and CUSO. Grant Wanzell told of being trapped in an anti-Ibo riot in Zaria, of hearing "a sound like chopping wood," and seeing an Ibo beaten to death while police stood by.[28] Gayle Cooper, another RV, travelled up and down the Ottawa Valley, speaking, putting on skits and exhorting the government at every opportunity. She and a group of others in Toronto decided to demonstrate in Ottawa.

About eight of us travelled to Ottawa by train, and we were joined by twenty others outside the Parliament Buildings. We had an appointment with an Opposition MP, but as soon as we got into the Parliament Buildings, we went straight to External Affairs Minister Mitchell Sharp's office and sat down on the floor. We amazed ourselves, and I think it's the only occasion there has ever been a sit-in in the Minister's office. After an hour the RCMP stopped us using the toilets, and about two hours after that, they carried us out. Taking our cue from reports of American sit-ins, we all went limp and they bumped us down the stairs. Two days later, we were still fasting near the Centennial Flame, and Sharp came out to 'dialogue' with us. He told us that we were badly informed about Biafra and that he had the complete picture from the Canadian High Commissioner in Lagos. The CBC cameras were rolling, and I told him that his High Commissioner had said to me that he thought the Ibos were getting everything they deserved. Sharp went absolutely white and fell backwards off my sleeping bag. He retained his composure and said, "Young woman, that is absolutely untrue."

"Well, he said it at the CUSO house in Ibadan in front of twenty other people," I said, and with that, Sharp retreated into the Parliament Building and the dialogue stopped.[29]

The pressure on CUSO to discontinue its Nigerian program was increasing, — with relentless lobbying of Board members, resolutions at CUSO meetings across Canada, letter-writing campaigns, and countless position papers, employing the purplest of prose. One RV, David Cayley, pompously accused CUSO of being "subservient to the interests of the Nigerian Government" which was conducting "a protracted and sanguinary jihad which has cost the lives of over a million Biafrans, most of them civilians." CUSO's program in Northern Nigeria particularly "after and in consequence of that region's murderous campaign against those whom convenience now impelled them to call their fellow Nigerians, was a tacit gesture of support for that campaign. That support should now be withdrawn."[30]

The intense lobbying in Canada provoked a response from CUSO volunteers working in Nigeria. A letter from the Nigerian field staff to Executive Director Frank Bogdasavich charged that the pressure campaign had nothing to do with the effectiveness of the CUSO program in Nigeria but was solely politically motivated.

It has only to do with the political aims of a group in Canada which sympathizes with the Biafrans in the current civil war and who wish to have CUSO take any steps which could be interpreted (and will be interpreted) as a gesture of support for their cause. To allow CUSO to be used in such a way calls into question the whole rationale for its existence and throws grave doubt on its continued operation in a number of other countries as well.[31]

The internal policy struggle continued, and in 1969, there was an effort to have the program 'frozen'. Such a move would have disrupted dozens of schools and institutions to which volunteers had already been promised that year and would have been seen by the Government of Nigeria as a political reprimand. CUSO Executive Director Frank Bogdasavich was uncertain of his own position on Biafra, so he consulted Dr. Geoff Andrew at the Association of Universities and Colleges of Canada. One of CUSO's founders, Andrew had a canny sense of politics and causes. He ordered the pro-Biafran AUCC representative on CUSO's Board to "go to a wedding or a funeral or something,'' and attended the meeting himself. Tim Brodhead, the new CUSO Field Staff officer in Ibadan, had been brought back for the showdown, and, armed with angry telegrams from volunteers in Nigeria, he made an impassioned plea for the Nigeria program. Bill McNeill, Director of CUSO's West African Program, said that freezing the program would mean expulsion for the 125 volunteers in Nigeria, and that many would probably be beaten on the way out. He promised that if that happened, all of them would attend the next Board meeting.

Abruptly, Dr. Andrew proposed a motion of support for the marvellous work being done in Nigeria by the staff and volunteers. Some members grumbled about the motion, and possibly about the spectre of 125 confused, vengeful volunteers crowding into the boardroom. Whatever it was, Dr. Andrew's motion passed, and the Board never raised the question again.

Ironically, it would be one of the most staunch pro-Biafran humanitarians who would do more than anyone else to bring Biafra down. Carl Gustav Von Rosen, a Swedish Count, was almost sixty years old. He had a chequered career behind him: as a long-distance flyer in the early days of marathon flight; as a World War II flying ace in Europe, and as a pilot for the desperate aid missions to the Ethiopians fighting against Mussolini, in Poland and Finland during the war and for the UN in the Congo.

Von Rosen flew his first aircraft into Biafra in August 1968 — A DC 7B loaded with Scandinavian relief goods and a few passengers, including Ted Johnson of the Presbyterian Church. Tremendously inspired by his discussions with Ojukwu, he spent the next few weeks travelling to Addis, Geneva, New York, Washington and Toronto to persuade government and church leaders of the need for urgent assistance. In September he was back in Sao Tome, 275 miles off the Biafran coastline, heading up what would quickly become the Nordchurchaid relief effort. Within a few weeks, however, he was forced out because of some highly publicized remarks about Biafra's need for guns as well as butter. Such statements lent weight to the Nigerian charge that the relief flights were also carrying weapons. By Christmas, Von Rosen was covertly discussing the 'guns' side of the equation with Ojukwu, and together they secretly planned to rebuild the now defunct Biafran air force.

With assistance from Tanzanian diplomats in Europe, a number of Swedish two-seater MFI-9B 'Minicon' aircraft were purchased and trans-shipped to Libreville via Paris. Von Rosen was there to meet them with a team of Biafran pilots and mechanics who would outfit the planes with weapons and rockets. Then, on May 22, 1969, five of the Minicons, the lead aircraft piloted by Von Rosen himself, appeared low over the airfield at Port Harcourt, and within minutes destroyed two federal MiGs and two Ilyushin bombers. Subsequent attacks on Benin and Enugu destroyed eleven Nigerian warplanes within a week. Air attacks on Nigerian oil fields in the Mid-West were combined with Biafran land raids, during one of which eleven foreign technicians were killed, and eighteen others captured and held for ransom in Biafra.

The sudden Biafran offensive shocked the Nigerian High Command, and caused an immediate change of policy. General Gowon had hitherto allowed the relief flights to continue, never putting Uli out of operation for more than a few hours. In fact, at the time of Von Rosen's raid, there had been no attacks on Uli for more than two months. That would change. One of Gowon's new commanders, General Olusegun Obasanjo, demanded a clear demonstration of Nigerian air authority. The pilot chosen was Bruce 'King' Gbadamosi, a Nigerian Captain trained in Canada, who was at the time dating the CUSO secretary in Kaduna. Occasionally, he would fly his MiG 17 low over the CUSO office to signal his return to Kaduna — sending files, secretary and Field Staff Officer to the floor with the roar of his engines.

On June 5, a Swedish Red Cross DC-7 was spotted on the radar, headed for Uli. Knowing its bearing, speed and time of departure from Sao Tome, Gbadamosi took off in his MiG and found it without difficulty, ordering the pilot to land at Port Harcourt or Calabar. The order was picked up as well by a Canadian pilot five minutes ahead. The Swede ignored the second call to alter course and land. Gbadamosi issued the final warning but the pilot remained on course and Gbadamosi brought the aircraft down in the bush near Eket.[32]

The ramifications were enormous, and marked the beginning of the end for Biafra. The ICRC immediately suspended all flights into the enclave, and they never resumed. Competent, low-key commanders like Obasanjo were placed at the front, with a clear mandate to advance. The incident of the captured foreign technicians badly tarnished attempts to polish Biafra's international image and its claim to recognition. "And Biafra was collapsing under its own weight of corruption," recalled its Director of Propaganda. "Relief goods were not getting to the people; army officers were commandeering property."[33]

On Jan. 10, 1970, with Nigerian troops advancing rapidly on all fronts and the Uli airstrip in imminent danger of capture, General Ojukwu flew out of Biafra "on a mission of peace," leaving most of his government and his generals behind to face the 'genocide' that had been written and spoken about for nearly three years. It was over.

At least it was over for the Biafrans. The foreign media, having predicted genocide for so long, now dispatched reporters to get the story. Among them were Peter Worthington of the *Toronto Telegram* and Robert Reguly of the *Toronto Star*. Along with the hundreds of reporters who descended on Nigeria that week, they vied for stories and for a place on the single F-27 made available for their travel to the former Biafran territory. Reguly didn't make it, and reported on whatever he could pick up in Lagos hotels and from the others when they returned. It didn't stop him or the *Star* from giving the impression that he was in the thick of the action: "There are widespread complaints that soldiers are looting and molesting girls in former Biafran villages . . . " said a report credited to Associated Press on Jan 21. "About 80 foreign journalists, most of whom yesterday painted a grim picture of starvation and misery, were expected to be released from confinement in Port Harcourt today," said a 'special' report the following day. "STAR'S MAN SEES REFUGEES TRAMPLED FIGHTING FOR FLOUR," shrieked a headline on the 23rd, and another on the 24th: "Nigerians looting Biafra of everything in sight."[34] Much later Reguly admitted that "conditions do not add up to genocide or systematic starvation"[35]— long after the hype of the headlines and the sensationalism of the articles had created just the opposite impression.

Worthington, who did scramble aboard the flight to the East, was more level-headed, though many of his reports were buried under emotional headlines such as "Newsmen Report Rape, Looting," and "Starving Biafrans Battle for Scraps."[36]

The newsmen, most of whom never reached the battle zones, were under heavy pressure from their editors; they were also suffering physical discomfort and hardships to which they were unaccustomed. Mort Rosenblum, former editor of the *International Herald Tribune*, recalled one saying, "During that long day under the hot sun, we rode, worked and squabbled, foodless, . . . How many of those purple passages in the popular press — 'the awful truth,' 'silent genocide' — which appeared during the following days had their genesis in our empty bellies?"[37] Worthington described the appalling misery and the desperate need, but he also recounted a sickening incident which characterized the worst in Third World 'firebrigade' reporting: "To their shame, several foreign television cameramen helped create scenes of riot by throwing Nigerian money in the air and letting the hungry masses scramble for it."[38] But Worthington, too, succumbed to the editor's appetite for massacre and genocide, reporting twice on "rumours" of a "My Lai" type massacre of seventy people that had "reportedly" occurred some time before the war had actually ended. The rumour was neither confirmed or denied, and disappeared in the welter of horror and starvation stories that Canadian readers had come to expect.

In Parliament, David MacDonald and Andrew Brewin, also anticipating the worst, were shocked and angered by optimistic reports brought back from Nigeria by Robert Thompson. The former Social Credit leader had himself worked in Africa for several years and had gone to Nigeria to assess the situation personally. When he stated in the Committee on External Affairs and National Defence that conditions in Biafra were under "commendable control" and that "charges of starving millions have been victory for skillful propagandists,"[39] David Lewis, then Deputy Leader of the NDP, stood and shouted that he was "presumptuous and arrogant." Storming from the Committee room, he roared that Thompson was "out of order, and as far as I am concerned, totally disgusting."[40]

Months later, as the former Biafran territory was pulling itself out of chaos and unhappiness, conflicting stories continued to appear in the Canadian press. A 'special correspondent' to the *Montreal Star* — probably a CUSO volunteer who remained anonymous 'for political reasons' — reported that famine was rampant and that people were worse off than they had been during the war.[41] By contrast, Jerry Okoro, an Ibo who reported for the *Times* of London and had returned to his home during the same period of time, viewed the situation much differently: "There is poverty in Iboland,'' he wrote, ''but there is no starvation. Food is cheaper in the East Central State than in any other part of the country . . . relief is reaching more people than ever before.''[42]

A month before, the last of several emotional debates had taken place in the Canadian House of Commons over the issue of government support for Canairelief. Prime Minister Trudeau took a cautious approach, saying, ''A starving child promotes an emotional response, and properly so. But that emotion must serve to assist the children and not the reverse . . . The Nigerian tragedy does not differ from others simply because some persons employ superlatives, or repeat accusation of genocide when these allegations have proved demonstrably incorrect.''[43]

Trudeau won no public applause for his position on Biafra, a position which was essentially consistent and diplomatically correct throughout the war. He had, in fact, earned the undying emnity of the Biafra supporters early in the war when a reporter had asked him what Canada's position was on starvation in Biafra. Giving one of his inimitable shrugs, the Prime Minister had replied facetiously, ''Where's Biafra?'' From that moment, and for the next two years, Biafra had become the biggest and most divisive foreign policy question in Canada, eclipsing even the war in Vietnam.

Tim Brodhead, the Field Staff Officer in Ibadan, felt that Biafra had generated so much passion and became such a major issue within CUSO because, for the first time, people had had to take stock of an issue which directly affected the organization: ''There were a lot of values bound up in it, a lot of political judgements and a lot of baggage: illusions about what Biafra meant and what Nigeria meant, complicated by some of the parallels drawn between Nigeria as a federation and Canada as a federation.

''The passion surrounded an issue which directly affected CUSO at a time when internationally — Paris, Berkeley, Vietnam — there was tremedous ferment, none of which touched Canada directly. Here was something that was our own.

''But the issues were not as straightforward as people presented them, and a lot of the people who had the most passion were wrong. The argument that we were assisting genocide was *wrong*. There was no genocide. It was not a conscious policy and CUSO was in no way aiding and abetting it."[44]

EPILOGUE

Jack Pierpoint, a twenty-four-year-old University of Saskatchewan graduate, posted in 1968 as a sociologist with the Ghanaian Volta Lake Research Project 500 miles to the west of Biafra, found that his 'research' would have to be both fast and practical. Relocating people from 760 villages into 52 new towns presented unique social and political problems, and his work, of necessity, focussed largely on problem-solving: surveys, so that land could be allocated to farmers who had been waiting through as many as three or four planting seasons; provision of sanitation facilities; health services; training in new skills; road building and designing new boats to replace traditional river craft unable to withstand the massive waves that the giant lake could generate within moments.

Then, one day in the Spring of 1970, a boat came up the lake with a telegram from Ottawa, asking Pierpoint if he would be prepared to go to Nigeria as a Field Staff Officer. The war was over, and CUSO intended to go back into the East. Within days, he arrived in a desolated Enugu, and with Felix Enang, CUSO's long-time Nigerian field assistant, he spent weeks travelling through former Biafran territory, enduring road blocks, food shortages, uncomfortable accommodation and the thundering onset of the rainy season.

"The economy had dried up," Pierpoint observed. "There simply wasn't any economy; there was no cash, no medium of exchange or goods to trade. The roads were in terrible shape and there was no capacity to fix them; there were tank traps and live shells still sitting in the middle of the road. Government offices had no vehicles, no equipment, no records, no money."[45]

"As we travelled around talking to officials and people in the villages," he said, "there was one thing without a single exception that I can recall: people said that they wanted to get their school going again. People were hungry; they didn't have much to wear. They had nothing, but their one overriding concern was their children who had been out of school in most cases for years. Going back to school meant that things were on the mend, and so they wanted those schools opened at any cost."

When talking to officials at the Ministry of Education, and visiting schools, he was almost embarrassed at the prospect of placing CUSO teachers. Most schools had been damaged by rockets or gunfire, or looted of their books, desks, tin roofs, and anything else that could be dragged away; the only thing they had in abundance, besides students, was teachers. Another teacher seemed the last thing they needed, but Pierpoint knew, as did the Nigerians, that besides bringing their skills, CUSO volunteers would also draw attention to the desperate needs of the region's institutional base as the relief began to dwindle.

So that summer, three years after Dan Turner had shepherded the last reluctant CUSO stragglers across the River Niger, a dozen carefully selected, hardy volunteers arrived in Enugu and then fanned out to their postings. In almost every case, they became the focus of a vigorous fund-raising effort back in Canada, and attracted funds, supplies and books which would otherwise have been beyond the means of their schools.

But the figures were tiny in relation to the dramatic economic problems and to other rehabilitation needs, which were met either very slowly, or not at all. Impatient with Canada's apparent policy of indifference, Pierpoint travelled to Lagos at the end of 1971 to remonstrate with the Canadian High Commissioner, Alan McGill. McGill, a thoughtful, experienced diplomat, was attempting to contend with both Canadian and Nigerian post-war political sensitivities, as well as with two massive federal bureaucracies with large appetites for proposals, clearances and permits. Gradually, however, he conceived of an idea as he listened to Pierpoint talk. If CUSO had some money to spend on rehabilitation in the East, he asked, how would it be spent? "I'd rebuild schools," Pierpoint told him. "I'd inject it into the local economy using local labour, local materials — nothing from outside." That way, Pierpoint thought, the money would serve a dual purpose: assisting the educational system, and even more important creating jobs and services and pumping cash into the local economy.

Pierpoint and McGill discussed the situation again. Looking out of his office window over the teeming Lagos harbour, McGill asked casually how much Pierpoint could spend. Pierpoint's pulse skipped a beat and he thought quickly, recalling an incident in Ghana two years before. He and another CUSO volunteer, Jean Pelletier, had approached the High Commission in Accra with a proposal for constructing water tanks on the parched Afram Plains north of the capital; the CIDA officer had balked because the $30,000 request had been too small to justify the paperwork required to process it through Ottawa. Pierpoint had asked how big was 'big' in CIDA's estimation, and he now recalled the answer: a million dollars. Sitting in Alan McGill's plush air-conditioned office, hundreds of miles from the wretched villages of Eastern Nigeria, he looked up from his coffee and said as casually as he could: "A million dollars."

Little more was said, but in March 1971, as Pierpoint remembered it, "suddenly it was announced — it was a million dollars!" Elated by the news, he began making plans for everything from building reconstruction to laboratory equipment and school farms; scouting office sites and warehouses; pricing cement, and surveying the local labour market. Almost daily, he would return to his Enugu flat and bang out lengthy memos to Ottawa. With an eagerness which completely outstripped anything CIDA had in mind, and long before the idea had even been suggested to Nigerian authorities, the basic philosophy of the project had taken shape in Pierpoint's mind: "I am convinced that our primary consideration should be how we can most effectively inject this cash into the existing economy, given the very broad parameter of education as a basic guideline. If this principle is accepted, then the direction of our input moves away from physical reconstruction and equipment supplies, towards items which maximize local input — such as furniture construction and ancillary projects."[46]

Pierpoint decided that he would need the services of a "financial wizard" in order to cope with the anticipated volume of transactions. He told Ottawa that he also wanted the services of Jack Lazareck, a CUSO engineer assigned to the Afram Plains Water Project and Jean Pelletier. Pelletier, the son of politician Gérard Pelletier had joined CUSO — for whom he taught French in Ghana — after failing to arouse a single response to his application to the Company of Young Canadians. "I think, since my father was Secretary of State," he said, "they thought it was a plan to get somebody into the CYC to spy on his behalf."[47]

The CYC's loss was CUSO's gain; by mid-April, both Pelletier and Lazareck had joined Pierpoint and had already done a reconnaissance of eastern Nigeria. The three men decided that, because UNICEF was roofing the primary schools, furniture should be the first CUSO priority. Because most of the 2,100 primary schools in East Central State were in villages, and because most villages had both sawyers and carpenters, the work could be done on a decentralized basis, by village artisans. While Lazareck was designing a three-student desk that could be made for less than $10, Pierpoint outlined the proposal to the Federal Nigerian Government and to state officials; and, in concert with the main CUSO office in Ibadan and the Ottawa secretariat, he began to work on official representations to CIDA.

Back in Ottawa, however, there were ominous rumblings from the CIDA mandarinate; despite an estimated approval time of four weeks when it was 'announced' in March, CIDA officials, by June, were dampening the initial enthusiasm with caveats, and procedures, and what development bureaucrats call 'conditionalities' — threatening to smother the project at birth. It was proposed that tenders might be called from commercial companies or UNICEF, or that CIDA might undertake the project itself. It was also seriously suggested that unless CUSO could demonstrate reasons to the contrary, the budget should be spent on Canadian goods and services.[48] It was another five months before a suitable contract would be signed with CIDA, by which time CUSO had already advanced almost $100,000 on startup costs, and a pilot project in Awgu Division had been all but completed.

It was during the pilot project that a third objective developed, almost by accident. Because the idea of centralized furniture production had been rejected, Pierpoint and Pelletier had to find a means of quality control and supervision for a project which would be carried on at hundreds of separate village sites; for without a costly bureaucracy and a huge staff, the opportunities and incentives for misappropriation were enormous in a post-war society. Pierpoint had already tasted it in Enugu, once the CUSO presence had been established. "People would come to my flat," he said, "and offer me a wide range of interesting propositions to help them; to be their friend."

Instead of attempting the impossible task of supervising all details themselves, Pierpoint and Pelletier developed the idea of local project management in each of the communities where furniture was to be built. They first assisted in the reconstitution of village education committees, and then made sure that the full details of the project were publicly understood. All project documents were signed by three committee members, and full details were made available to anybody who wanted them.

"Because we made it public," Pierpoint said, "and we were dealing with *the* priority in the community, there was no way anybody could make off with anything; community pressure to do it right was overwhelming." In fact, in the few cases where there was local misappropriation, the village committee covered the costs themselves, ensuring that everything in their contract was provided.

Besides the strong desire to see the schools reopened, the villages had another reason for ensuring scrupulous accountability. The CUSO team had provided an additional incentive which was not included in the CIDA project description and was barely mentioned in the final reports. They had made each community an offer: if the community could produce the desks for less than the $10 each allocated by CUSO, the difference could be kept by the village for other development projects. As a result — unbeknownst to the CIDA bureaucracy in Ottawa, which would have been aghast — the project also generated nearly $100,000 worth of small clinics, market sheds, wells, village farms and mopeds for visiting nurses. But by far the most important result was that villagers, demoralized and bankrupt by years of war and hunger, resumed responsibility for their own communities.

The project was not without difficulties. Because there were no functioning banks throughout most of the region, the delivery of cash was highly problematic, especially since armed highway robbery had become a commonplace post-war hazard. Pierpoint refused offers of armed police guards, which would have been both ineffectual and a dead giveaway to anyone watching when he emerged — as nonchalantly as possible — from the single bank in Enugu, clutching a briefcase bulging with cash. He would then make a highly furtive, top speed, day-long 'sprint' around the region, dropping off payments at intervals that were as irregular as he could make them.

On one occasion, a meeting in Aba was interrupted by armed men who fired off a few rounds and then escaped empty-handed. Jean Pelletier, affronted by their audacity, and propelled more by angry indignation than good sense, jumped into the CUSO van with four machete-wielding farmers, and took off in hot pursuit. Overtaking the miscreants on the outskirts of town and suddenly realizing his folly when he saw a pistol poking through the window of their car, he gunned the engine, passed the fleeing vehicle and sped on, finding the bandits now in hot pursuit of him. Rounding a bend in the road at breakneck speed, he spotted a knot of people at a roadside market, and breaking into a four-wheel skid, he jumped from the van, shouting, "Armed robbers are coming!"

There was a moment of stunned silence; then, instead of preparing to take a stand with Pelletier against the fast approaching thieves, the roadside vendors and their customers evaporated, 'running for bush' and leaving Pelletier alone beside his van. It must have been his immensely welcoming smile, his warm greeting and the overwhelming impression of simplemindedness he presented, as they pointed revolvers at his stomach, that persuaded them not to fire; in those days, armed robbery was a capital offence in Nigeria and few victims lived to identify suspects. In any case, Pelletier developed that day a respect for the authority of small arms that would remain with him throughout his stay in Nigeria.

In the end, CUSO reached more than a thousand schools in less than two years. Nearly seventy thousand three-seater desks were built, accommodating more than two hundred thousand children. An additional nine thousand teachers' desks were constructed and, to this day, children in eastern Nigeria are writing on CUSO blackboards and kicking footballs through CUSO goalposts. Administrative costs had been restricted to less than ten percent of budget, and when the final accounting was done and the last project vehicle sold, exactly $998,800 of the $1 million had been spent.[49]

"We never cancelled a single village program," Jack Pierpoint said. "We scared a few committees, but we never cancelled a program, and to the best of my knowledge, we never lost a penny . . . There were localized incidents where somebody made off with something, but the committees covered it; they simply wouldn't put the program at risk. It was too valuable to them."

For CUSO, the Nigeria Project signalled a major new direction in program development. Even before the project was completed, CUSO established a permanent Projects Division in Ottawa, headed by Jack Pierpoint on his return from Nigeria in 1972; over the following decade, it grew to forty percent of the organization's overseas activity, setting CUSO significantly apart from other volunteer-sending organizations.

The success of this project also convinced CIDA that a large-scale project could be developed efficiently and managed economically by an NGO — with an alacrity unknown within government. More importantly, it reached ordinary Nigerians in a way that few large governmental projects ever had. And the Nigerian schools reconstruction project was a vindication, to the extent that one was needed, of CUSO's decision to remain in Nigeria and to cast its lot, not with one political faction or another, but with ordinary people who simply wanted the same opportunities for their children as parents anywhere on the globe.

Chapter 6

The Bunker

In CUSO's formative months, anyplace where a poncho could be hung up or water boiled was home. Keith Spicer's apartment, Fred Stinson's Parliamentary offices in Ottawa, the International Student Centre in Toronto, the Ottawa offices of UNESCO; all served for a time as headquarters. In 1962, when CUSO came under the protective wing of the Association of Universities and Colleges of Canada, its Director, Geoff Andrew, made room for CUSO in his Ottawa office on Albert Street. When the AUCC moved to more spacious accommodation on Slater Street CUSO followed and sub-leased the entire tenth floor of the Burnside Building. With a tiny staff working in one corner of a cavernous void, it seemed like a precocious undertaking; but within five years the office would be jammed to capacity, and CUSO would eventually occupy half of the ninth floor as well.

Nicknamed 'The Bunker', or the 'Slaterbunker' — an ironic acknowledgement of being under siege from demanding, critical field offices — the secretariat was a portrait of CUSO in microcosm; it changed as the organization changed, reflecting its moods and trends and preoccupations. The 1984 floor plan bore the unmistakable hallmark of a voluntary agency as it had in 1974: over the years, spacious offices had been sub-divided into warrens of ever-shrinking nooks, clustered in labyrinthine disorder around the 'natural light' of coveted windows. The once tidy imitation of the Federal Government's 'open concept' — long abandoned — looked as though it had been reorganized by anarchists from the Paris Commune. Baffles of every shape, size and colour demarcated small territorial claims — none, as Conrad once observed of African housing, at right angles to anything else.

Everyone was always busy: photocopying, typing, shouting across ten thousand telephone miles, returning from 'The Field' or just about to depart, rushing earnestly — documentation (never papers) in hand — to one of the countless meetings that occasionally threatened to overwhelm all other activity in The Bunker.

A first-time visitor might well have imagined that the enterprise at hand was warehousing rather than international development, for everywhere there were boxes: outside the Medical Services Department were cartons filled with pharmaceuticals, snake bite kits and first-aid supplies destined for volunteer medical kits; in public affairs, boxes of newsletters, Christmas cards and publicity material lined the walls; and the corridor through the Orientation Department was often rendered impassable by cartons of books and audio-visual material either arriving from or being dispatched to a training program. For years, stacked cartons outside the Data Department aroused the ire of secretaries, who claimed that the pile had something to do either with centralized or decentralized filing — an idea that either had, or had not been properly implemented, and which, whatever the case, reflected badly on everyone. Fundraising was choked with boxes of flyers; Recruitment, with persuasive pamphlets, and everywhere was container upon container of documentation. Occasionally a missing file would spark a search through the cartons, and some of the boxes — long thought to have been destined for the legendary 'archives' in the fourth basement — turned out to be simply uncollected waste paper.

'Been-to' posters, brightly coloured kitenge cloth, ever-popular penis sheaths from Papua New Guinea, batiks, maps and souvenirs from hundreds of trips decorated the walls and room dividers. Through the years there was always at least one acrchetypal Che Guevara scowling down from the jumble of anti-apartheid, anti-imperialist and anti-nuclear posters which covered the Development Education ramparts; while at the other end of the office — and the political-bureaucratic spectrum — a benign image of Christ watched paternally over charts of volunteer statistics taped to the walls of the Data Department. Between these two camps, the walls were adorned with seductive tourist posters, emotive fund-raising banners and colourful announcements heralding obscure Third World events. The Cuban Ambassador once paused on a courtesy call to consider an arresting poster of a militant Miss Piggy, her fist raised defiantly, shouting, 'Pig Power'.

On the more conventionally organized ninth floor, a hermetically sealed, air-conditioned room was reserved for humming computer equipment and banks of terminals, whose operation was understood only by the omniscient Finance Department. Their quarters were shared with Personnel, and with a boardroom which always seemed too small for CUSO meetings and was always too hot, or too cold.

A telex machine on the tenth floor clattered day and night — spitting out messages which were always 'urgent'. But the most critical piece of equipment in the bunker was the photocopier; a ravenous monster, its ceaseless toil included covert weekend union duty and occasional late-night reproduction of the clandestine and highly irreverent *CUSO Underground*, whose masthead proclaimed boldly that "All the World is a Field." Second only to the photocopier in importance were the telephones, which jangled, whirred or bleeped — in accordance with their age and the organizational status of their keeper.

Down the hall from the photocopier, a spluttering coffee machine, surrounded by spilled sugar and Coffeemate-caked spoons, formed the nucleus of what was sometimes called the 'Dev Ed Boutique'. Profits from the overpriced and insipid coffee went to Development Education projects — as did proceeds from the sale of posters, buttons and pins comdemning or supporting important causes, ranging from Chile (against) to organic food (for). Plants lined the windows, dangled from macrame planters and perched on filing cabinets, competing for space with coffee mugs of every shape and size — most of them half-filled with yesterdays dregs. More coffee appeared to have been consumed by the carpet than by the staff.

Near the erratic elevators — objects of fear and loathing — a bulletin board announced job openings, meetings and ten-speed bicycles for sale; the nearby union board was always thick with notices of rallies, pickets and solidarity events across the city. When John Carson was Chairman of the Board, he labelled the draughty building a health hazard — a sentiment shared by the union, whose health committee complained about everything from the word processors to stains in the carpet and the absence of non-fluorescent lighting at every 'work station'.

On the other hand, a pot-luck lunch at The Bunker could be one of the most delectable meals in Ottawa, as staff members each produced their favourite recipes from around the world.

On Easter weekend, 1985 the office moved from Slater Street to new, more spacious, less expensive quarters in a former department store on Rideau Street; but to some 'The Bunker' would always be headquarters. To describe the Bunker as the heart of the organization would belie CUSO's enduring commitment to the Third World, towards which most of its energy was directed; nor was head office the muscle. Few staff would ever admit that it held the brains of the organization either, although it certainly was a nerve centre, and it housed, over time, some of the best and brightest of Canada's international development workers. Far removed from 'The Field', the Ottawa office sometimes seemed detached, as though it was peripheral to the real CUSO. On other occasions, it seemed like the centre of the universe: a coup, an invasion, an earthquake in a far-off land, and reporters would phone CUSO first, sometimes rushing TV crews with cameras and lights and microphones in search of a story. Thousands of out-going volunteers passed through its portals or, when the elevators failed, struggled up ten flights of stairs. Most staff were hired there, some fired, and in its boardroom many bid CUSO a sad farewell.

For those who worked in The Bunker longest, the corridors echoed with the sound of boardroom arguments, the static of overseas phone calls, press conferences, the occasional pop of champagne corks and snap of opening beer cans at Christmas parties; with the passion, the tears and the laughter that always underlined anything the organization did.

Chapter 7

The Mahatma

Between the idea and the reality . . . falls the shadow.

—T. S. Eliot

W hen the passion for social action and participatory democracy that overcame the Company of Young Canadians finally caught up with CUSO, it came in an unexpected form. It arrived in the 1970s, in the person of a soft-spoken, middle-aged Quaker who had spent two decades of his life in Asia. None of CUSO's Executive Directors, before or since, has excited as much passion, as much respect, as much concern as the man who was sometimes called 'The Mahatma' — Murray Thomson.

Murray Thomson's parents were missionaries in China from 1906 until the outbreak of war between Japan and China in 1937. Until he was 13, Murray's schooling alternated between China, Japan and Canada, and he developed an enduring love for the Far East. When World War II began, he returned to Canada to attend university and soon revealed a political bent that was unusual for the time; as a student politician, he defied authoritarian officialdom and successfully demanded student representation on the Victoria College Council. He was co-founder of a humanist club which championed the unpopular cause of the oppressed Canadian

Japanese Community. He became involved in the youth wing of the Cooperative Commonwealth Federation and was so impressed by the party's social conscience that, upon graduation, he sought employment in Saskatchewan, where the CCF had formed a government. While working there, in adult education, he began to study conflict resolution and its application to international affairs.

In 1955, Thomson accepted a UNESCO fellowship to study at the International Institute for Child Study in Bangkok. The eighteen-month experience confirmed his commitment to social action; there was no returning to Saskatchewan, or the academic life which had once attracted him. When he was offered a post in adult education at the Quaker Centre in India, he jumped at the chance. His five years there exposed him, more than ever, to peace-related issues; he met Gandhian philosophers, and talked with visiting activists such as Martin Luther King.

In 1962 Thomson returned to Toronto to initiate the post of Peace Education Secretary with the Canadian Friends Service Committee; during his seven years in this position, he developed an even deeper commitment to non-violence and social action.[1]

In 1964 he married Suteera Vichitranonda, a Thai biochemist who had been a delegate to one of the conflict resolution seminars he had organized in India. By 1969, they felt a need to return to Thailand. The Quakers were unable to provide a posting, so Thomson took his wife's advice and approached CUSO. The soft-spoken Thomson — round-faced, vaguely oriental in expression, and grey-haired at 49 — was offered a field staff position. Thailand was an ideal place in those years for a man with Thomson's sense of mission, for causes were not in short supply. Parliamentary democracy had enjoyed a chequered history in the 'Land of Smiles'; what Thomson found when he arrived in 1970 was a hesitant flirtation with elections and representative government, under the strict control of the watchful and conservative military elite. The government was engaged in an uneasy alliance with the escalating American military presence in Southeast Asia, and had converted Thailand into a giant, land-based aircraft carrier for U.S. operations in Vietnam. By 1970, there were fifty thousand American troops in the country. U.S. bases in the north and the northeast were used as jumping-off points for blistering air raids on Vietnam, Laos, and later, Cambodia. Thai cities and towns played host to hordes of G.I.s on 'R&R' — indulging greedily in the soldier's penchant for prostitution, violence, drugs and black marketeering.

Thomson was at first uncertain how he might function with a 'fair conscience' if he found himself unalterably opposed to the policies of the government. His first challenge, however, was CUSO, and its image with the Thai government; CUSO was not seen in Thailand as an organization concerned with social justice, but as a simple, apolitical technical-assistance agency.

Nor did many CUSO volunteers share Thomson's concerns about authority and democracy. Pre-departure CUSO orientations had repeatedly warned that Canadian perceptions and cultural values would not necessarily apply overseas, and that volunteers should refrain from involvement in local politics. And so, while Vietnam had become a major issue among young people at home, for CUSO volunteers — only miles away from the fighting — it had little significance.

"It just didn't bother me at the time," wrote CUSO volunteer Lyle Petch, "except insofar as the noise of the passing planes disrupted my classes. Insensitive? Politically naive? too much wrapped up in my own world to be bothered about the moral dilemma of war? I don't know; perhaps a combination of all three.

"I like to feel comfortable in a situation, and I don't think I could have faced two years of fighting a situation over which I had no control. So I pushed it to the back of my mind and spent my energies on matters which I could change. My job, therefore, became very important to me, I lived, ate, and drank the work I had been asked to do."[2]

But Thomson looked at 'the job' and the organization differently. To him, there were two ways of approaching CUSO, whether as a Field Staff Officer or as a volunteer. One could treat CUSO simply as a volunteer-sending organization, as the Thai government did, or it could be approached from a totally different perspective. "This is the world," Thomson once said, holding an imaginary globe out over the edge of a table, "poised on the edge of an abyss. My task is to make the organization as relevant to that as possible, regardless of what happens to the organization."[3]

Quickly shedding any momentary reservations, Thomson plunged into CUSO using this approach. He began to question the volunteers, visiting them at their posts throughout the country and challenging them in the same way that he challenged everyone he met. His wife's brother, a naval officer, had many heated arguments with him. He would descend on American air force bases as he travelled, seeking out the chaplains and prodding them on their tacit involvement in the war. To a chaplain at Udornthani, who was obsessed with the welfare of the countless Thai prostitutes, Thomson argued that prostitution was only a symptom of a larger issue: end the war, send the troops home, and it would decline of its own accord. He felt good about the encounters and confrontations, even though he realized, deep down, that "it was nothing." They were, in a sense, a necessary personal gesture in the face of the omnipotent force he sought to overcome.

Riecky Stuart and her husband Colin remember Thomson being at their wedding in Bangkok. A marriage between two CUSO volunteers was not an everyday occurrence, and the Canadian Ambassador had graciously hosted the reception on the lawn of the chancery garden. Among Colin's friends were some American air force personnel who had been helpful with supplies for the school where he taught. Thomson quickly identified one of them, and before long was engaged in an argument which took over the whole wedding. On another occasion, travelling with a friend in the northeast, Thomson thought seriously about going on to the air base they were passing, and lying down on the runway in an act of direct personal defiance, "to physically speak out about what I thought was happening." A lone Canadian, apprehended on a distant U.S. runway, would hardly have affected the outcome of the war one way or another, but to Thomson, the personal statement was almost more important than the effect. However, he knew very well, that it would have had a profound effect on CUSO: "That sort of act took a combination of courage, a willingness to take the consequences in terms of family and job, and a perception of how you should spend your time." Part of him regretted that he never went out onto the tarmac that day, and he always reserved a healthy amount of personal respect for those who made the direct personal statement in such situations.

Thomson's CUSO years in Thailand were not all high drama focussing on front-line world issues. There was an ongoing program of teachers, engineers and medical personnel to manage. Partly in an effort to educate himself, and partly out of commitment to his own views of how an organization should be operated, he arranged meetings of volunteers and invited interested Thais to participate. In October 1970, not long after he had arrived in Thailand, he convened the first meeting of a CUSO Thailand Committee, "to involve volunteers and staff in cooperative planning of CUSO projects, conferences, directions, and activities in Thailand."[4]

Not only did he feel that this was the best way to carry out his own function as a 'coordinator' of the program; he saw it as a means of making the volunteers more aware of some of the issues of development, and of involving them in the larger policy questions that would soon confront the organization — if he were successful.

His CUSO colleague in Thailand, Jim McFetridge, summed it up: " 'The Mahatma' provided the goals and the inspiration to build a genuine partnership in decision-making between volunteers, host nationals, and field staff. No one individual could dominate because of the Quaker style of group process and consensus-building, and it achieved both high morale and relevant programming".[5]

CUSO had never been a hierarchical organization in the conventional sense. From the beginning, its existence depended on the support it received from the Canadian university community. Its first constitutions, thrashed out by Lewis Perinbam and Bill McWhinney, ensured that the Board adequately represented a broad cross-section of Canadian university life, both faculty and student. When the returning volunteers started to become a factor, two guaranteed 'RV' positions were added to the Board. Later Executive Directors, Hugh Christie and Frank Bogdasavich, both had a sense of participatory management as it affected Canadian social service organizations through the mid-1960s. In CUSO, however, the changes were as much an acceptance of reality as a commitment to a new mood of management. The organization had grown tremendously, and the days were gone when an Executive Director could travel the world to manage programs, correspond with all volunteers and make all essential decisions. A more decentralized approach was unavoidable.

After Bogdasavich left CUSO in 1970, there followed a lengthy period of confused and conflicting management styles. His successor, John Wood, was an enigmatic man who, during his six-month tenure, was rarely seen in the Ottawa office. He had, in fact, never resigned from his United

Nations job in Malawi, and for six months he apparently moonlighted, travelling between jobs and continents.

During this odd, twilight period, management fell by default to the Director of Overseas Operations, David Catmur, and his Canadian Operations counterpart, Bill McNeill, two men with diametrically opposed styles. McNeill had been a volunteer in Nigeria, had joined the staff there and had become West Africa Director in Ottawa before taking over Canadian Operations. He believed in limited objectives and in ensuring that whatever CUSO undertook to do, it completed and did well. Clever, efficient and tidy, his image within CUSO had been damaged during the Biafran war. To the pro-Biafrans, McNeill had been little more than a lackey of the 'genocidal' Nigerian government — a man for whom the bureaucratic consideration was more important than principle. As well, he consistently maintained that CUSO was and should remain an apolitical organization; to take sides was to invite disaster. Thus, despite his demonstrated commitment to CUSO and his innovative programming talent, McNeill had become labelled: he was a 'pragmatist', which, in the long list of CUSO euphemisms, meant 'conservative'.

Catmur was different: he had never been a volunteer, and had had little contact with CUSO before Bogdasavich invited him in. The son of a Scottish mother and English father, he had served as a junior British officer in Korea, a tea planter in Assam, a CARE field worker in India during the Bihar famine, and a lecturer in agricultural economics at the University of Alberta. He respected bright people and new ideas, especially if they challenged the status quo; although, being something of a cynic, he usually left the commitment to others and gave it a wide berth himself. On the other hand, he loved the excitement of anything new, and to McNeill's chagrin, would often return from a field trip having approved ideas, expenditures, or new field staff appointments without any reference to budgets and procedures.

His taste for mischief was as strong as his taste for what he called "the wine of my mother's country," a predilection that often offended the more puritanical volunteers and staff. People either loved Catmur or hated him, but everyone had a healthy respect for the experience, skills and intellect he brought to the organization. As Dave Beer put it, "He was a tremendous catalyst. He challenged us and he terrorized us all the time."[6]

Catmur — rumpled, disorderly, looking down an inch of ash on a dangling cigarette — was the perfect counterfoil to McNeill, the clean-desk man in the blue blazer and knife-edge grey flannel trousers. That these two men recognized the contrast by no means made life any easier for them, however, and when the Board terminated John Wood's moonlighting, the internecine warfare began, culminating three years later in the appointment of The Mahatma as Chief Executive Officer.

Always amenable to new ideas, David Catmur saw a formalized kind of decentralization as both pragmatic and rational — consistent with his own approach to management and his total lack of interest in controlling faraway events and people. In an attempt to coordinate the growing number of ideas for participatory management in CUSO, he conceived an inter-regional conference — the first of its kind in the organization — of key players from Ottawa and CUSO programs around the world, to discuss future direction, policy issues, management options and programming matters. The meeting, held in Dar es Salaam, was the first opportunity most overseas staff had to meet with their counterparts from other parts of the CUSO world; in the sweltering meeting rooms of the threadbare Twiga Hotel, it was as if a new CUSO were being born — to Murray Thomson, attending from Thailand, it certainly seemed that way. Still new to an organization that he regarded as disagreeably hierarchical and 'apolitical', he was excited to find so much enthusiasm for decentralization. Catmur saw in Thomson the most eloquent spokesman for his own desire to shift decision-making to the field. After the Dar meeting, they continued a lengthy correspondence on the subject, eventually proposing a successful amendment to the corporate bylaws which gave the Thailand Committee full legal and voting status at the Annual General Meeting.

Although regional decision-making, especially in planning and budgeting, was a sensible and practical means of ordering priorities, it had a number of shortcomings. As a newly-appointed Field Staff Officer in Malaysia, former Lundu volunteer Peter Hoffman attended an Asia meeting in Bangladesh, a country he knew nothing about. "I was there four days," he said, "and I was making important decisions about the program in that country. I knew less about it than Head Office," — or than David Catmur, for example, who had once lived and worked there.[7]

It was the beginning of a lengthy period of confusion between decentralization and control from head office; in many cases, decision-making powers were allotted not so much to the country where CUSO programs were taking place, but to an amorphous group, held responsible to no particular authority, but standing foursquare between Ottawa and the program.

Murray Thomson would have a taste of how it could lead to problems. Not long after he attended the meeting in Dar es Salaam, Thomson proposed to the thailand local committee the CUSO attempt to make contact with ''or in other ways try to determine the policies of'' a band of Thai communist insurgents.[8] When the minutes of the meeting were circulated and copies reached the Canadian Embassy, cables were flashed to Ottawa and Thomson was called in for a dressing down by the Ambassador. Despite Thomson's argument to Ottawa that the guerillas merely represented a response to widespread social injustice in Thailand, Catmur ordered him to cease and desist. And he insisted that the offending minutes be destroyed, lest CUSO ''place all of its programs in jeopardy to salve the moral rectitude of a few volunteers and staff.''[9]

When the search began in 1970 for a new Executive Director, both Catmur and Thomson applied for the position. But Thomson was an unknown commodity, and Catmur was too adventurous for the Board of Directors; instead, they gave the jobs to a man who had not even applied for it, John Gordon. Gordon was an economic planner working on a University of Toronto contract in Tanzania. He was on home leave when a friend gave his name to the search committee and he agreed to allow his name to stand.

Soft-spoken, bearded, bespectacled and bald, John Gordon did not inspire the love, the hate, the passion that often became the nemesis of other Executive Directors. He was atechnician, a practical, down-to-earth administrator who saw his role as one of facilitation rather than innovation. He believed that the best administrators were not the 'idea people', the highly committed. Too often, he felt, they became involved in the debates themselves, to the detriment of their responsibility. To Gordon, the good administrator was ''someone who's not afraid to bring in good people, to allow them to work, to make it easy for them to work, and to channel, or coordinate their work in an effective way.''[10]

In this respect, he was successful on two important counts: he encouraged Catmur to develop a Projects Division, and assisted in obtaining a startup grant of almost a million dollars from CIDA — with few strings attached. And on the Canadian Operations side, he sanctioned the formal establishment of a Development Education Department and its ambitious startup projects.

At first, Gordon tried to ignore the growing schism between Catmur and McNeill. He recognized that conflict and new ideas were essential to the vibrancy of the organization, but he was uneasy about the clamour from Asia and East Africa for public stands on Vietnam and liberation movements. He distrusted the inexperience of youth, having reached his venerable mid-thirties; he disliked confrontation, and inattention to what he called "the restraints imposed on CUSO by its acceptance of government money." As far as politics went, he simply had no interest in the subject, "either in Canada, or in the development context."

Much of his time was, in fact, spent sorting out a deficit of nearly a million dollars which faced him on his first day in the office. That, and the growing conflict with SUCO (CUSO's sister organization), engaged him throughout his tenure, often ensuring that he was closeted far away from the gathering storm. To Murray Thomson, John Gordon was a cipher, a nonentity presiding over the Catmur/McNeill personality clash. CUSO had to rise above the pettiness and get on with the task: "Development is our business," Thomson wrote, "and development is disturbance; disturbance to ourselves and our organization, it means trying to define, isolate and attack obstacles, barriers, roadblocks to real development: trade barriers, arms races, greedy multinational corporations, elites (including ourselves) which are screwing up the process . . . the sooner we get on with tackling one or two of them, regardless of how the funding chips fall, the sooner we will be on the road to development."[11]

This was heady stuff, especially for other field staff who arrived in Ottawa for the now institutionalized, inter-regional meeting, in June 1973. By then, John Gordon had been seduced by McNeill's tidiness and was casting about for the means to rid himself of David Catmur. McNeill, too, was tiring of the endless bickering, but he blamed it on Gordon, whom, he said with customary acerbity, had "the imagination of a mynah bird."[12]

Thomson, in a further attempt at decentralization, organized a small gathering at the Quaker retreat on Grindstone Island for himself and the five other overseas regional directors. It was a beautiful setting on a peaceful June weekend; Thomson brought the rum and in the evening, they sat in front of a fire and agreed on a number of things. They agreed that Ottawa was a mess; the others agreed with Thomson that the overseas people were the heart of the organization, and, as such, had to provide the leadership. "Murray laid it on us and we lapped it up," remembers Chris Bryant, then Caribbean regional director.[13] It was like a pact betwen blood brothers in which they each agreed that if the opportunity arose, they would return to Ottawa to work on the problem.   For Thomson, the opportunity would arise in a matter of weeks, when cables reached CUSO field offices announcing the resignation of David Catmur — gone in an uncharacteristic flash of ruthlessness on the part of John Gordon, himself casting about for an exit visa. Days later, the way out came to Gordon in the form of the Directorship of the United Nations Volunteer Program in Geneva, and the CUSO search was on again. Once again, Murray Thomson applied, this time contending against the ascendant Bill McNeill.

But McNeill had made too many enemies along the way, and many of Catmur's erstwhile allies now fell in behind the Mahatma. McNeill's enduring commitment to international development was obscured by his acid tongue, which did little to endear him to the growing number of staff and volunteers who were composing resolutions, manifestoes and declarations about exploitation, Canadian culpability and liberation.

"They never did anything that was remarkable," McNeill said. "It was all rhetoric; they were given to the symbolic gesture." Regarding an East African CUSO 'development charter' which some staff wanted outgoing volunteers to sign before departure, McNeill snorted: "If I was a volunteer, I would have said, 'You're a bunch of loonies. You're running around with propellors on your beanies. You've got everything except a secret handshake.' "

So the scales tipped lightly in favour of Murray Thomson. Some felt he offered vision, a fresh outlook that reflected the overseas programs, a challenge — uncontaminated by the three years of office politics — that the organization needed. Murray 'the conciliator' could pour oil on troubled water. He could apply his training in adult education, conflict

resolution and group dynamics to a hapless administration, and to problems which extended beyond the CUSO secretariat — including the escalating debate with SUCO.

Within weeks of Thomson's arrival in Ottawa, the organization was
transformed; not because of anything he did in his first days on the job,
but because so many key players had suddenly disappeared. Catmur and
John Gordon were gone; early in the new year, McNeill resigned to
become Executive Director of World University Service of Canada. And
the SUCO 'star wars' culminated in the emotional resignations of the
Francophone Director and his Director of Overseas Operations. It was
as though a whole era was suddenly over.

The man from Asia arrived to a warm welcome in Ottawa, and was just
in time to attend the Annual General Meeting in November, 1973. A
former volunteer noted that he provided "a contrast to the timid bureaucrats who preceded him," recalling Thomson's earlier deprecation of
CUSO as a "slightly reformist, middle and upper-middle class organization."[14] Thomson had said that if CUSO people were unwilling to take
risks on matters of principle, they "would be putting the organization
ahead of the goals they are supposed to be working for." "It will be
very interesting," the RV noted cynically, "to observe whether Thomson's performance will equal his rhetoric."

When Murray Thomson took the job as Executive Director, he was
thinking of his father: as a missionary in China through the first four
decades of the century, the elder Thomson had faced every manner of
hazard, from illness and other physical discomforts, to bandits and war-
lords. Nevertheless, as the younger Thomson said, "you went in because
you had an idea, a cause."

Like his predecessor John Gordon, Thomson was quickly caught up
in the throes of day-to-day administration, and the internal difficulty
gnawing at SUCO. Ronald Leger, SUCO's Executive Director, was skid-
ding into a head-on collision with the francophone committee of the Board
— which saw him as a strict authoritarian, opposed by a well-meaning,
democratized and progressive majority of staff and volunteers. It was an
unfair caricature, but Thomson could sense an arbitrary streak in the
beleaguered Leger. In the end, he stood by and watched as Leger was

driven out, and he spent much of the next year working on a scheme to give the franchophones parity with anglophone Board members.

Thomson had enough problems of his own to worry about. CIDA, for example, became one of his larger concerns; annual negotiations for the government contribution consumed months of planning, preparation and argument. The delays and perceived intransigence by CIDA on the 1974-75 budget were such that Thomson involved the CUSO Board of Directors; and he threatened to publicize the costly delay. In the short run, the tactic was successful, but it created ill-feelings between CIDA officials and CUSO which would not soon dissipate. The following year, budget negotiations took a month longer, and when the figure was finally announced — six months into the financial year — it was almost a million dollars short of what CUSO had been expecting.

For Thomson, this sort of government-imposed disaster was to be expected. He had little regard for senior government officials, taking them for servants of the very *status quo* he was working to change. Lewis Perinbam, a founding father and CUSO's first Acting Executive Secretary, was now a Vice-President of CIDA, responsible for making the annual government grant to CUSO; but Thomson felt that Perinbam was never much of an ally. He thought that Perinbam was more concerned about perceived attacks on CIDA by CUSO's 'radical' political statements than he was about real development.

"Perinbam saw things in terms of the 1960s," Thomson felt. "He was always talking about innovations and new ideas, but when we came up with what we thought were new and innovative ideas, it turned out that he was more interested in his own ideas than in other people's." Perinbam, on the other hand, saw Thomson as "woolly naif" to whom CUSO was only a tool, a secondary concern.[15]

Brian Marson, who had helped establish the UBC President's Committee in 1961 and who had been an early Field Staff Officer in Asia, was now the Treasury Board analyst responsible for the CUSO submission. He paid a call on Thomson, not to offer support and encouragement, but to warn him that he had better make sure that CUSO remained on the tracks — and that the tracks were the traditional ones. And Romeo Maione, newly-appointed Director of CIDA's NGO Division, announced that CUSO's share of his budget was excessive, and that a much smaller rate of growth, or even decline, could be anticipated in the future. The confrontations increased, and where CIDA had previously been seen as somewhat benevolent (if paternalistic) it now became CUSO's favourite whipping boy, epitomizing all that was wrong with international assistance: it was bureaucratic, conservative, capricious, dangerous, and, above all, anti-developmental. Other branches of government were not viewed much differently and personal contacts with key decision-makers became more and more limited.

An increasingly tense relationship between CUSO and government was only one result of the conflict between Thomson's idealism and the day-to-day realities of his position at the organization's helm. Within CUSO, this conflict — often unresolved, as a consequence of Thomson's philosophy of equivocation — affected every aspect of the organization: funding, staffing, even the whole concept of voluntarism.

Thomson increased the staff of the Development Education Department; and he encouraged its new Director, Dave Beer, to take a more analytical approach to the subject; and he supported a program of financial grants to community-based education efforts to offset past programs in which CUSO took charge. Despite the larger staff, however, the development education budget was still small — restricted by CIDA's growing nervousness about the Department's increasingly activist stance.

As time went on, Thomson discovered that demands for unequivocal stands on controversial issues (such as he had made in Thailand) had to be tempered by a new context. Thomson supported the majority view that CUSO should be less financially dependent on CIDA — this would increase fund-raising from the public, foundations, and corporations; but he still espoused a 'development is disturbance' message and raised serious concerns about "greedy multinational corporations and elites." This dilemma had confronted others, and it was the bane of CUSO's fund-raising department. Accordingly, Thomson felt constrained to compromise, carefully tailoring the message to the audience he was addressing. He still hoped to sow a few seeds of controversy — no matter how slow the rate of germination — but he resisted the temptation to drag CUSO into the exercise.

Perhaps the most significant component of Thomson's tenure was a gradual but profound change in staff attitudes. Overseas programs began to decline as the numbers of volunteers fell from the high point in 1970. Some of the reduction was explained by increasing costs, a slowdown in the growth rate of the CIDA grant, and a demand for more highly specialized people, although the qualifications of people going overseas in 1975 were not appreciably different from those of five years before.

Quite apart from his larger questions about development, Thomson had already sown the seed of doubt about the relevance of volunteers, and Raymond Cournoyer who succeeded him as Asia Regional Director, took a further step in this direction. Cournoyer had little time for young Canadians, and saw CUSO's primary role as supporting Asian organizations in their own rural development programs.

In Latin America, which had never been an easy place to operate technical assistance programs, field staff began turning more attention towards project work than volunteer placements. And in East Africa, caught up in their own peculiar brand of participatory democracy, the staff and volunteers began to dismantle fifteen years of technical assistance programming.

One or two of the field staff in East Africa subscribed to a particularly doctrinaire view of development — seeing progress in terms of struggle, and development in terms of a class analysis; urging that 'contradictions' in society be exposed and heightened so that inevitably there would be change. To Thomson, such concepts posed no real threat: all ideas were worthy of discussion, and the suppression of ideas only led to conflict. He loved debate, and assumed that if proponents of class struggle pursued their ideas to the logical conclusion, they would see that violence was the ultimate outcome and would therefore modify or even abandon their positions. He believed strongly that if people were challenged to think through the consequences of their view they would would inevitably see the folly of anything that led towards violence.

"He was more interested in the ends than the means; he was interested in ideology as a means to an end," recalled Colin Freebury, one of his key staff members.[16] And if an ideology presented the answer to a problem its origin did not matter. "The tension over ways and means makes it easier to understand what is going on in the world, and get on with the problem-solving process," Thomson said.

But in some areas, the tension solved few problems and, instead, became and end in itself — a part of the development dialectic. Talk became a substitute for action, and where the number of overseas meetings increased, programs seemed to decline proportionately. And although 'democratic decision-making' was the order of the day, it was easily abused by a field staff with strong ideas.

Ray Clark had transferred to a teaching position in Zambia after two years as a volunteer in Jamaica: he attended a memorable CUSO meeting in May, 1974. The previous Christmas, staff had pushed for the creation of a local committee of volunteers. Many volunteers were simply not interested; they had gone to Zambia to do a job of work, not to become part of CUSO's administration. Nevertheless, the committee was formed, and at its first meeting that May, an Ottawa-based staff member, Lance Evoy, flew out to initiate an unexpected discussion on the future of CUSO's involvement in placing secondary school teachers and nurses. While the majority of teachers and nurses in Zambia felt CUSO should continue in this role, staff and others argued vociferously — in their new found 'awareness' — that by doing so, CUSO would be perpetuating an exploitative, elitist system.

Clark, who was the volunteer 'representative' from the Eastern Province, said: "There was a real snow job done at that meeting. It was one of those meetings where everybody gets involved in the heat of the discussion — decisions were whipping by — and then suddenly a vote is taken and people put up their hands. And then twenty minutes later they're saying, 'But wait a minute — we didn't mean to pull out of Zambia entirely; we meant to gear down, change direction, do something else, but not pull out . . . ' But Lance was there, waving the votes in front of us, saying, 'you just did it'."[17]

The next day, the volunteers organized a meeting of their own, without the CUSO field staff, in an effort to force a reconsideration. But it was too late. Some of the staff had already left. And so, Clark said, "We didn't have any more to say." And the Zambia program, once one of CUSO's largest, began to wind down, a victim of democratic decision-making.

In Canada, a year later, Thomson spoke publicly about world problems and how they related to CUSO and his own view of development. He argued for clarity of direction:

Are our directions clear? Are they consistent? Are we committed
to them? So often in looking at the world and its directions, I am
left with the sense that no one is in charge; neither the United Nations, nor specialized agencies, nor national governments nor
powerful organizations such as Ford, Rockefeller, the World
Bank, and certainly not the smaller NGOs such as the one in
which I have been involved . . . This is not an advisory function,
but it is an integral part of our planning efforts.[18]

Others would have put it differently. If it sometimes seemed that
no one was 'in charge' at CUSO, it was because Thomson deliberately
and systematically pushed the management function away from himself;
in the vacuum, rhetoric took the place of programs, which began to
disappear.

"People thought Murray was special," Jack Pierpoint said, "but it
was so difficult to get a decision on anything. It was an era of participatory
anarchy."[19] Pierpoint was Projects Director in Ottawa, and, like other
goal-oriented staff, he found his department increasingly in conflict with
Thomson. He and his staff would often sit up late at night plotting
strategies before a meeting with Thomson, sometimes just to ensure a
quick decision. For Pierpoint, and many others, it was an immensely
draining period, and personal frustration ran at a high level.

But often Jack Pierpoint would come away from a confrontation with
Thomson feeling somehow unworthy, especially after sitting beneath the
picture of Gandhi on Thomson's wall. "Jack wanted to talk about a
project and Murray wanted to talk about peace," recalled Chris Bryant.
"It was very, very frustrating in many ways. Murray was all over the
place, but he had a vision. We'd come out of a meeting where Murray
had driven us crazy — he couldn't grasp the point of needing as much
going in as you have going out . . . he was far beyond that. Every time
you came out of a meeting, you would feel vaguely dirty. Like you hadn't
really moved at the right plane . . . we were down there grubbing with
the numbers and the bodies and the dollars, and Murray was far beyond
that."

At the end of 1976, Murray Thomson's three-year contract came to an
end, and he did not renew it. He left CUSO to return to his prime interest

— working with Project Ploughshares, a small organization devoted to issues of peace and disarmament. The legacy he left CUSO was a complicated one which lingered for years, at least twice threatening CUSO with extinction.

Thomson had wanted an open organization and was happier arguing his ideas than seeing them prevail. But the commendable flourishing of ideas was offset by the polarization of ideologies, as what Thomson called 'the pragmatists' and the 'socialist roaders' squared off for battles that had yet to take place. A very special sort of Executive Director would be needed to deal with these conflicts, and transform Thomson's tentative first experiments with participatory management into a functional, effective system.

It was almost as though Thomson had reversed the dictum attributed to Conrad Black: "At a very early age I had to make the decision . . . did I really want to be Prime Minister? 'Shit, no,' I thought, 'I'd much rather be powerful'." Thomson had been more influential in Thailand: he cajoled David Catmur; badgered Bill McNeill; and ensured that his programming ideas, concerns about the war and concepts of participatory management were heard, attempted and implemented. In returning to Canada, he gave up his power in exchange for an ineffectual prime ministership.

Some would conclude that Thomson was too good for CUSO, too virtuous to occupy a gruelling and thankless administrative post that compromised and drained his real skills and talents. "I call Murray 'Mahatma'," said Jim McFeteridge, his CUSO colleague in Thailand, "because he has a spiritual quality about him, and he has unlimited love for people. There is no end to his forgiveness and trust."[20]

Thomson himself once said: "I have been more than a little pleased to bear that nickname; even in jest it is an identification I would like to be able to maintain."[21] He would always think of Mahatma Gandhi's words: "If you have doubts as to whether or not your work is effective, try to imagine the poorest, weakest person that you have ever met and ask yourself the question: 'will he benefit from your action?' "

Thomson might add: "Can our efforts be translated to the starving millions, not only the economically starving, but starving in terms of their dignity and their ability to be part of the process in which we are all caught up?"[22]

Chapter 8

The Gadarene Storm

> . . . and behold the whole herd of swine ran violently down a
> steep place into the sea, and perished in the waters.
> — Mathew 8: 32

Despite the rough ride of the previous three years, what Murray
Thomson handed over in 1976, could have transformed CUSO into
a unique, large-scale exercise in participatory management. The odds in
favour of success were not good, however. Volunteers and former volunteers who had either taken or had thrust upon them responsibility for
management decisions, drew on little more than the limited experience
of their own personal postings for insight into development planning.
Furthermore, the choices they thrust upon the organization were not
accompanied by the day-to-day responsibility for management, which fell
to the staff. Robin Wilson, Murray Thomson's successor, faced most
directly the issue of power without responsibility — what Kipling called
"the prerogative of the harlot throughout the ages" — by experiencing
the reverse. Wilson, more than any other Executive Director, found himself shouldering responsibility without power.

Managerial shortcomings in CUSO were not unique to volunteer committees. Many staff had little, if any, management experience when they

joined the CUSO payroll. On the positive side, this allowed for the high degree of flexibility that was essential to a people-oriented operation, and it permitted CUSO, in its early years, to experiment with structures and evolve systems to meet requirements as they changed. People joined the staff largely out of a sense of commitment and were willing to put in long hard hours in order to get the job done.

As the first full-time Executive Secretary, Bill McWhinney had taken a small, tentative operation and turned it into a major going concern almost single-handedly. He had a prodigious appetite for work, which he combined with a keen insight into problem-solving, and good judgement to pilot CUSO through a period of potentially hazardous unknowns. He was fortunate enough to have a small Board of Directors who believed passionately in the CUSO idea and who assisted greatly, particularly with fund-raising. But the task of organizing both the Canadian recruitment base and the initial overseas postings fell largely to McWhinney. In 1963, with ninety-seven volunteers departing for assignments in sixteen countries, he still worked with a total staff of only two secretaries. He corresponded with and personally met each of the volunteers, both before they left Canada and when they arrived overseas. In contrast, the German volunteer organization, with 133 volunteers in the field in 1964, had a staff of ninety, and the Peace Corps had a staff-to-volunteer ratio five times greater than CUSO's.

Rapidly escalating recruitment, the provision of RCAF flights for outgoing volunteers in 1964, and the first government grant in 1965, led to the expansion of the Ottawa office, although when McWhinney left CUSO early in 1966, its bureaucracy was still small and highly personalized. The next two Executive Directors after McWhinney each put an indelible stamp on the organization, both professionalizing it and drawing it some distance from its spontaneous, voluntary roots. Hugh Christie, McWhinney's immediate successor — formerly an official of the government's External Aid Office — was twenty years older than the staff and volunteers, and shared little of their volunteer ethic. Secretaries in the Ottawa office, whose shorthand he would test personally, called him "Mr. Christie" and often fled to the washroom in tears because of the demanding standards he set for them. Freed from the financial constraints of the past, Christie consolidated CUSO's funding relationship with the government, drawing on his personal acquaintanceships with senior officials; as well, he expanded CUSO's administrative base, bringing in other professionals without volunteer experience. Information and publicity staff were hired and a full-time fund-raiser was appointed. Office administrators and secretaries gradually took over many of the functions that had previously been provided free through the Association of Universities and Colleges of Canada.

Early in 1968, Christie was succeeded by Frank Bogdasavich, an RV who was anything but the archetypal volunteer. A lawyer, he had been Administrative Dean of Law at the University of Dar es Salaam before returning to Ottawa in 1966 to head up the rapidly expanding East Africa program. Given to conservative tailored suits and a rapid-fire, staccato management style, he continued the trend initiated by Hugh Christie — professionalizing and expanding the administrative complement and increasing the proportion of non-volunteers on staff. The emphasis on youth was downplayed and CUSO's original motto, "To Serve and Learn" gave way to "Development is our Business." Even the word volunteer began to fall into disfavour, and the ungainly term, cooperant, officially adopted by SUCO after 1969, was co-opted in a half-hearted way.

In the four years following McWhinney's departure, the number of volunteers tripled, from 341 working in twenty-nine countries to 1,110 in forty-two countries; the staff complement grew almost twice as fast, from ten officers to fifty. The original constitution was revised; the membership base was broadened; the Board of Directors was expanded and substance was given to both Christie's call for democratic processes and Bogdasavich's predilection for transferring decision-making to those involved in overseas programs.

As a result, Annual General Meetings were no longer intimate gatherings of the founding fathers, but large, brawling assemblies of returned volunteers, often radicalized by their overseas experience and the apathy they found on their return to Canada. Many were annoyed by CUSO's growing bureaucracy, its increasing dependence upon the Canadian government, its apolitical stance in the face of growing Third World problems and by what they saw as the complicit apathy of the industrialized world. Many wanted to slap the rose-coloured glasses off the technocratic face of development and say loudly what they had seen: that the gaps, rather than narrowing, were widening to reveal a terrible chasm of poverty and despair that demanded urgent attention.

The 1967 Annual Meeting was a case in point. Sixty-two resolutions were debated and passed on issues relating to every facet of the organization's activity. Two years later, the AGM had become even bigger and more virulent, and after Frank Bogdasavich made his farewell address, the meeting listened to a series of resolutions demanding that all plans and policies be open to scrutiny before implementation. There was concern expressed at continuing CUSO operations in Nigeria despite the horrific civil war; annoyance at the disproportionate number of male delegates to the meeting; a demand that wording in the CIDA agreement be altered ex post facto; and even a motion that the United Nations be asked to take the organization over; lock, stock and barrel.

Much of this, however, simply remained rhetoric, since the AGM had no formal authority, its resolutions serving only as recommendations to the Board of Directors. The Board, which met only four or five times a year, was much more concerned with budgets, bureaucracy, and CUSO-SUCO relations than resolutions on what it considered remote or hazardous issues. By 1976, the Board was spending most of its time on legalistic and financial battles between the anglophone and francophone wings, and very little on policy. Instead, real policy was being debated and developed by staff through the decentralized structures that Murray Thomson had helped to create.

Overseas local committees, dominated largely by staff but legitimized by a shaky and easily-manipulated volunteer base, made decisions and pronouncements and 'mandated' their staff representatives to carry positions forward to the semi-annual Inter-Regional Meeting in Ottawa. Although peer accountability had become an invaluable tool in planning and budgeting, the IRM was imbued with an underserved aura of democratic sanctity. At the height of the IRM's authority, Murray Thomson had felt obliged to treat its 'decisions' as binding, while his successor, Robin Wilson, squirming uncomfortably through the polemics of increasingly anarchic meetings, and attempting to reassert the authority of his position, would soon experience the wrath of the IRM scorned.

IRM delegates were drawn in equal numbers from the Ottawa office, the Canadian regions and overseas field staff. Although various complicated voting formulae were adopted over the years, the spectacle of the Executive Director — ultimately responsible to a Board and accountable to the government for a multi-million dollar budget — being 'voted down' by field people with no similar responsibility, seemed odd, not least to the incumbent. Had there been some reciprocation, the system might have had a chance, but the views of the Ottawa office and the Executive Director were ignored, or even rejected, in the field. The Latin American field staff, for example, became a law unto themselves, occasionally describing their staff meeting as a "collective." While their programs were more often than not beyond reproach, they became increasingly isolated from and suspicious of the rest of CUSO. As a result, CUSO's pioneering and often delicate work with rural groups in Bangladesh, for example, did not benefit from the experience of its Bolivian counterpart: more and more, each region acted as a completely autonomous operation. With Ottawa acting increasingly as cipher rather than coordinator, there was also a marked trend to compartmentalization and in-breeding among staff. The Latin America 'collective' not only had no interest in appointing staff from other CUSO regions; it actively worked to keep outsiders out.

The IRM, where everything came together like a semi-annual attack of space invaders, had become an institutionalized version of the Annual General Meeting. As such, its resolutions, while often no more sophisticated, were far more important and far more reflective of the organization's thinking. Although formal IRM agendas were inevitably consumed in groping with the annual budget and its various revisions, it had largely subsumed the role of both Board and Executive Director by the late 1970s.

To further confuse matters, Robin Wilson feared, with some justification, that the IRM and 'democratic decision-making' had become the main tools in what looked increasingly like a takeover bid by a group of staff with militant leftist views; a guarantee, he knew, of sure disaster in the CIDA cheque-writing department. Development education, for example, had been mandated to ". . . undertake a program of political education in Canada . . . using examples of struggles in order to sensitize and involve the dominated class in solidarity between nations." Canadian operations was urged to give "particular attention at pre-orientations" for outgoing volunteers, to "political and ideological awareness," and a remarkable East Africa Regional Meeting recommended that CUSO "contribute to continuing working class struggles in the region, Southern Africa and Canada."[1] Using a variety of techniques, serious proponents of these views — almost always a small minority — successfully cajoled, embarrassed or manipulated various 'democratic' forums into voting for them.

Overseas volunteer/staff committees became ends in themselves, and the dialectical 'process' — participatory management — was used to justify programs that field staff wanted, One regional meeting in East Africa at that time was held in the village of Serowe, in Botswana; at great cost, staff and volunteers had flown in from Malawi, Tanzania, Zambia and the Sudan. One of the issues they considered was the future of the CUSO program in Malawi; another was the possibility of opening new programs in Lesotho and Swaziland.

The staff position was clear: CUSO should remove itself from Malawi because its government was conservative, anti-developmental and pro-South African. New programs should not be considered in Lesotho and Swaziland, because these two countries were essentially hostages to the South African economy, and to assist them would imply approval of South African government policy.

The guest speaker was an African who had recently been released from detention in South Africa. He made an eloquent argument in favor of CUSO's presence in Lesotho and Swaziland; while the staff and volunteers listened politely, he talked long into the night. Blacks in South Africa, he told them, had been crucified twice: once by being born there, and a second time by white liberals who were not even willing to teach them to become mechanics. But when it came to a vote, the staff position held, because of peer pressure and staff insistence that CUSO make a 'statement'. And so, the Malawi program was terminated — despite the fact that volunteers in Malawi did not agree with the decision — and the question of new efforts in Lesotho and Swaziland was quashed. For some, it was a victory; a sign that CUSO was at last coming of age politically; evidence that participatory management really could work. To others, it was something very different.

"The volunteers had very heavy numbers done on them by the field staff," one of the Serowe participants felt, "and the field staff got their way. The way those decisions were made wasn't democratic at all."[2]

Thus, a middle-class organization, drawing its people and its support from a cross-section of middle class Canadian society and basically believing in a pluralistic approach to development, gradually took on the symptoms and appearance of a politicized, radical fringe group.

Untrained and unequipped (except by inclination) for the inevitable battle, Robin Wilson donned what managerial armour he could find, swung himself up into the Executive Director's saddle, and turned his high-strung steed onto the jousting course. A tall, personable Scot, Wilson had only a couple of years in Antigua and a YMCA background to assist him in the struggle for control of CUSO.

Already there was a "basic strategies" debate pointing in the direction of a worker-controlled organization, and the Board had momentarily broken away from its SUCO discussions to create something called "Task Force Five," which was supposed to recommend structural changes in management, participation and democracy. While most of the overseas programs went onto auto-pilot, the ferment and tension grew in the rarified air of the Slaterbunker.

Wilson's first mistake was to refer to the intensely serious 'basic strategies' discussion as the "B.S. Debate." His second, in a climate of confusion, distrust, and obscurantism, was to say exactly what he thought. His third was to put it in writing. Six months into the job, he issued a paper outlining his thoughts on CUSO's management structures. "Supervision," he said, "by definition has as one of its components, an element of authority." And authority had disappeared into the maw of the all-powerful Inter-Regional Meeting, which he said, had "neither the time, the setting nor the kind of relationships . . . to do anything that approaches effective supervision." To make matters worse, individuals had relinquished the authority that came with their jobs, "for fear of being perceived as opposed to the values we collectively espouse."[3] He said that the IRM could not deal effectively with budgets and planning, and that the regional structures were not providing the supervision necessary for effective management. For good measure, he took a swipe at the Board of Directors, which he said was not representative of the organization, and he even spoke well of CIDA, something no Executive Director had done for years.

The paper concluded with a restructuring plan which would convert the overseas regional "representatives" into "directors," responsible to him rather than to their amorphous regional groupings. A Personnel Director would be hired, and the Ottawa office would be reorganized so that there were clear lines of authority between the Executive Director and seven sub-directors. The IRM would continue to meet, but only "to discuss and develop recommendations to the Executive Director." The effect was like bullets in a campfire, with another explosion each time the words 'director' or 'authority' appeared. Even those in sympathy with Wilson's aims shrank from such unprecedented straightforwardness, finding common cause — for once — with those who seemed unable to utter a sentence without at least one 'democratic', 'popular' or 'collegial' falling from their lips.

And so began eighteen months of confusion, recrimination and paralysis, during which few of Wilson's recommendations would be implemented. He was criticized for authoritarian, undemocratic, unworthy ideas; for citing responsibility to CIDA and donors while ignoring responsibility to Third World beneficiaries; for neglecting the tireless voluntary efforts of the thousands of people overseas and in Canada who made the organization strong. The Board, increasingly weak and remote, burrowed furiously in the SUCO Problem, hoping vainly that the 'B.S. Problem' would go away.

CUSO has never been easy on its Executive Directors. Of the nine men who held the position in the organization's first quarter century, only two lasted longer than three years, and only one ever renewed his contract; two were fired, and three times a deputy had to stand in as acting Executive Director for periods of six months or more.

By the end of 1978, Wilson was effectively isolated from most of the staff; the left had reacted bitterly to the substance of what he was trying to do, while the majority objected to his tactics. Distant and unhappy, he felt that staff were working against him, both in lobbying the old board members and in stacking the election of new ones. He warned staff that Board members should receive information only through the Executive Director, while the Board found itself in some cases with insufficient information, or with data that contradicted what they continued to receive from staff anyway.

By January of 1979, Wilson had pinned the resurrection of central authority on a new personnel policy which would restore the Executive Director's long-lost power to hire and fire. To Wilson, it was essential; to many staff — unconsulted, worried, and willing to believe the worst — it represented yet another authoritarian directive from the top. For those with left-wing views, who could now sit back and let Wilson make his own enemies, it was simply the satin lining in his coffin. In fact, the new personnel policy was simple and reasonable; long overdue, it would neither have increased the power of the Executive Director significantly, nor would it have eroded the involvement of other staff in personnel policies and procedures. But the division had become so deep that the very life of the organization seemed to hang on this slender issue when it was presented to the Board of Directors on a Friday evening in January 1979.

Like an unsuspecting goat at the feast of Ramadan, Wilson entered the meeting unaware of the danger. It was a shambles. Many who were there do not even recall the issue, but they remember clearly a serious question of trust in the style and judgement of the Executive Director. Stan Percival, who had joined the Board only two months before, described it as a "blow-up — a real battle." The Board was evenly split on the personnel policy, and finally the Chairman broke the tie vote in favour of acceptance. But after Robin Wilson went home to prepare for the next day's meeting, some of the board members lingered, arguing long into the night.

The Board had little concern for Wilson's political problems; in fact, it barely conceded their existence. Most of the board members were, in any case, liberally inclined and accepted that the organization would inevitably attract a small radical fringe element. But regardless of whether the 'radicals' were a real power, Wilson's preoccupation with authority seemed to go against the grain of the consultative, 'family' way CUSO had of doing things, and the Board neither saw nor felt the threats that had isolated him so completely. "Robin wasn't in tune with the way people made decisions," Stan Percival said. "As an outsider, he didn't really have a handle on how decisions were made."[4]

The same could be said of the Board, which knew little of the internal debates, the soul-wrenching arguments and the reasons behind the utter paralysis that the power struggle had caused. But it hardly mattered. As the rump group argued on into that Friday night, several decided that they would resign the next day if nothing was done. In the morning, when the meeting convened in the Bell Canada building, high over a cold, bleak, snow-covered Ottawa, Wilson and other staff were asked to leave the room. For three hours the Board argued; then they called Wilson in and took the vote. Two of Wilson's strongest supporters were absent, and two members abstained. Six voted to release him, four opposed it. On a Board of thirteen members, six carried the day, and Robin Wilson's long and painful joust ended abruptly.

The fallout was swift and furious. Jim Griffiths, one of the absent board members, resigned, charging that "factions within the organization are destroying it."[5] Two other board members quit; one, Ria Zink, attended a meeting of fifteen Maritime universities and colleges, urging them to withdraw all support from CUSO. In her letter of resignation, another, Ann McRae, charged that CUSO "no longer has a Board of Directors. Instead it has . . . a group of individuals who are allowing themselves to be directed by staff, . . . and those making the decisions are not held accountable."[6]

There was much antagonistic media attention, and negotiations with CIDA on the 1979-80 budget ground to a halt. Romeo Maione, Director of CIDA's NGO Division, thought that "rads" and "trots" had finally done in the CUSO Executive Director, and that is certainly the way it looked on the surface. "The extent of dissatisfaction with CUSO's operation is the key to whether the organization receives money this year," he told reporters. "If the problem represents a struggle to the death, then we must think twice about putting money into a leaky pot."[7] And with that, CIDA locked its door, drew down the shutters, and waited to see what would happen.

One of the most immediate problems was the unpleasant renewal of the CUSO-SUCO battles, both over money and over SUCO's newfound anti-Zionist orientation. With several Board vacancies, and a severe crisis in public confidence, the Board also realized that it badly needed new blood. "Up to that point," said Stan Percival, "the Board was inept, split; it really did not function very well. In fact within the organization it was considered a bit of a laughing stock." Now it was forced to pull together, and to act for the first time in many years as a real Board of Directors. Within a few months, a number of experienced outsiders were brought in: John Carson, former head of the Public Service Commission of Canada; Gordon Cressy, RV, now a Senior Alderman in Toronto; Edmonton Alderwoman, Bettie Hewes; John Godfrey, President of King's College, Halifax; David Miller, Vice President of the Cape Breton Development Corporation; Bob Olivero, a former staff member with broad private and public sector experience. Almost overnight, the Board was transformed, and while not as representative of what some wanted the CUSO 'constituency' to be, it represented not only a good cross-section of CUSO interests, but also a fair slice of Canadian society. At last CUSO had a real Board of Directors.

The formation of a born-again Board of Directors, plus the appointment of a new Executive Director, a strong management team and CUSO's acceptance of a CIDA-inspired external management audit, helped re-establish government confidence in the organization. Nevertheless, when the CIDA grant was finally confirmed in September, almost halfway through the financial year, it was, as in 1974, nearly a million dollars short of the figure that had been agreed upon many months before. The immediate results were destructive, but in the long run, the cut had some redeeming effects; it heightened the financial bitterness between CUSO and SUCO, and hastened the inevitable divorce. CUSO was obliged to close its least effective overseas office, in Barbados, which forced a new and ultimately constructive re-examination of programming in the Eastern Caribbean. Within two years, the program there was both quantitatively and qualitatively more substantial than it had been for five years.

The Ottawa office took the brunt of the cut, restructuring itself along leaner, more efficient lines, and laying off a dozen staff. And the management audit led directly to a major constitutional overhaul which significantly broadened the membership base of the organization, giving policy access to all CUSO supporters rather than to the incestuous little groupings that had proven so susceptible to staff manipulation through the 1970s. Third World membership was encouraged as well, and six Board positions were created for overseas representatives — a move which would prove its worth many times over, even within the first year of operation. A maximum of three staff members could now be elected to the Board; thus, the CUSO Board of Directors became truly representative of the entire CUSO constituency, and a broad forum at last existed for serious policy formulation.

One of the most controversial effects of the CIDA cut was the beginning of a union within CUSO. Those who wanted a worker-controlled organization had lost incalculably in the aftermath of the Wilson departure.

The reorganization, the reassertion of Board authority, the layoffs, the budget cuts and the broadening of the constitutional base, had been handled with limited reference to the various staff 'collectives', regional groupings and the Inter-Regional Meeting.

Working on a fear among staff that further layoffs and authoritarian management were in the offing, the same group that had made life miserable for Robin Wilson began to envisage, in the creation of a union, a new route to organizational control. The debate was long and difficult, not least because of divergent perceptions of a union's role among CUSO staff.

Union organizers stressed that "democratic participation" was their ultimate purpose. But because their strength initially came from support staff in the Ottawa office, worried about conditions of employment and potential layoffs, "the interests of staff" also had to be considered. In order to bridge the gap between the two positions, the union first had to define 'management' — a concept its organizers had previously relegated to the 'collective' stratocumulus. Then, having defined it, they defamed it. "There is pressure from hierarchical/management-oriented senior staff to substitute themselves for participation and cooperation and to firmly entrench their decision-making powers into a top-down process." Quoting from an article entitled "On the Left in the CLC," the union newsletter condemned "business unionism" and said "the Left can form a credible opposition" to the "management/anti-union response" in CUSO.

The senior staff were perhaps unfairly disparaged. Most had long service as volunteers and staff in CUSO and other voluntary organizations, and some even had considerable union experience. Although there was no real anti-unionism among the staff or Board of Directors, there certainly was a great deal of unhappiness about a CUSO union. Many felt that a union had no place in an organization that worked with the rural poor of the Third World, and which sent Canadians overseas to face the most rudimentary conditions. CUSO had been founded essentially upon the principle of voluntary labour to assist development, and this was still the basis upon which the hundreds of volunteers worked both overseas and in Canada; indeed, this commitment is why most staff, particularly those overseas, were prepared to work long hours under difficult conditions. The intrusion of collective bargaining into an organization based on personal commitment seemed inappropriate, even mercenary.

There was little concern about "the democratic nature of CUSO programs" in 1983, when the union and management became deadlocked over union demands for a 13% wage increase, following CIDA's insistence that it be held to the 6% allowed all government and government-supported institutions. And the union never attempted to extend democracy to the dozens of locally hired CUSO support staff around the world, many of whom formed the basis of the organization's relationship to local government, its administrative strength and its skill in the reporting and management of money. Nor were the volunteers considered. Early union demands included significant increases in holidays, salaries and benefits; the new bargaining group also expressed concern about the filtering of air in the workplace, and insisted upon clean carpets and non-fluorescent lighting at every work station. Such concerns seemed very far removed from the day-to-day life of volunteers — living on subsistence wages, on a rural compound without electricity or running water — and overseas staff, most of whom could count themselves lucky if they had a fan to ward off the hot dusty harmattan* or the sweltering monsoon.

The union debate stretched out over many months. The worst sticking point was the definition of 'management' and 'management rights'. The union, at first, presented conditions which would have emasculated both the Executive and the Board of Directors, neither of which it deemed sufficiently democratic or adequately competent to be trusted with real authority, despite their election by a broadened CUSO membership.

Finally, in December 1981, more than two years after the process had started, a collective agreement was signed, and CUSO had its union. For all the protracted discussions, the agreement was, in the end, a reasonably straightforward document. Ironically, the formation of a union could not better have achieved the ends Robin Wilson sought when he first joined the 'B.S. Debate:' the management rights clause, far from limiting management, spelled out clearly, for the first time in a decade, the presence of a management function, who exercised it, and how it would be carried out. The agreement also provided for staff participation in various aspects of programming, as had always been the case in CUSO. But the mystical Inter-Regional Meeting — the subject of interminable debate during collective bargaining — was given no formal authority. It was simply a staff

---

* A seasonal dry wind on the Atlantic coast of Africa

meeting, one of many in the sometimes unfathomable constellation of CUSO gatherings.

The signing of a collective agreement in CUSO was, in a sense, the final entrenchment of a self-serving bureaucratic attitude amongst a fractious staff which hitherto had found its motivation and its safeguards in higher ideals. That those ideals had been manipulated and abused — by management, by ideologues and by incompetents on both sides — perhaps made unionization inevitable. As a substitute for flexibility, management now had clearly delineated authority; as a substitute for collegiality, the staff had interposed the protection of law and a clearly defined arbitration procedure for resolving disputes. And as a substitute for commitment, CUSO now had pages of rules defining half a dozen different types of leave and overtime.

In praising the positive aspects of the agreement, Board Chairman, Gordon Cressy, told the 1982 Annual General Meeting that collective agreements were not a panacea, nor were they a solution to all organizational ills. He recalled his membership on the Board of Directors of the Company of Young Canadians in the mid-1970's: The CYC had signed a collective agreement, but within a year, they were out of business, closed by arbitrary government fiat, not a single job protected by all the labour laws of the land.

He could also have recalled something Gordon Fairweather had written in 1969 when he was the Member of Parliament for Fundy-Royal. Fairweather had praised CUSO as a "smooth functioning organization which gets things done calmly and with a minimum of fuss," and he contrasted it with "the stumbling uncertainty of the CYC," in which problems centered on "leadership and responsibility in management."[8]

"Along with involvement must go responsibility," he added; a simple enough formula for success that CUSO had observed well in its first decade and had all but forgotten in its second. It was remembered just in time to ensure that there would be a third.

Chapter 9

To Serve and Learn: The Delicate Dialectic

Where is the wisdom we have lost in knowledge?
Where is the knowledge we have lost in information?
— T.S. Eliot

From the beginning, Development Education — the attempt to wean Canadians from outdated, paternalistic attitudes towards the Third World; to foster public awareness of development issues — was a fundamental tenet of the CUSO faith. It was the 'learn' part of the original motto, "To Serve and Learn"; it was etched indelibly into CUSO's Development Charter, and it was reaffirmed at every Annual Meeting after a Development Education Department was established in the early 1970s. Given such a mandate, the Department should have presented CUSO's vitally important message clearly, professionally, repeatedly — to the media, in schools, to professional and labour organizations, and to government. It should have been able to provide this essential education, building on the experience of thousands of returned volunteers, on CUSO's vast network of staff and offices worldwide, and on its own proximity to the seat of Canadian policy deliberations.

Instead, tragically, on the few occasions when Development Education's voice was heard outside the steamy little hothouse in which it came to rest, its message was lost; and it often presented an image of CUSO as narrow, amateurish, incompetent and hidebound. 'Dev Ed', as it became known, was as truncated in its imagination and its outreach as the nickname; it was reduced to an exclusive, almost rejectionist faction within CUSO. This harsh judgement would be unfair if it were applied — and it is not — to the individual and collective efforts of volunteers who returned to their communities with development messages. Like all generalities, exceptional examples of effective development education work by CUSO can be found to dilute its sting. But considering the urgency of the message, the universal desire within the organization to communicate with Canadians, and the assets which CUSO could bring to bear, development education was probably the organization's most prodigious failure.

The essence of development education was the volunteer's two year experience in another society. Life in an alien culture — thousands of miles from home, family and friends, and often under taxing physical conditions — began in trauma and was sustained like a battery on a trickle charge of tension throughout the assignment.

Glen Filson, who with his wife Vivian taught in a small Nigerian rainforest town, wrote about it: "The struggle of overcoming dependent, adolescent behaviour seems to involve baptism by fire as the person confronts the identity-disintegrating experience of anxiety, the depth of despair, the pangs of guilt and the peaks of frustration and anger. But, thrust into an environment which lacked the dependent, protecting values and comforts of home, these CUSO people were able to shed many of the shackles of independence as they developed and matured through change after change."[1]

Most CUSO applicants were ripe for change and escape: for some, the motivation was a flight from the career treadmill, the confinement and anonymity of suburbia and a drab job; for others, it was a combination of wanderlust and humanitarianism. CUSO staff took great pains, in the selection and orientation of programs, to temper romantic or escapist notions with a healthy dose of reality.

"I would say that CUSO orientation had a fantastic effect on me," said one Tanzania-bound volunteer. When several African resource staff suggested that volunteers might actually *harm* Tanzania, she was shocked. "I don't think I had ever considered this before; the thought that aid was harmful to those countries had never entered my mind. I was frightened by our Swahili teacher's suggestion. I really wondered if we should be going."[2]

Orientation programs were designed to inform volunteers about the conditions they were going to face; to give them a sense of reality and cross-cultural empathy, and to avoid disasters of the sort experienced by Peace Corps 1 in Nigeria. In 1961, at the very dawn of the bold new volunteer age, thirty-seven eager young Americans, lodged at the University of Ibadan, were undergoing a rigorous training program; among them was twenty-three-year-old Margery Michelmore, of Foxboro, Massachusetts. She was full of information, but lacked understanding of it: a common enough fault that, combined with circumstance, had disastrous repercussions.

One day, she accidentally dropped a postcard in the street; to a friend back in Massachusetts, she had written: "With all the training we had, we were really not prepared for the squalor and absolutely primitive living conditions rampant in both cities and the bush. We had no idea what 'underdevelopment' means . . . everyone except us lives in the streets, cooks in the streets and even goes to the bathroom in the streets . . . ."[3]

Copied, and distributed across the campus, her note provoked a virulent anti-American demonstration. Michelmore was fired, and the Peace Corps was left with a slow-burning Nigerian animosity which culminated in its expulsion from the country seven years later.

In their efforts to avoid similar disasters, CUSO orientations occasionally went overboard; in the late 1960s, some were so intense that many candidates would 'deselect' themselves before departure. The training in those days relied heavily on psychological testing, 'T-group' techniques, role-playing (to prepare volunteers for the anticipated 'culture shock'), and guest speakers strongly critical of neo-colonialism, neo-imperialism, 'do-gooderism' and aid in general.

The 1969 East Africa orientation reached either the zenith or the nadir of CUSO training programs — depending on the viewpoint of the participant. Among the guests were some prominent East Africans (including Peter Polangyo, the author of *Dying in the Sun*) and a number of black-power activists, invited for their perspective on North American society; the latter group, especially, spread doubt and guilt among the middle-class Canadians as though they were sprinkling herbicide on a weed bed.

Feelings ran high throughout the program and into the closing dinner.

The send-off 'banquet' was a grand affair, to which departing volunteers had invited friends and family for a final farewell. It should have been an occasion for some lofty after-dinner sentiments, and perhaps, a few tears. One of the more relentless black activists, however, would have none of it: rising to speak, he once again abused the volunteers, railing at their thinly disguised racism and their questionable suitability, not only for service in Africa, but for more general participation in the human race. Observers disagree on what happened next; some say that the speaker, excited by the power of his own words, concluded by picking up a chair and hurling it into the audience, striking one of the outbound volunteers. Her husband, simmering after days of systematic vilification, exploded, soared across the tables and began battering the speaker. He, in turn, was jumped by some of the African resource staff and the banquet ended in unhappy disarray.

Once the volunteers were overseas, however, even the worst excesses of orientation were seen as mere melodrama. Being exposed to poverty, disease, strife and political violence for the first time in their lives changed most of them forever. Attitudes towards everything, from family and food, to laughter and sex, had to be reconsidered in the new context. The major effect on most volunteers was greater self-awareness and confidence, as Western values either fell away or were reinforced. Ability to change and adapt was a prerequisite to survival; sheer force of circumstance made most of them less materialistic. Some, through introspection and homesickness, would become intensely Canadian, while others would become less so. And some, shocked by the huge gap between rich and poor, would begin to view political systems and processes differently.

Voluntary agencies like CUSO are based on altruism rather than politics, but practical action for human development — especially in the Third World — means that difficult choices have to be made; and such choices are inescapably political. All factors must be carefully weighed if money is to be spent effectively. Refusing to invest in a politically partisan cooperative movement, for example, is as much a political decision as investing in it. The simple act of sinking a village well or providing an irrigation pump can free farmers from the influence of a rich landowner who demands allegiance and social obligations as well as monetary payment. Projects which aim to educate women or provide them with gainful employment may seem straightforward; but, if successful, they will have a profound impact on society. Providing credit at reasonable rates of interest can liberate sharecroppers from the usurious clutches of village moneylenders who receive as much as four hundred percent interest per annum. Such projects, while manifestly humanitarian, involve clear political choices; carefully conceived and managed programs, whose aim is to benefit the poorest, cannot help but alter the balance of village power, perhaps for the first time in centuries.

Furthermore, development volunteers soon learned that changing the balance of power at village level, or at least tilting it more in the direction of the poorest, had little apparent impact at the national level; Third World Governments, regardless of their intentions and philosophy, found that solutions to the most intractable problems seemed to lie far beyond their grasp.

Access to international credit and capital was conditional and restrictive. Interest rates, western inflation, the arms race, the oil crisis, and tariff barriers to protect industrialized countries rather than primary producers, were all outside their direct influence. And, as the 'First Development Decade' gave way to the Second, foreign exchange became an all-consuming consideration in the Third World.

By the mid-1970s, most governments were focussing their talent and energy on increasing exports in order to finance the purchase of machinery, fuel, medicine, books — essentials for survival, not to mention development. Hugh Shearer, the Jamaican Prime Minister, made this dilemma clear when he visited Ottawa in 1968 to plead, not for aid, but for more reasonable trade terms. He pointed out that in 1960, Jamaica had been able to purchase a Canadian tractor with the revenue from the sale of 666 tons of sugar; by 1967, however, 1,500 tons had to be sold to pay for the same tractor. Regardless of Jamaica's later experiments in both socialism and free enterprise, external factors were the predominant influence on the economy; dramatic declines in world prices of sugar and bauxite, added to the cripling oil crisis of 1973-74, drove Jamaica into the arms of erratic and sometimes conflicting buyers, creditors and aid-givers — from the International Monetary Fund to Libya's Colonel Quadaffi. By 1982, the country's external debt was half as large as its Gross National Product, and interest payments had risen from U.S. $8 million in 1970, to U.S. $128 million. As a percentage of Jamaica's gross national product, this represented an eightfold increase.[5]

CUSO volunteers didn't need a degree in economics to know that something was badly wrong when even the most basic of locally made products were unavailable in the shops because they had all been exported in the quest for precious foreign exchange. They could feel the dramatic squeeze on their own earning power of a tiny shift in world prices of cocoa or bananas or palm oil; see their savings disappear overnight in an unexpected devaluation, or dwindle as annual inflation rates reached fifty percent and more. Although there was little they could do about such problems while they were overseas, many carried a message home with them at the end of their assignments.

As well, the volunteers were affected by political change, which often occurred quickly and violently in the Third World. One after another, the governments of Mali, Madagascar, Niger, Ghana, Nigeria, Bangladesh, Thailand, Peru, Bolivia and others fell to military coups; returned to civilian government; and changed back again. Ideologies would shift leftwards, then to the right, and back again without any apparent improvement in national fortunes; although volunteers were rarely affected directly, the changes were unsettling for Canadians who had previously been exposed to nothing more extreme than a Progressive Conservative leadership convention.

Many of them became emotionally involved. The massacres of Ibos in Northern Nigeria in 1966 profoundly affected the outlook of volunteers working in the Ibo homeland of Eastern Nigeria. The same was true for many of the volunteers in Thailand during the Vietnam war. Colin Stuart could sit in front of his house at Sakolnakorn in the evening and see the distant flash of American bombs exploding across the border in Laos. In his second posting, at Udorn, he and his wife, Rieky, began to reflect on it. "When you saw the effect on the school," Rieky said, "when you saw the money being poured into the base, when you saw the G.I.'s getting drunk in town, when you saw and heard the Phantoms taking off every twenty minutes and saw the waste of money on fuel alone, never mind in the machinery and the development of the equipment, it really did make you stop and think."[6]

Volunteers were often appalled by the official aid establishment; the huge, capital-intensive projects which emphasized foreign content; the resident expatriate community of British, American and Canadian aid 'experts': the bwanas and the memsahibs, surrounded by their coteries of cooks, houseboys, gardeners, drivers, ayahs and nightwatchmen. Generously salaried, supported by half-a-dozen different allowances, most closeted themselves in pristine air-conditioned isolation from the local culture, and in expatriate cliques, clubs, commissaries and cocktail parties.

Being a volunteer was different; it was based on service rather than profit, even if the 'noble sacrifice' was surprisingly more pedestrian than friends and family at home might have imagined. As Glynn Roberts put it: "In a world where human relations are steadily undermined by commercialism and materialism, a sacrifice — a genuine self-offering — can open man's mind to the realities of the need for human contact and brotherhood . . . the *spirit* of working-while-doing-without is central to volunteerism . . . to the whole problem of underdevelopment in which, as Gunnar Myrdal says, 'the rich countries want to help, but are not prepared to make any real sacrifice'."[7]

Tim Brodhead wrote about it after he returned from Nigeria to work in the Ottawa office: "Volunteering, finally, arises from the impulse to act rather than to stand idly by." But, he felt, there had to be more to it. "In the global struggle for development, isolated, individual actions are no longer enough; they must express a sustained commitment to overturn structures which permit the rich to profit from the poor, a commitment as relevant to our own societies as to others, as much reflected in our daily attitudes and lives as in exotic activities in far away places."[8]

In the late 1960s, CUSO Executive Director Frank Bogdasavich established a small research department in the Ottawa office. It commissioned some tentative studies on development issues and published a series of clippings compiled on economic growth, aid, trade and foreign policy. Spurred by the positive reception of *Readings in Development*, the Research Department undertook a more ambitious enterprise, a prestigious journal on development issues for a wide-ranging international readership.

The first issue of *NEWSTATEments* went to press early in 1971, with an international who's who of politicians, economists and activists as "associate corresponding editors." It was, the editors said, "a magazine about development."

In a world of increasing economic disparity, of extreme social and
human injustice, violence and frustration, we believe that 'radical'
analysis is necessary . . . chronic unemployment, overfragmenta-
tion of arable land, poverty, lack of capital for infrastructure development are all virtually universal 'problems'. To what extent
are these problems accidents of history and nature; to what extent
are they calculated policies? . . . . This is what *NEWSTATEments*
is all about — development in its broadest context."[9]

But NEWSTATEments didn't attract the type and size of audience its
editors sought. Circulation was unimpressive, and after a year both the
Research Department and *NEWSTATEments* fell victim to budget cuts
and internal criticism of their up-market style.

In their place, a project began which would have profound impact on
development education, from British Columbia to the Maritimes: the
"Mobile Learner Centre." This transportable, development-education
resource centre evolved out of CUSO's West Africa orientation programs,
which, after 1967, were held at the University of Western Ontario. Every
summer, the various faculties' libraries were culled for books, periodicals,
films and tapes ralating to West Africa; the material was then compiled
into a multi-media 'development library'. Gradually, the library began
to take on a life of its own: visiting experts were videotaped and recorded;
CUSO made substantive cash contributions; overseas staff sent artifacts,
newspapers, magazines and books. Such efforts produced one of the most
complete Canadian collections on West Africa.

The process of building this excellent resource bank, combined with
new techniques in education, had a profound effect on the way CUSO's
orientation programs were conducted; by 1971, the emphasis had shifted
from lectures and classrooms to what was becoming known as a 'learner-
centered' approach. Abstracts of each item in the multi-media library
were labouriously entered onto a Toronto-based computer, and volunteers
had quick and easy access, through a telephone hook-up, to whatever
information they required. By today's standards, there seems nothing
very remarkable about the system, but in the technological dark ages of
1971, before the advent of even the pocket calculator, this sort of technology applied to learning was revolutionary.

Excited by its success at the CUSO orientation, the originators set about expanding their idea. The result, in the winter of 1971 and the spring of 1972, was the "Mobile Learner Centre," jointly funded by CUSO and CIDA. The key elements of the original learner centre were duplicated, packed in specially built boxes, loaded onto a large rented truck, and shepherded through eight cities across Canada. As a direct result of the tour, more than a dozen new learner centres sprang up in other cities, most co-financed by CIDA's newly established Public Participation Program; by 1984, there were more than thirty in operation across Canada.

While some of the centres concentrated on the original idea of a 'learner centred' multimedia information bank, others applied it to a more activist stance on Third World and development issues. In Saskatoon, for example, a number of individuals involved with the United Nations Association, the Saskatchewan International Association, the Canadian Institute for International Affairs, and CUSO, applied for an Opportunities for Youth grant in order to set up their own modest centre. By the fall of 1973, the "One Sky Learner Centre" was established in an abandoned Talmudic School across the street from a scrapyard on the east side of town and Rieky and Colin Stuart, who had returned from Thailand in 1971, applied jointly for the sole staff position at the centre.

Sharing the salary of $10,000, which some of their colleagues thought too high, they began sifting through the mountains of boxes of files that had been accumulated, in an effort to emulate the original learner centre. They abandoned this idea almost immediately, concentrating instead on a more political approach and attempting to focus on local concerns and issues which could be linked to international problems. Native rights, working conditions, agriculture and food policies in Canada and Saskatchewan, the international grain trade and its impact on prairie farmers were all topics of concern as they "hooked into something people were interested in locally."[10]

They were typical of many others across Canada for whom the learner centre, whatever its form and function, became the focus of an approach to development based on local issues, rather than one which treated it as an isolated phenomenon taking place only in other countries. Dispensing information on international problems was not enough; 'the process of change' became as important as the change itself. They rejected the notion that development was simply a quantitative problem which could be overcome through aid, investment and other traditional approaches. Rather, underdevelopment was seen as the result of a system that used colonialism as its chief tool in the first half of the century, and, by the 1970s, had created a permanent form of dependency, ensuring that the rich remained rich and the poor got aid.

For many, development education became a more politicized 'process' than a discipline, using Paolo Freire's and Saul Alinsky's method of identifying local concerns upon which to build. As one study of development education put it, "The aim of this approach is not simply to master a body of knowledge, but rather to engage in analysing and understanding our own personal and societal need for development."[11]

From the mid-1970s on, CUSO's development education efforts began to concentrate on requests for financial assistance from learner centres and CUSO local committees, rather than on programs and priorities identified and operated by the organization itself. The decision on what to fund was influenced by the ebb and flow of political pressures within the organization, and increasingly by the imprecise principle of 'solidarity'. "Development requires a thoroughgoing change in the social and economic structures that sustain global dependency and social exploitation," wrote Brian Tomlinson, shortly before joining the CUSO staff. "Solidarity with struggles for social justice and change, whether in Southern Africa or Central America or the Caribbean brings a recognition of the dimensions and linkages of these same issues within our own society and the realization of Canada's actual economic and political relationship with the Third World."[12]

Like any large, social service organization CUSO was a coalition of views and personalities. There were impatient radicals, some sustained by an intolerance bred of rigid doctrine — which rooted easily in the fertile soil of development education; — there were liberals, and there were more cautious individuals, for whom social activism was a totally new experience. As time passed, it was the impatient who came to dominate CUSO's development education efforts; and they demanded that organizational security be relegated to second place. Development education staff often found themselves on the fringe, aligned against those who feared that increasingly controversial public positions would damage the organization's recruitment and fund-raising base, as well as its delicate relationship with government.

CUSO's long-time Board Chairman, Red Williams, said in 1976: "Idealism and youthful enthusiasm are not always sufficient justification for 'tilting at windmills' . . . . Innovative social and political reform may well be the fateful 'siren's call' on which CUSO will founder . . . to stop 'risking' in our programming will mean that we have lost our meaning, but to risk the whole corporation and abandon those we have already committed ourselves to assist . . . just to take a political stance, can often be poor judgement if not outright irresponsibility."[13]

There had been good evidence to justify Williams' concern. In 1973, Oxfam Canada nearly collapsed over support for liberation movements, and the publicity had a disastrous effect on fund-raising, which dropped by more than twenty percent.[14] In 1982, Cansave's controversy, over administrative costs and programming direction, became public, and the organization's patron, Anne Murray, jumped ship; donations plummeted.

Similarly, when Executive Director Robin Wilson straightened his tie and the red light blinked atop Camera Three in the CITY-TV studio one July night in 1977, CUSO's own inevitable date with disaster had arrived.

CUSO had hoped that publicity on the Morton Shulman television program would help remind corporations and the community of its existence; a major new fund-raising drive, headed by an IBM vice president, was scheduled to begin the following day.

Morton Shulman began the interview with Robin Wilson using a prepared list of questions. Within seconds of the first question, however, he abandoned it, and pointedly established that ninety-three percent of CUSO's funding came from government, and that CUSO and its francophone sibling, SUCO, were legally one body. He brushed lightly over CUSO/SUCO programs in Malawi, "where they're slaughtering tens of thousands of people because of their religion"; Cuba, where CUSO was "freeing their assets to be diverted to troops and other things"; and Morocco, where "CUSO-SUCO is recommending that (the) government be overthrown."[15]

He then homed in on Israel and the PLO. (Just as CUSO had identified with Southern African liberation movements, SUCO had found controversial causes of its own to support, often linking them with Quebec's domestic 'struggle' for independence. In 1976, the issue became Israel and the PLO. Restrained neither by political equilibrium nor by first-hand experience of the Middle East, SUCO's Montreal office began publishing pro-PLO anti-Israel articles in its newsletters, and promoting inflammatory resolutions at annual and regional meetings.)

"I was hit behind the knees," Wilson recalled. "He just blew me away by pulling out a number of publications and documents . . . presumably 'educational' material about Palestine and Israel . . . . which had been leaked to him from the SUCO office."[16]

"Let's just show you this one," Shulman said, waving a SUCO development education pamphlet. "It shows how the Jews across the world have driven down these poor Arabs. What have you got to say about this little piece of government propaganda, paid for by our Canadian Government?"

"I certainly disagree with it personally, strongly," Wilson replied.

"Well it isn't good enough to disagree with it personally. You're the Director," Shulman retorted.

Wilson attempted a half-hearted explanation about the mysterious workings of the CUSO board, the organization's curious federalism and CUSO's non-governmental status, but Shulman would have none of it, returning, like a terrier with a bone, to the "Hitlerian propaganda" and the almost total government funding.

"What would happen if we cut off the ninety-three percent" he asked. "Are you going to shut down?"

"I would think that the organization would shut down," Wilson agreed meekly.

"Well, if Joe Clark is listening and he shuts this place down," Shulman concluded, "I'll vote Tory."

With that, the interview, the corporate fund-raising campaign, and the attempt to rebuild lost public support came to an abrupt conclusion. It had taken Morton Shulman only a few moments on a summer's evening to demonstrate that outspoken political posturing, poorly presented and void of public support, had a ruinously high cost in lost credibility.

Globally, non-governmental organizations began to achieve international political standing in the 1970s. A growing body of literature recognized the legitimacy of NGOs alongside international sporting associations; and professional, promotional, and communal groups, concerned with peace initiatives, women's issues, ecology or the rights of indigenous people.[17]

In 1972, an NGO forum was mounted in Stockholm to coincide with the UN Conference on the Environment. This counter-conference attracted significant media attention and was successful in raising issues that might otherwise have been ignored by the official conference. As a result of the Stockholm success, the idea caught on, and from then on, NGO counter-conferences were held in conjunction with the Rome Food Conference, the Bucharest Population Conference, UNCTAD IV in Nairobi, the Habitat Conference in Vancouver and the 1985 Nairobi 'End of the Decade' Conference on Women. CUSO was an active participant in most — organizing, lobbying government delegates, and arranging 'report-back' techniques for a worldwide Canadian constituency.

But all the activity had a dead-end superficiality to it; UNCTAD IV being a case in point. A year before the conference, CUSO, along with most Canadian NGOs, had no knowledge of commodities, price indexing, buffer stocks, or any of the other critical issues involved in the makeup of the hoped-for New International Economic Order. A year later, CUSO was participating in the Nairobi counter-conference along with several other Canadian NGO representatives, while at home learner centres and local committees studied the issues, held workshops and sent telegrams to their MPs. UNCTAD IV, like its three predecessors, made little headway on most of the thorny issues, but a few doors were opened for future discussion and negotiation. However, when the first commodity agreements were being hammered out three years later, the NGO voice was silent; commodity issues had gone the way of the hoola hoop, and whatever legitimacy the Nairobi conference had given simply evaporated. At UNCTAD V in New York, there were virtually no Canadian NGO representatives.

CUSO's develoment education staff maintained that the organization's most appropriate role in such issues was to popularize them as they arose, and to demonstrate how they related to local conditions and problems. There was, therefore, only a transitory interest in long-term issues, and the tremendous network of staff, volunteers and returned volunteers was rarely mobilized for any sustained purpose other than the vaguely defined 'solidarity'.

For a brief period, the Develoment Education Department maintained an interest in the activities of trans-national corporations by joining the Inter-Church Task Force on Corporate Responsibility, which conducted research into the investment and labour policies of Canadian companies in the Third World. There were occasional confrontations at corporate annual meetings, and, for a time, the Department emphasized what became known as 'The Bank Campaign': a public exposure of Canadian bank loans to the Government of South Africa and its agencies. The campaign culminated in 1978, in a dramatic 'ultimatum' to the Royal Bank of Canada that all CUSO investments would be withdrawn if bank policies were not amended by a certain date.

The resounding silence with which the ultimatum was greeted was matched only by the hollowness of the threat: CUSO had no investments to withdraw. Indeed, the organization maintained its account with the Royal afterwards, and actually borrowed three-and-a-half million dollars for cash-flow purposes the following year. When CUSO eventually found an acceptable alternative in the Toronto Dominion Bank, the Ottawa manager of the Royal genuinely regretted that the Bank's policy on South Africa — of which he was totally unaware — had so annoyed one of his better customers.

While there were constructive and thoughtful Dev. Ed. projects over the years, the resonant 'solidarity' theme, which, in the 1980s, concentrated on revolutionary Grenada, Nicaragua and Cruise Missile testing, inevitably led to a decline in government support for develoment education. CIDA, watchful after the public controversies of the 1970s, gradually imposed tougher criteria on 'Public Participation' projects, requiring individual signed contracts for each, and refusing to finance those that CUSO had previously 'brokered' on behalf of learner centres and other organizations. As financial support fell, the Department's staff was reduced from three to two.

Internal debate also simmered, and occasionally flared into open conflict — not only because of public criticism and loss of income, but because of differing perceptions as to what should be done about development education. Kasper Pold, Director of the Queen's University International Centre and Chairman of the Kingston CUSO local committee wrote in 1981:

> The term 'develoment education' is meaningless. Most of what
> local committees lump into that category is not education at all, in

even a broad definition of 'education' . . . there is usually no pre-
planning or follow-up, no evaluation, and no continuity . . . this
reflects the hit and miss nature of development education and the
rather inexperienced approaches to it by well intentioned people
who expect that the sincerity of their convictions, the rightness of
their cause, and their own sheer goodness in volunteering effort is
going to have the desired effect . . . It isn't necessary to force
'radicalism' down people's throats; virtually all groups and individuals that start with mild curiosity looking at the Third World,
will inevitably come to certain conclusions and realizations of
their own . . . people should be afforded a self-educating process
by presentation of facts from which they can draw their own conclusions.[18]

In 1982, when he was President of CIDA, Marcel Masse sounded a
prophetic note. "If within the next ten or fifteen years we do not implement the necessary reforms to change the rules of the game between
North and South," he said, "circumstances will force us to do so. The
message we have to get across to the public is that this is now no longer
a question of religious values or humanitarian values or charity — it is
a matter of survival for the East, the South, the North and the West . . .
It is essential to show Canadians how the notion of interdependence must
not only affect their lives in the future, but is affecting them now."[19]

But despite a commonly perceived urgency for more effective development education, its future is clouded by the record of the past fifteen
years. NGOs, of which CUSO is the largest, generally see themselves
as a network: a broad chain of groups across Canada, in communities,
labour and professional organizations; polarizing issues; forging a better
appreciation of the world and Canada's role in it; engaging in school and
media activities, research, and solidarity work on special issues and at
selected pressure points in public policy.

In reality, development education has been an amorphous collection
of projects; some have made fleeting impressions on limited numbers of
people; but most have had virtually no impact on Canadian attitudes and
thinking. Efforts have been fragmented, repetitive and wasteful; the re-

sults have been unmet objectives, lost opportunities and burnout.   A broad survey of Canadian attitudes on international development, conducted on behalf of CIDA in 1980, revealed that 69% of those polled thought that Canadian aid should either remain the same or be increased. But this encouraging statistic was quickly dashed by statistical evidence of Canadians' appalling ignorance about development questions. Thirty-one percent of the respondents thought that Canadian aid totalled less than $10 million annually, and virtually no one cited NGO or church educational activities as sources of information about development issues. It was perhaps just as well, for despite the fact that 48% professed an awareness of CIDA, even more claimed knowledge of a totally fictitious organization called 'Canadian Overseas Assistance Agency'.[20]

Instead of reaching these people — ordinary Canadians — NGOs, CUSO included, have spent the better part of two decades in a peculiarly onanistic state — holding endless meetings, seminars and workshops dominated by a ubiquitous in-group, and churning out booklets, leaflets and pamphlets that would never be read. They have consumed a great deal of energy arguing about the terms and conditions of the tiny CIDA grants that gave most of them life; they have largely ignored the development of official aid and trade policies which helped justify the need for development education in the first place; nor have they spent much time trying to win support for their efforts. Often, perhaps frustrated by an unresponsive audience — Canadians, unable or unwilling to heed their warnings of trouble ahead — they would turn on each other, or retreat into endless recondite debates on the technique of their art.

Prone to all the development education trends, fads and weaknesses, CUSO suffered not so much from its differing perceptions of the need for change in society and the world, as from differing analyses of the need itself. The consequence of this self-indulgent polemic was a fragmented and tangential effort, exacerbated by further fragmentation of a development education budget that rarely exceeded one percent of CUSO's overall income. This money, spread over ten provinces and several dozen tiny groups, usually maintained a semblance of coherence, but was too little to buy continuity, professionalism or a sustained effort.

Despite CUSO's passionate belief in the importance of development education, when faced with the choice between effective action on important issues and principled but largely ignored prophecy, the organization usually allowed the latter to prevail. CUSO's most important development education program, and arguably the most important in Canada, was still the personal volunteer experience, the two years of life and work, of 'serving and learning' in another culture.

Chapter 10

Fatima Patel

I n 1965, at the age of forty, Fatima Patel left her native South Africa, and emigrated to Canada. It may have been the desire to 'help' that caused her to apply to CUSO shortly after her arrival; it may have been her personal response to an unwelcoming Canada; a wanderlust — or a combination of all three.

Fatima's first posting was to Chile, where she worked on a health project; she then travelled to Jamaica; and finally, in 1972, to Peru. There, she organized health courses for medical auxiliaries in remote areas and established jungle clinics, to which she most often travelled by canoe — its dubious outboard engine urging her and her supplies through the encroaching jungle to waiting patients.

Perhaps the most serious situation with which Fatima was faced was the problem of commercial baby food. Years before the tragic effects of Formula Food on the health of infants in the Third World became an international cause celebre, she saw the problem everywhere she went: even in remote jungle clearings and Andean mountain villages, the ubiquitous, colourful tins of baby formula and powdered milk would appear, often the only sign of modernity.

Sometimes a convenient breast-milk substitute for mothers who endured hard physical labour every day, baby food seemed an even more attractive alternative when a visiting salesman or clever advertiser told the women that the formula was superior to their breast milk. Advertisements showed strong, healthy babies being fondled by smiling, sophisticated, fair-haired mothers. Contrasting sharply with the squalor of jungle life and the heartbreaking reality of their own runty, sickly children, it was an appealing image for village mothers who had never even dared to dream of something better for their babies. In more populated areas, baby food manufacturers subsidized — and even owned — easily accessible, inexpensive maternity clinics, in which expectant mothers were given classes in various aspects of childbirth and post-natal care. Never far from the core of the curriculum was the message that formula food was superior to breast milk.

The problem with this message was not that commercial baby food was inherently bad, but that for families with limited income and little education, it was a very real danger: because of its cost, mothers would dilute it; once thinned, it lost its nutritional value, and by the time it became apparent that the baby was undernourished, it was usually too late to repair the damage or to return to breastfeeding. An even bigger problem was the use of water from the only available source — jungle rivers or unclean wells. Unless it was boiled, the water could render the formula lethal; it spread worms, disease, and the worst child-killer, gastroenteritis. And among mothers who knew enough to boil the water, the cost of fuel — added to the cost of the milk — increased the financial burden on the family.

The problem was not limited to Peru: by the mid-1970s, it had become endemic in most Third World countries in Africa, Asia, Latin America and the Caribbean. For Fatima Patel, after five years in Peru, the question of commercial formulas became a personal issue, impelling her to write a harsh letter to one of the biggest formula food companies in Peru. A copy of the letter somehow reached the Interfaith Centre of Corporate Responsibility; the centre, in turn, passed it on to the American 'Infant Food Coalition' (INFACT). INFACT and its European and Canadian counterparts — of which CUSO was a member — brought the problem to public attention, and it became an issue of great concern for several international organizations, including UNICEF. In the United States, a Senate sub-committee, chaired by Senator Edward Kennedy, was established to consider the matter, and Fatima Patel was invited to testify.

Fatima travelled to Washington in May 1978 at CUSO's expense to appear before the Senate sub-committee and testify on the dangers of indiscriminate marketing of breast milk substitutes in Third World countries. She called the infant formulas "deadly poisonous," and was supported by a doctor who testified that around the world, each year, an estimated ten million cases of diarrhea and malnutrition could be ascribed to breast-milk substitutes.

Nestles, one of the major corporate culprits, mounted a massive publicity campaign in its own defence; but in 1984, the company capitulated, agreeing to modify its marketing techniques substantially, in response to the development of a marketing code by INFACT.

The coalition had been effective, but it was because of the testimony of health workers like Fatima Patel, who had seen with her own eyes the disastrous effects of infant formula, that the campaign was a success.

Chapter 11

Smoke and Mirrors: Cuba

The Cuban embassy on Ottawa's Main Street is a large, brooding bunker, built for function and surrounded by grassy embankments, fifteen-foot iron fences, and hooded security cameras that constantly scan the perimeter. Sometimes, when the gates are opened, a large reception hall just off the main entrance, clad entirely in Cuban marble, becomes the scene of gay parties and elaborate receptions, always well attended by an eclectic gathering of Ottawa mandarins, businessmen, diplomats and Members of Parliament. Upstairs, away from the public areas, is the ambassador's office: fashionable chrome furniture; deep pile white carpets, steel shutters that can be rolled down to shut out external disturbances; an odd, sucking sound between the heavy double doors — hinting perhaps, of an independently controlled ventilation and filtration system for the executive suite.

The ambassador's residence, three miles away in tranquil Rockliffe Park, is a marked contrast. A gracious old home set back from a quiet street a block or so away from Stornoway (residence of Government Opposition leaders), its only apparent concession to security has been the removal of the glass in all the interior French doors and its replacement with — of all things — mirrors. It was here, on a warm summer's day in 1983, that the ambassador, former university president Carlos Amat-

Fores, hosted an elegant luncheon for senior CUSO staff, offering a special toast of friendship over well-aged French cognac and stout Havana cigars. The only hint of acerbity throughout the genial gathering was a lighthearted remark from a Canadian External Affairs officer, who unnecessarily reminded the Ambassador that some of Cuba's friends were not friends of some of Canada's friends. There was a moment of silence as the cigar smoke wafted upwards through the branches of the crystal chandelier and the guests unravelled the whimsical little riddle.

The revolution, the cane fields, the Bay of Pigs, the Cuban Missile Crisis, Fidel Castro, Che Guevara: they all seemed very remote that afternoon, as did the bureaucratic intrigue, government manipulation, interference and indecision that had characterized CUSO's Cuban program in the preceding years.

For more than a decade, CUSO was the only foreign voluntary agency working in Cuba. The CUSO program was, in many ways, a symbol of the organization's independence and its ability to create high-quality projects in countries with widely differing perspectives on government and development; and it demonstrated the tangible benefits that non-governmental activity can sometimes have for the Canadian economy.

In August of 1969, when Frank Bogdasavich, CUSO's Executive Director, visited Havana, Cuba's external image had undergone a number of subtle changes. The revolutionary expansionism of the 1960s seemed to have abated — perhaps making a CUSO program more acceptable an idea to a Canadian government, which would ultimately have to provide most of the funding — and the humanism of the Cuban revolution, along with its status as a Third World nation, made it widely attractive as a focus for international development.

In the early 1960s there were reasons for international concern about Cuban 'export of revolution': after the revolution, in 1959, there were forays into Panama, Nicaragua, Haiti and the Dominican Republic, and the Zanzibar Revolution of 1964, which was led by a man who had spent almost three years in Cuba studying the arts of revolution. In 1961, Cuba had set up a military training base in Ghana; Cuban troops were sent to Algeria between 1963 and 1965, during a border conflict with Morocco, and, before he went to Bolivia in 1965, Che Guevara had led contingents of guerillas into Zaire and Congo-Brazzaville. As well, during the mid-

1960s, hundreds of Africans were taken to Cuba for education and training.

But in the late 1960s, Cuban activity in Africa declined, as the 'revolutionary democratic' regimes supported by Cuba were supplanted by more conservative governments: in 1965, Ahmed Ben Bella of Algeria was overthrown by Houari Boumedienne; in 1966, Kwame Nkrumah of Ghana was ousted in a military coup, and two years later, Modibo Keita was similarly overthrown in Mali.

At the 1968 Tricontinental Conference in Havana, Castro said that revolutionary movements anywhere in the world could count on Cuba's unconditional support, but by then, Cuba's outward expansion was losing steam, especially after Che Guevara's attempt to enflame South America, and his death in Bolivia in 1967. The 1970 election of Salvadore Allende in Chile gave many leftists pause to reflect that goals could perhaps be achieved by less radical means than arms and bullets: a new era seemed to be dawning in Latin America.

Throughout the 1960s Canada's official relationship with Cuba was both cordial and profitable. The Royal Bank and the Bank of Nova Scotia were the only two financial institutions in Cuba that were not immediately nationalized in 1960, and when they finally were taken over, they were fully compensated. The United States imposed a trade embargo on Cuba in October of that year, but Prime Minister Diefenbaker said that "apart from the sale of arms, there can be no valid objections to trade with Cuba."[1]

He was perhaps keeping an entrepreneurial eye open for Canadian trade interests, which might benefit from an American embargo, but he also welcomed the opportunity to take a shot at the United States. Charles Ritchie, Canada's Ambassador to Washington at the time, remarked in his memoirs that President Kennedy keenly disliked Diefenbaker, "whom he regarded with supercilious aversion" — a sentiment more than adequately reciprocated by the Prime Minister.[2]

The Diefenbaker jowls shook with righteousness as he spoke in the House of Commons:

"While naturally Canada is most desirous of cooperating at all times with friendly nations, the decisions as to the course Canada shall take should be made by Canada on the basis of policies which we believe are most appropriate to Canada".[3]

Canadian balance-of-trade figures with Cuba rose dramatically through the 1960s. During the period 1959-63, Canada's trade surplus averaged about $9 million annually; between 1964-69, while Cuban exports to Canada declined, Canadian exports skyrocketed, and the trade surplus reached an average of $40 million annually.[4]

While Cuba's international image improved and Canada's official trading links grew more profitable, unofficial contacts by young Canadians and Americans vented the growing opposition across North America to the war in Vietnam. The Cubans fully exploited the phenomenon, recruiting thousands of young Americans and Canadians to the Venceremos Brigades which first appeared in 1969. Some went to Cuba for obscure revolutionary purposes, but most were attracted out of youthful curiosity and a wish to make a personal statement through the less-than-revolutionary act of cutting sugar cane; for those, the humanism and the achievements of the Cuban revolution were what counted. One theme of the Cuban revolution was *lucha*, or struggle — against colonialism, neocolonialism imperialism, bureaucratism, illiteracy, low productivity and so on — and the other, very much part of the revolution's great attraction, was the concept of utopia and the millenium. It was Fidel Castro himself who best described the joy of belonging to a victorious movement that heralded the utopian order of tomorrow:

It is not a man of the jungle that we want to develop; a man of the jungle cannot be of any benefit to human society. It is not that self-centered, savage mentality that can in any sense benefit human society . . . the old society fostered exactly those sentiments, exactly those attitudes . . . We want the coming generation . . . to receive the heritage of an education and a training that is totally devoid of selfish sentiments . . . The concept of Socialism and Communism, the concept of a higher society, implies a man devoid of those feelings, a man who has overcome such instincts . . . If we fail because we believe in man's ability, in his ability to improve, then we shall fail, but we shall never renounce our faith in mankind.[5]

Into this idealistic revolutionary milieu stepped the first CUSO volunteers.

Since 1962, there had been recommendations and Annual Meeting resolutions in favour of a program in Cuba; however, it was not until the spring of 1969, when the Cubans themselves expressed interest in CUSO, that serious attention was paid to the possibility of a program. "I always said," recalled Frank Bogdasavich, "that if the Cubans approached us — maintaining our principles that we were not making political judgements about the folk we were dealing with — we would have to look very seriously at such a request if it came. It came; we did."[6] Bogdasavich, who visited Cuba as a guest of the government, was given red-carpet treatment, as were all his successors who visited the island. (Before stepping onto the red carpet, however, he sounded out the Department of External Affairs: "Their response was that if we needed any assistance while we were there, our Embassy in Havana would help. That was it.")

A number of considerations were addressed before recommendation was made to the Board the month after Bogdasavich's visit: how would the Cubans view foreign — especially Canadian — technical assistance? How would the work and day-to-day life of CUSO volunteers fit within a communist society? How would other Latin American countries — and Canada — respond to the development of a CUSO program in Cuba? Answers were found to these questions — although the trickier problem of providing the Cubans with what they wanted from CUSO had yet to be addressed.

"Right from the beginning," Bogdasavich noted, "they wanted people with an expertise that was very high by our traditional standards, the kind of people that a government would normally request of CIDA. It was a big problem."

The Cuban demands also posed a problem for CUSO in other countries, where staff had often requested volunteers with wider qualifications — but to no avail. In Jamaica, Field Staff Officer Chris Bryant resented the excitement over Cuba. "You could almost see Cuba from Jamaica," he said, "but it might as well have been on the moon."[7] High-powered recruitment drives were begun to respond to Cuba's requests, but Jamaica continued to get only teachers.

In Canada, the opening of a program in Cuba made life a little easier for Frank Bogdasavich. "The Company of Young Canadians during those days was always thought of by young people as being the 'true movement of youth'," he said, "and we were the reactionary conservatives. Once the Cuba program was opened, that seemed to fall off.'' There were a few people, however, who told Bogdasavich that the Cuban involvement didn't count, ''because it was done too easily. We didn't actually challenge anybody; we didn't protest. We just went.''

In October 1970, CUSO chose Joe Vise, a former volunteer in Kenya, as the first Field Staff Officer in Havana. He left Ottawa full of optimism and enthusiasm for the development of the new program, but his mood soon changed. ''I've been here five months,'' he wrote on one occasion, ''and have received only two concrete requests.'' The reasons provided for the delays by Cuban officials were varied, but, continued Vise, ''I really have no idea what is going on. It is quite possible that the delay could be deliberate.''[8]

It seemed that the Cuban authorities had neither developed a system for dealing with CUSO that suited their internal bureaucracy and security requirements, nor even assured themselves of CUSO's capabilities. But finally, a senior Cuban delegation visited a number of Canadian universities to explore the idea of an exchange program that CUSO might coordinate.

Despite the industrial expansion that followed the Cuban revolution, there remained a major constraint: a lack of skilled engineers; the external assistance provided through UNESCO and from Eastern European countries had been insufficient to meet the growing demand, and the CUSO program focussed on developing the engineering faculty at the Ciudad Universitaria Jose Antonio Echeverria (CUJAE) in Havana.

A tentative program with CUJAE was finally approved in July 1971, and the first CUSO volunteer left Canada for language training in Mexico in October. Ironically, he was not one of the high-powered technical experts who had been the subject of so much discussion and debate during previous months; he was a swimming instructor assigned to work with the Cuban sports and recreation organization. By April 1973, two-and-a-half years after Joe Vise landed at Havana's Jose Marti Airport, and nearly four years after the Bogdasavich visit, CUSO's achievements remained limited: six volunteers on assignments of one or two years; seven on short-term assignments of one to four months, and twenty-two Canadian university professors on one-month contracts to the CUJAE Project at the University of Havana.

The CUJAE Program was the only clear success, and with the backing of Cuba, CUSO approached CIDA for special funding to expand the program levels envisaged by the university. The final CUJAE project, accepted in late 1973 received $1.1 million from CIDA, and involved the Universities of British Columbia, Waterloo, Toronto and Saskatchewan. The basic aims of the project were to upgrade Cuban industrial manpower through short-term training programs, improve the quality of the university teaching staff, and lay the groundwork for applied research in industry at the university. CUJAE selected and prepared Cuban graduate students, and took responsibility for the academic content of the program. Intensive immersion courses in English were given by CUSO teachers in Havana as part of the program, and Cuban students visited Canadian institutions under the supervision of the Canadian professor responsible for the project. The varied projects also included such activities as designing hydraulic devices for sugar cane harvesters, and developing heat exchangers for sugar cane juice.

By the time the project had finished, Canadian university professors had taught more than one hundred and twenty graduate-level courses at CUJAE, and seventy Cuban students and professors visited Canadian institutions in connection with 100 master-level research projects.

At an international UNESCO Symposium in Paris in 1979, Dr. Axel Meisen of UBC spoke enthusiastically about the project:

> In view of the size of the program, the CUJAE-CUSO project has operated very well and achieved its primary objective: CUJAE now has the capability of offering masters programs in all its engineering branches without foreign assistance . . . . Short-term graduate level courses by Canadian professors were particularly successful, the acquisition of material and equipment functioned smoothly . . . and the ordering and expediting were performed efficiently by CUSO.[9]

As the CUJAE project came onstream, CIDA's own Bilateral Program with Cuba began. CIDA President, Paul Gerin-Lajoie, had visited Cuba in 1974 with a senior Canadian delegation to put the last touches on negotiations for a full-fledged CIDA effort. Before he left, he was photographed doing what thousands of young foreigners before him had done: he went to the fields and cut sugar cane.

The CIDA program would terminate in 1978; in the intervening years, along with a contribution to the CUJAE Project, CIDA made grants of nearly three million dollars to assist in agriculture, fishing, cattle production and health; the agency also extended low-interest loans totalling $9.3 million.

In 1976, Prime Minister Trudeau visited Cuba, and at a mammoth rally, shouted in Spanish to cheering crowds: "Long Live Cuba and the Cuban People! Long Live Prime Minister and Commander in Chief Fidel Castro! Long Live Cuban-Canadian Friendship!"

Back in Canada, there was much criticism of his enthusiasm. But *Globe and Mail* reporter Geoffrey Stevens had seen the balance-of-trade statistics and described the Trudeau visit as "money in the bank."[10] The visit also helped strengthen Canada's image in the Third World as a country with an independent foreign policy, and reinforced Trudeau's earlier position on Cuba: "One of the best vehicles for understanding and closer relationship between countries is trade. The missionaries came first and the traders next."[11]

He could have added tourism to the list: by 1976, more than fifty thousand Canadian were flocking to Cuba every year to lie on Varadero Beach, and returning with thousands of bottles of seven-year-old Havana Club rum.

The honeymoon was in full swing.

Before the successful conclusion of the CUJAE Project, CUSO's field staff in Havana began to investigate other project possibilities through CUSO's regular channels, rather than through CIDA's funding mechanism. What emerged was a series of projects based on the CUJAE model — short-term professional visits to Cuba by Canadians, with reciprocal visits to Canada by Cubans.

A genetic swine reproduction and swine nutrition project involved more than seventy technical visits and the purchase of a variety of equipment in Canada; despite two major outbreaks of swine fever in the island during the five-year project, Cuban swine production increased forty-seven percent and the quality of herds markedly improved. A poultry project, begun in 1978, involved Agriculture Canada, the Ontario Ministry of Agriculture, Macdonald College and the University of Guelph in an effort to increase production and quality of broiler chickens. Two particularly virulent poultry diseases were better controlled by improved reporting procedures and the establishment of an isolation laboratory. A cattle research project produced a breed called the F-1, a cross between the Canadian-sired Holstein-Fresian and the Cuban Xebu: the result was one of the finest animals available in tropical countries. And other projects involved public health, tropical medicine and plant pharmacology. Almost every component of the CUSO program benefitted both the Cubans and the Canadians, some of whom extended their involvement over the course of several years.

Canada's trade surplus soared from $45 million in 1971 to a 1980 level of more than $225 million: much of the increase represented sales of Canadian cattle feed — a reflection of CUSO's involvement in Cuba.

In the summer of 1975, however, events were unfolding in Africa which would eventually bring the Cuba-Canada honeymoon to an end. The military coup in Portugal the previous year had paved the way for speedy decolonization of its African possessions, the most significant of which was Angola, an oil- and diamond-rich nation on the Southwestern edge of the continent.

Moscow's intermittent support for the Marxist-oriented MPLA* liberation movement of Dr. Agostino Neto increased: between March and July of 1975, the Soviet Union supplied an estimated twenty to thirty million dollars in armaments and military goods; this figure, which would skyrocket the following year,[12] and the presence of an estimated fifteen thousand Cuban troops by February 1976, were explained by the South African invasion of Angola.

Military success in Angola gave new impetus to Soviet policy in Africa and new skill to Cuba's revolutionary armed forces, which increased their capability for carrying out similar missions elsewhere. Late in 1977, Cuban troops arrived in Ethiopia to back up the massive material support that came from the USSR earlier in the year; by the spring of 1978, an estimated sixteen thousand Cuban troops were facing Somalian forces from the country's Ogaden region.

Whether Cuba acted in Africa as a surrogate for Soviet imperialism,

---

* Popular Movement for the Liberation of Angola

or acted on its own sense of solidarity with imperilled Marxist regimes, is something of a moot point. With Moscow increasingly dependent upon Cuban ground troops for the advancement of major policy initiatives in Angola and Ethiopia, Cuba was now able to secure major improvements in its economic agreements with the USSR; these included favourable new trade accords, new military equipment and the MIG-23, which appeared in Cuba not long after Cuban troops arrived in Africa. Some of Cuba's African activities, such as its support for Idi Amin, were clearly independent of Soviet influence, as was the use of Cuban troops to put down the apparently pro-Soviet coup attempt against Dr. Neto in Angola in 1977. But because of the Cuban intervention, Soviet policy-makers may have come to believe that socialist-oriented regimes in Africa were at last viable, and that further breakthroughs were possible. This belief, to the extent that it was shared in the West, had obvious and ominous overtones which made Cuba's emergence as spokesman for the Third World after the 1979 Havana Non-Aligned Conference particularly worrisome in Western capitals.

That year too, in Nicaragua, the Sandinistas overthrew the enduring and oppressive regime of the pro-American Somoza family. Many Sandinistas had trained in Cuba and the new government consolidated its position with the assistance of as many as two thousand Cuban technical advisers and teachers. In Grenada, Cuba agreed to build an international runway and airport for the newly established revolutionary government of Maurice Bishop, while Cuba's hand was seen in a series of revolutionary activities and violent upheavals, ranging from Libya, Algeria and Lebanon; to Syria, South Yemen and the Spanish Basque country. In short, Cuba's name, in Western capitals, was mud.

While Cuba's international reputation was sinking during the 1970s, Cuban activities in Canada were also the subject of concern. In the early 1970s, the CIA had begun to put greater emphasis on the activities of the Cuban Directorate of General Intelligence (DGI), which was reportedly operating its North American activities out of the Cuban Trade Commission in Montreal. In April 1972, a violent explosion in the Trade Commission killed one of the Cuban employees; RCMP officers had several hours to survey documents. According to John Sawatsky in his book *Men in the Shadows*, the Cuban code book was found, jeopardizing all intelligence traffic out of the Commission.[13] It was reputedly the RCMP's biggest catch since the defection of Igor Gouzenko in 1945; within hours, the material was transferred intact to CIA headquarters in Langley, Virginia. Sawatsky described the Canada-Cuba security relationship as an outlandish demonstration of the colonial status of both countries in the international security and intelligence community: Canada provided Cuba with an opportunity for covert activities aimed at the United States and often requested by the Soviet Union; while the Canadian Security Service, often at the behest of the CIA, ran aggressive intelligence operations aimed at both Cuba and the Soviet Union.

Occasionally, Cubans were expelled from Canada: a diplomat in 1976; three diplomats and a student in 1977. One of the Cuban officials asked to leave had been actively involved in protocol and visa work around the CUSO program; and among the dozens of CIA employees, agents and collaborators listed in Philip Agee's *Inside the Company: CIA Diary* was an individual who had applied for a CUSO field staff job in Latin America two years before.

"When you phoned Cuba," John Gordon recalled of his days as Executive Director, "it seemed that every time you went through a connection, somebody else seemed to be coming in and the power kept dropping; all phone calls had to go through Miami . . . ."[14]

CUSO, too, faced expulsions from Cuba: in the mid-1970s, two Field Staff Officers were asked to leave after a vague allusion to improper sale of a decrepit office jeep; however, there may have been more at issue — Robin Wilson, who visited the island when he was Executive Director, was surprised to see posters of Karl Marx and Che Guevara prominently displayed in the field staff residence, and offered an allegoric conjecture on the staff expulsion.

> If there was a comparable program, where Cuba was employing a Cuban Field Staff Officer in Canada, and Canadian authorities found that on the wall of his living room he had a life-size portrait of John Diefenbaker; and on another wall, a portrait of Pierre Trudeau; and on a third, John A. Macdonald, they might be justified in wondering about his orientation.[15]

No matter what the issue, the Cubans were always fiercely 'correct' in their dealings with CUSO; they were prepared to explain and discuss the official position on public events, but there was never a hint of proselytism, persuasion or ideology in any official dealings.

In May 1979, the Trudeau government was defeated at the polls, and Joe Clark formed Canada's twenty-first government. Among his cabinet and backbenchers were a number of MPs who either knew CUSO well, or had been directly involved in some way. Walter McLean, the Waterloo MP, had been among the founders of CUSO, and had later established the CUSO program in Nigeria. Cabinet members David Crombie and Flora MacDonald had helped CUSO with selection interviews in Toronto and Kingston. However, the more conservative elements within the Tory caucus were not well-disposed towards CUSO, and, buoyed by the swing to the right — both in Canada and south of the border — they claimed that some of CUSO's activities were excessively leftist for an organization receiving so much government funding. In the summer of 1979, CUSO was repeatedly attacked in the press for bringing Zimbabwean "terrorists" to Canada, and for its general activities in Southern Africa; Cuba was working its way up the agenda.

December 13, 1979 was a bad day for Flora MacDonald. That morning, after a hectic visit to Paris, the Minister for External Affairs arrived in Brussels to attend a NATO Ministerial Meeting. Moments after she entered the conference room, where NATO Secretary General Luns was already addressing the assembled Ministers, MacDonald was handed a note informing her that the secret presence of six Americans in the homes of Canadian Embassy staff in Tehran had been discovered by Jean Pelletier, *La Presse* Washington correspondent and former CUSO Nigeria staff member. At lunch that day, MacDonald met with Argentine officials to talk about the sale of CANDU reactors and with Lord Carrington to discuss the monitoring force overseeing the transitionary phase to independence in Zimbabwe; just before a scheduled meeting with U.S. Secretary of State Cyrus Vance to discuss the Pelletier problem, she received an urgent call from Prime Minister Clark: at 9.45 that evening, the government faced a vote of confidence on its budget, and she was needed back in Ottawa.[16]

The speech MacDonald was to make to the NATO meeting was never given; instead, sections of it were given to delegates and the press. Whether the transcribed speech was even noticed — in the confusion of the Minister's hasty departure and the government's subsequent defeat in the House of Commons — is debatable; at any rate, what MacDonald had to say to the meeting was not reported in the Canadian media.

However, the speech was apparently to have signalled a new, tougher Canadian attitude towards Cuba and the Soviet Union; a stance of which various branches of the Canadian Government had already been informed. Within days, CIDA officials informed CUSO that project funds for Cuba were frozen until there could be clarification of the speech, which said, in part:

> (The Soviets) have been using surrogates to further their interests, but just because they are sending boys to do a man's job, or should I say girls to do a woman's job, the betrayal of the spirit of detente is no less real . . . The Cuban adventures in Africa are well known . . . Of even more direct interest to Canada is the growing Cuban involvement in the Caribbean. They have been quick to try to exploit the opportunities provided by the overthrow of Somoza and the coup in El Salvador. The latest example is the assistance already given, and more promised, to Grenada. We all know that Cuba is a massive recipient of aid from Russia and yet they are turning themselves into the Santa Claus of the Islands . . . . We should make it plain that as far as detente is concerned, it applies not only in Europe . . . . it applies to the entirety of East Bloc actions all over the world. We have seen what concerted international action can do to influence the actions of Russia's puppets. We must ask ourselves what we should do as an alliance, *and as individual countries** to make the Eastern Bloc and particularly its leaders, play a more neutral role in the politics of the developing world.[17]

Up to this point, CUSO's program in Cuba and its project support work had required prior approval from CIDA for any expenditure using

---

* emphasis added to the original

CIDA funds. On the day of the NATO meeting in Brussels, four small projects — totalling less than twenty thousand dollars — were awaiting CIDA approval. One was approved (because of the perishable nature of the swine feed involved), but the others — the purchase of fresh and frozen boar semen — were rejected. In January 1980, a letter arrived from CIDA:

> A definitive comment is being awaited from the Minister. The NGO Division is urgently consulting with External Affairs on the whole question of CUSO operations in Cuba and (hopes) to be able to give you a final decision on the projects in the near future.[18]

The image of CIDA "urgently consulting" External Affairs on the subject of boar semen was reassuring to CUSO, but no decision was ever received. Instead, the matter became mixed up in the election campaign, during which MacDonald told CUSO officers that her Brussels speech did not signal a change in Cuban policy; the problem with CUSO projects was just another example of the overly zealous bureaucracy within External Affairs — overstepping its bounds or manipulating and otherwise misinterpreting her statements. However, there was no resolution of the question — despite the Minister's assurance that matters would be rectified.

In a matter of days, the election had returned the Liberals to power and a new Minister, Mark MacGuigan, took up office in the Pearson Building. With the return of the Liberals, CUSO's hopes were renewed: MacGuigan was known as a keen internationalist; a World Federalist; a member of the United Nations Association and the John Howard Society; former Dean of Law at the University of Windsor, and a founder of the Civil Liberties Association. However, everyone (including, apparently, the Prime Minister), was in for a shock. A new, conservative MacGuigan was quickly unveiled: cold, tough, hawkish on security matters, national defence and Central America — where the Reagan Administration was cranking up its anti-Sandinista and anti-Cuban apparatus. Because of his "meeting of minds" with U.S. Secretary of State, Alexander Haig — on El Salvador and Nicaragua, MacGuigan was quickly dubbed, "Al's

Pal," and, for the first time in a decade Canada found itself with a crusading cold warrior in the Cabinet. As it turned out, asking Mark MacGuigan to restore CIDA funding to the CUSO program in Cuba was a bit like asking Ronald Reagan to hum a few bars of the *Internationale*.

At a meeting in May, 1980, the Minister said he had no objection to CUSO spending its own funds in Cuba, but that as far as he was concerned, CIDA funds came from an aid budget, and Canada should not be providing official assistance to Cuba — not while Cuba had the wherewithal to maintain 50,000 troops in Africa and participate in other foreign adventures. However, this was "only a preliminary response," and MacGuigan promised a formal decision within two weeks.

The two weeks stretched into eight more months, and the process of equivocation and prevarication finally involved the Prime Minister and the entire cabinet. The Minister's office took the position that the matter was a CIDA decision; policy-makers at CIDA explained that they had made their recommendations to the Minister, with whom it now lay; and the ball was shuffled back and forth between CIDA and External all summer. In the meantime, CUSO staff and Board members approached those who had been involved with the Cuba Program — Agriculture Canada and provincial government officials, institutions, and individuals — and asked them to add their testimonials to the detailed and comprehensive dossier already compiled by CUSO for the Minister.

CUSO never tried to justify or explain Cuba's international activities. As with all other countries, CUSO took the position that its involvement with Cuba should focus on ordinary people rather than their governments. There may have been flaws in this approach, but as long as Canada maintained vigorous commercial and sports relations with Cuba; and as long as outstanding government loans continued to be extended and rescheduled, chopping the CUSO programs seemed pointless — even as a gesture.

In July, a senior official in the Minister's office confided to CUSO: "It's all decided now. It's in the Minister's hands, and you have no reason to be pessimistic." In September, the same official said he was "working on it . . . but very, very confidentially, no news is good news": a decision would be forthcoming, "possibly in a couple of weeks, but don't quote me."

In October, the matter came up during a Cabinet Committee meeting;

by then, External had received many briefs in support of CUSO, echoed by a number of members of the Cabinet Committee. Despite this the Minister recommended ending the program; his resolution was carried by the committee and then forwarded to the full Cabinet for its October 21 meeting. The Prime Minister is said to have questioned the recommendation and asked that the decision be postponed until his concerns could be answered. Trudeau's request may have related to a discussion he had around that time with New Democratic Party Leader, Ed Broadbent, recently returned from a visit to Cuba that included a meeting of almost six hours with Fidel Castro.

Broadbent's mission focussed on the increasingly dangerous Central American situation, but, in his meeting with Castro, he also raised the CUSO issue — having been briefed by the organization before his departure. Castro's response was indirect — perhaps out of respect for Canada's delicate relations with a virulently anti-Cuban White House; rather than addressing the political question, he concentrated on the CUSO projects. Surprising Broadbent with his detailed knowledge of the projects, he praised their quality and importance, not only to Cuba's development, but to a spirit of international understanding.

Trudeau was interested in Broadbent's observations, but non-committal about CUSO.

Finally, in November, CUSO was informed — almost casually — that a decision had been made. It was negative. Another two months would pass before the government would get around to an official notification; more than a year had passed since Flora MacDonald's visit to Brussels.

CUSO allocated private donor funds for the first two quarters of the 1981-82 program, and undertook energetic fund-raising efforts with a number of provincial governments, non-governmental organizations, and individuals associated with CUSO in Cuba over the years. CUSO's Latin American field staff contributed ten percent of their salaries to the effort, and several European organizations were contacted for support. Oddly, many of the universities, government departments and individuals who had benefitted from the Cuban exchange programs could not be reached, or did not return calls. Two dozen Canadian NGOs expressed polite interest on the phone — and even less, usually, in writing.

While government caution about Cuba was understandable, the cutoff was unique in its manipulation of a non-governmental organization, and might therefore have been seen as a dangerous precedent for others. But despite the courteous clucking, real support was sadly lacking: CUSO was joined only by her erstwhile sister organization — SUCO — by the Inter Church Fund for International Development — a consortium of Anglican, Catholic and other churches — and by Oxfam. While their support amounted to a total of only $50,000 in 1981-82, this was enough to allow the programs to continue. One of the major cost factors — airfares for scientists — was covered by the Cuban government through its regular Cubana flights to Montreal, and this assistance significantly reduced the financial pressure.

The long and painful journey leading to the desperate fund-raising attempts of the early 1980s was a sobering and costly one for CUSO. What the organization had known ever since it received its first government grant, in 1964, resounded with ringing clarity: CUSO was far from immune to the whims of its financial supporters. Recognition of the need for financial independence had echoed through the organization for nearly fifteen years; yet, for a decade, private donor funds had never amounted to more than ten or fifteen percent of CUSO's income, and had always been tied to the more attractive parts of the organization, such as small self-help schemes, rather than to the provision of volunteers or involvement in such controversial activities as the Cuba program.

One view of the Cuba affair is that the organization was an unwitting instrument of an uncertain and sometimes ham-handed Canadian government, sometimes eager to improve trade with Cuba, other times preferring to appease a belligerent administration in Washington.

Throughout the decade of CUSO's involvement, regardless of official relations between the two countries and despite Cuba's growing international profile, Canada's trade surplus continued to grow. By 1980, it reached $255 million — five times more than in 1970, when CUSO began its program. Some of the growth in trade and improvement in commercial contacts — especially regarding cattle and cattle feed — were assisted by CUSO, whose programs had improved and increased the herds, and whose field staff in Havana were always available to assist visiting Canadian government delegations as well as salesmen from the Canadian private sector.

But once the CUSO program had outlived its political value, or could by its decline better serve a new political purpose, it became expendable.

Except for the CUJAE project, funded exclusively by CIDA, CUSO's annual Cuba budget — including all administrative costs — never exceeded $150,000. This represented slightly more than one percent of the organization's total annual expenditure at the time. The Cuba program (severely curtailed) was subsequently maintained with CUSO's private income and the assistance of other NGOs. Canadian cabinet ministers continued to travel to Havana to sign contracts and exchange rum-laced toasts to international peace and understanding. And in the wintertime, thousands of Canadian tourists would clamber aboard Air Canada and Cubana flights, heading for Varadero Beach. Prime Minister Trudeau's 1969 dictum was still at work: "The missionaries came first and the traders next." For CUSO, the irony was that, by 1983, the first had become last, and the last had become first.

Chapter 12

Keith Bezanson

Keith Bezanson was understandably startled to discover that the patron of the Udoho Memorial School in Eastern Nigeria was the very-much-alive Chief Udoho, but dismay overcame surprise as the Chief dropped him off at his new posting in September, 1964. The school was a collection of half-finished ramshackle buildings without doors, blackboards, or even steps up to the classrooms. The Chief told Bezanson that the school was a memorial to his mother, also very much alive, but, as Bezanson later said, "the memorial aspect seemed more connected with the Chief's desire to establish a permanent source of financing for his private purposes than with any other single objective."[1] In fact, the Chief owned the school outright, and ran it solely as a profit-making enterprise.

The first day on the job at any CUSO posting is always one of the most traumatic, but Bezanson's was particularly so. His house had not been completed, so for several hours, he sat chatting with one of the teachers, who offered no hint as to where he might eat, sleep, or — as Bezanson began to think — simply survive. Late in the day, the Principal, Udo Essien, arrived and took Bezanson to his own quarters, a rented room in a thatched wattle-and-daub house. Only a few weeks into the job, Essien, himself a recent graduate of the school, had been enticed by Chief Udoho's offer of the Principalship and a salary higher than government rates. Essien was already disgusted, not least because the promised salary had proven as elusive as the most basic of educational elements: books, desks and chalk, and for the boarding students, beds and decent food.

As Bezanson's first day turned to night, Essien invited him to share his own dinner, and then to share his accommodation until his own house was finished. As they bedded down together that first night, Bezanson must have wondered what the future held in store for him. This emergency arrangement would last for several weeks, as it happened, but it was not an unhappy one. "Udo Essien and I became good friends in spite of the sleeping arrangement imposed on us, which was at total variance with our mutual and established heterosexual natures," he said.

Essien spent most of the next four months figuring out how to escape from his obligation to the rapacious Chief, whom he defamed when he and Bezanson commiserated each evening. But somehow, they and two other Nigerian teachers managed to provide 150 children in forms one and two with the rudiments of an education. Four months after Benzanson's arrival, Essien finally made good his getaway, and Bezanson found himself de facto Principal of the School.

Knowing what was expected of CUSO volunteers, he tried to rise to the occasion, ill-prepared though he was; in addition to his own teaching duties, he took on supervision of the school, organization of the timetables, feeding arrangements for the students and dealings with the Chief. "During the period from January to June 1965, Bezanson said, "I developed a relationship with Chief Udoho which was, at best, antagonistic. He came to the school only to collect the school fees and on a monthly basis to pay salaries. Requests to him for funds for books, desks, a reliable food contractor for the students met only hollow promises, none of which were respected."

Armed with what he called a "Presbyterian sense of the ethically absolute," Bezanson finally took matters into his own hands, and arranged with creditors and suppliers to pay them on the day the fees were to be collected. Desks, books, food and other supplies arrived early on the appointed day — earlier than the Chief — and Bezanson handed over the money, holding back only enough for salaries and a small contingency. "Not surprisingly," he said, "Udoho was outraged," and made personal threats. "Udoho's brother warned him that it would be in his own best interests to leave quickly, as the Chief had a reputation for vengeance.

And so, "Like an escaping convict, I left at night," Bezanson recalled. "I never returned."

What became of the Udoho Memorial Grammar School and its flamboyant owner is not recorded, but eventually the Nigerian government took over full responsibility for the management and support of all schools in the country, putting an end to speculative education.

Keith Bezanson was transferred to a school in Ijebu Ode, hundreds of miles to the west. "Life in Ijebu Ode was a stark contrast to the political isolation of my first CUSO assignment," he said. "One became aware of the extent to which the country was divided by social and tribal tensions, and I became convinced that the fragility of the political structure would inevitably result in a protracted period of unrest for the country."

His friends were people who were preoccupied with Nigerian politics, and his proximity to journalists, politicians and the urgent frenzy of Nigeria's two largest cities — Lagos and Ibadan — completed his transition from the naive enthusiasm with which he had arrived at the Udoho Memorial Grammar School, to a sadder but wiser cynicism. "If idealism continued to exist in me, it was certainly tempered by great scepticism," he said; when he was awarded a Ford Foundation Fellowship before he left Nigeria, he was convinced that he had been granted it because of the dismal picture he painted of Nigeria's future.

He was asked in his Ford interview what role he thought individuals and donor agencies could play in reducing the tribalism, corruption and political deterioration that he predicted. "There were many actions which could be taken," he replied, "which might increase the freedom of Nigerians to choose their future, but nothing which we would do individually or collectively would alter materially the nature of the choice that would be made in the short term."

Had his first position been more conventional and less frustrating, however, Bezanson might never have been challenged to apply for a fellowship in development studies. And far from putting an end to his interest in the Third World, the scepticism that Chief Udoho and a disintegrating Nigeria had superimposed on his initial idealism would lead instead to a career in international development work — including a vice-presidency of CIDA, and, in 1985 ambassadorship to Peru. His keen rememberance of the Udoho Memorial Grammar School, and of those first days and nights with Udo Essien, no doubt made a distinctive and keenly personal impression which helped shape his future.

Chapter 13

Into the Vortex: Bangladesh

> Make the revolution a parent of settlement and not a nursery of
> future revolutions.
>
> — Edmund Burke

Bangladesh. The name alone conjures images of disaster, starvation,
despair. Henry Kissinger once called it a "basketcase," almost
converting the flippant remark into a self-fulfilling prophesy by consigning
tens of millions of Bengalis to a year in hell while he and his president
"tilted" towards Pakistan.

For CUSO, the Bangladesh involvement began much as it had in other
countries, but the enthusiasm was tempered, this time, by the chastening
experience of the reconstruction project in post-Biafran Nigeria. Even
so, no one was prepared for Bangladesh. Its poverty and despair were
more deeply rooted, and monstrous, than anything CUSO had encountered
before.

The eastern part of Bengal has always been physically isolated from
the rest of the Indian sub-continent by the vast river network which fans
from the confluence of the Ganges, (flowing southeast from India) and
the Brahmaputra, swollen by the melting snows of the Himalayas. Together with the Meghna, these rivers drain the mountains of Tibet, Bhutan

and Nepal, and the entire Gangeatic plain of North India; they bestow on Bengal the most generous of nature's blessings, and the most terrible of its curses. Annual flooding regenerates the soil with upland silt, making it some of the richest in the world; its abundant produce includes rice, wheat, vegetables, fruit, pulses, and cash crops such as jute, sugar and tea. The rivers are also a natural highway for traditional marine transportation, and they provide bountiful harvests of fish as well as water for irrigation. But too little rain, a malevolent monsoon, a tidal wave or a cyclone can turn the delicate balance of nature against farmer and fisherman alike; all too often, natural disaster wreaks havoc on vulnerable rice seedlings, washes away fishing boats, drowns cattle and destroys already tenuous homesteads.

For generations an outpost of the far-flung Mughal Empire, with its court in far-off Delhi, Bengal languished as a tranquil, self-sufficient backwater, known for the beauty of its music, the lyricism of its poetry, and the delicacy of its white cotton muslin, which was of such fineness that even seven veils, it is said, could not conceal the beauty of a woman's face. Then, in the early 1700s, East India Company traders arrived, establishing factories for trading and weaving, and gradually developing greater influence throughout the region. The Company's control of the region climaxed on a June morning in 1757, when Robert Clive's ragtag army of 800 men faced the might of the Nawab of Bengal's 50,000 well-armed troops on a field at Plassey, 150 miles to the West of Dhaka,* the modern capital of Bangladesh. In a matter of hours, it was over, the Nawab's army in rout, thanks not to superior British tactics or prowess, but to a pre-arranged and well-financed abandonment of the battle by the Nawab's commander, who was later awarded the kingship.

Under East India Company rule, East Bengal became a supplier of cheap silk, cotton goods and handspun jute products to the British market. With the industrial revolution and British protectionism, however, the Bengal muslin industry suffocated; it was replaced first by indigo plantations, and then by greatly expanded jute cultivation for export in raw form to Scottish mills, and, subsequently, to their branches in Calcutta.

In 1905, the British divided Bengal in an effort to control religious

---

* In 1983 the spelling of Dacca was changed to 'Dhaka' to better reflect the correct pronunciation of the name.

factionalism; the predominantly Muslim province of East Bengal was created, despite the violent opposition of Hindu India. But only six years later, Britain cancelled the partition, leaving the Muslims increasingly discontented with their status. From 1940 onwards, the Muslim League — founded in Dhaka thirty-five years earlier in response to Britain's indecisive Bengal policy — sought independence from India. In 1947, they achieved their goal when the anomalous nation of Pakistan came into being.

Following the terrible communal bloodshed that erupted as hundreds of thousands of Hindus fled to India and equally large numbers of Muslims moved east, the former East Bengal became East Pakistan, separated from its western wing by two thousand miles of Indian territory. Until then, the cash economy, based largely on jute, had gone to the Calcutta mills; it now had to be completely redirected to internal production and Western markets. To make matters worse, the more industrialized, wealthier, but less populous West, treated the East as a colonial backwater, much as the Mughals and the British had. West Pakistanis occupied the most senior positions in government; West Pakistani businessmen dominated the fledgling economy and the jute industry, and Urdu, spoken only by a West Pakistani minority, was made the official language of the country.

Bengali nationalism, which had flared, often violently, during two decades of Pakistani domination, finally found its outlet in the elections of 1970, which were to return the country to civilian rule. Sheikh Mujibur Rahman, campaigning on a platform of greater regional autonomy, won 167 out of the 169 seats in the East, and an overall majority throughout Pakistan. But the military, unwilling to hand the reins of government to a Bengali nationalist, attempted to negotiate a deal which would have put Zulfikar Ali Bhutto, with his eighty-one seats, into the Prime Ministership. Not surprisingly, negotiations collapsed, and one night in March 1971, the Pakistan army began a bloody crackdown on the sleeping people of East Bengal. For weeks, rampaging troops murdered tens of thousands of Bengalis, concentrating their wrath on the Hindu minority, whom they assumed were in league with the traditional enemy, India. East Pakistani regiments of the army and police were decimated; crops were burned in the fields, and an exodus of refugees, who would soon number more than a million desperate men, women and children, began walking through the torrential monsoon towards the Indian border.

As the refugees reached Calcutta, with stories of the atrocities that were taking place within the beleaguered eastern province, world opinion was at first stunned, then outraged. In Canada, massive fund-raising operations began among non-governmental organizations and church groups, aimed largely at relief for the refugees pouring into India. Some of the few remaining CUSO volunteers in India offered their services in the Calcutta camps, and others, returning to Canada, attempted to stir public opinion and to press CUSO into action.

But Bangladesh never became the political issue that Biafra had been. Unlike the Biafra crisis, direct Canadian experience of East Pakistan was scanty; the CIDA program was administered from Islamabad in West Pakistan, and knowledge of the East was based on reports from other agencies and occasional visits. The only real Canadian presence was a small group of Protestant and Catholic missionaries, ministering to a tiny Bengali Christian community.

On December 3, 150,000 Indian troops crossed the border and began their sweep towards Dhaka; cut off and demoralized, the Pakistan army collapsed, and 100,000 troops surrendered on December 16. A month later, Sheikh Mujib was released from his prison cell in West Pakistan and returned to an exultant welcome in Dhaka.

"Joy Bangla!" cried the joyous throngs as the garlanded Sheikh passed on his way from the airport, tears of vindication and happiness rolling unabashedly down his cheeks.

"Joy Bangla! Joy Bangla! Joy Bangla!" cried a million voices as he stepped onto the podium in the Dhaka racecourse that sunny day, to address the sea of jubilant, upturned faces.

Three-and-a-half years later, the dreams of the young nation in ruins, he would lie dead on the steps of his house in Dhanmondi, murdered as much by his own failures as by the soldiers who fired the guns.

Not more than three months after Sheikh Mujib's triumphal return, Jean Pelletier stepped off one of the few commercial airliners servicing Dhaka; as he surveyed the sweltering confusion of the woefully inadequate airport, he gathered a first microcosmic impression of the fledgling nation. Pelletier, who had come from CUSO's post-Biafra school reconstruction project in Nigeria, had a simple mandate: to develop a Bangladesh program for CUSO as quickly as possible. He was shocked by what he found. There were terrible food shortages, little authority, and nightly gunfire across the city. Everywhere, there were people; searching for jobs, standing in line for relief food — watching, waiting.

In Nigeria, we knew where to start," he said. "In Bangladesh there was no government; it was a newly independent country; they had just gone through a bloody civil war . . . because of the sheer mass of the problem, no one knew what to do or where to start. It was far more depressing than Africa; people were simply dying in the street, something I had never seen in Ghana or Nigeria."[1]

Through some of the relief agencies, Pelletier began to make contact with the authorities. One person who helped was Terry Glavin, who had been a volunteer in Jamaica as early as 1962 and became Bill Mc-Whinney's right-hand man in the early days of CUSO. Glavin had joined CIDA in 1966, and in the early months of 1972, like Pelletier, was thrust into the maelstrom of relief and reconstruction in Dhaka. His job was to open a High Commission and develop a Canadian aid program as quickly as possible. For several months, as acting Canadian High Commissioner, he worked out of a small bungalow on Indira Road, wrote plans, fired off telexes to Ottawa, organized clearances for food shipments, and made longer term arrangements for development programs that would come on stream when the relief phase had ended.

Glavin was extremely helpful in arranging for Pelletier to meet some of the people to whom he had access, but the country was in total disarray. "Sheikh Mujib was still 'meeting the public';" Pelletier said. "There were long queues in front of his house every afternoon, and he would hold court and listen to their problems. And those huge rallies! I had never been in a country where you could hold a political meeting of two million people; it happened in Dhaka all the time; people came in trucks, by train, crowded onto the roofs of trains."

By now it was May; Pelletier had unavoidable commitments in the summer, and the pressure to meet them was mounting. He travelled extensively, trying to meet as many knowledgeable people as possible. Raymond Cournoyer, a fellow-Canadian who had arrived to set up a program for Oxfam, impressed him with his experience and knowledge of Bangladesh. "He didn't know exactly where he was going either," Pelletier noted, "but he had lived in the country before for so many years that he could sense there was no point in rushing, which was not the feeling I had."

Pelletier travelled south to Barisal on an ancient flat-bottomed, Mississippi-style side-wheeler — inappropriately named 'The Rocket' — jammed with people who gave him perspectives vastly different from those circulating in the capital. "There were people everywhere," Pelletier recalled of the journey, "on the benches, the decks, the floors, sitting and sleeping on tables. Coming back, I slept under a table in the dining room next to the Bishop of Dhaka — the top had already been taken — and I remember seeing in the morning that he had a big goat with him as well."

Pelletier had an open, though somewhat confused, mandate. He had been selected for the investigation in Bangladesh because of the success of the Nigeria project which had been based more on organization and cash than on traditional volunteer postings. "That contradicted, of course, the basic aim of CUSO, which was to send volunteers and provide Canadians with a new awareness" Pelletier said. So there was also pressure on him — although unspoken — to find placements for CUSO volunteers. "Somehow we reconciled these two ideas by saying we could do both in Bangladesh."

In only eight weeks, he developed what came to be known as the Village Technical Training Program (VTTP). Its purpose was to complement existing village structures with crash courses in irrigation, the use of fertilizer, tubewells, pumps, tillers; to encourage crop diversification, poultry farming, fish farming and animal husbandry. Three teams of CUSO volunteers, with expertise in these skills, would spend twelve months in each of twelve areas over a two-year period, covering a dozen of Bangladesh's 400-odd thanas (counties), training counterparts as they went, and providing cash or material input for projects that would complement the training.

The idea was simple and straightforward, and addressed the urgent need for a technical infrastructure at the village level if the country were to realize its most urgent priority: self-sufficiency in food. The country had a population density twice as heavy as India's; somehow, seventy-five million people were going to have to eke out an existence on 144,000 square kilometres, an area roughly twice the size of New Brunswick. "Too many people are competing for too little land," wrote Pelletier, stressing job creation outside as well as within the agricultural sector. "There is a great need for diversification of the production base of the predominantly rural economy of Bangladesh . . . by creating more employment opportunities in small-scale industry as well as the traditional industries like hand loom textiles, improved agricultural implements and simple consumer items.''[2]

The plan for twenty volunteers was modest in comparison with the needs of Bangladesh, but it was a bold one nevertheless. David Catmur, CUSO's Director of Overseas Operations, had spent six months in the country himself, so he understood the magnitude of the problems and knew better than to expect too much. The project began with a special CIDA grant of $235,000 and the first volunteers arrived in August of 1972, ready to begin their Bengali lessons; with them was the newly-hired Field Staff Officer, Georges Leclerc, who had worked as a missionary teacher in India, and who already spoke fluent Bengali.

For the next two years, the project ran like a high-performance engine on low-grade octane. Recruitment efforts in Canada were successful at first, producing an agriculturalist, an experienced construction foreman, a welder and a machinist with thirty years' experience. But there it stopped. A doctor and a physiothereapist were recruited for postings outside the VTTP, and others, with less specific or less relevant skills were thrown into the program in the misplaced hope that they might be able to help; there were several early returns.

Jean Pelletier had discussed his original proposals with enthusiastic senior government officials before many of the major agencies had appeared on the scene. By late 1972, when the CUSO volunteers arrived, there were more than a hundred foreign voluntary agencies swarming over Dhaka and the rural countryside, searching out projects. Dozens of embassy and agency officials, and consultants with bulging attaché cases and sugar-plum visions, lined up day after day outside the understaffed and inexperienced ministries. Even the minimal local support planned for the tiny CUSO effort — housing for the volunteers, and salaries for Bangladeshi counterparts — was beyond the government's meagre resources. The proposed Thana committees, which were to work with the VTTP teams, were never formed, and even selecting project thanas proved impossible. While the first volunteers diligently practised Bengali in Barisal, Georges Leclerc searched desperately for alternative postings.

Pelletier had made it clear that he would not be available to CUSO beyond the summer of 1972. Had he been able to stay on and adapt a program to the changing situation, it might have been different. "I had returned to Canada determined that a program should be initiated in Bangladesh," he said, "but my biggest failure was giving in to the pressure to place volunteers . . . the only approach we should have taken was to open an office with money and a project director, and go very slowly in posting people; at that point in Bangladesh's history, things were changing from week to week."

Leclerc, left to pick up the pieces of a program that was now clearly a failure, both from the Canadian and the Bangladesh perspective, shifted the volunteers into projects run by other agencies: an agriculturalist was assigned to a rural health project to work on a nutrition program and locally produced baby food. Another was assigned to the Catholic Organization for Relief and Rehabilitation, for whom he supervised the sinking of tubewells in a project northwest of Dhaka. Several were sent to the town of Comilla, 100 miles southeast of the capital, where massive injections of pre-war American aid had helped create an agreeable but totally unreplicable model of rural cooperative development. Pierre Markhon, assigned to an irrigation project which advanced at a snail's pace, persuaded Leclerc to finance an experiment on a bio-gas generator and a solar cooker. John Warren, ostensibly managing a rice mill for which there was little rice, and a tractor workshop for already cannibalized tractors, became involved in health projects and a seed-distribution scheme.

More of the volunteers left early, feeling hopelessly frustrated by the chaotic Bangladeshi infrastructure, and surrounded by starvation and despair on which they felt they had little impact. With Catmur and Pelletier now out of CUSO, Leclerc, who had no previous experience in the organization himself, found his situation increasingly difficult; he demanded assistance, but got little more than authorization to hire a Bengali project officer.

He was able to bring in a few more volunteers, and provided some relief in the form of seeds and cattle vaccine after the 1974 floods. In two villages near Dhaka, he assisted with training and equipment for pottery projects. But by the time Leclerc's two-year assignment was ending, it had become clear that a new approach would be needed if CUSO were to justify further expenditure in the impoverished nation. At this point, the country was also suffering the worst drought in a generation. A CUSO 'task force' visited the country, and stated that "even a cursory perusal of letters, memos and cables between Dhaka and Ottawa would reveal a story fraught with frustration and heartaches . . . . often generating more heat than light."[3]

"The prospects of developing a new CUSO program in Bangaldesh are not without promise," their report continued. "The needs in the country are, beyond question, of highest urgency."

Then, in the manner typical of so many 'task forces', 'missions' and 'consultancies' to the Third World, the report concluded with a range of platitudes, suggesting vaguely that what was needed was "levelheadedness in resetting CUSO's sights (sic), redefining its targets, laying out a feasible work plan, and seeking for the human and material resources that are required."

As bewildered as Georges Leclerc and the volunteers had been by the magnitude of Bangladesh's worsening problems, the task force then packed its bags and flew away, having overlapped for one day with the newly-appointed Field Staff Officer, Raymond Cournoyer.

Raymond Cournoyer — Brother Raymond of the Order of the Holy Cross, 'Raymond Bhai' to his Bengali friends — was quite unlike any other person to enter the ranks of CUSO's field staff. Gruff, uncompromising, a chain-smoker; physically, he was a cross between a Sumo wrestler and Paddington Bear. His penetrating eyes, thundering voice and mercurial temper, combined with a love of argument, often frightened those who didn't know the softer side of his nature, and it disappointed him that many would defer to his sometimes outrageous opinions without debate. His age, his background, his experience and his temperament equipped him with the special skills that would be necessary to make sense out of CUSO's enfeebled ambitions in Bangladesh.

Cournoyer was a child of the thirties, the last of seven children born to a struggling farm family in rural Quebec at the start of the depression. His mother, who had been a teacher before marrying his father, instilled a special love of education in him as a child; ultimately he was the only one of the children to go beyond Grade Three. By his twelfth year, the family's financial situation had improved, and Raymond's father sent him to a Catholic boarding school where he came in touch for the first time with the Catholic Action movement that would eventually have such a profound effect on the leaders of Quebec's 'Quiet Revolution'. The essence of Catholic Action for the young Cournoyer was, he said, "very simple and very basic, with three key words: 'see', 'judge', 'act'. It was not selling models or recipes; it was a tool for analysis, for drawing conclusions, and for doing, if the conclusions called for action."[4] It was an approach that would remain with him, and it would form the basis of his future interest in what he called "human development."

"In those days," he said, "such human development work took place pretty much exclusively in the field of teaching . . . . and in the Catholic Province of Quebec, teaching was done through priests or teaching brothers." So, in 1951, after much study and contemplation, Cournoyer entered the Order of the Holy Cross as Brother Raymond, and three years later, graduated as a teacher. The Order had a number of mission schools in East Pakistan, and although Cournoyer had never thought of himself as a missionary, in 1958 he found himself on an aircraft bound for Asia.

His assignment, first as a high school teacher and then principal, would keep him in East Pakistan for seven years without home leave. Before long, he found himself rebelling against "the club," as he called it, of older Canadian priests and brothers; they had, he felt, an outmoded proselytizing view of their role as ministers to the downtrodden. He challenged their concepts of education, organization and religion. In his own words, he "opened the Catholic ghetto that were our institutions, and (surprisingly) received unfailing support from the non-Catholic community." He created local school management committees, and despite the direst of warnings from his Canadian colleagues, found not only that there was no improper interference from the non-Catholic participants, but that the community itself was willing and able to support small development projects without the financial assistance of the mission. It was a revelation to Cournoyer, a lesson that would make itself felt again and again in his future development work.

Not surprisingly, he and the small community of Catholic missionaries grew further apart on a range of issues, and eventually, Cournoyer returned to Canada knowing that he would have to pursue his development ideas outside the formal structures of the church. He joined Oxfam as a fund-raiser in Quebec; when Oxfam/UK agreed that the Canadian branch could nominate a Field Staff Officer in recognition of its growing financial contribution, Cournoyer was an obvious choice.

His area of responsibility was massive: the Indian states of Orissa,

Bihar, Uttar Pradesh and Assam, as well as all of Nepal and East Pakistan. Less than four weeks after he arrived in India in 1971, hoping to put some of his long-nurtured ideas of development into action, the Pakistan army began its bloody crackdown in Dhaka. As the refugees started flooding across the border into India, Cournoyer, true to his training and his temperament, made judgements and acted decisively on them. He knew the size of the Hindu minority that was being singled out for special brutality, so he predicted — contradicting Oxfam's expert British advice — that the refugee numbers would soar.

When they did, and as agencies with various interests and specialities arrived in Calcutta to assist with children, health, sanitation, clothing, feeding, and drugs, the confusion and duplication of effort became rampant. Oxfam was quickly discovering Cournoyer as unconventional to its cherished self-image as had his order, but because his predictions had been right, it heeded his advice; he urged against the traditional practice of funding other agencies and suggested Oxfam take on complete responsibility for 'centres' of 100,000 people each. Even more heretically, he proposed that foreign managers were not required; he could find enough workers in India and among the refugees themselves to manage the camp without a lot of high-powered, expensive expatriates. "If we start bringing in foreigners," he said, "we won't have any time to care for the refugees."[5]

When the war ended, Oxfam could foresee an even more Herculean task inside the new Bengali republic; Cournoyer was dispatched from Calcutta in a Land Rover, with a budget of $2.5 million and promises of more. He had extracted a guarantee that he would not have to get involved in relief handouts. One of his first ideas was to restore the country's shattered transportation network, which was essential for distributing food and supplies. Hundreds of bridges had been blown up by the retreating Pakistan army, making relief deliveries almost impossible, and raising the spectre of the first post-independence harvest left stranded and rotting. Cournoyer purchased simple truck ferries in kit form, had them shipped to Bangladesh and assembled at the river side. Within weeks, the main road between Calcutta and Dhaka had been reopened to civilian use, courtesy of Oxfam. Thereafter, ferry construction in Bangladesh followed the simple but practical Oxfam design. Cournoyer also provided some of the first funding for two local groups whose impact on

the development of Bangladesh in the coming years would be incalcu-
lable. Gonoshasthaya Kendra — People's Health Centre — was still little
more than a collection of tents and ideas in the mind of Dr. Zafrullah
Choudhury, a young medical doctor who had returned from Britain to
work with the Freedom Fighters during the civil war.

"His perspective on medical care," Jean Pelletier had said, "was to
me the realization of everything Ivan Illich had been writing about medicine; that many health needs can be met by local people themselves if
you can provide the education and have medical personnel actually living
in the rural community." But actually handing over money to a Bangladeshi organization without some sort of foreign control and without
direct expatriate involvement, was a radical, almost unthinkable idea at
the time.

For Cournoyer, however, the time to support local initiative was long
overdue, and he had no compunction about providing some of Oxfam's
millions to assist the struggling medical centre. Another group, the Bangladesh Rural Advancement Committee (BRAC) also received support at
a critical point in the early development of its health and adult literacy
programs in Sylhet.

Cournoyer was highly critical of the traditional approach to development among the foreign NGOs. Despite all the rhetoric of "helping people
to help themselves," the endless talk of "the grass roots," "integrated
rural development" and "basic human needs," he found them as paternalistic and as far away from the people as "the club" of priests and
brothers had been for him fifteen years earlier. Their attitudes were reflected in their names: they had come to wage a 'War on Want', to 'Save
the Children', to 'CARE', provide 'Food for The Hungry', to be 'Brothers
to All Men'. There were nearly two hundred foreign agencies in Bangaldesh, each with its own office, staff, and vehicles; each in search of
opportunities for "real grass roots development," but few willing to take
any risks with Bangladeshis of proven character and experience.

By mid-1974, Dhaka had become a madhouse of foreign aid missions.
Housing prices had skyrocketed and a building boom in luxury homes
began as older embassies expanded, newer ones opened, and even more
relief and development workers arrived. The city swarmed with foreigners, from the representatives of the more impoverished NGOs who rode
through the streets in rickshaws — kurtas and saris blowing in the smut-

laden air — to the suited diplomats in their air-conditioned limousines: flags flying, horns blaring, shaded windows rolled tightly against the filth and heat and noise of the streets. The most impressive vehicle of all belonged to the embarrassed Canadian High Commissioner — a huge, Canadian-made living-room-on-wheels, tastefully appointed in plush velour; a metallic blue behemoth with contrasting vinyl roof and tinted opera windows.

Trucks seemed to dominate the traffic: ancient lorries, survivors of the Second World War, carrying jute from the countryside to the mills at Narayanganj and returning to the countryside laden with food; relief trucks — 700 huge white ones brought in by the UN, reduced for want of spares to fewer than a hundred within two years; ten-wheeled U.S. army surplus monsters that averaged six miles to the gallon; depression-era Swiss army trucks that had been taken out of mothballs and donated to the Catholics; all belching black bile into the air as they carried their precious cargoes of food to the hungry.

And the hungry were legion. Dhaka's street were crowded with them, as were other towns across the tiny nation: rural people without work and without food; people who had moved to the urban job centres in hopes of a better life or any life. The hapless Bihari minority, which had sided with the Pakistan army, was now huddled into disgracefully inadequate 'refugee camps' where life itself had become an atrocity. Bustees* would appear overnight in a park or a vacant lot, crowded with hovels and hutches constructed of cardboard and sticks and rags, housing whole families, or, more often than not, a widow and her children. The residents would spend their days scavenging for saleable bits of broken glass or plastic or paper, and for twigs to fuel a small cooking fire for whatever edible scraps they had been able to find, or beg, or receive in a relief line.

The most shameful of the bustees was not the largest, but a rather small one that sprang up in a vacant lot on Mirpur Road, next to the United Nations relief headquarters and not far from the CARE office. The white jeeps and lorries would arrive and depart all day, loaded with food and vigorous young expatriate relief workers. As the sun rose, it would cast a shadow from the highest mast in the tangle of communication

* A word originally in Urdu and commonly used throughout South Asia, meaning slum.

antennae on the UN roof, tracing an accusatory finger across the shame and degradation of the tiny bustee and its sad inhabitants.

Food was the major concern in Bangladesh, and it would remain so for many years to come. But many aid agencies seemed more concerned about supplying food than in expanding the capacity for local production. There were relief ration shops in the cities, relief handouts in the countryside, and hundreds of ''food-for-work'' projects. During Bangladesh's first decade, food aid constituted more than 66% of Canada's official assistance program; the 1.6 million tons of wheat had a value of over $300 million dollars. And yet this incredible amount represented only 15% of total food aid from all donors to Bangladesh during that period.[7] Population growth was another concern shared by many foreign donors, particularly the United States. Demographic and fertility statistics and projections were alarming. The 75 million Bangladeshis at independence in 1971 were projected to become 90 million a decade later, and were expected to reach 156 million by the turn of the century. Already dependent upon food aid for 10% of its total requirement, and barely able to expand local food production at the rate of population growth, the country was staring into a statistical whirlpool of human disaster. So family planning became, for a time, a key item in some aid agency portfolios, and massive education campaigns were undertaken, highlighted by giant jamborees in the countryside at which women were signed up for the pill and men were cajoled into vasectomies by persuasive Elmer Gantry-style doctors and politicians offering gifts of rice, baubles and cash.

But history has shown, world-wide, that smaller families are the result of improved economic conditions, not better family planning education. In the words of the 1983 Brandt report, *Common Crisis*:

> Unless broadly based development reaches and changes the lives
> of ordinary people, rapid population growth will continue. Only as
> education spreads, and health programs keep existing children
> alive, as families have secure incomes which do not depend on
> increasing their numbers, will incentives for large families disap-
> pear and population growth be kept within manageable bounds.[8]

Until such levels of living are available to couples in the Third World, they are unlikely to heed the pleas of politicians and aid donors who exhort them to think of the nation as they huddle in their shelters at night and worry about tomorrow.

Late in 1972, Raymond Cournoyer left Dhaka to take up a fund-raising assignment for Oxfam in Canada. It lasted only a few months, partially because of Cournoyer's unhappiness about Oxfam's portrayal of the Third World and its use of starving-baby images for its fund-raising. To him, it belied the reality and the dignity of the hard-working people he had now lived with for more than a dozen years, and it smacked of the same paternalism he had railed against in Bangladesh. So when Jean Pelletier, now Director of SUCO's Overseas Programs, offered him a job in Africa, he jumped at it. A year later, dissatisfied, he responded to a CUSO job flyer, advertising for Asia staff.

Murray Thomson and Cournoyer had a long discussion about the Bangladesh position, and Cournoyer was strongly tempted. "I said I would go to Bangladesh with the understanding that I would not have to find jobs for Canadians if Bangladesh didn't need Canadians," Cournoyer said. "I would go to find out what CUSO could do best to help with Bangladesh's development, but I didn't have a clue what it would be." In view of CUSO's growing predicament in Bangladesh, Thomson had little alternative but to agree, and in September, 1974, Raymond Bhai set forth once again for Bangladesh.

When he arrived in Dhaka in September, 1974, Raymond Cournoyer found a CUSO office, housed in the former Canadian High Commission in Indira Road; an enthusiastic young project officer named Faruque Ahmed; the remains of a few small projects, and a couple of volunteers whose contracts would be completed within a few months. His first observation was that despite the vast growth in the number of foreign agencies and their activities since he had left two years earlier, there was tremendous duplication, wastage, self-interest and failure, and the few projects that were making any impact on the poorest, were those that were operated by Bengalis themselves. BRAC and Gonoshasthaya Kendra had grown and were pointing the way to new approaches in health, literacy, and rural job creation. The Quakers had established a successful project south of Dhaka at Madaripur, now entirely Bengali-operated.

Among the foreign agencies making effective contributions were the Mennonites with their winter vegetable and crop diversification project in Noakhali; others were concentrating on irrigation, housing, winter wheat or pisciculture. Cournoyer, however, saw an even more hopeful development base in the 20,000 organized Bangaldeshi groups formally registered with the Department of Social Welfare, few of whom had any contact with foreign aid agencies. While most of these groups originated as sport or recreation clubs, there was still a tremendous wellspring of nationalistic enthusiasm for Bangladesh, especially among the young; Cournoyer began to see in such groups the potential for a more broadly based development effort than any in the past. If CUSO could in some way facilitate a link between these groups and co-opt the development efforts of the BRAC's, the GKs and the foreign agencies, perhaps a significant contribution could be made to economic development in Bangladesh.

Furthermore, Cournoyer wanted to extend this coordinated effort to the landless, who formed the largest part of the Bangladesh population and whose plight was most desperate. By 1977 almost half of the population was functionally landless, eking out a meagre existence as farm labourers at fifteen or twenty cents a day, or as sharecroppers — forced to take all responsibility for labour, seeds, fertilizer and pesticides, and then to share half or more of every harvest with the landowner. It was this growing category of peasant, further victimized by usurious money-lenders, on whom most development programs foundered.

The traditional western 'trickle-down theory' of development was best enunciated by USAID:

(The rural problems of Bangladesh) can be resolved if the society can be organized to apply modern agricultural technology. More intensive cultivation of existing land is the primary means of narrowing the food grain gap . . . key program elements include modern inputs sich as fertilizer and pesticides; improved irrigation, flood control and drainage; small farmer credit; agricultural research; multiple and double cropping of land; rural public works.[9]

For sharecroppers, however, forced to bear all the input costs as well as moneylenders' interest rates of at least ten percent *per month*, investment in new technology was an impossible dream and the trickle-down theory a hollow promise. The British land tenure act of 1793, perpetuated in the Indian subcontinent in various forms over two centuries, had preserved a feudal system in which half the population, tilling the soil for absentee landlords, had no stake in expanding production, and was in fact, actively discouraged from it. This was borne out in the experience of development workers, who found that tenant farmers and those owning extremely small plots of land, were neither willing nor able to assume the risks and costs of the new technology. The result was that foreign assistance inevitably had the greatest impact on those with the largest amounts of land.

An obvious conclusion was that without land reform and suitable public policy, technology alone could not create equitable development. As the authors of one study put it:

> The numbers of persons who have little stake in preserving the
> traditional agrarian structure already represent the majority of rural
> Bangladeshis. This fact, coupled with the gradual erosion of the
> authority of rural elites, surely provides grist for the mill of any
> who would attempt to transform rural discontent into overt forms
> of disruptive behaviour.[10]

It was clear to Raymond Cournoyer, and to other people who knew rural Bangladesh well, that the transfer of technology would only benefit the landless, when they were able to deal more effectively with landlords and moneylenders, and to form themselves into groups and cooperatives which could become the basis for influence and the foundations for savings and credit.

Cournoyer began fleshing out an idea for a CUSO program that would address both the organizational requirements of the poor, and subsequently the technological requirements. At first, he called it a "Logistics Centre," a place which would provide training in group-building, co-operative formation and "human development." He saw BRAC, GK, the Mennonites, and others as "laboratories," to which trainees might be attached for on-the-job training, rather than unrelated technological training. Once the associated consciousness-raising and skill training had taken place, CUSO would then be available to provide project support as well. A small group, for example, might approach CUSO for assistance in wheat farming; CUSO's response would first be a course in group skills and cooperative development tailored to specific needs, followed by an arrangement for individuals to be assigned to other organizations with wheat projects for periods of a few days to a few months. The applicants would then return to their village, reconsider and possibly redraft their original proposal, and resubmit it for financial assistance from CUSO.

As Cournoyer developed the idea for the Logistics Centre with CUSO's Project Officer, Faruque Ahmed, and later with a former BRAC employee, Rahat Uddin Ahmed, the country was going through its worst post-independence crisis. Blistering drought had scourged the countryside for months, driving tens of thousands off the land and into the cities where Sheikh Mujib's government, once the bright hope of 75 million people, had been stunned by the oil crisis and rendered impotent by its own terminal corruption and mismanagement. By March 1975, rice had peaked at six-and-a-half times the January 1972 price, and starvation stalked the land. It will probably never be known how many died during the famine that occurred once the relief supplies ran out, but they numbered in the tens of thousands. The disorder marked a final public disenchantment with the Sheikh. When he was gunned down by soldiers that August, few mourned, and fewer condemned the coup which aimed at a moral as well as an economic regeneration of the nation.

Declaring a policy of *swarnivar*, or self-help, the new government stressed community participation and self-help projects rather than the relief mentality fostered by the previous regime. The policy accommodated Cournoyer's project perfectly. At about that time, the Logistic Centre held its first course for a group of village boys who wanted to set up a small plantation of fruit and coconut trees in their village. The early courses stressed functional literacy, organization analysis, group dynamics and project planning; the following year the Centre began to shift its focus towards the landless poor in the rural areas. By now, Rahat and Faruque, both of whom had themselves attended special training programs in India and the United States, were beginning to envisage a centre that might some day become independent of CUSO. They discussed their aspiration with Cournoyer, who agreed readily, encouraging them to formalize the concept by registering a separate organization. Proshika, incorporated in 1976, was a Bengali acronym: 'pro' stood for *proshikhsan* (training); 'shi' for *shikhsa* (education); and 'ka' for *kaj* (action) — a centre for practical and intellectual development.

"Proshika is really concerned with human development," Cournoyer said at the time. "The whole idea is to get people to think for themselves. If there's one thing Asia has taught me, it is that development must belong to the local people. Once they have a scheme, then you can share your knowledge with them, discussing and questioning their ideas to deepen their involvement." At Proshika, he said, "all are teachers, and all are learners."[11]

Initial funding for Proshika was modest, and came out of surplus funds set aside for the original VTTP program. By 1977, however, Proshika's growth indicated a potential far beyond CUSO's funding capacity. Again, CIDA stepped in, and over the next four years, committed more than half a million dollars to Proshika, an amount which was quadrupled when the project was renewed in 1981.

With funding, the programs were able to expand rapidly, and the house on Indira Road which had been the first Canadian High Commission, was no longer large enough to house Proshika, the CUSO office and Cournoyer's own residence. He and CUSO moved to a new location, and Proshika's training programs expanded to include trainees from Caritas, UNICEF and other organizations. A woman's project and beekeeping operations were also begun, while Rahat and Faruque began to search for a rural site which might become a more permanent and appropriate home for the organization.

The projects varied, but were usually small, rarely requiring more than a few hundred dollars: a loan to lease some land over a cropping season; money for seeds or fertilizer; fish breeding. Many groups would borrow money to buy or lease a pond which they could stock with fish fingerlings, keeping some of the grown fish for village consumption and selling others to repay the loan and provide future income. A group of women borrowed enough money to purchase ten cows — one each. They fattened the cows then sold them for profit at a festival, repaid the loan keeping a share for their families, and reinvested the balance.

Through 1977 and 1978, so many groups were forming that a centre had to be established at Comilla to meet some of the demands from the eastern part of the country; smaller area-development centres were also set up to assist and monitor the new projects that were rapidly coming on stream. By early 1978, the staff had grown phenomenally, thanks to the enthusiasm that Proshika engendered amongst young people and the generous CIDA grant. And Proshika was able to keep its essentially personal character, although it now touched the lives of hundreds of people.

Canadian Member of Parliament Doug Roche made an extensive tour of China, Indonesia and Bangladesh in the fall of 1977, looking for development success stories as well as failures, and probing official and unofficial Canadian aid projects. He wrote extensively about what he saw, first in *Reader's Digest*, then in a book entitled *What Development Is All About*. Although he earned the enmity of the Canadian High Commission for his scathing attacks on a Canadian-built earth satellite station, he spoke glowingly of Proshika, saying that in his travels through Asia, ''I did not see a better use of Canadian aid.''[12] It was an important tribute from this Progressive Conservative who had made international development the cornerstone of his Parliamentary career — especially because it was an observation based on travel and personal discussions in the villages, rather than on the diplomatic cocktail circuit.

'For three-and-a-half hours,' wrote Roche of one excursion, ''Rahat and I bounced along Bangladesh's Highway No. 1 in a Land Rover. The early morning sky was black when we finally stopped in the jungle, sixty miles out of Dhaka. ''Follow me,'' said Rahat, as he hopped out. We had gone scarcely 300 yards along a winding trail before I found myself in a cluster of mud huts: the village of North Rampur. About 30 men stood waiting for us . . . . they had been landless peasants — broke, disorganized, despondent before Rahat came to the village and persuaded them that they must work together and help themselves. Under his guidance, they pooled their labour and they were soon vaccinating cattle, raising chickens and stocking two fish tanks. In a year, their credit union had accumulated $1,800 which was lent to three members to buy a little land. Then the group bought ten cows,

later selling them for a profit. Now, they said, they were negotiat-
ing to lease one acre of land for each member of the cooperative
to work, one third of the proceeds going to the landlord, two
thirds to them'.[13]

Rahat took me to a second Proshika village where I met fifteen
young men who started a cooperative with a total of $6. They
bought fish to stock an unused ditch, and later sold the fish for a
profit. Then they started a common vegetable garden, and with the
profits, enlarged the garden and started a new fish pond. I asked
one man what the co-op meant to him. 'I know I am better off,'
he replied. 'I do not deal with moneylenders any more. I feel
more secure.' Small accomplishments, yes. But as I looked into
his face and saw his pride and hope — which I had certainly not
seen in the slums of Dhaka — I felt exhilarated. I felt that I was
looking at a liberated man, who would have a chance to realize
his potential in life. Foreign aid doesn't need to be big. And it
can be beautiful.[14]

By now, Raymond Cournoyer had moved on to become CUSO's Regional
Director for Asia, based in Singapore; and CUSO's role with Proshika
had been reduced to one of general advice and liaison with CIDA. "CUSO's
role from now on will be very much at the back of the stage, where it
should be for a foreign agency working in a developing country," Cournoyer said. Proshika's continuation and expansion after Cournoyer's departure was, as Roche said in his book, "the ultimate tribute to an aid
officer."
    There were unavoidable problems and setbacks along with the success.
Proshika was criticized for its heavy dependence on external revenue
while promoting a self-reliant thesis in the villages. Occasional disputes
with CUSO or CIDA threatened Proshika's ability to retain its own sense
of values and direction. Simplistic political formulas and the desire for
speedy solutions tempted some Proshika trainers away from the concept
of a truly village-based development process. And internal strains between
the Dhaka and Comilla groups eventually led to a formal split and the
development of two separate organizations.
    But the difficulties could hardly overshadow the immense achieve-

ments. A 1977 Bangladesh Government evaluation estimated that Proshika had provided training in the previous year to 278 groups and had dispersed project funds and revolving loans that benefitted more than 25,000 people.[15] One of its biggest successes was to help farmers ward off *Mohajans* — moneylenders. In some areas the *Mohajans* had reduced their interest rates by half, and were even offering interest-free loans in order to keep farmers borrowing from them. It was reported that in a part of Comilla district *Mohajans* offered one of the Proshika staff a bribe of 20,000 taka ($1,400) to pull Proshika projects out of the area, a telling tribute to the organization's success.

An independent 1981 evaluation quantified the achievements of the previous three years: 368 trainers, of whom 261 were volunteers, had provided courses for more than 5,000 individuals, representing groups whose membership was estimated at more than 50,000 people. The revolving loan fund had distributed $268,000 to 1,500 projects, to which villagers had contributed $55,000 themselves; another 1,200 projects had been started with funds from other organizations now providing assistance to Proshika.

"Proshika has shown," the evaluation stated, "that the powerlessness and exploitation of the rural poor can be broken by organizing the landless labourers so they can challenge the structures, institutions and policies which keep them exploited and oppressed. All of this is being done within the law. In fact the landless groups are challenging the lawlessness of the traditional leaders in the villages who have manipulated the local courts, misappropriated food-for-work wheat and development funds, abused their position of power and influence in all village institutions, and physically beaten employees without any fear of reprisal."[16]

CUSO developed other projects in Bangladesh over the years, but few compared in scope and importance with Proshika. Although it was Rahat and Faruque, and dozens of other Bangladeshis, who developed and built Proshika, CUSO could take justifiable pride in its own catalytic role. Raymond Cournoyer had been the right man, in the right place, at the right time; Proshika's success vindicated his approach to development and his faith in people. Characteristically self-effacing, he said that Proshika was simply a logical response to the context and circumstances of the time. "If I went there now to develop a program I might try something quite different," he concluded. "It is not a moral but an experience. It will change and evolve in years to come."[17]

Proshika, of course, could not solve the problems of Bangladesh; at best, it could provide some examples, a model, a signpost of what was possible. Despite the quantifiable indicators of success, it is too early to judge the organization, except in comparison with the thousands of failed 'trickle down' projects that have brought so little in the way of real hope to the millions who subsist on the edge of existence in Bangladesh.

As for Bangladesh, political stability has proven elusive, and rural landlessness, natural disaster and poverty continue apace. However, there has been some progress: food production has almost kept pace with population growth, and relief imports are half what they were ten years ago. Winter wheat, almost unknown in Bangladesh a decade ago, is now widespread, and wheat harvests in excess of a million tons are not unusual. There is evidence that aid programs are becoming more responsive to real needs, and even the largest donors are now beginning to model some of their plans and policy recommendations on the hard won successes of voluntary organizations like BRAC, Gonoshasthaya Kendra and Proshika. It has taken great amounts of sweat and money to keep Bangladesh afloat over the years since Sheikh Mujib returned from Pakistan, and it will take a great deal more. Life there hangs in a perilous balance that can be all too easily, and fatally, altered.

The Bangladesh national anthem is based on a poem written four generations ago by Nobel laureate, Rabindranath Tagore: "Amar Sonar Bangla" — My Golden Bengal. Some say the poet, when he spoke of gold, referred to the exquisite sunset over the Bay of Bengal. Others say it was the endless fields of mustard flowers, the sheaves of rice at harvest time, or jute, "the golden fibre." Whatever he meant, substance will be given to his vision only by sustained achievements that reach all Bangladeshi communities and offer people the chance to survive and prosper through their own efforts.

Chapter 14

Ray Clark: Prince For a Day

There were several people who remained involved with CUSO over the years, or who were lured back on different occasions by an enticing assignment or a fresh opportunity for adventure. One of the most durable was Ray Clark. Despite the near-termination of his career on his fourth day in Jamaica — when his landlord's dogs were slaughtered in an attempt to frighten him away — he survived, eventually transferred to Zambia, and in 1977 was in the middle of his third posting, this time teaching at Fatima High School in the Western Highland Province of Papua New Guinea.

Unlike his schools in the Caribbean and Africa, Fatima High School was part of an experimental program that emphasized village life rather than the standard academic preoccupation, which tended to encourage students to leave the villages for larger urban centres. At Fatima, students and teachers divided their time equally between the classroom and a large school farm, where they grew vegetables and coffee, and raised pigs, poultry and ducks. Groups of students were each assigned an area of the farm where they could build houses in the style of their own village, and where they were basically free to do anything, as Clark put it, "except sleep in them or burn them down."

On Saturdays, Clark travelled to Mount Hagen to shop, and, during the harvest season, to sell the coffee. One Saturday in the Western High-lands is much like another, but on one particular morning, as he set off for Mount Hagen with Brother John and Brother Joe, two of the Australian teachers, Clark knew they might run into some difficulty on the road. Prince Charles was in the midst of a royal tour of Papua New Guinea, and was expected to pass along the Highlands Highway some time that morning.

As though they had timed it, they encountered a huge crowd awaiting the Prince at the junction where the school road met the highway, and the route ahead had been closed by the police. So the trio from Fatima High School was forced to wait. It was enjoyable enough, seeing so many people in their finery — huge feather headdresses, copious grass skirts, brilliant head-to-toe paint jobs, spears and arrows of all shapes and sizes, and drums ready for a sing-sing as soon as the "big man" arrived. It was not entirely clear who the big man was — they called him "Big Pella Man im Pickaninny Bilong Missis Queen Bilong England" — but with a name like that, he was bound to be important, and so the crowd waited in eager anticipation.

Suddenly, a guard vehicle with a loudspeaker appeared, chugging up the gravelly Highlands Highway, warning loudly that "Big Pella Man he come!" And then a shiny black convertible, so wide and so grand that it virtually straddled the highway, eased noiselessly into the junction. In the back sat the Heir to the Throne.

Instantly, singing, dancing, shouting, and general pandemonium broke out. As the full motorcade arrived at the crossroads, officials, police, spectators, dancers, Australian Brothers and one CUSO volunteer surged forward. The Prince seemed to enjoy himself, smiling broadly and shaking hands with all assembled, including Ray Clark. Clark was impressed; normally the junction was a pretty quiet place, not somewhere you would expect to run into the Prince of Wales. But it was already ten o'clock and he worried about getting to Mount Hagen before the banks closed at noon. Finally, the motorcade set off — the loudspeaker vehicle first, followed by the Prince, then the entourage and finally, Brother John and Brother Joe in the Toyota Scout, with Ray Clark sitting out in the back on top of the sacks of coffee beans.

As the procession wound its way through the mountains, they were greeted by frequent displays of dancing and drumming and excitement.

At the next official stop, everyone alighted from the vehicles and the Prince once again availed himself of the opportunity to shake Clark's hand. The motorcade was ahead of schedule, a common occurrence according to the Prince's valet Stephen Barry. "Frequently we would find ourselves sitting in a lay-by because the Prince was early," he explained, "something that made him frequently fume because it meant that whoever had worked out the trip had allowed for normal traffic conditions — forgetting that the authorities would clear the roads for him."[1]

Because they had time to kill, the Prince and valet decided to make a brief visit to a nearby village. "We were both enchanted," said Barry, "by the sight of a stunning black lady, dressed in a black wrap with a superb, heavy necklace — made of Coca-Cola bottle tops." As soon as the royal party had plunged off into the bush in search of exotica, however, Ray Clark saw a chance to make a move. "Brother Joe," he said, "Let's get out of here and shoot ahead now."[2] And with that, they were off.

What they had not reckoned on was the lead vehicle with the loudspeaker, which had not been informed of the royal pause, and was still ahead of the school jeep, announcing that "Big Pella Man he come."

"Everybody started to drum and shout and jump up and down as we passed," Clark said. "And Brother Joe caught on and started to honk and point to me sitting up on the coffee beans in the back."

Despite his unprincely jeans and a bushy moustache, Clark was fit, and good-looking, and white, and could just conceivably have been the pickaninny bilong Missis Queen, especially given that he had begun to take advantage of the situation — standing erect amidst the coffee beans as Brother Joe slowed to a more regal pace, and waving majestically to the crowd. Prince Charles and his motorcade followed, but by the time he passed, everyone had gone home and the welcome along the rest of the road to Mount Hagen was decidedly tepid.

Outside Mount Hagen, at the junction to the airport, the much-cheered, one-vehicle motorcade from Fatima High School came to a halt. Because the Prince was flying out, everybody from town had driven to the junction, and the road into the town was hopelessly clogged with people and dancers and buses and cars. So Clark and Brother John and Brother Joe were forced to wait. Eventually the official motorcade caught up with them, and, no doubt pleased by the sudden improvement in the level of welcome, the Prince descended once again from his huge black car and shook hands all round, greeting Ray Clark for the third and final time. The banks in Mount Hagen had closed by then, but it didn't really matter. For Ray Clark it had been a nice day.

Chapter 15

South by Southeast

East, Central and Southern Africa did not initially present as many programming difficulties as CUSO encountered elsewhere in the world, although it was slower than other programs in getting away from the starting gate. In the summer of 1962, Duncan Edmonds took a Canadian Crossroads group to Southern Rhodesia, and, at the request of Lewis Perinbam, spent two weeks travelling dervish-like through Northern Rhodesia, Nyasaland, Tanganyika, Kenya and Uganda, investigating possible placement opportunities for volunteers.

After graduating from the University of Toronto in 1959, Edmonds had spent a year at the London School of Economics where he had come under the spell of Barbara Ward, C. P. Snow and L.S.E.'s growing school of Africanists. When he returned to Canada, he joined the staff of the Liberal Opposition Leader, Lester Pearson, and helped establish the African Students' Foundation which became active in providing scholarships to Canadian universities for African students. In 1962 he joined the faculty of Carleton University, where his work included representational duties on behalf of CUSO. Being so close to the tiny CUSO Ottawa office, it was natural that Lewis Perinbam — then CUSO's acting Executive Secretary — would suggest that he add two weeks of CUSO activity to his summer in East Africa.

What Edmonds found there in 1962 seemed light years away from the Africa of today. Most of the countries he visited had not yet become independent and still bore their colonial names. In most capitals, he found British civil servants acting as Ministers, Permanent Secretaries and Chief Inspectors of Education.

In Kenya, on the eve of the colony's independence, white settlers warned him of the imminent 'Armageddon', and Edmonds reported that the political situation was "anything but stable." But he found most countries eager for CUSO teachers, and able to meet the local financial obligations; he was impressed by the hospitable attitudes and surroundings, and the absence of any "serious medical difficulties or problems of disease." He also met a number of Canadians already working in Africa who were eager to assist; over the coming years, many of them would develop and maintain an interest in CUSO and would form the backbone of Canada's early activities in the region.

In Dar es Salaam, the Principal of the University College, Dr. Cranford Pratt, was a Canadian, as was the Dean of the Law School, who eagerly requested a CUSO volunteer tutor. In Uganda, Jane Banfield, who had been with the Canadian Commission for UNESCO, the body which had provided CUSO with its first year of administrative support as well as the services of Lewis Perinbam, was now working at Makarere College. At the Mindolo Ecumenical centre in Northern Rhodesia, which Edmonds said was "without doubt one of the most exciting places in Africa,"[1] Rev. Garth Legge, seconded by the United Church of Canada, was Chairman of the Board, and Professor Douglas Anglin (from Carleton University) was teaching a summer course. The plummy tones of Edmond's report — the "grand opportunities," the "splendid venture," the "fine contribution," the "strong determination and fervent spirit," — have a wistful, almost nostalgic ring to them, and for all their relevance to the East Central and Southern Africa of today, might as well have described an Arthurian Camelot.

But Duncan Edmonds' enthusiastic recommendations would not bear immediate fruit. Bill McWhinney had just taken over from Lewis Perinbam, and would spend late 1962 and early 1963 consolidating the Canadian recruitment and fund-raising base required to support commitments already made in Asia, the Caribbean and West Africa. In the spring of 1963, McWhinney made a tour of Asia and Africa which took him over some of the ground Edmonds had covered the previous year, re-establishing contacts with ministries — already more Africanized — in Kenya, Uganda, Tanganyika and Northern Rhodesia. It was not until the summer of 1964 that the first full-fledged CUSO contingent arrived in East Africa: thirteen were bound for independent Tanzania; five for Uganda, and four to the former Northern Rhodesia — now Zambia.

One of the Zambia contingent was Dave Beer, who had trekked with Guy Arnold across the Rupununi Region of British Guiana in 1960, and had later gone to Jamaica as a volunteer. Arnold, continuing his odyssey through the Commonwealth, had left Canada for Zambia where he began to develop what would eventually become the Zambia Youth Service, an attempt to mobilize Zambian youth and train them in animal husbandry, crop management, and technical trades. Arnold corresponded with Bill McWhinney, asking for CUSO volunteers, and wrote to Beer, asking if he would like to be among them.

Zambia was in many ways more challenging for Beer than Jamaica had been. Jamaica in 1964 had little of the racial tension that permeated Zambian society. Jamaica had a national culture, a shared history and a sense of nationalism that most East African countries did not enjoy. And because of the ethnic diversity and the multiplicity of languages, most African countries were forced to use the former colonial language — a second tongue to all — as the language of government and commerce. But because Zambia was such a new country, with the future spread at its feet, it was an exhilarating time:

"Zambia was a wonderful place to be," Beer said, "President Kaunda was an extremely inspirational person, copper was about to boom, everybody was fresh and everything was happening."[2] One of his first jobs was to organize a sports display of national youth for independence day. "The greatest thrill of my life as a volunteer was on that day leading five hundred young Zambian men and women onto the tarmac before over one hundred and fifty thousand people. The excitement and feeling of freedom was high at that time in Zambia's fledgling history."[3]

In Tanzania, President Julius Nyerere was emerging as one of the more thoughful and eloquent spokesmen for Third World development; he had already become something of a *guru* to internationalists worldwide. "Africa must change," he had written; "change from an area where people eke out an existence and adapt themselves to their environment, to a

continent which challenges the environment and adapts it to man's need . . .
a revolution has begun in Africa. It is a revolution which we hope to
control and channel so that our lives are transformed....the choice is not
between change and no change; the choice is between changing or being
changed by the impact of forces beyond our control.''[4]

It was heady stuff, particularly for young CUSO volunteers like Hugh
Winsor, already an experienced journalist, who had come to help establish
a national news agency. He had imagined himself as a kind of ''czar of
the printed word'' in Tanzania, and possibly even a ghost writer for the
President's speeches. ''Knowing little more about the country than I did
about the assignment,'' he said, ''I packed into my suitcase two years'
supply of razor blades, only to find that one of the first buildings on the
road from the airport into town was a razor-blade factory!''[5] He went on
to discover that his colleagues were experienced, literate journalists; that
Dar es Salaam had four daily newspapers — more than Toronto or New
York — and that President Nyerere, far from needing his assistance as
a ghost writer, had already written several books and had even translated
some Shakespeare into Swahili.

Frank Bogdasavich, having passed his bar exams after a year of ar-
ticling in Saskatchewan, was posted to the University College of Dar es
Salaam as a tutor in criminal law. Before he finished his assignment, he
would become Administrative Dean of the Faculty, and would also act
as CUSO's first part-time Field Staff Officer in Tanzania.

In 1965, Kenya was added to the CUSO program in East Africa;
in 1967, the first volunteers were posted to Malawi and Ethiopia.
Colin Freebury was in the first Malawi group and had been asked to
act as CUSO coordinator in addition to his duties at a teachers'
college near Lilongwe. ''Up until 1967,'' he said, ''programs or activities
were more or less the result of tours made by somebody from Ottawa
who met the odd minister and said, 'Yes, we can place somebody at this
school . . . '.''[6] But with more than two hundred volunteers in East Africa
alone, by then, and the numbers increasing quickly, the need for more
full-time field staff was apparent.

The political scene in East Africa as a whole was also changing rapidly
during those years. Guerilla wars in the Portugese colonies were heating
up, while hopes for majority rule in Rhodesia were dashed by Ian Smith's
Unilateral Declaration of Independence in 1965. Smith closed the border

with Zambia, cutting off its supplies of food and fuel. Britain's Prime Minister, Harold Wilson, said it would be over in a matter of weeks, and David Beer felt a surge of national pride as he watched Canadian Hercules aircraft flying oil from Kinshasa into Ndola, in order to keep Zambia afloat while the matter was settled. But the matter was not settled, and the Canadian aircraft stopped coming. And gradually, the whole 'liberation phenom', as Dave Beer called it, began to encroach on the thinking of everyone in the region. Until the ties with the white south could be replaced; until the colonial sores and the racist cancers could be expunged, they would remain uppermost in the minds of the governments and the people of East, Central and Southern Africa.

Chapter 16

Portugal: The First to Come, The Last to Go

> (The signatories) respect the right of all peoples to choose the
> form of government under which they will live; and they wish to
> see sovereign rights and self government restored to those who
> have been forcibly deprived of them.
>
> — Atlantic Charter, 1941

In 1970, Portugal; small, poor, overpopulated and underdeveloped, found itself maintaining a colonial empire nearly twenty-five times its geographical size. The country was fighting three vicious wars and supporting 160,000 soldiers in Africa — five times, per capita, the number of U.S. troops in Indochina at the height of the Vietnam War. A decade after other European colonial powers had shed their African empires, Portugal hung on tenaciously.

The first phase in the African experience of Europe had been one of mutual discovery, in which the Portugal of Prince Henry the Navigator was undoubtedly the pioneer. Before the birth of Columbus, the Portuguese had reached the Senegal River and Cape Verde; in 1497, Batholomeu Dias rounded the Cape of Good Hope, and the following year, Vasco da Gama sailed northwards from the cape to touch the coast of

Lewis Perinbam

August 1961: Therese Spicer, Keith Spicer and Fred Stinson, M.P., wave farewell to the first COV volunteers.

BILL McWHINNEY

1963: (l. to r.) Francis J. Leddy, CUSO's midwife; Msgr. J. Garneau; Lester B. Pearson; Bill McWhinney and Geoff Andrew, one of CUSO's most undersung heroes.

DAVE BEER

1963: Dave Beer at Cobbla Camp, Jamaica

GORDON CRESSY

Christmas 1963: Canadian Christmas Trees being loaded aboard BWIA at Barbados for the strangest flight down the Windward Islands.

Dave Beer, Guy Arnold David Milne on the Esiquibo River, Southern British Guiana, August 1960: the start of CVCS.

DAVE BEER

Smiling Faces Going Places: the 1966 East Africa group on the steps of Montreal's City Hall shortly before the racial brawl

1971: Carpenter Emmanueal Eze with desks he made for the Nigeria Schools Project.

McFETRIDGE

(Above) Jim McFetridge and students near Nakorn Dawan, Thailand

(opposite) Murray Thompson – The Mahatma

(Bottom) 1980: Iona Campagnolo (center) at CUSO press conference following her visit to Kampuchean Refugee Project. Sharon Capeling (left) became CUSO's Public Affairs Director; Ian Smillie (rt.), Executive Director 1979-83.

CUSO

CUSO

PIERPOINT

Jean Pelletier, much as he looked
shortly before his final departure
from Madagascar.

CUSO

Chris Bryant served in Grenada,
Barbados, Jamaica and Papua New
Guinea before becoming Execu-
tive Director of CUSO in 1983.

Lagos Airport, 1966: Michael Sinclair (l.) says farewell to Keith Bezanson
(r.) as the East Africa volunteers continue their journey. Bezanson was
later reluctantly appointed Principal of a school in Nigeria; in 1985 he was
appointed Canada's Ambassador to Peru.

DAVE BEER

Darrell Martindale up the creek in Bolivia

Ron Wensel working on an electric plant in Bolivia.

1971: The Nigeria Schools Reconstruction Project; CUSO desks in a war damaged school

1983: Marlene Green (rt.) in Grenada (return to CUSO)

Bolivia: a woman sorts through rocks looking for pieces with tin; these will later be smashed by hand

1964: Bill McNeill with Senior Students, Sancta Crux Secondary School, Nigeria

Mozambique, sail as far north as Malindi in what is now Kenya, and turn eastward to India.

At first, the Portuguese were content to trade; they treated the Africans as partners and encouraged them to send ambassadors to the court at Lisbon. King Mbemba-a-Nzinga, who reigned as Dom Alfonso I during the first half of the sixteenth century, adopted Christianity and encouraged Portuguese priests, artisans, printers and teachers to live in his country. Iron, copper and other metals, as well as pigs, sheep, poultry and cattle, were traded for ivory, gold and spices.

But this partnership soon turned to enslavement: the Spanish, Portuguese and British colonies in America demanded innumerable Africans to work the mines and plantations of the New World. Their demands were met: between 1530 and 1600, Spanish slave contracts alone accounted for as many as eight hundred thousand slaves; by 1700, ten thousand slaves were being shipped annually to Brazil; and by the 1830s, near the time Britain announced abolition, an estimated four million men, women and children had been exported from Portuguese colonies — three million from Angola alone.

The third colonial phase, after abolition of slavery, centered on imperial expansion and rivalry. The Portuguese, slow to accept the abolition forced on them by the British fleet, exported twenty-five thousand slaves annually between 1840 and 1850 and extended the process until 1878, replacing slavery with a system of forced labour which survived (despite the occasional international outcry) until 1960. Shipments of Angolans to the cocoa plantations of Sao Tome, at the rate of two thousand to four thousand annually, became a scandal during the First World War, but continued nonetheless. In Mozambique, thousands of people were indentured to the mines of South Africa, and countless numbers of them died. One report revealed that of 418,000 men sent to work in the mines between 1905 and 1912, 87,000 never returned.

Portugal's brief dream of trans-African empire — from Angola in the West to Mozambique in the East — was dashed by Cecil Rhodes, who carved out a Cape-to-Cairo swath for Britain; and by the Berlin Conference of 1884, which deprived Portugal of half its claims in the Congo and Angola. Yet Portugal's role in the European grab for Africa was foremost in rapacity, denounced even in the British House of Commons for moral and legal iniquities which "fetter the activities of trade with shackles of a truly mediaeval type."[1]

Development in the colonies between the wars was largely left to private enterprise and huge trading companies — the Mozambique Company, the Niassa Company, the Zambesia Company and others, financed mainly by international, rather than Portuguese, capital. The Salazar regime, with its concept of a 'Third Empire', glorified the Portuguese mission in Africa and established a policy of sharp distinction (as if one had been needed) between 'unassimilated' Africans, whites and 'assimilados', the latter status out of reach for most Africans, who had little access to education. State schools were run largely for the white community, and mission schools provided few opportunities beyond the primary level. In 1958, there were only 511 Africans in high school in Mozambique; by 1960 — the year that eighteen other African countries achieved independence — there had been little improvement on the 1950 census figures, which showed fewer than thirty-five thousand assimilados in the population of more than ten million in Angola and Mozambique.

It was only in 1951 that Portugal, in an attempt to integrate the colonial economies with its own, began to make an effort to bring about any real change in the colonies. Eager to please the West, after placing itself somewhat ambiguously in the fascist camp during the Second World War, Portugal not only encouraged renewal of American military installations in the Azores, but also became a member of NATO. In 1951, as a step towards Portuguese membership in the United Nations, the colonies were declared 'provinces', so that Portugal, on admission to the UN in 1956, could state that there was nothing to decolonize.

There was also a concerted effort to attract foreign investment in the colonies and encourage increased emigration and settlement. In the 1930s, there were fewer whites in the Portuguese colonies than in Prince Edward Island today; however, between 1940 and 1960, the white population of Angola grew from 44,000 to 200,000, and, in Mozambique, from 27,000 to 85,000. As a result, the few opportunities still remaining for Africans disappeared; even the menial jobs went to immigrants who had fled the poverty and backwardness in Portugal.

African opposition to Portuguese entrenchment was slow to begin and slower still to become known internationally; state control of the media and a secret police force effectively muzzled political opposition. Ironically, it was in Portugal — not Africa — that the opposition began, in the 1940s and 1950s. Among African students in Portugal was a small group of assimilados — young men who had forsaken, but not forgotten, their language and culture: they included Agostino Neto, a medical student and poet; Amilcar Cabral, a student of engineering hydraulics; and Mario de Andrade, a literary critic. At first, they concentrated on a rediscovery of the Africa they had left behind. They formed a Centre of African Studies in Lisbon, which, among other endeavours, encouraged and published poetry. They began to study the effects of colonialism on their homelands. They were reformists; Neto even worked for the Presidential election campaign of a moderate opposition candidate in Lisbon in 1951. When the candidate was forced to withdraw from the election, Neto was arrested; the Centre was outlawed; and the group was forced to disband.

Unlike African students in France, Britain and other European countries, the group found few sympathizers among the Portuguese — organized opposition being either non-existent or underground. Their only allies were the outlawed Portuguese Communist Party and one or two other anti-Salazarist groups; as a result, Marxism became an important part of the development of their revolutionary ideas. As Neto recalled it, "We learned from the sharp conflicts that existed in Portugal; they provided us with useful lessons."[2]

After being released from prison, Neto finished his medical degree and returned to Angola to rejoin Andrade.

The founders of the MPLA,* and FRELIMO** in Mozambique, probably started from a philosophic base of non-violence — as had other African nationalists such as Nkrumah, Nyerere and Kaunda. "At first," wrote Nkrumah, "I could not understand how Gandhi's philosophy of non-violence could possibly be effective....the solution of the colonial problem, as I saw it at the time, lay in armed rebellion . . . After months of studying Gandhi's policy and watching the effect it had, I began to see that, when backed by a strong political organization, it could be the solution to the colonial problem."[3]

"Our preference," said Nyerere, "and that of every true African patriot, has always been for peaceful methods of struggle. We abhor the suffering and the terror, and the sheer waste of time, which is involved in violent upheavals, and believe that peaceful progress is worth some sacrifice in terms of time. But when the door of peaceful progress is

---

* Popular Movement for the Liberation of Angola
** Front for the Liberation of Mozambique

slammed shut and bolted, then the struggle must take other forms; we cannot surrender.''[4]

The Portuguese did shut and bolt the doors to reform in their African colonies. Economic deprivation among Africans was now endemic, and lack of opportunity for advancement was increasingly intolerable — particularly within the general context of African decolonization. The most modest expressions of political discontent and desire for moderate reform were met with violence, arrest and imprisonment; more violence was bound to result.

The flame that set off the conflagration in Luanda was sparked in 1960 with a demonstration against another arrest of Dr. Neto. Thirty strikers were killed when troops opened fire, and more than two hundred were wounded. The following year, thirty more people were killed in riots; widespread rebel attacks in the coffee country followed, forever extinguishing the image of a 'happy and peaceful colony'. A rigid news blackout was imposed, and a violent military crackdown ended in the loss of between ten thousand and thirty thousand lives, and the exodus of more than one hundred fifty thousand refugees to the Congo.

A background to the Portuguese experience in Africa is essential to understand the liberation movements and to appreciate their frustration and anger at arguments favoring an evolutionary approach over armed struggle as a means of gaining independence. For the nationalists, bludgeoned and suppressed at every turn, there was no longer any choice: a gradual approach could only consolidate Portugal's African foothold — and would not facilitate the orderly attainment of independence envisaged by some Portuguese allies.

As the fighting began, Canadian involvement in the Portuguese colonies began to change from a nominal role to aggressive trade development. What Prime Minister Trudeau once said about trade with Cuba, External Affairs Minister Mitchell Sharp echoed with reference to Angola and Mozambique: "We believe in the Canadian Government that trade helps bring about contacts that do in fact help influence policy."[5] However, Canadian trade seemed to have as little influence on Portuguese policy as it did on the Cuban position; as Canadian trade with Portugal increased, so did war in the colonies.

In 1960, Canada purchased only $200,000 in goods from Angola and

Mozambique; by 1972, the volume had increased to $49 million in coffee, cotton, tea, cashews and sisal — all at competitive prices achieved through repressive labour practices. Also by 1972, one-third of Angola's oil was being refined in Canada, and Canadians, through lucrative Alcan contracts, were involved in the construction of the Cabora Bassa Dam in Mozambique. This huge hydro-electric, irrigation and strategic development scheme would help expand plantation development, industry, and foreign investment — and, in turn, European emigration. Angola and Mozambique would be fully integrated into the modern commercial world — a world which would eventually help Portugal keep the liberation movements at bay.

By 1970, Portugal had 160,000 troops in Africa[6] but the possibility of their defeat could not easily be dismissed. Portugal's foreign debt was ten times higher than it had been in 1961; the defence budget had tripled between 1960 and 1968. While Britain, France and Belgium began to feel that early independence was the best chance for Portugal to retain some influence and to stave off the growing radicalism of liberation movements, the United States maintained that the wars were a Portuguese affair. Between 1962 and 1968, however, the U.S. gave Portugal $39 million in military assistance and $124 million in economic assistance.[7] Among Portugal's many silent partners, most significant was South Africa, which saw Mozambique, Angola and Rhodesia not only as important allies in maintaining white Southern Africa, but also as military buffers against guerilla forces which might penetrate the Republic's own borders from hostile neighbouring states.

Many CUSO volunteers in Africa saw the issue as it was presented by Julius Nyerere in an address to the General Assembly of the United Nations in October 1970:

> Africa has no choice but to side with the freedom struggle of
> Southern Africa . . . but what of other non-African nations? They
> all claim opposition to apartheid and to colonialism. Yet the sad
> truth is that — far from using their power for justice, many na-
> tions represented in this Assembly give continuing and expanding
> practical support to South Africa and to the Portuguese colonial
> war effort. Does anyone imagine that one of the poorest states of
> Europe could, unaided, fight colonial wars in three territories,

which are together twenty times its own size? On the contrary; its NATO membership allows it to meet an otherwise intolerable burden. And things like the planned foreign investment in the Cabora Bassa Project enable Portugal to increase its exploitation of Africa.[8]

Late in 1970, Southern Africa made headlines when it seemed Britain's planned resumption of arms sales to South Africa might destroy the Commonwealth. British Prime Minister Edward Heath was persuaded to change his plans during the Commonwealth Heads of Government Meeting in Singapore in 1971 — but it was a close call. Prime Minister Trudeau warned that if a long-term view of African racial questions were not taken in both Africa and the West, a situation could develop within ten years that would not only be "disastrous for Africa, but disastrous for the world." He spoke of "the moral indignity, the moral abomination of racial discrimination, which debases not only the states who practise it, but those individuals who have it in their hearts. It poisons the relationship between human beings. It makes peace in the world a less possible matter, a less possible eventuality."[9]

In March 1971, as part of a Canadian initiative to find peace in Southern Africa, External Affairs Minister Mitchell Sharp left on a two week trip to Africa to explore possibilities for a 'dialogue' between black countries and the white south. Two CUSO RVs were in the entourage. Jon Church was a volunteer in India and Ghana before joining the Ottawa staff; he resigned from CUSO to run unsuccessfully for Parliament in the federal election of 1968, and he became Mitchell Sharp's Executive Assistant not long afterwards. The other RV was a member of the press corps — Dan Turner, the former volunteer and FSO who had been expelled from Nigeria after evacuating the volunteers from Biafra, was now a correspondent for Canadian Press.

"Mr. Sharp expressed himself as quite impressed with President Felix Houphouet-Boigny's dovish views on dealing with racism in Southern Africa," reported the *Globe and Mail*, after the Minister's first stop in the Ivory Coast. Houphouet-Boigny, the report continued, "advocates that black Africa involve itself in a dialogue rather than a confrontation with white minority governments in South Africa, Rhodesia and the Portuguese colonies."[10]

Sharp went on to Nigeria, where the Head of State, Yakubu Gowon, dealt summarily with the question of 'dialogue' with South Africa. "There is no question of dialogue with a person that doesn't think someone of my race is fit to be a human being," Gowon told the Minister bluntly. Dan Turner reported that he had been even more succinct in private, telling Sharp, "To me, that stinks."[11]

By the time Sharp arrived in Zambia, the idea of Canadian involvement in the promotion of inter-racial African dialogue had already been erased from his mind. Dave Beer recalled meeting the Minister's aircraft when it arrived at Lusaka's international airport. One of the first off the plane was Jon Church who, sensing Beer's own antipathy towards 'dialogue', greeted him with an urgent, "It's not true! It's not true!"[12]

President Kuanda put the clincher on the whole matter by saying that the West was helping the Portuguese, the South Africans and the Rhodesians "to oppress us, to kill us, to destroy us."[13] Canada, obviously, would have no part of that.

At the same time, many Canadian voluntary agencies, churches and special interest groups began to look more closely at Canada's involvement in Southern Africa. During the summer of 1971, a number of studies and briefs were prepared, in response to public involvement in a government-created 'Foreign Policy for Canadians', and wide-ranging hearings by the House of Commons Standing Committee on External Affairs and National Defence.

By then, twelve hundred CUSO volunteers had served in East, Central and Southern Africa, many of them going on to senior management positions within the organization. It was inevitable that CUSO would seek to influence government and public opinion on the subject: in the late 1960s, a number of CUSO RVs formed the Committee for a Just Canadian Policy Towards Africa; the group sponsored *The Black Paper, An Alternative Policy for Canada Towards Southern Africa*, published in 1970. Its authors, including RVs Rick Williams and Hugh Winsor, repudiated Canada's policy of 'dialogue', which they found both meaningless and ineffective:

Canada's pious and uncritical repetition of such platitudes as
"Canada remains committed to the cause of peaceful change in

Southern Africa'' has become irrelevant and only serves to destroy
our credibility....the violence to be deplored in Southern Africa is
the violence now exercised in the name of the state. When an oppressed people to whom one cannot honestly suggest any other alternative finally reacts to that violence and strikes out in the name
of values which are our own values, one can hardly then deny the
legitimacy of their struggle.[14]

In CUSO's brief to the Standing Committee, strong concern was expressed that the hollow piety of official Canadian policy on the subject
might be directly related to Canadian investments in Southern Africa.
CUSO's postion was clear and simple:

The Canadian Government should state publicly that it considers
the nationalist movements in Southern Africa, as recognized by
the Organization of African Unity, to be more representative of
the people of these countries than the governments and administrations presently in control. Furthermore, Canada should move towards giving official recognition to the liberation movements . . .
and should offer funds for relief and educational work in Tanzania, Zambia and Congo-Kinshasa for refugees who have fled from
Southern Africa.[15]

When it came time for Commonwealth Heads of Government to gather
again in the summer of 1973, the issue of Southern Africa was even
higher on the agenda than in 1970, and because the meeting was to be
held in Ottawa, the Canadian Government wanted an active role in the
discussions. Despite acrimonious debate on the subject (characterized by
British intransigence on a number of key points) the final communique
of the conference, which Canada unhesitatingly accepted, marked a significant departure from previous policy. There was reference to "the
efforts of the indigenous people of the territories in Southern Africa to
achieve self-determination," and to the need "to give every humanitarian
assistance to those engaged in such efforts." The heads of government
also "recognized the legitimacy of the struggle to win full human rights
and self-determination."[16]

However, the Canadian government was slow to act on this policy of
humanitarian assistance to liberation movements. Late in 1973, when the

Canadian Council of Churches requested funds to support FRELIMO, MPLA and PAIGC through the World Council of Churches, it seemed an ideal test case — and test case it was. When Toronto's *Globe and Mail* learned of the plan, it ran the story under front page headlines: "Ottawa to Give Aid to African Guerilla Groups." While not totally unsympathetic, the *Globe and Mail* article sparked a torrent of editorial outrage across the country: "Canada Gives Aid to Terror," said an *Ottawa Citizen* editorial. The *Toronto Star* called it a "two-faced policy in Africa" and the *Toronto Sun* wrote about "How Canada Aids Terrorism."

Within two weeks, External Affairs Minister Mitchell Sharp had issued a 'clarification' which put the policy into a four-wheel skid. He said that CIDA would be "authorized to consider requests for assistance in support of projects within Southern Africa provided such projects are sponsored by reputable Canadian non-governmental and international organizations and provided such projects are of a humanitarian or developmental nature." He talked of "strict control" and "full accountability" but, he explained, no grants of this sort would be made "until the estimates of CIDA for the year 1974/75 . . . have been approved *by Parliament*."[17]

Dave Beer, now in charge of CUSO's Development Education program in Ottawa, was furious, and began to organize a letter-writing campaign, saying that "the Minister's sudden delaying mechanism" meant that the negative lobby had been successful and that "policy makers in External Affairs and politicians have not heard from those who support the policy in enough strength."[18]

At an urgent Toronto meeting with church representatives, CUSO and other organizations made a statement urging the government to proceed with the policy it accepted at the Commonwealth meeting: "By this new policy of humanitarian assistance, Canada takes its place with a great many countries including Denmark, Sweden, Norway and Holland, where both governmental and non-governmental agencies are carrying out programs of assistance to the liberation movements."[19] The debate was on; the Standing Committee again entertained submissions and presentations, which showed much more support than anticipated for the policy; endorsements came not only from the NGO community, but also from the Canadian Labour Congress, churches, university professors and Members of Parliament from all parties. The opposition remained static.

The day of the final hearing was laced with special drama and poignancy. Dr. Agostino Neto, MPLA President, came to Canada on a speaking tour arranged by Oxfam and SUCO — CUSO's now somewhat distant sister organization; Jacques Roy, a former CUSO volunteer devoted to the Angolan liberation movement, supplying the SUCO connection. On April 25, Oxfam staff appeared before the Committee as witnesses; with them was Dr. Neto. Although Dr. Neto's status had been significantly altered the previous day, when a military coup toppled the government of Portugal and paved the way for speedy independence in the Portuguese colonies, Mitchell Sharp refused to meet the future President of Angola on the grounds that he was not "a government representative."[20] However, Jean Pelletier, now SUCO's Overseas Operations Director, arranged a private meeting for Neto with his father, Secretary of State Gerard Pelletier, and Prime Minister Trudeau.[21]

But within two weeks, the Canadian government had been brought down over its budget proposals, and the Southern Africa question simply disappeared. It was not an issue in the election that followed, and would have to await the presentation of government estimates in October. By then, "It was an anti-climax," wrote Paul Ladouceur, a former CUSO Board Member, "for both the proponents and the opponents of humanitarian aid for Southern Africa. When CIDA's estimates once again came up for discussion in the Standing Committee, not one word was said on the subject and the estimates were approved by Parliament shortly afterwards."[22]

By January 1975, $200,000 in CIDA grants had been allocated to humanitarian projects organized by the liberation movements, including $100,000 to the World Council of Churches for the MPLA in Angola and FRELIMO in Mozambique. As far as the MPLA and FRELIMO were concerned, however, it hardly mattered, for the Portuguese empire in Africa was already finished.

EPILOGUE

In the searing heat of a September day in 1983, Brian Rowe, CUSO's Regional Representative for East, Central and Southern Africa, stood on the banks of the Limpopo River at a point in Mozambique where farms had once flourished. Shielding his eyes from the sun, he peered through the shimmering haze to the opposite bank, more than half-a-kilometre distant. Because of the river and the irrigation it provided, this part of the country had been the breadbasket of Mozambique. What Brian Rowe saw now was an endless expanse of brown: "The river was virtually dry; the trickle of water was brown; the fields were brown; the sky, because of the wind, was brown. Everything was covered with a light film of brown dust."[23]

Four months later, still staggering under the worst drought anyone could remember in Southern Africa, Mozambique was unexpectedly hit by a devastating hurricane. Sweeping violently across the Mozambique channel from Madagascar, it destroyed thousands of cattle, swine and poultry and wiped out almost all existing horticulture in Maputo Province. Hundreds of people lost their lives.

On top of the natural calamities, man-made disasters also conspired to mock the enthusiasm that had greeted independence from Portugal only nine years before. In June 1975, John Saxby, once a CUSO Zambia volunteer, and John Saul, a former lecturer at the University of Dar es Salaam, both tireless supporters of FRELIMO, stood proudly with other official guests of the new government as the Portuguese flag was lowered in Lourenco Marques for the last time. They alone represented Canada; the Canadian Government, so tardy in its appreciation of the Portuguese eclipse, had not been invited.

But the jubilation in which they participated gave way to shock and dismay. Nine out of every ten Portuguese residents left Mozambique, taking with them their assets and skills; because Africans had been virtually excluded from schools and universities, there were now only six doctors left to care for the entire population of ten million people. All Portuguese plantations collapsed, industry faltered, and the infrastructure deteriorated. The new government's ambitious plans outstripped both its own ability and the willingness of foreign donors to assist. Western nations, wary of the government's outspoken Marxism-Leninism, hung back. Eastern European nations moved into the breach, but much of their assistance proved inadequate or inappropriate. Huge communal farms, fashioned out of abandoned Portuguese estates, became barren testaments to the limitations of high technology and mechanized agriculture. Rusting Bulgarian tractors and threshers dotted the fields where they had stopped like unwound clocks.

FRELIMO, once the victorious guerilla army and now occupying the seat of government, was itself faced with a guerilla threat from the South African backed MNR — the Movement for National Resistance. By 1984, the MNR either controlled or threatened vast stretches of the national highway and railway network; again, Mozambique, was a nation of enclaves, fighting for survival. Once the proud standard-bearer of Southern African liberation, FRELIMO now courted aid and economic investment from the West, sought greater economic integration with its African neighbours, and formalized an accommodation with its racist enemy in the south. Largely ignored by aid-giving countries, tormented by South Africa and scourged by nature, poverty-ridden Mozambique seemed the most unhappy of nations. Looking for positive signs was not unlike trying to see through the haze that obscured the Limpopo River that year.

CUSO was there from the beginning, as it had been in Nigeria, newly independent Bangladesh, and a dozen other countries. An agreement had been signed with the new government in 1977, making CUSO one of the first foreign voluntary agencies to begin working in Mozambique. A few months later, the volunteers arrived: Dr. Stephen Helliar; nurse's aide Mary Healy; teacher Ona Stonkus, and geologist Guy Masson. Because the need for technical assistance was so great, more volunteers followed the appointment of a Field Staff Officer in 1980: Don Kossick organized cooperatives for the production of badly needed pit latrines in the barrios of Maputo; Linda Simard established an orphanage outside the capital on the road to Swaziland; and they were joined by dozens of agriculturalists, communications technicians, architects, electrical engineers, computer scientists, literacy trainers and teachers.

For several years, the program was a joint CUSO-SUCO operation, with equal numbers of English and French-speaking volunteers. To avoid the linguistic problems afflicting French-English communication in Canada, the 'cooperantes' conducted their work and their meetings entirely in Portuguese. All suffered the hardships caused by shortfalls in project supplies, food shortages, restrictions imposed by the guerilla war, and dramatic changes in government policy; but many, convinced of the value of their contribution, would stay for a third and fourth year.

There is a tendency among development workers to want fast results. It is a human tendency, but among aid agencies it is accelerated and compressed into two-year packages, the average length of an overseas assignment. Political, social and technological revolutions, however, do not occur quickly — even in the computer era; even under optimum circumstances. Despite the natural calamities, political problems and well-publicized mistakes, great events are also taking place in Africa, and future societies are being formed. Mozambique, in its agony, was not significantly different from many of the countries in which CUSO worked; the mix of circumstances was different, but the calamity was no more devastating than the tragic circumstances of the drought-stricken Sahelian nations, of Bangladesh, or of Bolivia. What made Mozambique special was what made the others special: the indomitable human will to survive, to grow, to make life better for the children. This, along with the pure, unalloyed hard work of Mozambicans in the hot African sun, was what gave CUSO volunteers the strength to stay, and to make their own contribution, no matter how small it may sometimes have seemed.

Chapter 17

Zimbabwe: "The Happiest Africans in the World"

> If there is no struggle, there is no progress. Those who profess to
> favour freedom and yet deprecate agitation, are men who want
> crops without ploughing up the ground. They want the ocean
> without the awful roar of its waters.
>
> — Frederick Douglass

I an Smith, who laboured fourteen years as Prime Minister of Rhodesia,
must have grown to regret his oft-quoted remark: "Our Africans are
the happiest Africans in the world."[1] It was as though he were discussing
contented cows and it was palpably untrue, even to the most casual visitor.
African grievances were real, and they were rooted in an unhappy relationship with whites that stretched back three-quarters of a century.

In the summer of 1962, Duncan Edmonds spent six weeks in the
country — then the colony of Southern Rhodesia — and investigated
possibilities for a CUSO program. It was a tense period; the old Federation
of Rhodesia and Nyasaland was foundering on the rocks of white intransigence in the south, and on the demand for independence and black
majority rule in Nyasaland and Northern Rhodesia. Edmonds was received
cordially in Salisbury, and spoke of the "fine human beings," he had

met, "both black and white working to achieve a non-racial society . . . (but) it is a very open question whether or not their dream will be achieved."[2] By 1964, when the first volunteers were ready to depart for East, Central and Southern Africa, the Rhodesian situation was already out of control, and it would.be many years before CUSO would be welcomed back to Salisbury.

White settlement in Rhodesia was a relatively recent phenomenon. Apart from a very few explorers, travellers and missionaries, the five hundred miles of territory between the Zambesi and the Limpopo Rivers had been largely ignored by the colonial powers until the Berlin Conference of 1884. The ensuing scramble for occupation and consolidation propelled the troops and police of Cecil Rhodes' South Africa Company into Mashonaland in 1890 and Matabeleland in 1893. The Africans viewed the arrival of the military, and the gold prospectors who followed, as a curiosity, not realizing that to the British, the exchanges of gifts, signatures and pleasantries, signified their right to stay and take control of the land. Too late, the Africans reacted, and their 1896 uprising was crushed under the full force of Imperial righteousness and its modern weaponry. From then on, Rhodesia was British. Fifteen million acres of prime agricultural land were expropriated immediately and the inhabitants evicted; by 1898, 38% of the Matabele people had been forced into reserves where traditional life simply died out.[3] In 1961, one-third of Southern Rhodesia was owned by whites, then accounting for approximately 5% of the population, and land had become the single most burning African grievance. Barely 8,000 European farmers controlled most of the best agricultural property, cultivating only 3.5% of it, compared with 10.4% under cultivation in the less arable African lands which had to support far larger populations.[4] Overworked and undernourished, the African lands declined in productivity and some parts of the country came to resemble a dustbowl.

For whites, however, Rhodesia was truly a land of opportunity; the soil was fertile, education and health services were good, the sun shone and things worked. What had been a difficult life for the early settlers gradually improved between the wars, and as investment increased, so did immigration. Between 1941 and 1951, the white population nearly doubled to 135,000, and it reached a quarter of a million in 1961. By that time, one white family in five living in Salisbury had a swimming pool, and everyone could afford African servants.[5] It was a paradise for those emigrating from the drabness and the bleak prospects of post-war Britain.

But for Africans, it was different. Access to education, health care and other forms of social welfare were severely limited. While the government could boast in 1971 that it was spending more in absolute terms to educate blacks than whites, the actual per capita expenditure for whites was sixteen times higher than for blacks. Fewer than thirty thousand Africans out of a population of almost five million completed primary school in 1960, and less than seven thousand gained access to secondary schools.[6] By 1972, only one African child out of 500 completed secondary school.[7]

African wages during the mid-1970s averaged £22 per month in urban areas, half of what was judged to be the poverty line in Rhodesia at the time,[8] and in 1976, there was one government hospital bed for every 1,261 Africans, compared with one for every 255 whites.[9]

The well-organized, all-pervading discrimination touched and tainted every facet of life, confronting Africans with humiliation and dead ends at every turn. It was as though a small group of people, as many as live in Iceland, had taken control of a country the size of East and West Germany combined, banning five million of the original inhabitants to poor farm land, or to urban slums from which they might commute to jobs paying half of what it cost to live a decent life. Contradicting all the logic that modern history could offer, Ian Smith proclaimed that he did not foresee majority rule within a thousand years.

The nationalist movement began peacefully in Rhodesia at the end of the 1950s. The African National Council was formed in 1957, with Joshua Nkomo as its President, but its initial optimistic zeal was dashed within two years when it was banned and a national state of emergency declared. In 1961, The Zimbabwean African People's Union (ZAPU) took its place, again with Nkomo at the helm; a year later, it too was banned. By now, many of the nationalists were going abroad for organizational training, for studies and in search of financial assistance. Robert Mugabe taught in Ghana after it became independent in 1957; in 1963, he persuaded Ghananian President Kwame Nkrumah to provide military training for fifty men who would eventually return to Rhodesia to take up the armed struggle that now seemed inevitable. That year, too, there was a falling out among the ZAPU leadership, and a breakaway faction — the Zimbabwe African National Union (ZANU) was formed.

Ian Smith made his famous Unilateral Declaration of Rhodesian Independence in November, 1965, and despite international economic sanctions, enormous external political pressure and the apparent growth of the liberation movements, he was not seriously challenged for almost a decade. Canada followed the British lead by closing its trade mission in Salisbury and applying sanctions against what had been, in any case, minimal commercial activity. But these measures accomplished little. The breakaway regime received overt assistance from South Africa and Portugal, and the many foreign conglomerates holding Rhodesian interests violated the sanctions covertly. The Unilateral Declaration fostered greater economic self-reliance. Even the bravado of the liberation movements had to be largely discounted; despite a few attacks on isolated farms and outposts, no whites died as a result of guerilla activity between 1967 and 1972.[10] There were, in fact, probably more casualties within the liberation movements from internal power struggles than were inflicted on them by Rhodesian security forces. Even during 1979, the worst year in the war, statistics did not suggest a major military debacle: seventy white civilians — mostly farmers and their families — were killed, along with 146 members of the security forces. The Rhodesian estimate of guerilla deaths that year was put at 4,542,[11] not including casualties in cross-border raids into Mozambique and Zambia.

Such statistics, however, did not tell the whole story. Although the guerillas were too weak to fight the Rhodesian forces in conventional battle, their hit-and-run tactics and surprise attacks terrorized the population and kept the government increasingly preoccupied and off balance. Guerilla activity was geographically widespread; attacks included using ground-to-air missiles on civilian aircraft. The sparse white population was always on edge and a large army had to be maintained, with every able-bodied white male required to serve in the reserve forces. The government placed ever more draconian controls on the black population; in an imitation of British policy in Malaya, it created a series of "protected villages" into which Africans were herded to prevent them from supporting guerilla bands. By 1974, 70,000 people had been forcibly moved into thirty-six protected villages, from which they had to walk long distances daily, to their farm plots. Four years later, there were 580,000 people crowded into 200 of these depressing encampments, the 'protected' population having long since lost whatever confidence it may have had in the Smith regime.

The independence of the Portuguese colonies in 1975 added new international pressure to the growing military threat. South Africa, reacting to the Cuban presence in Angola, decided that a moderate black regime in Salisbury was preferable to the radical, Soviet-backed alternative. The economic sanctions began to hurt when the former Portuguese colony, Mozambique, cut off Rhodesian access to the sea; and even more when South Africa throttled supply lines from the south. There were many months of talks, meetings, and shuttles between London, Washington, Salisbury and Pretoria. Even Henry Kissinger became involved, flying to Pretoria to inflict a private diatribe on the feckless Ian Smith, who was finally abandoned to reality by kith, kin and even those whose political outlook he had long admired.

Like their counterparts in the Portuguese colonies, few of the nationalist groups in British Africa began as liberation movements. Caught up in the tide of African independence, they talked at first of liberty, justice and human dignity, in a context of reform and evolution. By the mid-1960s, however, when it had become abundantly clear that the white south would not be dislodged by appeals to justice and democracy, a more revolutionary cry began to ring through the movements, striking fear into the heart of Western officialdom. In the Portuguese colonies, in ZANU and ZAPU, and later in the Namibian and South African movements, the idea of reform was gradually abandoned in favour of armed struggle.

Ironically, guerilla warfare was first successfully practised in modern times by Boers fighting the British Empire on the South African veldt; Mao Tse Tung later put the strategy into the context of class struggle:

> When the Red Army fights, it fights not merely for the sake of
> fighting, but to agitate the masses, to organize them, to arm them
> and to help them establish revolutionary political power; apart
> from such objectives, fighting loses its meaning and the Red
> Army its reason for existence.[12]

There is a clattering echo of the same theme in the ZANU statement appointing Robert Mugabe to the party leadership in 1975:

> The principle objective of our revolution is the seizure of power by means of destruction of the racist political-military machine and its replacement by the people in arms in order to change the existing economic and social order . . . Armed revolutionary struggle constitutes the fundamental and principle form of our revolution . . . guerilla warfare as a genuine expression of the peoples' armed struggle is the most adequate form of waging and developing revolutionary warfare.[13]

This sort of rhetoric was perhaps inevitable, given that the only sources of training and supplies for the liberation movements were China, the Soviet Union and Cuba, countries which must have rejoiced at the western investment in Rhodesia, the timid calls for moderation and the toothless sanctions. "We appealed to the Western nations before we even knew the way to Havana, before we even knew the way to Moscow, to Peking, to Prague," said a ZAPU official during a visit to Canada. "We have been appealing to the Western nations and we were rebuffed. The socialist countries are prepared, and were prepared, to give us weaponry, educational grants and material assistance....were we supposed to fold our arms and get exterminated by not getting arms from Cuba?"[14] And so, by the time Henry Kissinger realized that someone had to give Ian Smith hell, it was too late to alter the ideological balance or to ignore what David Caute called, "the nightmarish purity of Mugabe's Marxist invective."

It is hardly surprising that the ideological question would create problems for CUSO. In one of the more scurrilous attacks, long after majority rule in Zimbabwe, Paul Fromm, Research Director of a small right-wing lobby group, stated baldly that "CUSO is part of the terrorist support network," referring particularly to the relationship with liberation movements.[15] CUSO's Executive Director, Chris Bryant, replied that there were only three choices: "We can support the status quo, the forces for change, or we can do nothing." Referring particularly to South Africa, he said:

"Like many others, we find that apartheid is impossible to support. We believe that to do nothing is to condone apartheid, and we find that is unacceptable too. We are left with no choices — we must work where we can to dismantle apartheid . . . When change comes, the West — by aligning itself with the racist regime — seems likely to reap the very result it does not want: a socialist regime."[16]

For more than twelve years, this was the underlying principle behind CUSO's support for the liberation movements; it was an ethical question reflecting the liberal and humanitarian values at the foundation of Canadian society and Western democracy. The principle was sorely tested over the years: by a Canadian government that tacitly supported most of the white regimes in Southern Africa; by a right-wing lobby that seemed to prefer a sub-continent in flames to any political or racial concession, and by the strange bedfellows under the many blankets of the Southern African support community in Canada.

For example, the Toronto Committee for the Liberation of Southern Africa, (TCLSAC) was often a source of political embarrassment. Founded in 1972 by returned CUSO volunteers and others, TCLSAC raised money for humanitarian assistance to the liberation movements and helped CUSO to establish a program in newly independent Mozambique; at the same time, it saw 'liberation' in more generic terms than might be contained in notions of independence, majority rule and an end to apartheid. John Saul, indefatigable orator, writer, CUSO RV and key TCLSAC organizer, worked both sides of the winding ideological street, condemning liberalism but praising the liberal church and NGO groups which funded and vocalized the liberation issue in Canada. In a speech on Canadian bank loans, Saul spoke highly of groups like CUSO which had, in their moderate and reformist manner, pressured the Canadian government and chartered banks to alter their lending policies on South Africa. On the other hand, he eagerly belittled Canada's "unrepentantly capitalist system . . . our political (and uncritical) encapsulation within the 'western alliance' under the thumb of the United States . . . our cultural imprisonment within the ideological framework of modern liberalism . . . (the) imperial dictate, capitalist rationality and bourgeois dominance which shape, in the last analysis, our South Africa policy."[17]

He sounded a shrill theme which reverberated through TCLSAC papers and booklets. *Words and Deeds*, published by TCLSAC in 1976, dealt with the inconsistency of Canadian policy towards Southern Africa. It concluded that the timorous official attitude towards Southern Africa, the inconsistencies and hypocrisies, were endemic to the system:

> There are serious questions here for the Canadian left. Clearly we must ask what methods of ideological work will enable us to present such realities in terms immediately accessible to ordinary Canadians. This means in the first instance, cutting through the slogans of official liberalism, but it should now be apparent that there is an even deeper challenge here — the simultaneous necessity of undermining the very liberal culture which gives these slogans such acceptability as they have".[18]

Undermining the "very liberal culture" of Canada may also have held some attraction for CUSO's antagonists on the far right; it was never central, however, to CUSO's own thinking on Southern Africa. Between the two political extremes, there was a body of opinion which thought, or at least hoped, that the new government leaders in Mozambique, Angola and Zimbabwe might, through their protracted struggles, have developed the capacity for a broad-based approach to development, rather than the elitism of Africa's first two disappointing decades of independence. These latter-day Fabians formed the consensus within most NGOs and church groups. For most Canadian supporters of the liberation movement, the question of Southern Africa was a question of ethical and moral principles, not political and ideological issues; it was the simple injustice of racism, institutionalized by white minority regimes, that sustained their effort.

Despite its concern about Southern Africa, CUSO's financial contributions to the liberation movements were always small and far outweighed by the administrative time it took to ensure adequate monitoring and reporting. In 1983-84, only one fifth of one percent of CUSO's overall budget ($32,000) was allocated for humanitarian support to liberation movements. It had occasionally been higher during some of the bleakest times before Zimbabwean independence. In 1979, there were 60,000 Zimbabwean refugees in Zambia, most under the care of ZAPU. Their living conditions were deplorable, and the Zambian government, already stretched beyond its own economic limits, could provide very little support. In 1978, CUSO united with the Canadian save the Children Fund to build dormitories and other facilities for 200 children and expectant mothers at Victory Camp near Lusaka. A day care centre, a creche, a kindergarten and a pre-school facility were added when the child population soared to 1,300 within a year.

In another project, CUSO and the United Church of Canada joined with German, American and British agencies to construct school buildings at two camps with a combined student population of 20,000. School books were translated and printed in the Shona and Ndebele languages. Oxfam, SUCO and a Belgian organization cooperated to establish an agricultural complex at Freedom Camp. $14,719 was spent on chickens and pigs to establish the stock for a farm which would eventually help to feed 11,000 girls at Victory Camp, and emergency food supplies were purchased for a small ZANU refugee camp when World Food Program shipments temporarily ran out.

Rhodesian commando raids posed a constant threat to the refugee camps. In 1977, jets and troops attacked a complex of ZANU camps near Chimoio, eighty kilometres inside the Mozambique border, killing 1,200 Zimbabweans in the space of a few minutes. Many of them were women and children who had been strafed, bombed, burned or shot at point-blank range. In October 1978, Rhodesian forces attacked three of the five ZAPU camps in Zambia, killing 300 young men and women; further raids, including attacks on targets in the Zambian capital, were commonplace throughout 1979. The CUSO office in Lusaka, never far from the threat of physical danger itself, refinanced some of the original projects after clinics and school buildings were flattened in the Rhodesian raids.

In the summer of 1979, CUSO, two other NGOs and the United and Anglican Churches jointly funded a visit to Canada by two representatives of the Patriotic Front — the umbrella organization for ZANU and ZAPU. The two men, Saul Ndlovu and Dr. Dzingai Mutumbuka, travelled across Canada and spoke in fifteen towns and cities across the country over a four week period; they tried to explain what was happening in Rhodesia and what they hoped to achieve, and they solicited donations for the Canadian NGOs that were assisting the refugees. The trip was a moderate success; the two men were widely quoted in the press and were, on the whole, treated fairly themselves. The story was different for CUSO however. The *Winnipeg Free Press* attacked CUSO for spending "$2,500 to send two terrorist spokesmen on a tour of Canada,"[19] and torrents of clippings, soggy with vitriol, piled up in the Ottawa office. The media for the most part ignored the other NGO and church participation and, once they had their claws extended, ignored the issues the two men had come to discuss. They also ignored the fact that all NGOs regularly brought project holders to Canada to meet with donors, Board members and government officials, and that tours by Third World speakers were commonplace. If anything, the need for openness and communication about the liberation movements was even more important than for conventional projects. But Rhodesia was somehow different: Ndlovu, a music teacher, botanist and former journalist; Mutumbuka with his three British science degrees — to most editors they were nothing but terrorists.

By 1978, a dim light had finally blinked on in the bunker of the Rhodesian mind; the Smith Government, in a gesture to the inevitable, arranged an "internal settlement" on majority rule. The 1979 election, boycotted by ZANU and ZAPU and based on electoral rolls derived from a ten-year-old census, returned Bishop Abel Muzorewa as the new Prime Minister of "Zimbabwe-Rhodesia"; as guardian of a new constitution which entrenched and preserved almost all white power and privilege. It was far too little, and it was far too late. The guerilla wars escalated, in a furious reaction to the sham that had been perpetrated, and diplomatic activity increased proportionately.

The Commonwealth Heads of Government Meeting in Lusaka that summer was the scene of fierce diplomatic activity, during which CUSO hoped to bring influence to bear on the official Canadian delegation as well as the Canadian media. Historically, Canada played a valuable conciliatory role at Commonwealth meetings; this time, however, there was a rookie delegation: Prime Minister Joe Clark, elected only a few weeks earlier; External Affairs Minister Flora MacDonald; Senator Martial Asselin, in the new portfolio of Minister of State for CIDA; Doug Roche, Chairman of the Parliamentary Standing Committee on International Affairs and Defence; and a coterie of nervous government officials, uncertain about the new Canadian leadership. Among them was Michel Dupuy,

President of CIDA, a man who owed his job to the previous Liberal government and whose name was reportedly high on the Tory hit list. Close behind the neophyte delegation was a group of Canadian reporters. Some were seasoned, but most had never been to Africa in their lives; all would now be faced with one of the most complex news events of the decade.

For CUSO, it was a fortuitous opportunity to put Zimbabwe clearly before the Canadian public. Never before had there been access to so many Canadian journalists, top officials and politicians — and in such proximity to the issue. Weeks in advance, Zambia FSO Dave Beer had offered the Canadian High Commission CUSO assistance in organizing an itinerary for the visitors. He had assembled a package of information on Zambia, including projects which had received Canadian NGO support; to it, he added the names and addresses of all the locally-based liberation movements, with descriptions of CUSO-supported projects — the ZAPU Freedom Camp farm north of Lusaka, and Victory Camp, the refugee settlement to the west for women and girls.

Beer wrote to journalists he knew in Canada, saying that he was attempting to organize background meetings and perhaps a small group interview with Joshua Nkomo, the President of ZAPU. "I know that he and his colleagues want to present a strong and constructive position to the new Canadian Prime Minister," Beer wrote, "and to the Canadian media — at least to those who will listen . . . I am quite worried that the Canadian press corps will contain more people who do not have a clue about our part of the world, and we need to have some good, constructive reporting on the situation here."[20]

In Ottawa, Doug Roche asked CUSO for a pre-departure briefing and said that he would like to visit the refugee camps; he stressed the importance of CUSO interaction with the official delegation as a chance for the organization to regain credibility in the wake of its management debacles earlier in the year.[21] Back in Zambia, Beer began to make arrangements with ZAPU for the anticipated camp visits; permission was essential, as most of the camps were heavily guarded after the Rhodesian Air Force attacks.

At first, things went even better than planned. Steve Wadhams of the CBC cabled Beer to ask about an interview with Nkomo; Doug Roche made contact almost as soon as he arrived, and other reporters began to call for contacts, ideas and meetings. Senator Asselin officiated at a CUSO function, ceremoniously handing over the keys to a new vehicle designated for a local project group. Beer had been unable to arrange an appointment with Michel Dupuy, so he simply outwaited the CIDA President and accosted him in the lobby of the Ridgeway Hotel for a frank discussion about CUSO's association with the liberation movements; he explained that CUSO support was in the form of humanitarian assistance for refugees, mostly women and children, and that payments were monitored to avoid their being siphoned off for military use. Beer wanted CUSO's work with the movements clearly understood, so that it could be maintained and perhaps even increased.

He was delighted when Flora MacDonald unexpectedly altered her plans and spent a busy afternoon with the CUSO people on the day before her departure. While most of the Canadian journalists were relaxing at a poolside lunch hosted by the Canadian High Commissioner, the Minister of External Affairs drove west to Victory Camp, where she inspected a nursery project being funded by CUSO and Cansave. She was welcomed in song by hundreds of girls, and, touched by the warmth and spontaneity of their greeting, she told them that if any of them ever came to Canada to study, they should come to see her. "Just ask for Flora," she said.

But CUSO's euphoria over her visit soon turned sour. Much of the media coverage was shallow, concentrating on the Canadian delegation, whose performance was lacklustre; actually, the real initiative at the conference had passed quickly and decisively to Australia. Norman Webster's article for the *Globe and Mail* was entitled: "To CUSO, Guerillas are not Terrorists." Much of his story was as emotive as the headline. "Many Canadians" he wrote, "think all members of the Patriotic Front are terrorists. Dave Beer, from Newmarket, has them over for dinner. He also hands over lashings of Canadian government money to them."

Although more or less factual, the article gave the misleading impression that CUSO was writing blank cheques on the public purse for a dangerous terrorist army. "There is no doubt we've made a political decision," Mr. Beer says. "We are supporting movements that are waging wars in Zimbabwe, Namibia and South Africa . . . my own personal view, having lived here for more than ten years, is that the rebel is (Ian) Smith, not the Patriotic Front. The terrorists are the (Rhodesian) security forces, not the Freedom Fighters."[22]

Four days later, the *Globe* ran a stinging editorial attack on CUSO, demanding to know on whose authority Beer was "scattering substantial sums of public money in highly partisan, extremely dubious ways." The newspaper reminded readers that CUSO had come close to being cut off by CIDA earlier in the year and had, as a result, agreed to ensure that "its budget would not continue to be splashed around on a succession of chic or strenuously partisan causes. And now this. Has the message not registered with CUSO? External Affairs Minister Flora MacDonald should make certain that the message is repeated. Loudly, clearly and soon."[23]

At the same time, the *Toronto Sun* was making a firestorm out of dispatches from its reporter in Lusaka, Robert MacDonald. "Canadian-funded 'farm' Off Limits," bawled the headlines. The story centered on Doug Roche who, the report stated, had been unable to visit a CUSO funded, Patriotic Front 'farm'. "Roche said CUSO Zambia Director David Beer told him he could not get permission to visit the operation, located at Chikumbi, north of Lusaka.

"It makes you wonder what it really is — if its a farm, you would wonder why a visit is prohibited, commented Roche."

"The prohibition threw more suspicion on the real role of the 'farm', especially since the place was attacked by Zimbabwe-Rhodesia fighter planes on June 27th with the claim that it was a guerilla camp for Joshua Nkomo's Patriotic Front forces."[24]

The next day the *Sun* ran an editorial calling CUSO a "frightful body which attracts zealots and ideologues and armchair revolutionaries . . . The wrath of the Canadian government should fall on CUSO . . . and especially on the arrogant young zealot who heads CUSO in Zambia and boasts that aid to the Patriotic Front is a 'political decision . . . ' Clark should put the kibosh on the whole CUSO-SUCO program and start over."[25] Beside the editorial was a cartoon in which a well-armed, barefoot Nkomo played a ukelele while Joe Clark danced to his tune: "Old Nkomo had a farm, CIDA and CUSO; with a bang bang here, and a boom boom there, here a bang, there a boom, everywhere a bang, bang."

In Ottawa there was unmitigated panic at CIDA, as junior officials, blasted from above, telephoned CUSO to find out what had gone wrong. Negotiations on the CIDA grant, already four months overdue, came to an abrupt standstill, and the conning tower at 151 Slater Street was battened down in anticipation of a long slide to the bottom.

Sharon Capeling, now CUSO's Director of Public Affairs, was finally able to reach Dave Beer in Lusaka by telephone.

"Did you take Roche to the Camp?" she demanded across the static.

"Of course I did," Beer responded.

"Did *you* go with him? Did he actually go?"

"Yes, I'm telling you he went," Beer said, confused by the suspicion and the urgency.

"Are you *absolutely* sure?" Capeling demanded once again.

"Absolutely," Beer replied, incredulous at the line of questioning.

The *Sun* kept its diatribe going for another two weeks, reporting that Michel Dupuy planned to mount an investigation into the secrecy at Freedom Camp. The same story was repeated a week later, reporter MacDonald again attacking the 'farm'; "Beer claimed it was a . . . . farm growing food for refugees. But Roche was turned down and left justifiably suspicious."[26]

By now, the story had been picked up by the wire services, and anti-CUSO articles and editorials appeared across the country. Doug Roche, the one man who might have dispelled the gloom at CUSO and corrected the *Sun* story, was incommunicado — en route somewhere between East Africa and Sri Lanka.

Dave Beer, stung by the criticism and by the jeopardy in which it had placed CUSO, wrote querulous, plaintive letters to the *Globe and Mail*'s Norman Webster, to whom he had talked at great length in Zambia; and to Michel Dupuy, whom he had tried to inform about the purpose and method of CUSO's work with the liberation movements. Dupuy never replied, but Webster did — several months later. "On re-reading," he wrote, "I regret using the word 'lashings' in the opening paragraph; it does seem loaded. Aside from that, I think the story is fair and accurate . . . Obviously some people in Canada — and certainly the editorial writers — don't agree with what you are doing. It would have been naive on both your and my part to think they all would, and that there would be no reaction."[27]

When Doug Roche finally returned to Canada at the end of August, he wrote a long letter to Michel Dupuy, saying that he had indeed visited the farm. "I was impressed," he said, "with the agricultural operation, accomplished with minimal resources, and in the face of bombings by the Rhodesian military. I satisfied myself that the ZAPU farm is a humanitarian operation, with the food destined for refugee camps.'' He said that this project and others were deserving of CIDA support, and he went on to commend Dave Beer, whom he said, ''represents all that is best in the Canadian aid effort.''[28]

The *Sun*'s destructive falsehood, however, was never corrected; it was a bitter and sobering experience, one that would make other CUSO field staff wary of itinerant reporters in search of 'the truth'.

By October, 1979, the issue that had given rise to all the passion and fury was reaching its climax. Talks on the Rhodesian crisis were under way at Lancaster House in London; negotiations which, for the first time, involved all parties and factions. By December, it was all over; direct British rule was reassumed under the Governorship of Lord Soames. Such were the many ironies of the Rhodesian tragedy that, two decades after the 'winds of change' had blown across the African continent, an African Prime Minister handed power to a Governor representing the British crown. Robert Mugabe, Joshua Nkomo and the other leaders returned, and under the watchful eyes of Commonwealth observers, London bobbies and hordes of international journalists, a new election was held in March, 1980. ZANU, led by Robert Mugabe, won sixty-three percent of the popular vote and fifty-seven seats in the new Zimbabwean Parliament. Joshua Nkomo's ZAPU won twenty seats, and Bishop Muzorewa only three.

Years before, in 1965, John and Claudia Gishler had gone to Kenya as CUSO teachers, only eighteen months after the whites of that country had been forced to cross the rubicon of independence. Thousands had sold everything and fled, ''convinced that Kenya would descend into chaos at 12:01 on December 12, 1963,'' John Gishler wrote. ''Surprisingly, when the Union Jack came down and the red, green and black Kenyan flag was run up at midnight, the ground did not open up and swallow all the Europeans. President Kenyatta did not order them to leave; instead, he called a meeting of the European farmers and assured them personally that Kenya needed them — if they would support the new government.''[29]

Something similar happened in Zimbabwe the day after the elections. 'Comrade' Robert Mugabe, the dreaded Communist 'terr' — now discovered to have six university degrees — appeared on television screens across the nation. "We will ensure that there is a place for everyone in this country," he said. "We want to ensure a sense of security for both the winners and the losers."[30] He spoke of international non-alignment; he reassured farmers that their land would not be nationalized, and he guaranteed the pensions of civil servants. "Let us forgive and forget," he said. "Let us join hands in a new amity."

On April 16, less than a month after Zimbabwe's elections, Dave Beer set out on the journey from Lusaka to Salisbury. It was only a six-hour drive, but for years it had seemed infinitely further away — a world apart. His last visit had been fifteen years before, and now everything seemed to have changed. Abandoned farms and villages, burnt houses, and derelict fields lined much of the journey, but in Salisbury, lying pristine in the African sun — its skyscrapers and neon signs testament to the success of corporate sanction-busting — white soldiers and police directed the traffic jams created by incoming independence guests, controlling the rush-hour exodus of blacks heading for crowded southern townships and whites hurrying back to the tidy white suburbs of Borrowdale, Avondale and Mount Pleasant.

The new government had invited CUSO to attend the independence ceremonies as an official guest, and Beer, who had worked for so long in the region, was CUSO's chosen representative. It was an emotional event for him, he remembered being in the Lusaka stadium for Zambian independence sixteen years before; now, in Salisbury, the Rhodesian forces, with their medals, plumage and brightly-coloured dress uniforms, marched smartly into the stadium to the polite applause of thousands of spectators, guests and assembled heads of state. But the crowd showed where its heart lay when three or four units of ex-guerillas entered. "The place went nuts," Beer said. The people's heros wore plain green or grey uniforms and simple berets, drab in comparison to what had gone before, but as Beer recalled it, "The thing that got me was that the lights on them only caught one place, and that was the Freedom Medal that each of them wore . . . it was a very moving thing."[31]

CUSO had been placed in the category of "solidarity group," and Beer received his credentials only after some confusion, finding himself placed among "the Polish this and the Nicaraguan that." To ensure access to all events, he had also sought accreditation as a journalist, representing the Canadian University Service and its prestigious international publication, '*Forum*'. Harried white officials, bewildered by the array of strange and unlikely delegations swarming over their once inviolate stronghold, dutifully stamped all papers proferred by outstretched hands.

CUSO had also been invited to attend the Prime Minister's first formal function, an independence luncheon at Government House. "There was a wonderful big coloured tent, and people were going through a short line where I met Mugabe and some others," Beer said. "I had a moment to say how pleased CUSO was to be represented here . . . and then I walked out onto this empty lawn where people had drifted towards other tents. You were very much alone as only one person from each of the national delegations was invited . . . and there I was in a borrowed suit."

"I knew some of the cabinet ministers and I was chatting with them . . . when of all things I see a black limousine with a Canadian flag. Out gets little Mark MacGuigan, the Minister for Extenal Affairs, and he goes through the line, and there he was, just like me, standing alone on this expanse of grass. He looked so lost as he walked across the grass that I thought I had better go and catch him. We talked for maybe twenty minutes and then he asked if I could help him by pointing out some people; so I introduced him to the Foreign Minister of Zambia and a couple of new Zimbabwean cabinet ministers . . . "

It was a rare irony for Beer, who along with CUSO had been so vilified in the Canadian press only months before for "sloppy, puerile" support for terrorism. He had to restrain himself from pointing out that the new Minister of Education was none other than the 'terrorist', Dr. Dzingai Mutumbuka, who had barely been able to get the time of day from Canadian officialdom on his CUSO-sponsored visit to Canada exactly twelve months before.

Chuckling to himself, Beer moved on to the hors d'oeuvres. As he reached for the shrimps, "a woman's hand came forward at the same time. It was Indira Gandhi." "Holy Jesus!" Beer said. "You had to pinch yourself."

"And then Mugabe gathered us around." Standing with Lord Soames, British Foreign Minister Lord Carrington, and Commonwealth Secretary General, Sonny Ramphal, the Prime Minister addressed the gathering. Beer, distracted by the august company, remembered only that Mugabe was effusive in his praise of Lord Soames. "There were all these heads of state and prime ministers, four deep, crowding in to see," he recalled. "I was squeezed in behind this beautiful Nicaraguan translator whispering into Daniel Ortega's ear . . . to my right, the enormously tall Australian Prime Minister, Malcolm Fraser; Kuanda was ten paces to the right, and there was Josh standing over a little further. It was just incredible."

POSTSCRIPT

Not long after the independence of Zimbabwe, CUSO began a program of development activities centered on the Zimbabwean Women's Bureau and the Organization of Rural Associations for Progress. An initial series of small projects gave way to a CIDA-supported fund of $500,000 that would be used to assist further rural activities between 1982 and 1986. In addition, volunteers and funds of $3.9 million over three years would be provided to assist with the development of 140 producer cooperatives for ex-combattants, in an effort to get as many as possible back to the land and productively employed. Physiotherapists and occupational therapists would also be assigned to projects for the rehabilitation of former soldiers.

It would have made a happy ending to a long and bitter story, if CUSO could have reported that all was well within the new republic, now that majority rule had been achieved. There is, to be sure, a strong tendency within NGOs towards an optimism that cannot always be supported by facts. It is somewhat understandable; the NGO, barraged by a constant diet of negative Third World media coverage and depressed by public apathy, thirsts for the big success story, and sometimes has a heart too soon made glad. The early days of independent Tanzania were a case in point: Julius Nyerere's bright, lucid vision of a cooperative African utopia excited development workers and made Tanzania the object of countless academic and journalistic pilgrimages. Within CUSO, Tanzania was talked of in reverential tones, and the volunteers assigned there in the 1960s were thought to be among the development elect, despite the country's obvious problems and shortcomings.

Zimbabwe inherited the mantle briefly in the early 1980s — the struggles had been too long, too bitter, for Zimbabwe to fail. Nevertheless, CUSO managed to take a relatively balanced position in Zimbabwe. In 1982 and through 1983, as Robert Mugabe consolidated his political position, troops of his North Korean-trained Fifth Brigade went on a violent rampage in Matabeleland, the stronghold of Joshua Nkomo's opposition ZAPU. Women and children were murdered, villages razed, and food shipments halted, while the troops sought out "dissident elements." CUSO, along with eight European, American and Australian organizations joined in a strong appeal to the Prime Minister.

"We do not contend the need for security forces in the area. However, there are reports which suggest that the forces of law and order . . . are themselves the instigators of atrocities on local people, including women and children . . . We face the dilemma of reconciling our humanitarian concerns and our commitment to newly independent Zimbabwe with the alleged violations of human rights being perpetrated by the security forces."[32]

Two weeks later, the agencies met with the Prime Minister and his security officers, and made their concerns even more clear. The discussion was strained, and it is difficult to say what effect the combined international grouping had. "It's all very well to talk of human rights and the government violating these," the Prime Minister said, a dark echo of previous regimes, "but you must appreciate what we are trying to do . . ."[33] A more detailed brief on the issues was later submitted; the government, whether in response to these appeals or on its own good intentions, did lift food restrictions and there was a brief decline in civilian complaints from Matabeleland.

The direct effect on government policy (if any), was one thing; that the intervention happened at all was quite another. It was a sign of a new and more honest maturity in CUSO's approach to the political questions, which all too often override and forestall real development efforts at the village level; it showed a willingness to recognize that development and growth would be no easier in the new Zimbabwe than anywhere else.

Chapter 18

Karl Swinimer

A lthough it recalls Hemingway and sounds challenging, climbing Mount Kilimanjaro is relatively straightforward if you follow the trail and the signs which mark the way to the summit. It is a well-trodden path, and guides are readily available for the many tourists who make the romantic pilgrimage. But for Karl Swinimer, Mount Kilimanjaro proved something of a challenge. Swinimer was posted to Tanzania in 1972 as a math teacher, and the following March, he and another volunteer set off on the four-day climb with a group of students. The problems began on the last stretch.

"We started out on the final climb to the top at night," Swinimer recalled. Climbers always started at night so that they could reach the top at sunrise, when presumably, all of Africa would lie resplendent before them. But Swinimer was not a climber, and in the thin air and the darkness, the trail was difficult. "It was extremely cold," he said, "and after five hours of climbing, I was exhausted. Some of the party had already gone down and I decided to turn back too."[1] But he was not seeing very well; his vision was blurred, and as he cut across the switch-back trail, he missed the hut where they had left their knapsacks and food, ending up far below.

It didn't take Swinimer long to realize that he'd made a very serious mistake. At first he attempted to find the trail by switching back and forth across the rocky slope. When that proved futile, he decided to find his own way down, ending up at the bottom of a valley with only his clothes and a single orange. Days passed. The Tanzanian Air Force was scrambled and helicopters raked and combed the mountainside. The CUSO office in Dar es Salaam was alerted; Ottawa was notified; the Swinimer parents in Yarmouth, Nova Scotia were informed after several days and told that the chances of finding their son alive were slim. Meanwhile, Karl had finished the orange, and was sampling the vegetation in the fastness of his private valley. He found that it did not agree with his stomach. Finally after almost two weeks, with little more than water in him, he started to climb out of the valley. It was the thirteenth day of the search, and the Tanzanian Air Force was on the point of quitting, when Swinimer was spotted perched atop a massive rock. "The search helicopter flew overhead at just the right moment," he said in his understated fashion.

The CUSO field staff were tempted to send Swinimer home, but, after a few days in hospital, he convinced them that he was well enough to continue his work, and that he would be more careful in future. They believed him.

A year later, in 1974, as his contract was coming to a close, Swinimer travelled to Dar es Salaam to inform the CUSO office that he had fallen in love and planned to marry. His fiancee was a Russian volunteer, and he though he should mention it in case there were any questions from the Russian Embassy. Not long afterwards, back at the village, Swinimer and Svetlana were married by the Justice of the Peace; the following day they flew to Dar for their honeymoon.

"For some reason," Swinimer said, again understating the case, "the Russians were suspicious. They were watching for us; four Russian cars blocked the driveway as soon as we reached the CUSO office and the Russians rushed up the stairs demanding the release of our Russian 'captive'."

The temperamental phone in the office was working that day, and soon the Tanzanian Ministry of Foreign Affairs was involved, along with a distraught First Secretary from the Canadian High Commission. After a four-hour standoff, the Russians agreed that the siege could be transferred to a downtown hotel, where Karl and Svetlana were soon closeted in a luxury suite. "We spent six days there," said Swinimer. "It was rather an interesting honeymoon. The Russians were constantly calling up and telling us that Svetlana's father was sick and her parents worried about the whole business.'' The thoughts of Swinimer's parents in Yarmouth are not recorded.

The Russians finally hit on a solution, at least one that suited the beleagured couple: why not go to the Soviet Union where a nice job would be arranged for Karl? Well, if you've been stuck at the bottom of a valley for thirteen days with nothing but an orange, you know there are worse things than a job in the Soviet Union. ''Usually it takes about three weeks to get a visa to visit the Soviet Union,'' Karl observed. Within a few hours, however, the newlyweds were airborne, bound for their new life in Moscow. Or so they thought.

Karl's job proved as elusive as a visa renewal, and a month later he was homeward bound, leaving Svetlana behind in Moscow. He settled in Ottawa, as close to the Department of External Affairs as possible, filing papers for Svetlana's emigration from the Soviet Union in August, 1974. External was not optimistic, but then External is never optimistic, and if there was one thing Karl knew, it was the virtue of patience. Karl won; on a cold January day five months later, an aircraft bearing Svetlana Swinimer at last set down on a Canadian runway.

Before he left Tanzania, Swinimer made several (successful) ascents of Kilimanjaro, perhaps to prove a point. Once he even acted as a guide for a party on the same route that had earlier eluded him. ''So I saved a bit of face,'' he said. And in the summer of 1977, he, Svetlana, and their new born son, Georgi, returned to Moscow for a holiday. ''We've had no problems since,'' said Swinimer, a tiny hint of what might be taken for wistfulness in his voice.

Chapter 19

Frank Talk in the Interregnum — South Africa

> The most peculiar thing about South Africa is that you have 28 or
> 29 million people living in the same country, and 24 or 25 million
> don't exist. They're virtually foreigners in South Africa, without
> any rights. Immigrants can come from Europe or Latin America,
> and in two years become citizens, participating in rule over people
> who have been there for generations.
>
> — Oliver Tambo

T he story of CUSO and South Africa, and of the International University Exchange Fund, may seem peripheral to CUSO's main work; but it had important implications for other CUSO activities. South Africa, itself, although negligible in terms of CUSO's programs and spending, consumed vast amounts of intellectual, emotional and political energy.

CUSO was fascinated with the largest liberation movement, the African National Congress, to the exclusion of almost all other forms of opposition to apartheid. This fell neatly into the South African government's preferred strategy: which was to demonstrate — no matter what the cost in dollars, truth or lives — that the issue was not one of apartheid, but one of righteous Christianity in a manichean struggle against bloodthirsty communist hordes.

The organization's blinkered approach severely restricted its ability to influence both Canadian public opinion and official policy on South Africa, and in the early 1980s, South Africa became the issue on which the organization was most frequently judged by its more conservative critics.

For Canadians who cherish freedom, justice and democracy, the dilemma presented by the South African situation should always have been simple. It should not have been difficult to see through the veneer of South Africa's pro-western, free-enterprise facade, nor to understand that the talk of reform and liberalization of antiquated race laws was only talk. The country flourished on foreign investment that took eager advantage of cheap labour; and its government survived by diligently maintaining a Stalinistic system of pass laws, treason trials, forced population removals, security police, espionage, intimidation and torture. All this has been carefully documented, and it has been exposed time and again by countless black South Africans. Some of them, such as Nobel laureates Albert Luthuli and Bishop Desmond Tutu, and political activist Steve Biko, have, in their pain, become known to the West. The stark horror of racist repression has also been dramatized by white writers — Alan Paton, Athol Fugard, Nadine Gordimer, Donald Woods, J. M. Coetzee. And yet, the clearer the message becomes, the more difficult the choice seems to be; for if it is accepted that the South African government is not, in fact, liberalizing; is not quickly or even gradually moving towards majority rule; and if it is assumed that the West will continue with its hands-off policies — then the only obvious alternative for black South Africans is bloody revolution and war.

Internal opposition to apartheid and its precursors has a long history. One of its strongest opponents was the young Indian lawyer, Mohandas K. Gandhi, who practised law in South Africa for twenty-one years. After years of black protest and futile appeal to the Imperial government in London, the African National Congress was founded in 1912, to help the cause of black people in the newly-independent Dominion of South Africa. For the next seventy years, the ANC was at the centre of the struggle for universal franchise and equality; during its first half-century — longer than most independence parties in Africa have existed — it was devoted to non-violent opposition. The egalitarian aims of its 1955 Freedom Charter were irreproachable; universal franchise, equal rights, return of the country's wealth to the people, free and compulsory universal education, housing, security, employment and human rights for all, equality before the law. But the killing of sixty-nine black protestors during the Sharpville and Langa anti-pass law protests of 1960 was the final straw for the ANC: with its leadership banned, imprisoned, exiled or dead, it finally turned — as had others in Africa, — to armed struggle.

Had the West been genuinely interested in reform in South Africa, there were clear opportunities for action during the critical years of the 1960s and 1970s. Investments in South Africa might have been restricted, or linked to social reform; loan and preferential trade arrangements could have been used as pressure points; sanctions might have been considered; arms embargoes more effectively implemented; conditionality attached to IMF loans. The toolshed of western diplomacy is full of such implements, and they are often brought to bear in the cultivation of relations with eastern bloc countries and the Third World.

But South Africa was deemed to be different; and the final excuse for inaction, after most others had been exhausted, was that the blacks would be the first to suffer if there were economic crackdowns. Bishop Desmond Tutu, General Secretary of the South African Council of Churches and later, Bishop of Johannesburg, acknowledged that this was probably correct, but he had two rejoinders: "A cynical one is, when did whites become so altruistic? After all, they have benefitted from black misery engendered by low wages, migratory labour etc. for so long. The less cynical is that blacks would probably be ready to accept suffering that had a goal and purpose and would therefore end, rather than continue to suffer endlessly."[1]

It is hardly surprising that the African National Congress, driven underground, and having come to equate black misery with foreign investment and capitalism, would become attractive to a broad non-racial spectrum — ranging from Africanists to Marxists. Perhaps its most controversial alliance was its accommodation with the banned South African Communist Party, one of the few political groups in the Republic with the courage and foresight to stand up, in its clandestine way, and be counted. Communist involvement in ANC strategy and policy formation, combined with the Marxist literature coming from the ANC printing presses, suited the South African government's anti-communist defence of its racial policy, it helped cast the struggle in east-west terms and made South Africa appealing to conservatives in the West. "It is a struggle of the Christian, western civilization," said Prime Minister P. W. Botha, "against the powers of darkness and Marxism, and not just a black-white struggle."[2]

The SACP had not always been in the vanguard of racial equality. In 1922, communist organizers had promoted a strike among white South African mine workers with the slogan, "workers of the world unite and fight for a white South Africa."[3] Thirty blacks died during the racial violence that ensued. But times and strategies change; in 1976, Joe Slovo, a leader of the ANC's military wing and longtime SACP member, stated that: "national liberation in its true sense, must . . . imply the expropriation of the means of production (monopolized by a bourgeoisie drawn from the white group) and the complete destruction of the state which serves them. There can be no half way house."[4]

It is still the communist and Marxist influence in the NAC that complicates what is essentially a straightforward moral question. Liberal opponents of apartheid have generally dealt with the complication in one of two ways: by remaining silent, or by pretending that it is either not true or is vastly overplayed. Nadine Gordimer describes the current period between unchallenged white supremacy and the inevitable majority rule as an interregnum. "I am silent," she says, "because in the interregnum, any criticism of the communist system is understood as a defence of the capitalist system which has brought forth . . . apartheid. The choice for blacks cannot be distanced into any kind of objectivity: they believe in the existence of the lash they feel. Nothing could be *less than better* than what they have known as the 'peace and security' of capitalism."[5]

Less honest, and therefore more advantageous to the South African government, is the liberal suspension of normal critical faculties, in order to accept the argument that liberation movements have been forced to go to Moscow or Peking or Havana for arms — rather than for ideology — simply because the West has refused to help. Hugh McCullum, Editor of the *United Church Observer*, travelled extensively in Southern Africa in 1981, and discussed questions of armed struggle and Marxism with ANC President-General, Oliver Tambo. Tambo answered, speaking not of ideology, but of the base of his support — which comes, in fact, as much from Western countries (Sweden, Holland, West Germany) as from the Soviet Union. "I wonder why they don't describe us as the 'Swedish dominated ANC'?" he asked.[6] And so McCullum wrote of the "*propaganda* that Marxism is the predominant ideology of the liberation movement leadership," not only begging the question of ideology, but fuelling the tendency to substitute it for the bigger question of what the west — governments and individuals — could and should do to end apartheid without bloodshed.

In CUSO, the same speak-no-evil tendency prevailed. Such seeming gullibility, combined with CUSO's project support for ANC-sponsored refugees in neighbouring states, and the occasional ANC publicity or 'education' project, made the organization a favourite punching bag for the pro-South African lobby in Canada.

But the International University Exchange Fund was different, and in the mid-1970s, it seemed to have found a middle ground between the scylla and the charybdis of the South African situation. The IUEF was founded in 1961 and that year helped twenty Southern African refugees with scholarship assistance. By 1972, the Geneva-based organization was supporting more than a thousand people, and by 1980, more than 2,000 African refugees and 600 Latin Americans were under its care. As well, it supported projects over the years — schools, clinics and hospitals for refugees. CUSO's involvement with the IUEF began in 1970 when two of CUSO's Zambia field staff were asked to represent the IUEF at the Organization of African Unity's first conference on refugees. A year later, the CUSO presentation to the Standing Committee on External Affairs and National defence spoke of assistance to the liberation movements in Rhodesia and the Portuguese colonies, but not South Africa (the ANC was still something of an unknown factor). The brief made recommendations on trade and sanctions against the apartheid regimes, and asked that Canada follow the lead of Norway, Denmark and Sweden, which granted a total of $485,000 to the IUEF that year. CUSO asked "that the IUEF should be considered as a particularly effective channel of Canadian aid to refugees from Southern Africa."[7]

Paul Ladouceur, a former CUSO Board Member, served on the IUEF Board of Directors. Tim Brodhead, a former CUSO staff member, moved to Geneva in 1972 to head the newly established International Agency for Cooperation in Overseas Development under the aegis of the IUEF, with which he would work closely. And following the Organization of African Unity (OAU) refugee conference, contacts between CUSO and the IUEF began to develop in Europe and Africa. The Canadian connections undoubtedly facilitated CIDA support for the IUEF; in 1972, even before the government had an official policy on support to liberation movements, a grant of $30,000 was made to the IUEF for refugee scholarships. Over the next six years, CIDA grants would total almost half a million dollars.[8]

Through the latter part of the decade, CUSO assisted the IUEF, particularly in Zambia — scouting, monitoring and evaluating projects, and assigning volunteers to staff the Lusaka office. As the IUEF grew, so did support from Scandinavian governments, Holland, Britain and Canada. As a 1980 report stated, donor governments "channeled funds through the IUEF for good practical reasons, but also with political intent — to participate, even when this could not be done directly for one reason or another, in struggles for liberation from different forms of oppression in different parts of the world. The aim has always been that through the IUEF, a contribution — sometimes indirect — could be made to the liberation movements."[9]

But the IUEF was dealing with much more than liberation movements. To the annoyance of the ANC, it also supported the other OAU-recognized liberation movement, the Pan African Congress (PAC). More importantly, it began in the early 1970s to provide direct assistance to opposition groups within South Africa itself. The National Union of South African Students (NUSAS) was a pro-black grouping of white, English-speaking students. Two black groups became progenitors of what would soon emerge as the Black Consciousness Movement — the South African Students Organization and the Black People's Convention. And despite growing efforts within South Africa to discredit such movements, a number of prominent black leaders began to emerge, the most vocal of whom was Steve Biko, a medical student who occasionally wrote under the pseudonym, Frank Talk. By the mid-1970s, the ANC had almost totally eclipsed the PAC, but it did not have a broadly-based, popular organization within South Africa. Hit-and-run raids and the occasional bombing were becoming more frequent, but real internal opposition was being generated by the Black Consciousness Movement and leaders like Steve Biko.

The IUEF's support for the BCM was regarded with suspicion by the ANC, which saw the BCM's policy of non-violence as a step backward from the armed struggle that most liberation movements now avowed; furthermore, the BCM was not doctrinaire. In a 1977 interview, Steve Biko explained that Black Consciousness was the cultural and political revival of an oppressed people. He spoke of the difficulty blacks had in seeing their identity in terms other than those defined by whites; and he was straightforward in saying that western investment in South Africa was a key element in the care and feeding of apartheid.

> Many persons within the liberation struggles look upon the Marx-
> ist analysis of oppression as the proper diagnosis of their situation.
> And on top of this, there is the overwhelming evidence of Ameri-
> ca's involvement in the Third World for the sake of its own eco-
> nomic self-interest. Russia has no investments to protect in
> Johannesburg. American does....But in being so critical of the
> economic self-interest in the Third World on the part of American
> capitalism, I at the same time have no illusions about Russia.
> Russia is as imperialistic as America. This is evident in its inter-
> nal history as well as in the role it plays in countries like Angola.
> But the Russians have a less dirty name; in the eyes of the Third
> World they have a cleaner slate. Because of this they have had a
> better start in the power game. Their policy *seems* to be accepta-
> ble to revolutionary groups. They are not a 'taboo'. Here we are
> probably faced with the greatest problem in the Third World to-
> day. We are divided because some of us think that Russian impe-
> rialism can be accepted as purely an interim phase, while others,
> like myself, doubt whether Russia is really interested in the libera-
> tion of black people.[10]

Frank talk, indeed, and unlikely to endear Steve Biko either to the ANC and some of its unconditional supporters, or to the South African government, for whom he was proof that much of its opposition was robustly independent of the supposed Kremlin puppet-masters. Sooner or later, Biko's deviation from standard revolutionary rhetoric and his growing strength and popularity was bound to bring down the wrath of the authorities on the Black Consciousness Movement.

It began in June, 1976, in the black township of Soweto, when students walked out of their classrooms to protest a government edict that they should be taught some subjects in Afrikaans instead of English. It seemed like a small thing at the time, but it was one straw too many. The bloodletting, looting and killing that ensued over the next eight months demonstrated, more clerly than Steve Biko ever could with words, that South African blacks were determined that change would come.

The final death toll was something between five hundred and one thousand, and more than ten thousand people were injured. An official one-man commission of inquiry reported straightforwardly that "the government's race laws, official bungling and police unreadiness were to blame for the uprising." More specifically, it cited the "bitterness and frustration among blacks over racial laws which included influx control, segregation rules and social injustice."

But the causes were of little interest to the government. Soon after the rioting began, dozens of BCM leaders were detained; among them, Steve Biko, arrested on August 18, 1977. After a brutal beating and callous lack of medical attention, he was driven — naked and comatose in the back of a police Land Rover — the 740 miles from Port Elizabeth to Pretoria, where he died in prison on September 12. His death and the subsequent inquest outraged international opinion and drew attention to the fact that twenty-two other non-whites had died while in police custody in the year since the riots had begun. Death in South African Police cells was not uncommon, but the spate of 'suicides', 'heart attacks', 'suffocations' and defenestrations in that single year outnumbered all similar prison deaths over the previous thirteen.

The riots, bannings and detentions closed many of the IUEF's channels into South Africa. In June 1977, in an attempt to rebuild the network, the IUEF's Swedish Director, Lars-Gunnar Eriksson, hired a white South African exile to be the organization's Information Director. For a while, things improved. Craig Williamson was well known to the IUEF, having been a vice-president of NUSAS and an outspoken student activist before he fled to Botswana. He was soon promoted to Deputy Director, a position which placed him in direct contact with the leadership of the ANC and other liberation movements, and gave him responsibility for developing links with the World Council of Churches, donor governments and other NGOs. But through 1978 and 1979, things began to fall apart. Serious administrative and cash-flow problems developed within the IUEF. In 1978, a BCM courier was arrested while carrying IUEF funds from Lesotho into South Africa. Renfrew Christie, a white South African doing sensitive 'research' on South Africa's nuclear capability (his work partly funded by the IUEF) was arrested in 1979. Winston Nkondo, an ANC member travelling to Lesotho using IUEF travel authorizations, was arrested in Bloemfontein when the plane stopped there. And there were suspicions that Steve Biko's arrest and death were not unconnected with his use of IUEF funds.

Then, on January 6, 1980, a story appeared in the London *Observer* about Arthur McGivern, a South African agent who had defected and who was gradually exposing some of South Africa's best-kept espionage secrets. In a second article a week later, McGivern explained how the Bureau of State Security, spooked by the Soweto uprisings, had suspected both communist and CIA destabilization. BOSS officers had begun to bone up on their Fanon, Freire and Marcuse; they read Stokey Carmichael long into the night; and they eventually came to the conclusion that the danger lay in community development: cottage industry, literacy courses, clinics and creches, funded by outside organizations such as the IUEF and their suspected backers — starting with the CIA and moving right across the political rainbow to the Socialist International.[11] The article seemed patently incredible, but when Craig Williamson failed to show up for work in Geneva the following day, apprehension began to pulse through the IUEF. There was no word from Williamson for several days. Then, on January 17, he telephoned Lars-Gunnar Eriksson in Geneva, and asked him to come to Zurich for a meeting the following day. The two met at the Hotel Central and from there they moved along the wintry streets to the Hotel Zurich. After some random conversation, Williamson blurted out that he was a member of the South African Security Police. He said that he wanted his cover to continue for a while longer so that he could complete his work against enemies both he and Eriksson had in common — the communists. At that point, an incredible thing happened. Brigadier Johann Coetzee, head of the South African Security Police, entered the bar and sat down at their table. The report of a later inquiry into the event picks up the story:

In the course of the subsequent discussion, Coetzee allegedly
made certain threats against Eriksson, his family and against the
organization. He proposed to Eriksson 'a deal' which involved
Williamson being kept in the IUEF for up to six months in order
to complete his mission of penetrating the ANC and the SACP,
after which Williamson would return to South Africa with as few
complications as possible for the IUEF and for Eriksson. [12]

Instead, Eriksson blew the whistle, going first to the press, then to the
Swedish government, which in turn asked for Swiss police protection for
Eriksson. By the time the Swiss security police were adequately informed
of events, both Coetzee and Williamson had vanished.

Williamson had decamped with important files, which listed all of the
IUEF's contacts within the Republic. There was no knowing what damage
he might have done, both inside and outside the country, though his first
months back home were spent compiling evidence and testifying against
some of the people already detained in connection with IUEF-sponsored
work, including Renfrew Christie. Five years later, details of his petty
infiltrations, his political voyeurism and his payoffs were still coming to
light.*

The security police had called it 'Operation Daisy', and in South
Africa, Williamson was feted as a hero: 'Our Man in Moscow' proclaimed
a bold headline in the Johannesburg *Sunday Times*; ''He spied on the
KGB; he sent back vital data; he visited terror bases; he was a real James

---

* *The Guardian* of April 7, 1983 reported on the British trial of a Swedish journalist,
allegedly paid £1,000 monthly by South African security services to assist with a burglary
of the London PAC offices and to infiltrate the Anti-Apartheid Movement. Major Craig
Williamson was his handler. In August, 1984, Auret Van Heerden, like Williamson a
former NUSAS activist, charged the police with torturing him while he was in detention.
At the trial, Williamson was produced to testify that Van Heerden had himself been a
secret service agent and that the police therefore had no need to torture him. It was
Williamson who explained to reporters why South African troops had raided the Botswana capital of Gaberone in June 1985, killing a dozen people in their beds, and it
was Williamson who was charged with 'investigating' a 1985 South African press
allegation that Mozambiquan rebels were still receiving South African support, despite
an official 'cease fire' between the two countries. At about that time, it was reported
(Observer, June 30, 1985) that Williamson's name had risen to the top of the ANC hit
list.

Bond!'' He bragged to the press: ''You've got to be what I always call . . . a controlled schizophrenic . . . perhaps the most vital tool of the agent is supreme self-confidence.''[13] And he posed — pudgy, clean-shaven now, smiling over a South African Sunday barbeque.

Within the IUEF, recriminations flew thick and fast; there were a number of senior staff departures and Eriksson resigned. He had built the organization from a small scholarship fund into one of apartheid's most formidable non-governmental enemies outside South Africa. Liberation movements were quick to issue statements saying they had always known Williamson was a spy, in order to 'prove' that it was impossible to work with the BCM because it was so riddled with agents and 'contradictions'. The major donor agencies and governments that had sponsored the IUEF for years (including CIDA), suddenly withdrew their support, pending numerous hastily-arranged audits and investigations; and financial mismanagement was alleged. Among the members of a Commission of Enquiry, which investigated the incident, was David MacDonald, former Canadian Secretary of State.

How had Williamson been so successful? What sort of man was he? Tim Brodhead had known him as well as any of the Canadian confidants of the IUEF, and found him ''rather unpleasant. He was in my view a rather conventional ideologue and consequently rather boring. Now I can see why, but then I couldn't understand how anybody could sit through meetings of endless solidarity conferences and tirelessly redraft statements that would go nowhere. But for him, that was bread and butter; it didn't exactly make him a scintillating companion.''[14]

The IUEF had become a prime target once the South African government identified it as the major external supporter of the enemy — black advancement. ''The South Africans picked the IUEF,'' Brodhead said, ''because it was a social democratic organization. Its support came largely from the social democratic governments of Scandinavia; it had a coherent strategy — it wasn't just going in to 'do good', it wasn't just helping the victims and the oppressed. It was specifically working to develop a non-Moscow-oriented internal opposition to apartheid, and in that sense it was the greatest threat.''

The Commission of Enquiry submitted its report in the summer of 1980, and might have proven helpful had donor agencies been willing to continue their support; but with the IUEF having lost its rationale, most of the major donors saw little reason to continue funding it. Some of the organization's NGO members remained faithful, but many, including CUSO, made themselves scarce. Perhaps they had never understood the IUEF's political rationale, or perhaps in their 'purity', they wanted to put as much.distance as possible between themselves and the IUEF's besmirched reputation so they could continue working with the ANC. In any case, the IUEF was finished.

The Commission concluded that, "at the simplest level, we felt required to establish that there was no risk that the South Africans were still using the organization for their own ends, or could do so again in the future."[15] This naive objective was obviously not achieved. Not only was the Commission unable to reestablish donor confidence in the IUEF, but it acknowledged the success of one of Williamson's most obvious goals:

> In relation to (a wide variety of exiled black South African groups) with which he established contact, Williamson's aim may have been not only to penetrate the organizations as far as he could, but also to encourage the organizations to form links with the ANC — which could easily result in *all* opposition to the regime being depicted in South African propaganda as 'communistic'. This would also concentrate opposition in a disciplined, centralized organization which the South Africans may have felt they could cope with more easily than a more diffuse opposition made up of many groups with varying activities.[16]

In hindsight, the mistakes of Lars-Gunnar Eriksson and the IUEF seem legion; but at the time, few participants were able or willing to offer constructive advice. The IUEF was the only NGO to pose a real threat to South Africa, and it had to blaze its own trail. Few of the European and Canadian NGOs, which supported the IUEF understood the enormous potential of the Black Consciousness Movement. They missed the implications of the Williamson affair and proved themselves incapable of defending the IUEF in its hour of need.

But the fate of the IUEF also underscored a structural deficiency common to many NGOs: it is inevitably the staff, rather than the Board of Directors, who make most decisions: directors are continents — and oceans — removed from programs. The IUEF directors were willing to accept as incontrovertible the arguments put forward by staff members for a course of action. They rarely debated either the broad political implications or the details of the strategy. Although they were fully appraised of the thrust of the IUEF activity, none had the day-to-day involvement, personal commitment and individual contacts that Eriksson had — much as he unwisely shared them with Williamson.

Most NGOs seem genetically infused by a willing suspension of disbelief if the right words are spoken: Williamson spoke the language, knew the incantations, and thus became an acceptable member of the inner circle. The cause of the Black Consciousness Movement had been a staff concern, orchestrated almost exclusively by Eriksson — until he embraced the viper.

In its twelve years of liberation-related activity, the CUSO Board of Directors — not unlike the IUEF in its naiveté — rarely had a detailed discussion on the purpose and philosophy behind the organization's support for liberation movements. They never went beyond simple humanistic statements of opposition to minority rule: there was never a serious discussion of the possible implications of various forms of activity; or the logical consequences of a viable threat to a totalitarian regime; or an association with one form of opposition rather than another. When the IUEF collapsed, the CUSO Board of Directors received the news in a staff report, which didn't discuss the implications for CUSO's own work in the region. There was tacit acceptance that IUEF's demise left no course of action open except support for the ANC.

Ironically, it was probably the collapse of the IUEF that reduced the size of CUSO's support to ANC refugee projects. In 1981 (its pluralistic funding arrangements with the IUEF defunct), CIDA decided that it would provide no further matching grants for joint CUSO-ANC projects; the available pool was reduced to a few thousand dollars for token support. And while international church and labour organizations began to provide increased assistance to their counterparts within South Africa, CUSO elected to remain unilateral in its limited financial 'solidarity' with the ANC, its armed struggle, and its underground labour wing, the South African Congress of Trades Unions — SACTU.

CUSO's connection with SACTU is worth examinating because it demonstrates the short-sightedness of people who are too close to an issue. While the importance of SACTU in the history of the labour movement in South Africa is undeniably significant, the congress had become all but irrelevant by 1981. In 1969 — five years after SACTU was driven underground — there remained only 16,000 black union members in South Africa. By 1981 — without SACTU — the labour movement had mushroomed: there were 250,000 members of black and non-racial unions, as well as 370,000 members of the multi-racial Trades Union Confederation of South Africa.[17] But SACTU, affiliated with the ANC, remained important to CUSO staff in the region who ignored the strength of the genuine labour movement in South Africa. CUSO support was engineered for SACTU through tiny grants made out of discretionary regional budgets, or through the Development Education Department. In 1981, for example, CUSO financial assistance, allowed two Albertans (Ken Luckhardt and Brenda Wall), to research and publish a ponderous 520-page history of SACTU, giving it a credibility far beyond its peripheral circumstances.*

As well, much of CUSO's potential for real leadership on the South African question was consumed by irrelevant debates, such as often occurred at East Central and Southern Africa staff meetings. At one celebrated gathering in Tanzania, a full day was spent arguing about whether the local PAC representative should be invited to speak. The PAC, thought to be racist, corrupt, less 'progressive' than the ANC (and therefore divisive), remained unheard. In Ottawa, serious discussion was inhibited by ignorance of the issues, and by a small group of ANC torch-bearers who attacked any suggestion of activity beyond support to the ANC as unworthy — or even supportive of the South African government.

By 1985, CUSO was still giving halfhearted artificial respiration to SACTU, and its assessment of the situation in South Africa still relied mainly on the ANC's point of view. Meanwhile events in that country had once again overtaken the CUSO position. When Bishop Desmond Tutu received the Nobel Prize in 1984, rising church opposition to apartheid gained new and powerful international exposure. Black Conscious-

---

* The London-based Catholic Institute for International Relations estimated in 1981 that SACTU could "count on probably less than 300 active supporters, mostly shop stewards and radical unionists belonging to other unions." *South Africa in the 1980s*, CIIR, London, 1981, pg 35

ness was revived in the shape of dozens of militant new groups operating under the umbrella of the National Forum: the non-racial United Democratic Front claimed membership of 1.5 million; the growing trade union movement had helped convince organized business to start freeing itself from apartheid. In the West, it was the likes of Edward Kennedy, Stevie Wonder and Amy Carter (visiting the country, writing songs or getting arrested outside South Africa's Washington embassy), who began to convince even conservative politicians that the time for sanctions had come.

Reports of riots and killings began to emerge from South Africa almost daily. In the first four months of 1985, South African police estimated 1,500 injuries and 381 black deaths — double the 1984 figure. The massive escalation of black protest; the riots; the murders of black councillors, policemen and suspected informers, were answered in July 1985 by the imposition of a State of Emergency and even more draconian repression. It was perhaps not the start of the long-expected revolution, but it was a sure sign that South Africa was hurtling past the point of no return.

Prime Minister Trudeau was not far wrong when he predicted, in 1971, that South Africa could become "another Vietnam" in a decade. Thousands of Cuban troops in Angola; South African incursions into Mozambique, Botswana and Angola; battles in Namibia; guerillas — training, arming and growing in strength and purpose; and international alarm over South Africa's probable impending nuclear potential: all signs pointed to a terrible international failure and impending holocaust. That CUSO's stance on the issue was consistently 'progressive' and 'correct' hardly compensated for its ineffectual posturing and shortage of imagination.

The President of Zambia, Kenneth Kaunda, should perhaps have the last word on South Africa, for he among 'front line' leaders lived closest to the issue for more than two decades:

> Apartheid's challenge not only to South Africa, but to all humanity is so absolute that if there is no other way, we must face up, as the free world has done before in this century, to a long hard struggle . . . only South Africa herself has the power to avert what is rapidly becoming inevitable, by demolishing the whole vicious structure of apartheid, setting all her peoples free from cap-

tivity to the past, and offering her immense talents and energy in the service of the development of the whole continent. I am not optimistic, but I have faith in the provenance of God. That alone seems to stand between us and the void.[18]

Chapter 20

Bruce Edwards and Elisea Mori: Wings of Hope

For Bruce Edwards, flying was a hobby. By the time he was twenty-four, he had his commercial pilot's licence; but with an engineering degree from the University of Toronto, and experience as a part-time teacher and refrigeration technician, his application to CUSO in 1978 might well have destined him for a classroom posting. However, a small humanitarian air service in Peru — Wings of Hope — had requested a pilot, and within a few months Bruce Edwards was flying rickety single-engine Cessnas over the Amazon jungle to Peru's eastern interior. When he arrived in Peru, he was one of four North Americans with the air service; by 1980, he was the only foreigner and had become Wings of Hope's chief pilot — flying medical emergency missions, evacuating produce, rushing a doctor to a remote village, even transporting an entire football team across the jungle for an important game.

"We operate in some of the most rugged, isolated and inhospital terrain in the western hemisphere," Edwards wrote from Peru. "In the course of a week's flying I could be cruising over the treeless peaks of the Andes at an altitude of up to 18,000 feet; a few days later, I might be touching down on an unnamed jungle river in a forgotten corner of Peru in one of my float-equipped Cessnas."[1]

The river landings were often the most dangerous, especially on the deceptively tranquil Amazon. ''It is in fact a pilot's nightmare. The river is a treacherous monster complete with whirlpools, shifting banks, uprooted trees and even floating islands.'' The fierce currents could easily wrench control of the aircraft from a weary pilot; a branch could rip into a pontoon, making takeoff impossible.

On a typical day, this one in May 1980, Bruce Edwards finished some business in Lima and boarded a commercial flight to Iquitos where a Wings of Hope seaplane was based. He had spent much of the previous six months rebuilding the aircraft ''down to the last nut and bolt,'' following 7,000 long hours of jungle flying. Now it was ready for the air again.

''As soon as I arrived, I heard there was an emergency in a leper colony named San Pablo,'' he recalled. Loading the plane with medicine and supplies, Edwards and his Peruvian student pilot took off, returning to Iquitos after three hours in the air, with a tetanus patient who had convulsed on the return flight. Edwards described the next trip of the day:

> In thirty minutes we had the plane gassed up and were off to pick up another accident victim in Yanashi while the boy from San Pablo was slowly dying of lockjaw. In Yanashi I left behind a load of mail, books, medicines and fresh vegetables for the Canadian Mission. On the return flight we flew back a smiling young boy with two broken arms. It was strange to find anyone grinning so much after a tree had fallen on him and broken a few bones, but apparently this was his first ride in a seaplane with a 'gringo' pilot and he was quite looking forward to the adventure.

After filling his tanks again and loading the aircraft with medical supplies, school books and machine parts, Edwards took off for the last flight of the day, a four-hour journey to the Upper Napo river, landing just as dusk was settling over the jungle. For Bruce Edwards, it was the end of another routine day. He spent the night there in a one-room grass hut near the river's edge, listening to the vibrant night sounds of the river and the jungle. In the morning he would breakfast on bananas, rice and

coffee before inspecting his aircraft. Then, trusting to luck and the tremendous skill he had developed, he would gun the throttle, and, gaining
speed, blaze past cheering Indian children on the riverbank; he would
pull back on the stick and then he would be airborne once again, pointing
the nose towards Campo Serio where a woman with a gangrenous broken
arm waited with her family by another riverbank for the Wings of Hope.

Unlike most CUSO volunteers, Elisia Mori was not a Canadian. She was
born in the Peruvian jungle, and moved with her family to Lima when
she was thirteen. In 1979, at the age of twenty-six, after interning and
working in the slums of Lima, she received her medical licence and
applied to CUSO. Dr. Mori wanted an opportunity to go back to the
jungle and serve the people she had lived with as a child. She was posted
to the town of Satipo, to a twenty-five bed hospital which served the
8,000 inhabitants of the town and another 30,000 people scattered over
an area of 20,000 square miles.

"I am the doctor responsible for community visits on the hospital's
three-person medical team," she wrote in 1980. She described her work
in the field:

> My work might well be considered a medical free-for-all because
> as well as examining and diagnosing patients, I must also person-
> ally administer and control treatment, prepare my equipment for
> rural visits, clean and sterilize it upon return and handle many
> other activities normally carried out by auxiliary medical person-
> nel. Out in the field, I might attend a birth or a Caesarian section,
> re-attach a semi-severed limb, or perhaps amputate it with a chain
> saw. I frequently perform operations I had only read about
> once . . .

Even back at the hospital she was always short of equipment and
supplies. There was no microscope, and staff were attempting to construct
their own incubator and other basic equipment for the diagnosis of a range
of endemic diseases: yellow fever, typhoid, hepatitis and leprosy, which
were often spread by insanitary conditions.

Her principal concern was preventative medicine, vaccination and education campaigns. Vaccination was rejected by the population at first but had slowly gained acceptance.

Around the small village of Otica, preventative programs aimed at reducing malaria and tuberculosis were established through community schools. CUSO provided funding to build a health post at Otica and for the training of auxiliaries. Travel to outlying villages was by boat, or with the assistance of Wings of Hope, which Dr. Mori said was "worth its weight in gold many times over."

It was slow, difficult and often intensely frustrating. Dr. Mori had to cross the language and cultural barrier with the Amerindian population, just as Canadian-born volunteers would — learning Quechua and Campa, and coming to terms with life in the jungle where calendars and timetables were non-existant. She described the priorities:

> Our actions depend on those of the communities; the day everyone goes fishing for example, all other activity stops. Weather is another factor: bad weather and torrential rains can hold up a project for days or weeks, and delay transportation of badly needed materials. Health promotion activities are difficult in native communities rooted in their own customs and traditions.
>
> My work progresses slowly, slowly, because we are dependent on the generosity of others to develop our work. Slowly, as we wait for the production of the more nutritious foods that we are teaching the people to plant and grow . . . Slowly as the people and communities awake.

Without Wings of Hope, the Otica project would probably not have been possible. Bruce Edwards would often fly Dr.Mori on regular flights from Satipo to Otica, and occasionally on emergency missions to more remote villages. If she heard the engines of his Cessna across the jungle on an unscheduled flight, Dr. Mori knew that it was "a sign of some problem." But more and more frequently, it was also the sign of a visit from Bruce Edwards.

Perhaps it was the jungle that drew them together, a shared idealism, a common sense of purpose, or just love. Whatever it was, Elisea Mori and Bruce Edwards extended their contracts, and were married in the summer of 1980.

Chapter 21

Rollercoaster: The CIDA Connection

We are ruled by laws so we will not be ruled by men

Jean-Jacques Rousseau
Social Contract

A propellor-driven Hercules aircraft on its flight from Britain to the Falkland Islands has a difficult refuelling problem. It can complete a certain part of the journey unaided, but the stretch after Ascension Island — the final takeoff before Port Stanley — is vast, and without landing rights between, the plane's dependence upon jet tankers is total. The docking operation for any in-flight fuelling is precarious and fraught with danger; the timing and positioning must be perfect, the judgement of the pilot flawless. But on the Falklands run it is even trickier, for the top speed of a Hercules is less than the stalling speed of a tanker. In order to accomplish the perilous operation, therefore, the Hercules must climb to its maximum altitude and then increase its velocity in a long seaward dive as the jet draws close and injects the precious fuel, through a coupling, into its tanks. For a fill-up the operation must be completed several times.

The "rollercoaster," as it is known, is not unlike the delicate symbiosis between CIDA and CUSO. Although they work in the same general service, they take their instructions from different airfields and travel at different speeds and altitudes. One is normally independent of the other, but for a brief moment in the difficult journey from budget to budget, the survival of one and its ability to continue is decided entirely by the actions and intentions of the other. The consummation, without which the flight cannot continue, usually takes place beyond the point of no return, at high altitude, and after long and arduous travel. And the success of the operation is based not only upon the goodwill of both crews, but on the degree of attention, skill and experience they apply to the tasks of navigation, piloting and communication. The slightest error in judgement, timing or signals can mean that the entire operation must begin again, and for one of them, delay can be fatal.

The first approach to the Canadian government for assistance to a volunteer scheme was made in 1955, by the young Malayan-born General Secretary of World University Service of Canada. Lewis Perinbam had already coordinated two of WUSC's international seminars — one in India and one in Indonesia, and was struck by the growing Canadian interest he encountered in the newly independent countries of Asia. Seeing the success of the Australian Graduate Volunteer scheme in Indonesia, he envisioned the possibility of a similar Canadian effort. But in Ottawa, he met a brick wall of indifference within the Canadian Colombo Plan offices. "I got a flat refusal," he said, "I couldn't even see the head of the operation. It was a bureaucracy, and they simply weren't capable of understanding the idea."[1] Undaunted, but further impressed by subsequent WUSC seminars, and especially by keen interest on the part of the newly independent government of Ghana, he wrote a more definite proposal, submitting it in 1959 to the same authorities. Again, the answer was negative.

Keith Spicer, working on his own idea for a volunteer program, had been warmly received by Prime Minister Diefenbaker in 1959, but any notion of government financial assistance was politely dismissed. Early in 1961, when the Canadian Overseas Volunteer group was about to make its first placements, an approach was made to government under the auspices of the Royal Commonwealth Society, requesting a subsidy of $50,000 in order to place twenty volunteers in Asia. This time, the refusal was based on concern that if the government supported COV, it would open a Pandora's Box of worthy organizations, all equally deserving of support. Even with Progressive Conservative MP Fred Stinson as President, COV made little headway with government, beyond general statements of praise and congratulations.

In answer to a question in the House of Commons, Diefenbaker had allowed that COV demonstrated a "foresight and spirit of cooperation in international development that deserves the widest commendation . . . Insofar as the question of finance is concerned," The Chief continued: "The External Aid Office and the Canadian missions abroad will extend to them, in their initiative, every administrative support and assistance."[2] But no cash. When CUSO operations were underway in Ottawa with Lewis Perinbam acting as the organization's first Executive Secretary, the government was similarly fulsome in its praise, and equally parsimonious. Howard Green, Minister for External Affairs, said, "CUSO seems to me to be a particularly commendable example of action taken by private individuals without waiting for government assistance."

By 1963, however, a number of things had changed. First, there was a new government, and the CUSO Executive Committee had much better connections with the incoming Liberal administration. Geoff Andrew had served in External Affairs with Lester Pearson during the immediate post-war years; External Affairs Minister Paul Martin represented the riding of Windsor, where Francis Leddy, Chairman of CUSO's Executive Committee, was now president of the university. Duncan Edmonds had served on the CUSO Board, acted briefly as Executive Secretary before Bill McWhinney's return from Ceylon, and helped scout the first posting in East Africa; he now reappeared as Paul Martin's Executive Assistant.

More importantly, CUSO was beginning to emerge as the single national volunteer-sending organization; it had joined with COV in 1963, and would incorporate the Canadian Voluntary Commonwealth Service the following year. CUSO was becoming known because of overlapping enthusiasm for the highly publicized American Peace Corps; and, on its own, it was attracting widespread campus support — including many more applications than it could handle — and media attention.

The *Regina Leader-Post* had written, "In its own quiet way, Canada is developing a practical program to provide much needed knowhow to aid the development of less fortunate countries. Created this summer....CUSO is going to send young Canadian graduates abroad to serve in Asia and Africa . . . the plan merits public support.'' The *Montreal Star* spoke of the ''generous idealism of some of our many young people willing to offer some years of their lives to help the people of underdeveloped countries . . . a portion of government aid appropriations would be a worthwhile endorsement of CUSO.''

The *Toronto Star*, in March 1962, wrote: ''Here is young Canadian idealism at work. The volunteer students who often work alone in remote villages, under rough conditions, receive only their fares and a small subsistence allowance . . . This enterprise — humanitarian, practical and beneficial — is deserving of government support.''[3]

Meanwhile, private fund-raising continued. In 1963, $135,000 was raised from the private sector; but the following year, donations dropped to $95,000, and a consultant's report warned that CUSO would be unable to raise more than $250,000 annually in the forseeable future. Set against a projected 1964 budget of $295,000, this prediction presented the Board with a challenge to liberate government funds as a means of ensuring the organization's future.

Although there were differences of opinion as to the wisdom of seeking government support, the Board now knew that CUSO could place many more than the two or three hundred volunteers under consideration. There was, as Bill McWhinney put it, ''an inevitable demand pull on the organization. The only reason the Board would ever have thought about government support was the fact that it was not expensive to put volunteers in the field and look after them; the overseas demand to have volunteers was strong and there were a lot of Canadians who wanted to volunteer. Government support was simply an obligation.''[4]

Geoff Andrew, active on the CUSO Board, knew that universities were providing rent-free accommodation, salaried workers and secretarial assistance to the CUSO effort; and he estimated its value at more than $500,000. This assistance, he argued, was an indication of private support, which warranted financial support from the government. He arranged to discuss the matter with Prime Minister Pearson.

Paul Martin, however, was not well-disposed to the idea. Like Diefenbaker, he worried about the precedent and the requests that would probably come from other agencies — particularly church organizations and missionary efforts, with which he felt government should not be associated. He and his assistant, Duncan Edmonds, were present at the Prime Minister's meeting with Geoff Andrew and Bill McWhinney.

"We made our pitch to Mr. Pearson," Andrew said, "and I told him about the monies we had already collected from the private sector and that the private sector felt very strongly that these monies should at least be matched by the government. He eventually seemed favourably disposed and turned to Paul Martin and said, 'I think we can help them, Paul'. But Paul, who is an awfully nice fellow, hates like hell spending his own or anyone else's money, and he resisted." Finally, pleading another appointment, the Prime Minister concluded by saying, "I think we *will* help them Paul," and that ended the meeting.[5]

It wasn't quite that simple however. "The problem," as Duncan Edmonds saw it, "was that Pearson didn't say how or why, or make any funds available. All he did, in effect, was soften Martin a little bit and make other ministers realize that in taking some initiative, the PM would support them."[6]

Within the bureaucracy, there was a great deal of opposition. The External Aid Office had no mechanism for providing funds to a private organization, and Herb Moran, its Director, regarded CUSO as idealistic and amateurish. As well, Moran was only getting negative feedback from some of Paul Martin's advisors after the Prime Minister's vague commitment; this reinforced his own concerns about the inviolate nature of private agencies.

Duncan Edmonds discussed CUSO's dilemma with Bill McWhinney: it seemed to Edmonds that in the short run, the organization's biggest single expense was air fares for volunteers. He knew that ultimately, the intransigence of the External Aid bureaucracy would have to be overcome, but, he recalled, "I began to see that if we could solve the transportation problem in the short run, that would establish the principle of general assistance, and once we had that, we would be able to go on and get the grants and the more substantial funding from government." The possibility of sending volunteers out on RCAF flights had already been explored; the idea had been turned down for what Edmonds felt were bureaucratic reasons — the impropriety of flying civilians in military aircraft, questions of insurance and so on. Now, however, with the Prime Minister's tacit approval of CUSO, he felt he could raise the matter again.

Edmonds went to Defence Minister Paul Hellyer, and discovered that Hellyer, who was impressed with CUSO, would give favourable consideration to a request from Paul Martin for the flights. He drafted the necessary letter, and tried to get Martin to sign it. The Minister of External

Affairs refused. Officials within External Affairs prevailed on him — at least temporarily — by simply reiterating their concerns about CUSO and referring to the earlier RCAF objections.

Edmonds then returned to Hellyer's office, where he and the Defence Minister's secretary drafted a response to the request that Martin had refused to make. "If you would sign this reply, I think I can get Mr. Martin to sign the request," he told the Minister. Hellyer agreed, and not long afterwards, Edmonds placed the signed reply (and the unsigned request) before the Minister for External Affairs. "Martin looked at me, winked, smiled, and signed the request."

And so, in the summer of 1964 ("appropriately converting swords into ploughshares" as Keith Spicer put it), the outgoing volunteers travelled aboard noisy, lumbering, RCAF Hercules — and CUSO saved $80,000 in air fares. For Geoff Andrew, who had meanwhile arranged a fifty percent rebate in cash donations from Canadian Pacific Airlines, it seemed something of a Pyrrhic victory, but, as Duncan Edmonds realized, it was a foot in the door: that was the most significant thing.

Securing a cash contribution to CUSO was the next step, and it was Francis Leddy, now Chairman of the CUSO Board, who turned the trick. On a winter evening early in 1965, Leddy had dinner in Windsor with Paul Martin, and renewed the appeal for funds with his usual and unrelenting vigour. Martin dismissed his plea out of hand, and Leddy pouted, both disappointed and irritated.

"I left with him for an evening reception in his honour downtown," Leddy recalled. "Suddenly it occurred to me that Duncan and I had been taking the wrong tack with him. We had been emphasizing the general merits of CUSO, and had been neglecting to stress the political advantage for him and the government in helping us. Accordingly, I bluntly raised the matter again, early in the reception, expressing regret that he was missing the opportunity to be given credit for an imaginative innovation. We would now be compelled to turn to several of his cabinet colleagues whom we were aware were well disposed. 'Who are you thinking of?' he asked. I replied: 'Maurice Sauve and Alan MacEachen'." Martin did not respond immediately, but Leddy was counting on cabinet rivalry and latent party leadership ambitions to do their work. Just before he left the reception, Martin caught up with Leddy and said, "Francis, I think I see a way to help CUSO financially."[7]

Leddy's meeting fortuitously coincided with the submission of a comprehensive CUSO brief that Bill McWhinney had prepared, and an increasing number of glowing accounts of CUSO from overseas missions. Chester Ronning, Canadian High Commissioner in New Delhi, sent his views on the organization to External Affairs. "We originally had serious misgivings as to the value or desirability of such a program in India. I am glad to be able to report, therefore, that the CUSO volunteers have proved to be an impressive, self-reliant and dedicated group of young Canadians, and have, I think, been a credit to their organization and to Canada."

"If the organization as it presently exists really needs to be placed on a better financial basis in order to preserve its existence," he continued, "I think it would be appropriate for the government to provide some necessary financial assistance."[8]

Barraged from all sides — by the Prime Minister, the media, his ambassadors overseas, his friends and his own Executive Assistant — Paul Martin had little choice. In April 1965, he announced that the government would support CUSO's budget with a contribution of $500,000, allowing the organization to send 250 volunteers that year. Further support would contribute to a growth in numbers over the following three or four years, by which time 500 volunteers would be dispatched annually, and a thousand maintained in the field.

Paul Martin made the grant against his better judgement, and always maintained privately that it had been a mistake. In announcing his agreement to the military flights the previous year, he had spoken highly of CUSO, but had sounded a prophetic warning: "It is from its voluntary and non-governmental character that CUSO gets its spirit and its impetus, and we must do everything to make sure that this spirit and this impetus remain undiminished."[9]

CUSO had received a one-time grant from the government, but the means of institutionalizing the funding had not yet been found. Duncan Edmonds pondered the problem through 1964; he and John Turner, and Judy LaMarsh had knocked around an idea — not only for a funding mechanism, but for something much larger and more ambitious than CUSO. The little "ginger group," as Edmonds called it, wondered "if there wasn't more we could do to encourage the ideal of service and involvement in their community and the broader world community on the part of young Canadians. We spent many months trying to formulate an instrument of government that would stimulate primarily young people to give of themselves some service in exactly the same concept as CUSO.'' Judy LaMarsh gave it a name, and it was outlined in the April 1965 Throne Speech, a week before the first CUSO grant was announced: it would be called The Company of Young Canadians.

Initially, the concept was vague, although Edmonds, who was named Secretary of the Organizing Committee for the CYC, saw it as ultimately an umbrella organization for both domestic and international programs. Its unique relationship to government — answerable to Parliament through a minister — was modelled on the Canada Council and would give it unparalleled autonomy. And it would at last provide CUSO (which would fall within its purview), with the arm's-length, regular funding base it required. Going far beyond the original mandate of CUSO, however, the CYC would expand the 'serve and learn' concept into Canada's own underdeveloped communities — rural areas, urban slums, the north, Indian and Metis communities.

But within CUSO there was profound shock and consternation when the objects of the CYC were announced: ''to support, encourage and develop programs for social, economic and community development in Canada *or abroad* through voluntary service.'' There was fear that the government planned to take CUSO over entirely and suspicion that Duncan Edmonds was carving out an empire for himself, of which CUSO would be a part. And there was fear, that even if CUSO remained independent, the CYC would become involved in competitive international programs. To the sceptical, the timing of the announcements of the CYC and of CUSO's first grant was more than coincidental: they saw a clear intent to marry the two concepts.

Geoff Andrew in particular, was appalled at the idea, and at the fact that Edmonds had inveigled Francis Leddy to chair the working committee that would flesh out the CYC over the summer of 1965. Perhaps Leddy, the great moderator, saw in the CYC an opportunity to play midwife, as he once had with CUSO, to what looked like an exciting idea; whatever it was, Andrew was annoyed. ''Frank is a hell of a nice guy,'' he observed, ''and he was a good Chairman of the Board for CUSO, but he enjoyed holding offices more than doing much with them, and so he never really realized when Duncan persuaded him to take the Chairmanship of the Organizing Committee of the CYC that he was in a situation of conflict of interest.''

He was even more annoyed with Duncan Edmonds. ''Duncan never understood that all the effort I put into fund-raising for CUSO was worth-while,'' he said. ''We disagreed profoundly on whether you could have a successful organization under government sponsorship if government provided all the money.''

But Edmonds ploughed ahead regardless — travelling across the coun-try; holding high-level consultations; and requesting that CUSO submit its 1966 estimates through the CYC. CUSO nervously obliged, but the panic button was fully depressed and the CYC was the central item of discussion at every CUSO Board meeting that year. What would become of CUSO if the CYC ever fell foul of the government? What would happen to CUSO's recruitment base if the CYC became unpopular on Canadian campuses? Would the CYC have veto powers over the CUSO submission to government? Would CUSO be subject to budgetary or programming whims of the Company?

Meanwhile, there were fierce battles raging within the tiny CYC Sec-retariat and its advisors over the kind of organization it should become: a radical, participatory democracy, run by its volunteers, as some ad-vocated; or a body reflecting ''the goodness of dedicated youth and vol-unteerism'' and ''the best qualities of initiative and enterprise of the young people of Canada,'' as Edmonds and Leddy saw it.[10]

Then, in August 1965, Lester Pearson called a general election in an ill-fated attempt to get a majority government, and Duncan Edmonds was taken off the CYC Committee to work on the campaign. By the time he returned in November, everything had changed. Not only had he been undercut by CYC insiders, but Geoff Andrew had been at work in CUSO's interests, trying to forestall the CYC-CUSO merger. ''I had to go to the cabinet behind Duncan's back,'' he said, ''to have that quashed.'' He reminded his highly-placed friends that Canadian universities were now making in-kind contributions worth approximately a million dollars an-nually to the CUSO effort. ''I said, 'If you attempt to put CUSO under the CYC, you're going to have a revolt by all the universities that have supported CUSO'.'' He added that as Executive Director of the AUCC, he would ensure that the CYC had to pay for all the services now rendered free to CUSO if the merger went through.

Edmonds maintained that CUSO had not understood what he was trying to do, and that without CUSO, the CYC had lost much of its original raison d'etre. "I think they were misguided and short-sighted." he said of Andrew and McWhinney, maintaining that the CYC funding mechanism would have been preferable to direct government support from the External Aid Office. If CUSO were really afraid of being too dependent on government money, through the CYC, "they didn't have the same fear about being almost totally funded through the External Aid Office," he said. That Andrews, McWhinney, Leddy and he — a successful team in the past — had been unable to pull it off together, was, for Edmonds, a tragedy, a failure in communication on a grand scale. "The CUSO support would have made an enormous difference to the CYC . . . instead, it got taken over in too narrow a way, by too narrow an ideological group, too preoccupied with domestic radical change techniques. It never had the balance of the international dimension and the experience of CUSO to assist it."

Although Edmonds would serve on the CYC's first Advisory Council — with Maurice Strong and Marc Lalonde, among others — the Executive Director's job eluded him. "It was a very unhappy time for me," he recalled years later, "because I felt shunted aside. I took all the risks, provided all the vinegar, all the aggressiveness, all the political lobbying and campaigning and pushing over an eighteen month period, and when it all ended up, I felt I had got a raw deal on the thing."

When the first Interim Executive Director was named, he was not drawn from the CYC's inner sanctum, but from the front ranks of its antagonists. "It's pretty hard to turn down a Prime Minister," said Bill McWhinney.

Ironically, it was the appointment of Bill McWhinney as Interim Executive Director that secured CUSO's freedom from the CYC. Geoff Andrew had done the background work and McWhinney, having stated the CUSO position often enough, had no desire to perpetuate the problem once he was at the CYC. Within days of McWhinney's departure, CUSO's new Board Chairman, King Gordon, met with Prime Minister Pearson to clarify the issue once and for all. A few days later, Pearson issued a statement in which he said, "CUSO continues to be the principal Canadian agency devoted to providing opportunities for young Canadians to serve as volunteers on long-term contracts in developing countries....The government will continue to add its own substantial financial support to the very necessary contributions received from the public at large . . . in order to encourage this significant Canadian service to developing countries.''[11]

And so, with the issuing of a press release, the perceived threat from the CYC had disappeared, and CUSO's shaky financial situation was placed on as firm a footing as it ever would be.

By 1967, CUSO's placements had increased dramatically and the government grant had grown to $1.8 million. But there was still no formal mechanism for making the contribution, and as Paul Martin had predicted, other voluntary organizations were lining up at the trough.

The External Aid Office itself had been in a state of uproar since the arrival in 1966 of its new director, Maurice Strong. A self-made millionaire, and former cabinboy, prospector and stock promoter, Strong worked in the Far East and Africa in the early 1950s and set his sights on an international career until External Affairs turned down his job application in 1954. Working his way through Dome Petroleum and Canadian Industrial Gas and Oil, he was only thirty-five when he became President of the rapidly expanding Power Corporation ten years later. When the top job in the External Aid Office opened in 1966, Strong exerted all of his considerable influence to get it. Once in the saddle, he began to mould and shape the organization to fit his idea of what Canada should become in the field of international development.

The EAO originated with the Colombo Plan, a consortium of white Commonwealth countries formed in 1950 to provide assistance to their South Asian Commonwealth counterparts. Canada's contribution was small in comparison with the $2 billion it had given for European reconstruction after the war, but in the early 1950s, aid was seen as a short-term phenomenon that required neither large inputs of cash nor a complicated bureaucracy to administer them. By 1958, however, the concept was changing: many more grants were being given to UN agencies; and a Commonwealth Caribbean program was set up, followed not long afterwards by a Special Commonwealth Africa Assistance Program.

The creation of new departments, branches and programs without development of a long-term approach to international assistance made policy formulation and planning almost impossible. Keith Spicer, in his 1966 book, *A Samaritan State?* said that the myopia only served to undermine sound administration. "Called to execute tentative and shadowy policies, civil servants could do little more than stumble from budget to budget, responding peristaltically to each sporadic batch of project requests."[12]

Finally, in 1960, the government created the External Aid Office in an attempt to bring order out of chaos; to centralize the administration of aid programs; and to give recognition to the long-term nature of the aid phenomenon. Between 1951 and 1960, Canada spent $420 million on aid programs; much less per capita than the United States and most of Canada's European allies. Between 1960 and 1965, the EAO doubled the rate of spending, contributing $558 million. It concentrated largely on commodity and food aid, and on infrastructural projects, but techncial assistance also became a priority, and the numbers of Canadians serving abroad under government programs increased from forty-eight in 1960 to 418 by 1965.[13]

When Strong took over, he expanded and professionalized the operation, bringing in new blood with experience in the Third World to complement or replace some of the bureaucrats. He had a special interest in non-governmental organizations, and was determined to establish a larger and more reliable funding base, from which to expand NGO activity. He asked Lewis Perinbam, now working at the World Bank in Washington, to return to Ottawa and work on the problem. Perinbam agreed to a six-month contract in 1967; he discovered that NGO activity had proliferated in the few years that he had been away. Eighty-two Canadian organizations were now raising annual funds of about $34 million for international development; with missionary activity included, they were maintaining as many as 6,500 Canadian workers overseas.[14] Perinbam thought that if Canadians were willing to contribute that much (in addition to the tax dollars that went towards official external aid), a logical case could be made for matching grants from government. Despite the predictable objections from External Affairs, Strong liked the idea, and his political influence prevailed over the bureaucrats who had years before ignored Perinbam's proposals for a volunteer-sending organization.

The Canadian International Development Agency, which Strong unveiled in 1968, had a Non-Governmental Organization Division; Lewis Perinbam was its director.

CIDA's NGO Division got off to a slow start; the first five grants (announced in June 1968), totalled $4.12 million, most of which went to CUSO. In 1969, the CIDA grant to CUSO was $3.2 million, but the money went a long way. CUSO volunteers, who cost $5,000 per man-year, were much less expensive than CIDA 'experts', who cost the government $36,000 each and often found themselves working at the same institutions as CUSO volunteers, filling similar positions. That year, for example, CIDA had sixty-seven teachers working in Tanzanian secondary schools, each one costing roughly seven times more than a CUSO volunteer — of whom there were 115.

The late 1960s and early 1970s were the halcyon days of CUSO's relationship with CIDA, and Maurice Strong's door was always open to the CUSO Executive Director. Frank Bogdasavich found that CUSO's financial picture was as good as its budgeting. "If we were right in our cost estimates, we got the money," he said. "Maurice Strong believed there was a role for the NGOs, and CUSO was the flagship . . . He was always extremely supportive, but he was demanding on principles of accountability and audits, and his officials leaned on us to professionalize a lot of that."[15]

The CIDA grant kept pace with CUSO's growth, and even during the management debacles of 1970 and 1971, CIDA asked few questions. Lewis Perinbam's budget had quadrupled by 1972, and the annual CIDA agreement with CUSO, written in the form of a contract, was tied to the number of volunteers placed overseas in a given year. It was a simple, per-capita head count, unencumbered with questions of early returns, extensions, administrative costs and overheads. These were detailed in the CUSO budget submission upon which the grant was calculated, but for the purpose of convincing Treasury Board of its worth, the best calculation was still the man-year figure; no one could beat the CUSO cost.

But the easy days were drawing to a close. In 1973, CUSO/SUCO suffered a combined $700,000 overrun, and although much of it was attributable to SUCO rather than CUSO operations, it was even more damning than it appeared, because large surpluses from the previous year were also spent. By now, there was a great deal more competition for CIDA funding; in 1972, contributions were made to more than a hundred groups and organizations. Far from being a 'flagship', CUSO was now viewed by some as having an unfair advantage over other NGOs; ninety percent of its budget came from CIDA while most organizations were restricted to equally matching grants — at best. On top of CUSO's management and financial problems in the early 1970s, CIDA was drawn into the political embarrassment of SUCO's pro-separatist "Operation Angola" and a controversial visit by Madame Allende in 1973. Members of Parliament, and the media, were beginning to ask questions about what CUSO/SUCO were doing with the government's millions; and CIDA, no longer the small, highly personalized operation it had been in 1966, was now a complicated bureaucracy, ever more demanding in its rules and regulations. As the NGO Division became bigger and more complex, Lewis Perinbam, now a CIDA Vice-President, increasingly left relations with CUSO in the hands of inexperienced, junior officers.

All these factors conspired, in 1974, to an inordinate delay of the CIDA grant. CUSO's new Executive Director, Murray Thomson, unable to develop a rapport with CIDA, and faced with a delay now stretching into the second quarter of the fiscal year, finally called in the Chairman of the CUSO Board. The chairman intervened with Perinbam, and threatened to publicize the delay if action were not forthcoming.[16]

The tactic was successful in the short run, but it further strained relations between CIDA and CUSO: in 1975, preliminary discussions on the budget were not held with CIDA until mid-April, two weeks after the fiscal year had begun. At the end of May, CUSO was told it could expect a decision by mid-July. By the end of July, CUSO was operating on bank loans totalling $1.45 million and by the end of August, with still no decision yet in sight, the loans reached the $2-million mark. It was not until the end of October that Treasury Board finally approved the grant, and the figures agreed upon with CIDA six months earlier were severely reduced. With less than five months remaining in the fiscal year, spending levels had to be decreased drastically.

To give CIDA its due, the problems and delays were not always of its own making. Aid policy by the mid-1970s was formulated not so much by CIDA — which in any case was answerable not to its own minister, but to the Minister for External Affairs — as by a variety of inter-governmental committees, drawn from six different departments: External Affairs, Industry Trade and Commerce, Agriculture, Finance, the Treasury Board Secretariat, and CIDA. Each department brought to committee meetings its own special axe for grinding, and despite the government's stated commitment to the "economic and social development of developing countries as the primary objective of the Canadian development assistance program,"[17] it was only CIDA, of the six, that was primarily concerned with Third World interests.

The normal route for CUSO's budget submission was through analysts at CIDA's NGO Division, past Vice-President Perinbam, and to the Project Review Committee within CIDA, where it would be examined, questioned and defended at the most senior levels of the agency. From there, it would proceed to the Minister for External Affairs who, depending on personal proclivities and the advice available, would seek clarification or amendments, or simply sign it. Then, it would be examined by Treasury Board analysts who would consider it in the light of whatever guidelines had been established by cabinet and Parliament; finally, it would go to the Treasury Board — a committee of cabinet ministers — which would approve, reject, or alter it, according to its best judgement and departmental advice. Apart from discussions with CIDA's NGO Division staff, there was little opportunity for CUSO to participate in the process; and none, once the document left CIDA. CUSO's own submission, often 200 pages in length, and replete with the most minute detail, was reduced by unseen hands to a few sheets for Treasury Board analysts, and further reduced by analysts to a few paragraphs for cabinet ministers.

Such a system made rational and early acceptance of the CUSO budget almost impossible; it guaranteed administrative confusion within the organization, and generated understandable hostility towards government. Lewis Perinbam felt the hostility acutely. "There is a sort of adversarial notion of the government among NGOs," he said, "There is an assumption that the government must be against them . . . They don't realize that we don't get up in the morning and say 'What are we going to do to the NGOs today?' " Peter Hoffman, who had worked as a CUSO volunteer, a Field Staff Officer and in the Ottawa office before joining CIDA, agreed: "It's too bad there has been so much paranoia about the government in CUSO. Yes, we're incompetent — you could find a million examples of how difficult it is to work with CIDA. But there's no sinister plot. Even when we give CUSO a hard time and it looks as though people have come together and rationalized a decision . . . really it's a muddle, often based on personalities rather than a rational judgement."[18]

Goodwill and benevolent muddles notwithstanding, CUSO paid more than $60,000 in interest to the Royal Bank of Canada in 1979 while it waited for the various gears of government to clank into action. When they finally did, six months into the financial year, the CIDA grant was almost a million dollars short of the original estimates, and a dozen staff had to be laid off in order to make up the difference. It was as though the ghost of Duncan Edmonds, with his simpler, more autonomous model, was coming back to haunt CUSO.

The 1979 CIDA grant was supposed to be the first installment on a three-year contribution. CIDA had agreed that CUSO's multiple-year operations needed a sounder footing than the annual granting mechanism in order to surmount the inherent delays of the bureaucracy; but when CUSO's Executive Director was fired in January of that year (to the full accompaniment of a public outcry for investigation), the three-year budget, prepared with great care, fell among thorns and nettles.

In order to bolster confidence, a full management audit of CUSO was undertaken at CIDA's behest by the accounting firm of Coopers and Lybrand. After exhaustive research and investigation, they confirmed that a three-year budget cycle was essential to effective management. So in the spring of 1981, CUSO's field staff began again, preparing plans for the 1982-85 period. Projections were agreed upon with CIDA, and after much analysis and scrutiny, a three-year plan and budget were submitted in January 1982, three months before the beginning of the period they were meant to cover. The proposal languished in CIDA for six months, after which Treasury Board analysts — rattled by Alan MacEachen's 1982 budget and its attack on spending — ripped into the CUSO request. At the end of November, Treasury Board decided to approve only two of the three years, cutting $250,000 off the first year, and $500,000 off the succeeding one.

There seemed little choice for CUSO but to close a program: Tanzania was reluctantly selected, and was only saved at the eleventh hour by CIDA's unprecedented decision to appeal the Treasury Board action. The appeal was finally heard in March 1983, and most of the cuts were restored, but the cost to both administrative efficiency and morale had been high. CUSO's first multiple-year contract, for the period 1982-1984, was signed on March 29, 1983, two days short of a year into the period. When it was all over, Chris Bryant, who was trying to run the Papua

New Guinea program with uncertain budgets, constantly changing formats, and requests for ever more detailed information, wrote to Ottawa: "I recall when I ran a Jamaica program of sixty-five volunteers with a part-time secretary. We didn't even have a calculator or a photocopier. CIDA gave us the money and we spent our time programming. I knew almost nothing about programming then, but I had the time to learn. Now I know a lot about programming, but all my time is spent filling out forms and calculating the telephone bills for 1986."

Over the years, contractual problems also arose. The basic formula in the CIDA grant to CUSO had not changed; it was based essentially on the number of volunteers overseas, although it had been refined to encompass host national and short-term volunteers, as well as extensions and early returns. After 1978, it also included a penalty clause, in the event CUSO fell more than five percent short of its placement target. Some in CUSO felt that the contract placed undue importance on the number of volunteers rather than on the quality of the programs; nor did it seem to take into consideration the fact that CUSO now administered hundreds of projects each year, and functioned as much more than a volunteer-sending agency.

Neither CUSO nor CIDA could be very specific about CUSO's objectives, however. "Development is our business," Frank Bogdasavich had said — but despite its positive ring, the phrase was utterly (and conveniently) intangible. A 'development charter' spoke of awareness, lifestyles, sensitivity, involvement, and identification. A set of operating principles stated that the organization would "respond to needs" and "promote" the use of local resources, host national participation and cooperation. But specific, limited, clearly-defined targets, priorities, and deadlines: these were highly problematic, except in terms of volunteer numbers and certain administrative costs.

Education is the 'business' of a school, but it must satisfy more than the educational needs and aspirations of a society (however they are defined). It must also satisfy students, teachers, administrators, parents, the school board, unions, taxpayers and the government. CUSO faced a similar dilemma. So attempts to alter the CIDA contract proved futile: no alternative formula with quantifiable indicators could be found, and CIDA suspected that without checks, balances, and a penalty clause, CUSO would probably do less — not more.

There were also philosophical differences which exacerbated the bureaucratic delays and misinterpretations. The disillusionment that many returned volunteers felt about the slow pace of development work at the village level was underlined by the 1969 Pearson Commission Report on World Development.

After his retirement from politics, Lester Pearson chaired a prestigious international body of economists, politicians, labour and business leaders who spent two years, under World Bank auspices, trying to diagnose Third World ills. The report, *Partners in Development*, was one of the first comprehensive, semi-official statements on development issues; it proposed tougher, more concerted action by both developed and developing countries. The Pearson Report was a hopeful sign, but little was done with it; and it soon became a dust collector on government shelves — its most salient recommendations ignored.

Some volunteers would see at first hand how large, capital-intensive bilateral projects simply bypassed villages. For many, the only contacts with official Canadian aid were the CIDA experts: often these 'experts' were cynics with little more experience than the volunteer; they were cloistered in expatriate ghettos; they were highly paid; out-of-touch; bitter, sometimes to the point of racism, about the futility of their projects. And occasionally a volunteer would come in contact with an itinerant third secretary from the embassy, taking an annual up-country pilgrimage in a chauffeured car to check out projects and attend to the complaints of the 'pampered experts'.

To look at CIDA's side of the question, it was hard for the agency to be critical of the 'great job' being done by the 'CUSO kids' — although many an embassy official must have gagged on the sanctimony, the lost passports, and the outraged letters volunteers would sometimes send to cabinet ministers, MPs and hometown newspapers about Canadian aid snafus in the Third World. There seemed to be little understanding of CIDA's own difficulties with the bureaucracy of government, and the apparent lack of CUSO support for the agency was often a source of resentment. Even CIDA-financed development education projects were sometimes critical of Canadian aid programs, much to CIDA's irritation.

But some of the mutual misunderstandings went beyond mere annoyance. CIDA apparently assumed that CUSO spoke with one voice and that policies formed of thousands of individual experiences could emanate from a single source. Annual general meetings, where returned volunteers proposed, debated and passed resolutions on everything from baggage allowances to Canadian membership in NATO, became an annual source of friction between CUSO and CIDA. For an AGM in the 1970s, thirty or forty resolutions were nothing. Years later, they read like a compendium of idealistic, radical-chic, and progressive causes. Although it is easy to find amusement in much of this, the meetings themselves were intensely serious; the issues were real, and the RVs felt passionately about them. Despite the passion, the politics and the pain, resolutions passed at an AGM were only recommendations to the Board of Directors; later, in comparative peace, the Board could consider them objectively and with the advice of the Executive Director and staff.

CIDA often forgot this and regarded some of the more extreme resolutions as imprudent policy statements, or just plain craziness. Robin Wilson and SUCO Director, Yvon Madore were once summoned into the presence of CIDA President Michel Dupuy to be told that Dupuy knew the difference betwen development and politics, and hoped that they did. Unfortunately (or perhaps fortunately), he did not explain this difference.[19]

The days immediately following an AGM would inevitably be difficult, as MPs, reporters and government officials besieged the Slaterbunker to demand explanations of the more controversial resolutions. Through the years, it was every Executive Director's nightmare (and the bad luck of some) to be confronted before a microphone by an overzealous interviewer who had dredged up a series of questionable 'whereases' and the inevitable, totally inexplicable 'be it therefore resolved that . . . ' from the murk of some long gone AGM.

The only way to understand the peculiar dilemma that such resolutions presented to the organization was to experience it at first hand; for while the organization could hardly support ill-formed resolutions on irrelevant issues, neither could it repudiate its own membership. The equivocation that often resulted was annoying to CIDA, frustrating to the RVs, and entertaining for CUSO's critics and the media.

While CUSO has been a thorn in the flesh from time to time, it has — in the long run — served Canada well. CUSO programs, in much of Latin America, Zambia, Botswana and other countries, came long before official Canadian aid, and even paved the way for the CIDA bandwagon. In many countries which received little or no official assistance from Canada, the Canadian government could point with pride to CUSO's presence and achievements.

CUSO has long been the only visible Canadian presence in Bolivia, Papua New Guinea, Vanuatu, Sierra Leone, the Sudan, Mozambique and parts of the Caribbean and Central America. CUSO undoubtedly contributed much to Canada's healthy trade surplus with Cuba. And there is no question that CUSO's then-controversial support for humanitarian projects of the Zimbabwean liberation movements made a post-independence High Commission and official protocols easier to establish than might otherwise have been the case.

And there are other examples. CUSO's school reconstruction project in the former Biafran territory of Nigeria established a Canadian presence in the region a year before official aid programs began; and when CIDA diversified funding arrangements with NGOs on larger rural development projects, CUSO led the way with a successful North East Thailand Rural Development Project.

Occasionally, CUSO could even bail CIDA out of a tight spot: when private Canadian consulting firms botched the development aspects of large bilateral projects, CUSO would sometimes be invited to help pick up the pieces. For example, a major project in Togo might have left an embarrassing legacy of rusting Canadian pipes and dry pumps — had CUSO not assisted with training and extension programs long after CIDA thought the water project was well in hand.

Another example of CUSO's assistance to CIDA was in 1972, when a non-resident Canadian ambassador, on a rare visit to Liberia, told President Tolbert about Canada's marvellous development work in Africa, (apparently forgetting, momentarily, that Liberia was rated privately in Ottawa as a 'minimal interest' country). When the President asked for examples of Canadian aid, the ambassador talked fulsomely of CIDA's educational programs. Logically, Tolbert then asked for Canadian teachers and CIDA, fearing diplomatic embarrassment but not wanting to embark on an official aid program with Liberia, asked CUSO to assist. On such occasions, when CUSO could help, the effort seemed taken for granted — despite the cost in time, effort and dollars to scout and support

a few placements in a country where the organization had no representation. On the other hand, it seemed that when CUSO felt it could not
assist, it was seen as recalcitrant, ungrateful and overly bureaucratic.

Part of the friction between CUSO and CIDA was a function of the
changes that had taken place both in CIDA and in CUSO.

By 1985, Lewis Perinbam had been Vice-President of CIDA for several
years, presiding over an NGO and Special Programs budget more than
thirty times bigger than what he started with thirteen years earlier. CIDA
had grown from the relatively small, personalized operation over which
Maurice Strong presided in 1966, to an agency of more than over 1,100
employees, with a 1984-85 budget of $2 billion. And CUSO itself
had 110 employees and a projected three-year budget of $59 million for
1984-87.

CIDA's NGO Division, unlike other government departments, was
now staffed almost exclusively by men and women drawn from the NGO
community. Their experience and commitment created a special climate
of support and understanding for NGOs; but there were drawbacks: NGO
Division staff, often frustrated by government bureaucracy and cut off
from direct involvement in projects, were more interventionist, more
conscious of detail than their counterparts in bilateral programs. Many
just ignored the invisible (but critically important) dividing line between
government and the non-governmental sector: they became too involved
in projects and organizations they might never fully understand; and they
sometimes behaved as if they wished they were their own clients.

The problems between CUSO and CIDA were certainly not unique,
but they were of a magnitude greater than those between government and
most other NGOs. The funding relationship was a faustian bargain of
sorts: CIDA incorrectly gauged CUSO's willingness to conform to government priorities; CUSO unrealistically assumed that it could chart a
completely independent course without regard to its source of income.

CUSO, of course, would never have survived (much less become
Canada's only world-class NGO), had the government not intervened at
a critical point in its history. And the subsequent creation of CIDA's
NGO program was a master stroke which has given Canada and Canadian
organizations a capacity for development work far exceeding that of their
counterparts in much larger countries. The story of a mid-air fuelling

therefore — difficult as it often was — is only a small facet of the entire story, which would have been much different (and much shorter) without the creative and catalytic role played by CIDA.

The concerns of Geoff Andrew and Paul Martin — the danger of dependence on government — had to some extent been justified. But it was not the issue of government funding that became the problem; it was CUSO's subjugation to cumbersome, multi-tiered government requirements, and the mass of contradictory policies and procedures. And it was of little consolation to either partner that CUSO itself, in its occasional bouts of managerial and political experimentation, was far from blameless in contributing to the situation.

Some in CUSO may have felt that the Edmonds model of a Crown Corporation; built as a buffer between CIDA and the NGOs; free of the governmental chain of committees, analysts and procedures; and modelled on the Canada Council or the International Development Research Centre, made sense after all. Indeed, CIDA itself would always be subject to the policy-and-procedure constraints of the government as a whole. But in creating the NGO Division, Maurice Strong and Lewis Perinbam breathed new life into a spontaneous activity that had been of good service to Canada, and, more importantly, the Third World. After almost two decades, it was perhaps time to find a new means of freeing it from the rollercoaster, so that it could regain altitude and continue on its important journey.

Chapter 22

Ray Clark: On the Road Again

In 1957, the Gold Coast, a British crown colony, became independent Ghana, the first of dozens of African territories to become sovereign nations during the following decade. Ghana was special: unlike any other country in Africa, it had universal primary education; it was blessed with an abundance of natural resources; and it had, in its charismatic Prime Minister, Kwame Nkrumah, a leader of international repute. But history would be unkind to Ghana. Bold experiments to break colonial trading patterns crippled the inherited economy, while misplaced investments failed to produce anything significant in its place. The soldiers stepped in, followed by new self-serving civilian regimes which were succeeded in turn by ever more draconian military governments. By 1981, Ghana, the former leader of African independence, had been reduced to a caricature of a nation, beholden to international creditors and aid donors, devoured from within by a quarter-century of mismanagement, corruption, and misguided, unfulfilled aspirations. Parched as well by severe drought, it seemed to be a country where nothing worked; where the daily search for food was the most important task of the day; where the cedi, once at par with the dollar, had become virtually worthless; where a full day's wages bought little more than a handful of rice or yam.

Ghana had been one of the first countries in which CUSO worked but in the spring of 1982, the field staff and volunteers, weakened by chronic illness, frustrated by extreme food shortages and frightened by the latest military takeover, met to discuss the possibility of a pullout. Of the twenty who were there, thirteen decided to throw in the towel; seven, along with one Field Staff Officer — a Sierra Leonean named Victor Brandon — remained. It was agreed that a detailed review and evaluation was necessary, and Ray Clark was asked if he would do it.

After his last volunteer assignment in Papua New Guinea, Ray Clark had joined the staff in Ottawa, and then in 1979 had taken a field staff position in Nigeria, his fourth overseas posting with CUSO. In 1982, he was back in Canada enjoying a leave of absence when the call came. By September, he was in Ghana, attempting to work out a prognosis for CUSO and to recommend, clearly, either continuation or closure.

He was surprised by what he found. "Nothing was working," he said, "and CUSO was just a semblance of what it had once been there. But I had never been in a country where so many of the local people were committed to change and improvement. Time and again I'd go into a farm or a health project and find hard-working, committed Ghanaians saying they didn't want fertilizer, they wanted information; not technology, information — we'll do it ourselves, they told me."[1]

He met a Ghanaian doctor in a small up-country hospital and asked him why he wasn't in the capital, Accra, where he could doubtless make a fortune; why he hadn't followed the tens of thousands of emigrants leaving for Nigeria or Europe or North America. "Ghana needs me here," the doctor told Clark. "I'm willing to put in two years in a rural area — they need doctors here as much as any place else."

Clark was also impressed that groups of Ghanaians, united in their hardship, were making connections between health projects, women's activities, literacy and agriculture in a way that had not been the case when resources were more plentiful. "They were meeting together, and working together, and starting to solve a lot of their own problems."

But by the end of September, after weeks of travelling through the country, Clark still did not know if he could recommend to CUSO that it continue its programs. On the road back to Accra, after a gruelling journey to the north, he and CUSO's Ghanaian project officer, Besa Amenuvor, made their last stop at a hospital in Nkawkaw, 100 miles north of the capital, to determine its suitability for a CUSO doctor. Then, as they headed south out of Nkawkaw, a sequence of events began that helped Clark towards the clear decision he had to make.

The CUSO car, a Peugeot Station wagon, was in bad condition, and had been kept on the road only through the genius of Ghanaian mechanics working with little more than bailing wire and ingenuity. Not long after they had set out from Accra, the entire exhaust system had fallen off; beyond repair, it was roped to the roof and they roared on through the countryside. "I don't think hens laid for a week after we passed," Clark observed.

Then the trip nearly ended when the bolts all but sheared off one wheel. As with everything else, replacements were unavailable, so they took one bolt off each of the other wheels and crossed their fingers. At Nkaw-kaw, they bought as much fruit and as many vegetables as they could find, for these were either unavailable in Accra or were prohibitively expensive, and they crammed them into the back along with their luggage and five jerry cans full of gas. Heading into the home stretch, they descended the steep winding road from the Afram Plains with Besa at the wheel. They had just reached a straight stretch of road and Besa had accelerated to the accompaniment of a throaty, unmuffled roar, when suddenly, as Clark put it, "all hell broke loose."

"I thought the car had exploded," he said, but it was only one of the threadbare tires. "Besa tried to keep control, but I knew he was losing it." Clark was amazed at how much time he had to think — about how he should brace himself for the impact, about how, if they were lucky enough to go nose first into the bush they might not flip. "Then it struck me that we weren't going to hit the bush head on, and I knew we'd roll, and we did. I thought, "Raymond, keep your eyes open because this is an accident and you're going to want to remember every detail," and I did — as we rolled over I saw all the windows busting out and one of the jerry cans flew into the front seat. Besa and I actually made eye contact on one roll and I said to him, "Good luck," and then I thought, "Stupid bugger, you're upside down and you're going to get killed, and you're saying 'Good luck'."

By then Clark was halfway through the windshield, but he managed to grasp the rear view mirror with one hand and push on the hood with the other; he levered himself back into the car just as it hit the road upside down for the second time, squashing them down into the seat. "Then we rolled a third time, and my last thought was, 'Do I have on clean underwear?' ", a recollection of the mysterious connection his mother had always made between personal hygiene and traffic flow.

After the terrible noise, suddenly everything was still. Somewhere, Besa shouted to see if Clark was alive, and in the silence, unhurt, he wasn't at first sure. Then reality began to encroach on the near dream; he was covered with both petrol and blood — mostly Besa's, as it turned out. Besa had suffered a deep gash to the wrist, and from the way his hand dangled, it was clear that the tendons had been severed. Clark dragged a sheet from their luggage, and tearing it into strips, made a tourniquet and a bandage; then he began to survey the damage. The car, long overdue for the scrapheap, was finished, smashed beyond recognition, and for three hundred yards down the road there were bananas, yams, plantain, oranges, cassava, suitcases and CUSO files.

Four days after the accident, Clark wrote to Ottawa: "Ghanaians are truly *wonderful, wonderful* people. Had this accident happened elsewhere, Besa would probably have bled to death. Almost as soon as it was over, cars started to stop and people tried to help — not rob us or stand gawk-eyed." A pharmacist took Besa back to Nkawkaw, to the hospital where they had thought of placing a CUSO doctor, and an ancient taxi, loaded with people and luggage, also stopped. The driver, with the unlikely name of Carleton, had seen the CUSO sign on the station wagon, and because he had been taught by a CUSO volunteer, was eager to help. His passengers disgorged themselves from the vehicle and all of them helped gather up the fruit and papers. Two insisted on staying behind to guard the wreckage while Carleton drove Clark to the nearest police station.

The taxi was, if possible, in worse condition than the CUSO car had been, but eventually they pulled up at the police station — "a little hovel with a tin roof," as Clark described it, "painted pink on the outside, with a shined-up officer and a brand new Land Rover." Seeing an *obruni* covered with dirt and blood and stinking of petrol, the officer's first reaction was similar to the others Clark had so far received: "God bless you," and, "God has saved you; you are lucky today."

Unfortunately, the accident had occurred outside the jurisdiction of this police station, so the officer was unable to handle the case. He was prepared to offer Clark a drive back to Nkawkaw, however, but sadly,

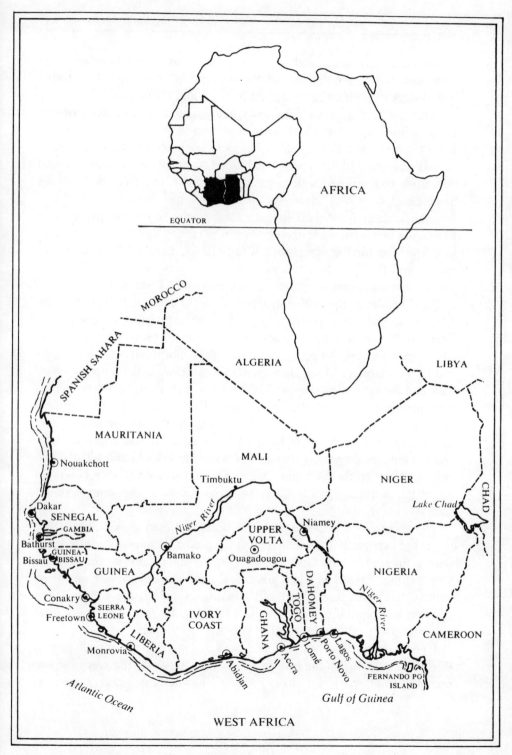

EQUATOR

AFRICA

MOROCCO

SPANISH SAHARA

ALGERIA

LIBYA

MAURITANIA

MALI

NIGER

CHAD

Nouakchott

Timbuktu

Lake Chad

Dakar

SENEGAL

Niger River

Niamey

GAMBIA

UPPER
VOLTA

Bathurst

GUINEA-
BISSAU

Bamako

Ouagadougou

NIGERIA

Bissau

GUINEA

Niger River

Conakry

SIERRA
LEONE

IVORY
COAST

GHANA

DAHOMEY

TOGO

Freetown

CAMEROON

LIBERIA

Lagos

Porto Novo

Monrovia

Abidjan

Accra

Lomé

FERNANDO PO
ISLAND

Atlantic Ocean

Gulf of Guinea

WEST AFRICA

Maps taken from Lila Perl, *Ghana and Ivory Coast; Spotlight On West Africa*, William R. Morrow, New York 1975.

UPPER VOLTA

UPPER REGION

Bolgatanga ●

Black Volta River

White Volta River

Wa ●

MOLE
NATIONAL
PARK

NORTHERN   REGION

Tamale ●   Yendi ●

Damongo ● ● Yapei Port
Bole ●

IVORY COAST

GHANA

ASHANTI REGION

Volta Lake

TOGO

DAHOMEY

Sunyani ●

Tano River

Bonwire ●
Kumasi ●

Lake Bosumtwi

Ho ●

Akosombo
Volta River

AKWAPIM
HILLS

Ankobra River

Obuasi ●

Aburi ●   SHAI
HILLS

Pra River

Accra ◉

Tarkwa ●

Tema

Ada

Keta

Saltpond
Anomabu
Cape Coast
Elmina

Half Assini

Axim

Takoradi

Atlantic Ocean

GHANA

he had no petrol. Petrol was the one thing Clark had plenty of, and while the police driver put on his new uniform, they gassed up the shiny Land Rover. As dusk settled across the countryside, they roared off at top speed towards the accident with the siren blaring out over the somnolent African bush. "There's something backward about this," Clark thought to himself. "I should be screaming *away* from the accident, not going back to it."

At the site, his heart went out to the people still patiently guarding the wreck and the priceless food he had been carrying. The officer decided that the vehicle should be hauled out of the bush to reduce the danger of looting, and after much struggle and several broken chains, the station wagon came to a rest upside down in the middle of the highway, a considerably greater traffic hazard than it had been in the bush. At Nkawkaw, the police graciously offered to radio Accra so that Victor Brandon would know what had happened; fearing that a garbled message would only upset Brandon, Clark said that he would prefer to give them a written message in the morning. Out of kindness, however, the police sent the message anyway after Clark had left to find Besa in the hospital, and what Victor Brandon heard later that night was that Ray Clark had been seriously injured and Besa Amenuvor was missing. As was the lot of so many CUSO field staff before him, Victor Brandon spent a long and sleepless night, unable to leave for Nkawkaw because of a military curfew.

In the morning, after dividing the fruit and vegetables among the people who had guarded the car, Clark and Besa set out with a doctor who was travelling to Accra. On the road, they encountered Victor Brandon roaring up the highway towards them, and together the three made their way back to the city.

The next day, it was as though nothing had happened; just another busy day in the life of a CUSO Field Staff Officer. "Besa's hand will be OK," Clark wrote to Ottawa, "it was his left one fortunately . . . as for me, I feel extremely fortunate; another worst fear lived through. I made sure to drive myself around Accra the last few days — no ill effects; I'm still the same. I'm a bit homesick though. I was due to go to Togo this week but Ghana has closed its borders — reportedly another coup attempt — I may get out by Wednesday."

And he reflected more deeply than he had, on Ghanaians. "Despite the fact that hordes are in exodus because of the harsh conditions here, the reality is that there are an amazing number of Ghanaians in rural areas aware of what they need and really trying to do it. Self-sufficiency, cooperation and hard work are not news here. I've met more Ghanaians committed to rural development and self-help than I have anywhere else.'

Not surprisingly, the final recommendation of his journey to Ghana was positive. "CUSO has been involved in some good work here; it should be continued."

Chapter 23

Curtains: The SUCO Connection

The relationship between the anglophone and francophone wings of CUSO is a tale of intrigue, mismanagement and confusion. It is a story of missed opportunities, ruined careers and the death of a dream. It is about racism and separatism, money and power; it is about the lure of socialism's radical fringe and liberalism's suicidal optimism. In short, it is a story so Canadian in its substance and its evolution that many who have never heard of CUSO will know the tale as though it were a family legend.

CUSO/SUCO had always been envisaged as a bilingual national organization, open to both anglophone and francophone applicants. To this end, Quebec universities and fledgling francophone development organizations participated with their anglophone counterparts in the founding meetings of 1961, and care was taken to ensure proportional francophone and anglophone representation on the early Board of Directors. But in programming terms, work in the French speaking countries of Africa was slow in starting. In 1962, twenty teachers were sent to Congo-Kinshasa, and another six to the Republic of Guinea; but the assignments, arranged through Marcel Cloutier, Chairman of the CUSO committee at the University of Montreal, had been concluded on the basis of full-salaried expatriate contracts rather than the volunteer terms and conditions upon which CUSO's foundations rested.

Guinea presented major financial and administrative problems, and the Congo, quickly descending into anarchy and civil war, had an obviously limited future for placement purposes. Though a few opportunities opened up in the Ivory Coast, Rwanda and Burundi in 1964, there were fewer placements in French-speaking countries that year than there had been in 1962. As a result, it was agreed that the Vice Chairman of the Board, Louis Berubé, should make a tour of French-speaking African countries to investigate the potential for CUSO development. It was a gruelling two-month journey that took him from Conakry on the west coast of Africa, south to the Cameroun, east across the continent to Madagascar and north through Burundi, Rwanda and Ethiopia. He visited more than a dozen countries and learned at first hand of the difficulties that would always hobble programming efforts in francophone Africa.

The first problem was that the francophone nations, excluding only Guinea and the former Belgian colonies, were still tied into the French sphere of influence in a way that was significantly different from the more independent-minded former British colonies. Most of them received considerable assistance from France, which included both experienced 'cooperateurs' and 'Volontaires de la Paix' whose salaries and allowances, (completely covered by the French government), made CUSO's terms and conditions seem comparatively onerous. In any case, the local salary for government teachers was generally far below anything a CUSO volunteer could live on, as Berubé discovered in the Cameroun. Government teachers there earned only $25 a month, whereas expatriate-style food alone could cost four times that amount. Berubé also sensed a condescending attitude towards CUSO, which was clearly seen as an inferior Canadian product.

"All CUSO volunteers considered for service in French-speaking countries must be very carefully checked and screened for the quality of their spoken French," he warned in his report, adding that "some of the volunteers (already overseas) are not sufficiently careful of the way in which they speak French."[1]

Although Berubé met with ministers of education across the continent, it became clear that postings in government institutions were not likely to amount to much. Yet, in most countries he visited, he found French-

Canadian priests and nuns, often in positions of significant influence within the educational network. Brother Bertrand Cloutier smoothed out his arrangements in the Ivory Coast, taking him up-country to visit the two volunteers who had arrived the previous year, and assuring him that further mission postings could be easily accommodated. In the Cameroun, he found four schools operated by Canadian missionaries, who were eager to have volunteers; and while he met with a cool reception from government officials in Madagascar, the man in charge of the seventeen Canadian-run mission schools, Brother Trudel, said that he could use as many as ten CUSO teachers immediately. In the former Belgian colony of Rwanda, where there were already eighteen CUSO volunteers and a part-time CUSO coordinator — Jean-Yves Tremblay — Berubé discovered that finances, again, were the major problem. Tremblay lived in a single room, travelled the country on a scooter and somehow survived on a salary of $147 a month, while the government nagged that volunteers were costing too much.

Berubé's conclusions were straightforward: if CUSO was serious about working in the former French and Belgian colonies, the cost would be higher than in other countries. More experienced, better qualified people would be necessary if they were not to be disparaged in comparison with their French counterparts. And most postings would probably have to be made through mission schools and hospitals.

Thus were sown the seeds of an approach to programming which was different in methodology and cost from the anglophone program, and which would eventually lead to philosophical difficulties both within the francophone wing, and between the French and the English. By 1967, there were ninety volunteers in francophone Africa, and two years later, the number had risen to 166. Most of them worked with French Canadian missionaries, and many found the social life difficult. Denise Chamberland had already taught for four years in Canada before she arrived in the Ivory Coast and found herself incarcerated in a maisonette under the careful watch of Canadian nuns. "This allowed them to keep a discreet check on the times of my coming and goings, as well as the friends I was able to invite to my place," she said. The nuns would lock the gates at eight in the evening and only reluctantly gave her a key if she wanted to stay out later. She ate with the sisters, and found the prayers and the readings from the *Imitation of Christ* before meals upsetting.

"After the meal there was a reading from the gospel or Roman martyrology, followed by the *De Profundis* for the nuns of the order who had passed away. Believe me, the atmosphere was really go-go!"[2]

Paul Hitschfield and other SUCO volunteers faced an unexpected problem in Zaire when they went to sign their contracts with the Ministry of Education. Zaire did not accept "do-good" volunteers, only professionals. The SUCO people were therefore — ipso facto — professionals, not volunteers, and would be paid full professional salaries. "Many of us protested that this was too high," Hitschfield recalled, "but the Ministry representative got very annoyed at us." Later, the SUCO staff officer proposed a project fund to which the volunteers might contribute, say, 'a few thousand each'. "I remember the silence in the room as he talked about this," Hitschfield said, recalling the fast-waning ardour for poverty — "all of us wanted on the one hand to support this thing and become 'poor' like the others, but on the other hand we were not willing to give up our cash . . . the development fund got nowhere."[3]

In Madagascar, Andre Guindon began to question the "momentary process of westernization" that he was part of, a westernization which created in his students, a "blurred feeling that their studies have no logical follow-through,"[4] while Normand Tellier, who taught in Rwanda between 1964 and 1966, saw the posting only as a means to an end.

"CUSO and myself are two, without deep bond," he had written from his posting, but after his return to Canada, he began to see the importance of creating a bond which would prevent the organization from becoming an overly bureaucratized, "perfectly running but purposeless machine."

"If we are not attentive," he said, "this bureaucracy will make civil servants of our leaders, mere files of our volunteers, and of CUSO a skeleton. Let us search and continue searching until we have found the formula which will make every one of us a leader and each leader a volunteer, so that CUSO itself might become an opportunity for fulfilment and the overcoming of limitations, to the end that we may finally say: 'We are CUSO'."

What sounded like a rallying cry, was in fact more a plea: it addressed the rapidly growing francophone program, which was still proscribed by the strictures Berubé had outlined several years before; but its larger context was Quebec's Quiet Revolution, by then in full swing.

When Frank Bogdasavich was appointed Executive Director in May,

1968, he had a different vision of CUSO; and a vision of Canada that was more in tune with the maître-chez-nous feeling growing within SUCO. Charles Morin, the newly appointed francophone director, was a Catholic Brother in his mid-forties who had worked in Africa for several years as a teacher. He had a proud, paternalistic attitude towards 'his' volunteers, and a condescending, almost apathetic posture towards the anglophones. Like Bogdasavich, he wanted to make something of his organization — to put it on the map. For Bogdasavich, this meant a greater organizational awareness of what constituted development, as well as physical growth and a more sensitive, streamlined form of management. For Morin, it meant growth, but also greater autonomy for the francophone sector.

Bogdasavich had great respect for Morin's francophone nationalism, which suited the mood of the times. While the francophone board members discussed the question of greater autonomy with their anglophone counterparts, Morin talked to Bogdasavich. "He was a very quiet, soft-spoken man in the European intellectual tradition," Bogdasavich felt. "He certainly influenced my thinking. I found his counsel to be wise and I relied on his judgement in staking out my own position."[5]

Bogdasavich's position was clear: the organization had grown very quickly, and had reached the point where it could no longer be run by one person; the relationship between both the Ottawa office and the Canadian regions and between Canada and the overseas programs had to be modified. In his opening remarks to his first Board meeting, eight weeks after taking office, Bogdasavich said that he did not intend to be the spokesman for the entire organization: he stressed decentralization, greater participation by the constituent wings:

The Executive Secretary of CUSO-SUCO is often told that 'we had better keep the French and English together'. To achieve that little directive means we had better know where it's at or within a half decade, not only will CUSO have excluded itself from French Canadians or vice versa, but many others will have been excluded as well . . . The development of a powerful French program is not to be viewed as a special status or a concession to French Canadians or to any other Canadians for that matter. It is an integral part of the program as a whole.[6]

Morin encouraged Bogdasavich's effort to avoid the French/English divisions that pulled most national bodies asunder in those years.

Thus, in 1969, CUSO's constitution was rewritten, creating a Francophone Committee of the Board, which would, under the general supervision of the entire Board, oversee the operations of the Francophone wing of the organization. Charles Morin became Associate Executive Secretary, and from then on, 'SUCO' stood for an increasingly distinct, autonomous operation — not just a translation of 'CUSO'.

"My total preoccupation was the overseas operations," Bogdasavich said later. "It would, I felt, harm the anglophone wing of the organization if we didn't give French-Canadians a profile of their own. I believed you could do that and still have one organization, but to do it, your executive management and Board would have to be sensitive because it was always a moving event; it was never static. There was always a risk that it would drift right out, and if it did, there was nothing we would have been able to do to stop it." The next two or three years were, in a sense, the calm before the storm. SUCO continued to grow, doubling its placements to 350 between 1969 and 1972, and operating programs in fourteen countries. Morin took a long lease on a large office in Montreal and gradually moved much of the recruitment, selection and orientation function away from Ottawa, creating an impressive 'documentation centre' and encouraging SUCO's first efforts in development education. SUCO opened recruitment centres throughout Quebec, in New Brunswick and even in Sudbury, establishing a network as impressive as CUSO's and twice as costly. It was the cost factor that inevitably led to argument between the two sectors.

CIDA, unwilling to condone a final *de facto* split along ethnic lines, insisted that the organization submit only one budget as long as it was legally a single body. And as francophone costs mounted, the anglophone staff and Board balked. Board meetings became bitter wrangles — over money, over what was perceived as inappropriate anglophone meddling, and then over the need for yet another constitutional reform. Francophone members complained that they attended their own SUCO annual meeting where they elected their own board and set their own policies, and then were obliged to participate in a full Board where anglophones held the majority.

"The subordinate position of francophones and their insufficient control over their own program and future have provoked a structural malaise in SUCO,'' wrote Henri Sire, who had been called in to study the problem. ''This malaise is manifested by a strong will for autonomy. Francophones want to escape from a guardianship which they consider to be false and unrealistic . . . people are concerned about autarky and autonomy for Third World countries, and yet they seem to have little interest for the same type of social justice within their own association.''[7]

By the summer of 1972, relations had further deteriorated between the two branches. Frank Bogdasavich had been gone for eighteen months, and much of CUSO's ability to communicate with SUCO had departed with him. Throughout 1971 there had been little leadership within CUSO. John Wood, the elusive new Executive Director, spent less than two months in the office before being relieved of his job. David Catmur, who filled the position on an acting basis, had neither the time nor the inclination to spar with SUCO. In 1971, Charles Morin had also departed, leaving SUCO, too, in the hands of a six-month interim management.

But when the two new Executive Directors were at last in place, they were culturally, if not temperamentally equipped to understand each other even better than Bogdasavich and Morin had been. John Gordon had been brought up in a bilingual family atmosphere in Quebec; Ronald Leger came from a bilingual family in New Brunswick. Both spoke the other's language, and both had CIDA experience: Leger in Ottawa, and Gordon in Tanzania. They had fundamentally different dispositions, however, and communication would always be a problem. John Gordon was a technocrat's technocrat; calm, unemotional and studied in his approach to whatever crisis arose. Ronald Leger was as flamboyant as Gordon was reserved, as impetuous as the other was cautious. He approached SUCO with enthusiasm, and the question of development with both commitment and passion.

Leger had gone to Madagascar as a teacher in 1966, dividing his time between a small village school and part-time coordinating duties for SUCO. In 1968 he was appointed full-time Field Staff Officer for another year, before returning to post-graduate studies at Laval University. While at Laval, he became a member and then Vice Chairman of the SUCO Board of Directors, and then joined CIDA a year later. When he was appointed Executive Director of SUCO in mid-1972, he brought with him a keen desire to transform the organization. He felt that while Charles Morin had strengthened it in innumerable ways, it was little more than a large version of what it had been years before: an exporter of technical assistance, tied in large measure to missionary efforts which had failed to come to terms with post-independence Africa. Many of the volunteers were teaching in private schools for expatriates and the rich; in Abidjan alone, a city with more than fifty-three thousand Europeans, there were a dozen volunteers. He wanted SUCO to become more dynamic; he wanted it to become involved in project development and administration, as CUSO had done in Nigeria and Bangladesh; he felt that development education should have a higher priority than it had been given. He wanted to involve more locals overseas and, eventually, make each SUCO program an autonomous body, with the head office acting in a service capacity to a truly international network. Knowing of Jean Pelletier's experiences with the Nigeria Schools Reconstruction Project, and in Bangladesh, Leger persuaded him to become SUCO's Overseas Director. And on the Canadian side, he brought in Michel Blondin, an 'animateur sociale' in Montreal, who had been a volunteer in Bolivia.

Their first problem, however, was an enormous one: CUSO/SUCO had run up a deficit of almost a million dollars, most of it on the SUCO side. "We had to rationalize that budget," Jean Pelletier said. "In Morin's days it was incredible, the amount of money they would put into all kinds of things — that huge office in Montreal; a magazine that cost something like $75,000 to print, and all kinds of silly expenses."[8] SUCO had actually bought a house in Hull, just across the river from Ottawa, in order to provide a meeting place away from the anglophone intimidation of the Slaterbunker, and SUCO staff had increased to ninety, not including the overseas assistants and secretaries. Leger sold the house in Hull and laid off almost half his staff. He allowed other offices to atrophy and asked CUSO for assistance.

But John Gordon was not sympathetic, especially in view of the 'anglo-bashing' in which SUCO Board members seemed to revel. While he felt that there was "no real problem" on the anglophone side of the Board, it was different on the francophone side. "Many had probably never seen more than $3,000 together at one time, and were students or grad students in a very politicized Quebec," he said. "There was a basic difference in understanding of how things function," he added, echoing SUCO's own generalized preconceptions about anglophones. "The Gallic question of rationality and the need to have things in writing is very much part of the French tradition. . . . "⁹

The CUSO attitude towards SUCO was as paternalistic as it was unsympathetic, just at a point when one of the last opportunities for dialogue and cooperation presented itself. Perhaps a different approach would not have mattered, however, for other forces were at work which would make 1973 one of the organization's most difficult years, with calamities and misunderstandings raining down on SUCO like a monsoon. Ronald Leger had already begun to discover that his political problems did not lie entirely, or even predominantly in the separatist inclinations of his staff and board.

"It was not so much a question of separatism and nationalism," he said, "it was 'des revolutionaires verbaux': people who had read maybe one volume of somebody writing about Marx but had not read Marx themselves," — what George Orwell once called "fellow travellers of fellow travellers." "It would have been easier to sit down and have working arrangements with a thoroughly purebred Marxist group, but who were intelligent and who had a purpose, than with these. It was impossible to have any kind of precise discussion because I don't think they had a very clear ideology . . . they knew what they wanted to destroy, but not what they wanted to do, and that's where my expression, 'verbal revolutionaries' came from." ¹⁰ He shared John Gordon's evaluation of his Board, telling them on one occasion, "You couldn't administer a case of beer. You could drink it, but you couldn't administer a case of twenty-four."

The problem, at least in part, was Michel Blondin, who had begun staffing the Quebec offices with people he had known in the labour movement; people, Jean Pelletier said, "who had never been overseas, never been in CUSO, never served a term on a Board of Directors anywhere"; people who shared Blondin's political outlook on life.

"I remember a fellow in Three Rivers — he had been an organizer for the CSN and now had a salary of $13,000 — good at that time — as the SUCO rep in Three Rivers. But the guy had no clue of what to do. There was no question of recruiting volunteers. There were requests by the dozen, but they weren't going to do that. They would say, 'Our mission is to explain to the people of Quebec that they are in solidarity

with the exploited masses of the world'. I remember asking for a physiotherapist and they said, 'What do you want a physiotherapist for?
She'll come from Canada and she'll have bourgeois values. And what
will she give to the people? Bourgeois values. This is negative development'.''

Gradually, Blondin, Jacques Fournier and a small group of others on
staff built up a network across Quebec, bringing like-minded people into
local committees which in turn controlled the appointment of delegates
to the annual meetings where the Board of Directors would be elected.
It was the kind of takeover that was happening regularly in unions and
other Quebec organizations at the time, and in SUCO, naively idealistic
and easily beguiled by nationalistic fervour, it was like taking candy from
a baby. Of Blondin, Pelletier said, "Leger brought about his own destruction in hiring that guy."

The story of Jacques Roy is deserving of a book in itself. He had gone
to Tanzania as a CUSO teacher in the late 1960s and, as legend has it,
soon decided that there was a more important cause in which he could
become involved: the liberation of the Portuguese colony of Angola.
Unlike so many, for whom Angola and the Portuguese colonies was one
in a long series of political 'struggles' to be fought in posters and resolutions and rhetoric from the safely and comfort of home, Jacques Roy
marched into Angola on foot, made contact with the MPLA — the Popular
Movement for the Liberation of Angola, and asked how he could help.
He spent much of the next five years travelling back and forth between
Canada and Africa, raising funds for refugees and for training projects;
he talked to hundreds, perhaps thousands of small groups, attempting to
convince them of the rightness of the Angolan bid for independence. It
was Jacques Roy who arranged for Dr. Neto, the MPLA leader and later
President of Angola, to come to Canada on a speaking tour — which
began, ironically, on the day of the Portuguese coup that led directly to
the independence of all Portuguese colonies.

Ronald Leger met Jacques Roy and became convinced of his dedication
and sincerity, and the justness of his cause. "He was being kept alive
because people were giving him $25 to make a speech! When I discovered
his dedication, I gave him a salary to continue some of his work, and to
orient it and place it in a context of public awareness . . . I felt it was

damned important that Canadians discover what was going on, and Jacques Roy was the only one who could do that." Pelletier agreed to support some of the overseas projects by supplying medicines and tools, and Michel Blondin said he would launch a program of support in Quebec.

"And then," said Pelletier, "Blondin came out with his goddamned poster." A large poster featuring maps of Angola and Quebec, prominently joined by the word 'Libre', it created a political uproar. The first Leger knew of it was when his telephone started ringing — along with alarm bells at CIDA, External Affairs and CUSO. Blondin, Director of Information explained meekly that no executive had been in the office to veto the poster when it came up for approval; turning the argument against CUSO, he said, "CIDA officials associate SUCO with separatism. The problem between CUSO and SUCO began when CIDA stepped in and demanded that we cease our domestic activities. Only then did CUSO begin to think we were a menace to the whole organization."[11]

CUSO huffed and puffed, alternating between internal indignation and public contrition, while in a foretaste of the formal response to even bigger blunders, the Board voted to "congratulate the staff for their involvement in 'Operation Angola'."[12] Only John Gordon, fearful of the implications, voted against it.

The next imbroglio was the Allende visit. Salvadore Allende Gossens, a Marxist, was elected President of Chile in 1970; he set out to transform the economic and social structures of the country, but encountered strong opposition within the Chilean legislature. As inflation mounted and reserves declined, the country fell into economic and political disarray; covert CIA activities (well-documented), exacerbated the chaos. In September, 1973, the military carried out a bloody coup, in which Allende was killed. The rightist government arrested innumerable people, and thousands were simply never heard of again; overnight, Chile became one of the worst violators of human rights, and an international bête noire.

Leger and Pelletier watched the brutality and rising death toll with horror. Over the years, large numbers of refugees from Hungary, Czechoslovakia and other communist countries had fled to Canada, but a month after the Chilean coup, only twenty refugees had been admitted.

The Canadian ambassador to Chile was in Argentina buying himself a new car when the coup took place; he rushed back to Santiago to announce Canadian recognition for the junta even before External Affairs had considered the matter. He was supportive of the coup, but his cables were so contradictory that Prime Minister Trudeau felt obliged to dispatch a high-ranking External Affairs officer to Chile to find out what was actually happening. Meanwhile, in Ottawa, the cabinet was split, fearing a public backlash if they rushed to allow ''leftist refugees'' into the country. External Affairs told Leger and Pelletier privately that the cabinet might be moved to open the doors if there were advance proof of public approval.

An idea was formed: bring someone to Canada to speak publicly about what had happened in Chile; give substance to the problem and do something practical. (And outstrip the 'revolutionaires verbaux' in the SUCO office, where engines were already revving on the Chilean issue.)

They would bring Mrs. Allende to Canada! It was a simple idea, and it worked. Leger arranged for her to travel to Montreal, Toronto, Ottawa, Winnipeg and Vancouver; unable to persuade John Gordon of the plan's merit, he paid her air fares from SUCO funds. The meetings, some of which were huge, were well covered by the media, and local costs were borne by the sponsoring agencies in each city. Hortensia Allende had been an actress before she married, and was not a politician; she spoke simply of events as they had happened, and of the plight of her husband's supporters in Chile.

The 'revolutionaires verbaux', however, were not happy with the tour, for Mrs. Allende was not the hard-hitting politico that they would have wished for; they dogged the enterprise at every step. ''She had been the wife of a head of state, and we put her up at the Queen Elizabeth Hotel,'' Pelletier said of the Montreal stop, where she was to speak at The Forum. ''Blondin made a big fuss because he said she was representing the oppressed masses — he wanted to put her up in St. Henri in some sleazy hotel. So we had to settle for a compromise; she ended up at the Windsor, which was becoming seedier by the hour.''

The risks were enormous — there was an attempt on her life only weeks later in New York — and Leger knew what could happen in Canada. ''Ronald was so concerned that no fuck-up should occur on this one that he travelled with her across Canada,'' said Pelletier. For Leger, it was the most difficult undertaking of his life and, incidentally, one that caused him to miss the CUSO/SUCO Annual General Meeting. Although the Allende visit helped open Canada's doors to large numbers of Chilean refugees, it backfired within the organization. The 'verbaux', already disenchanted with Leger and Pelletier, were disgusted with what they felt was a lame approach to the political question in Chile. John Gordon on the other hand, was outraged that Leger had engaged in such a high-profile event without Board approval; spent upwards of $5,000 on it without authorization, and missed the most important meeting of the CUSO/SUCO calendar, "under the guise of development education."

The continuing push for greater SUCO autonomy was now welcomed by Gordon — almost as a gift from heaven. "We put a lot of pressure on SUCO to leave if they wanted to become involved in development education, in the political process as they saw it . . . the attempt to force SUCO to either move out or compromise was in fact an attempt to control the radical push within SUCO. It was hoped that if we could bring SUCO to the brink . . . it would have a moderating influence." It is hard to determine the source of CUSO's unsympathetic attitude towards the Leger cleanup attempts; its apparent ignorance of SUCO's internal battles over 'Operation Angola', and its negative reaction to the Allende visit. There could be no mistake, however, about what was going on at the SUCO Annual General Meeting in the autumn of 1973. The gathering was stacked with 'verbaux' delegates, many of whom had no experience of the organization whatsoever. Leger was accused of a multitude of sins: he was not collegial; he did not circulate documents that should have been made available; he was opposed to development education; he had a major conflict of interest because he was on a leave of absence from CIDA. The Chairwoman of the Finance Committee moved that SUCO should not be bothered with fund-raising, and Blondin agreed that his department would henceforth not participate in fund-raising; he added that he did not believe sufficiently in SUCO to make a personal donation.[13]

Pelletier was angered that people had been imported to the meeting "from nowhere." "Why do you dig wells in Niger?" Pelletier recalls one asking. "These people are bourgeois and that money is only going to serve colonization!" Pelletier, cursing Blondin for his chicanery, wanted to shout back 'Bullshit!', but fettered by his own liberal courtesy, he held his tongue.

The cap to the meeting was the debate on public education. The assembly and the board members wanted it to have a vastly increased budget, but Leger demanded to see concrete plans first. "There was never a content debate on what public education actually was," he said. "Any debate was always turned political." When he stuck to his position, he was accused of opposing public education; despite his opposition, a budget significantly different from his own was approved — with twenty percent devoted to public education activities.

John Gordon, now only weeks away from his own escape to the greener and safer pastures of the United Nations, wrote to some of the CUSO field staff with his observations:

> I don't think there is any doubt that the underlying philosophy of the francophone Regional Meeting was a simplistic form of Marxism . . . I personally do not feel that this is compatible with the present CUSO philosophy and programming. I think the majority of anglophone staff and RVs would agree that technical assistance is still the prime goal of CUSO. Consequently, I feel that the SUCO model can only lead to strife and I would prefer to see a separation take place now while it can still be done with good will on both sides.[14]

By now, Leger knew he was on very dangerous ground; the "tactics of the left — control of assemblies, passing resolutions, dividing groups between the 'good' and the 'bad', isolating people who were not 'true' Third World supporters," had gained the advantage. The time had come to dig in, but he had been outflanked in his earlier skirmishes and no longer held the high ground. Unsatisfactory as it was, a stand would have to be made over the budget for 'public education'.

"I was determined not to live through another year of ambiguities," said Leger, referring to the $635,000 that the annual meeting had voted for public education. "It wasn't so much the total amount; it was that there was no precise content or purpose." In fact, it was aimed largely at bolstering SUCO's huge Quebec network and the bulk would go towards meetings, salaries, travel, telephone and office costs. "SUCO was better structured," Leger said, "with money, personnel, and offices . . . than the Parti Québecois and many of the unions. . . . It was impossible. On the one hand they wanted to do imaginative, revolutionary things with *six hundred and thirty five thousand* government dollars — and they didn't want anyone to say no — and on the other hand they refused to raise money publicly.'' Public education's chief architect wasn't even willing to contribute personally to the cause.

Until 1972, the Malagasy Republic seemed to be a quiet island of seven and a half million people; its conservative government was closely allied with the former French colonial masters. But this peaceful surface belied the country's economic and political malaise; what began as a wave of student protests flared into full-scale revolt against repressive government measures. Demonstrations, strikes, government retaliations, and police shootings finally forced President Tsiranana to hand over power to his army Chief of Staff, Gen. Gabriel Ramanantsoa. In contrast to the obsessive anti-communism of his predecessor, Ramanantsoa established diplomatic relations with the Soviet Union and broke all ties with South Africa. French teachers were replaced in large number by Malagasys, and a move began to have French troops and other examples of lingering colonial subservience removed.

The extreme political shift in Madagascar (a country which had been hitherto ignored by SUCO's ever vigilant 'verbaux') suddenly thrust it into new prominence, and in the summer of 1973, an 'Operation Madagascar' was begun as a complement to the ill-fated 'Operation Angola'. Leger did not pay it much heed, concentrating his efforts instead on trying to ensure that the growing hostility towards French teachers in Madagascar didn't jeopardize SUCO's program there; he went to the island to visit the volunteers, to discuss events with the Field Staff Officer and to meet with senior government officials. After three hours with the Minister of the Interior, he came away moderately satisfied that SUCO could remain aloof from the country's rapidly changing political scene. Before leaving Madagascar, Leger invited SUCO's Malagasy Deputy Coordinator to the SUCO Annual Meeting, hoping that she might eventually become part of the 'nationalization' of SUCO that he had in the back of his mind. It was an invitation to a disaster.

At the SUCO meeting, the Malagasy woman and four other international staff visitors were badly treated. ''There was even a resolution forbidding them to speak,'' said Leger, ''because they were not true representatives of 'the people'.'' Although Leger found it 'insulting and outrageous', the visitor from Madagascar harboured an even deeper resentment which she carried home with her. Within weeks, signals began to arrive in Ottawa that all was not well with SUCO in the Malagasy Republic. The government apparently had serious reservations about a project that SUCO was developing, and one of the volunteers was fired and sent home.

Jean Pelletier was hurriedly dispatched to assess and untangle the problems. The country was in turmoil, and several political factions, all vying for the title of 'most revolutionary', were jockeying, sometimes violently, for position. Pelletier met with the Interior Minister, who told him that some of the volunteers, unnamed and unspecified, were involved in political activities. "These people shouldn't be involved in our democracy," he told Pelletier.

Pelletier then met with the Prime Minister, a man who was to lose his job and his life three months later to the Interior Minister's special version of Malagasy democracy. Pelletier was able to make an agreement with the Prime Minister about SUCO's role and responsibilities in the country. "So we shook hands, had our pictures taken, and I went to the volunteers and told them that everything was OK," he concluded.

"But in my bags I foolishly had Blondin's last report on liberating the masses, oppression around the world and so on. I arrived at the airport with my suitcase. The guy looks at my passport, takes me into a small room and asks me to undress. I undress, and I'm bare naked, and they search my papers and they find this report. Since the report was marked confidential, they naturally took it away. Eventually a civil servant returns, and he says, 'You can take the plane, but we have to keep this document'." "I took the plane and a day later they expelled everyone for trying to undermine the revolution."

It was the first and only time that CUSO or SUCO was ever expelled from a country — in marked contrast to the Peace Corps, which was often used as a political football, sometimes moving in and out of countries several times in a decade. To CIDA, External Affairs and CUSO, it was further confirmation of SUCO's troublesome radical proclivities.

Murray Thomson, who had now taken over as Executive Director from John Gordon, was vague about the causes for the expulsion, saying privately that the Madagascar government, itself anti-imperialist, had obtained some SUCO documents "filled with rhetoric about imperialism and exploitation.''[15] But the irony of the situation was overshadowed by the further damage done to SUCO — and its relations with CUSO.

Murray Thomson was new to the job, but unlike his predecessor, he felt that ''it was terribly important to keep CUSO and SUCO together if at all possible.''[16] He tried to present the differing factions as fairly as he could:

> There is no consensus within the constituency as we begin 1974.
> A large segment of CUSO believes that we should continue to do
> what we have always done — promote high quality manpower to
> overseas countries — only do it better . . . Part of this segment,
> too, supports development education as long as it does not jeop-
> ardize placements and projects . . . Another large segment of
> CUSO is asking that we make a shift of direction and emphasis in
> 1974 . . . Not a lurch or a drastic change but a shift towards more
> public identification with the unrepresented of the world; the poor,
> the oppressed, and the powerless.[17]

He was correct: many felt that CUSO's traditional role remained valid, and many within that group felt that development education was also an essential part of the organization's mandate. But development education was not a hypothetical proposition, for CUSO had by that time been involved in projects with schools and community groups for almost four years. Nor did the organization ignore 'the poor, the oppressed, and the powerless' as Thomson's analysis might have suggested; rather it had tended to view 'education' as a long-term process which would not be advanced by revolutionary rhetoric, faddism and armchair demonstrations of solidarity. One CUSO committee expressed it clearly enough:

> Essentially, we do not differ from SUCO and returned volunteers'
> views about what needs to be done to create social and political
> awareness at home and abroad . . . (but) we do fear that ap-
> proaches such as SUCO's would lead to a reduction of even the
> little bit of good that CUSO can do in the present and in future
> programs abroad. We feel that Canadians will not respond posi-

tively to the sort of confrontation politics advocated by
SUCO . . . we feel that it might well swing public opinion against
the Third World and development.[18]

Thomson, fresh from his posting in Thailand and eager to bind up the
wounds of the organization, was willing to give the benefit of the doubt
to the good intentions of Leger's 'revolutionaires verbaux'; Leger himself,
he found, "effective but authoritarian," the antithesis, in the latter point,
of his own approach to leadership.

Ronald Leger's battle with his Board of Directors, in March 1974, was
fraught with tension, high drama and overwrought soliloquies. A first
SUCO budget was presented, reflecting the massive increase for public
education, voted in at the Francophone Annual Meeting. Leger opposed
it, defending his own more modest proposal. The anglophone members,
uncomfortably aware of their disagreeable and untenable position between
the francophone Executive Director and his Board, searched in vain for
something to hide behind. A feeble attempt was made to discuss the
comparative merits of the proposals, but the francophones simply refused
to entertain any debate.

"It was a terrible fight," Jacques Fournier said. "In the same room,
there was the French Director agreeing with the English. We told them
that if they wanted to deal with the SUCO constituency, we would just
sit back and watch."[19]

The francophones charged racism: "There is anglophone prejudice
towards the French businessman. The anglophone board members in
particular feel that we don't know how to spend money, even though the
audit reports prove we can," said René Leduc. "The anglophones try to
adhere to the myth of pragmatism while the French adhere strictly to
values and principles."[20]

They charged interference and anti-democratic behaviour, accusing the
anglophones of "interfering in the affairs of the francophone sector by
refusing to approve the francophone budget . . . which had been approved
unanimously (except for the Executive Director) as submitted by the
Francophone Committee."[21]

"The English do not feel the Board is responsible to the general assembly, where the French feel the people give them a mandate to which they are responsible," said Leduc.[22]

It was the same indirect censorship that CUSO had experienced in arguments about development education, about unqualified support for the African National Congress, over formation of a staff union and in the 'B.S. Debate'. The pattern was always the same: it began with self-censorship of the majority of those involved; then, deliberate suppression of arguments advanced by the enemies of the faith; then, if they persisted, by discrediting their motives; and finally by overt attacks, accusing them of being destructive, frightened, bureaucratic, conservative, or in this case, anti-developmental, anti-democratic, and anti-French.

Leger insisted that the substance of the budget required discussion; his Board refused. "They refused any debate because they knew they could always get the anglophones on the political level; they could always win by saying, 'You can't understand Quebec', and of course if I tell someone from Vancouver he can't understand Quebec, what can he say? It's an ad hominem argument — it doesn't stand up to reason, but he can't even speak French, so they could always shut out any debate."

The francophones demanded Leger's resignation. He refused. Jean Pelletier was watching the Chairman of the combined Board, Red Williams. "Red was so torn," he said, "he was suddenly aware that Canada was two cultures; something he had read about somewhere but had never lived. The whole atmosphere was 'You fucking English; you're not going to screw one French Canadian here!' And the English all felt stupidly guilty. They felt, 'These guys are bastards, but why should we judge them? why should we be involved?' "

The question was finally called on the budget, but before the vote could be taken, the francophone members stormed from the room, leaving Leger to vote with the anglophones who maintained both a quorum and a majority. Leger had won the battle, but he had lost the war.

The Francophone Committee went straight to the media with a press statement denouncing the anglophone intrusion into its affairs — a particularly resonant theme in Quebec in those days: "The impasse illustrates the profound difficulty for pan-Canadian organizations to function where francophones are in the eternal minority."[23] Clement Boulanger, Chairman of the Francophone Committee pronounced himself acting Executive Director, charging Leger with insubordination, maladministration and conflict of interest and suggesting that anglophone interference threatened the very existence of the organization. Leger responded, saying, "this approach persists in threatening the Board with a split in the event it should refuse a blind approval, that is to say *without discussion, without examination, .without participation* of any sort, in any alternative budget presented by the Francophone Committee."[24]

It soon became apparent that the anglophones were not prepared to maintain their support for Leger. Murray Thomson proposed that an external facilitator be brought in, that Blondin not be fired — as Leger, too late, now proposed to do — and that if no agreement was worked out within eight weeks, Leger should resign.[25] It was clear to Leger that the anglophones, in order to be rid of their unwanted responsibility, were willing to concede that the debate was an internal SUCO matter that revolved around his own 'undemocratic' behaviour and lack of support for the motherhood issue of development education. Leger resigned, citing breach of contract.

A small group of SUCO volunteers and staff reacted; they demanded that the 'Blondin-Fournier clique' be exposed as "revolutionaries who claim to know exactly what the Third World needs, who it needs, and especially which Third World is 'good' and which is 'bad' . . . The time has come for returned volunteers to put an end to the reign of the Blondin-Fournier junta . . . which has done harm enough to SUCO by using it for their own mean purposes."[26] But the anglophone board looked the other way. The francophone Committee simply ignored the charges and moved the entire SUCO office, lock stock and photocopier to Montreal — partly to draw attention from internal staff ructions.

Jean Pelletier quit, despairing of the Board. "When I resigned", he said, "I was waiting to see CIDA clamp down on SUCO. It took ten years. Ten long years."

At the previous Annual General Meeting, one in a relentless progression of constitutional proposals had been accepted. It had suggested a model which became known as DAPDUC — Deux Associations Paralleles dans Une Corporation: two parallel associations in one corporation. The DAP-DUC proposal was simple: there should be parity in numbers between the anglophone and francophone board members, ensuring (with full attendance) that one side could never outvote the other. For some DAP-

DUC became 'Daffy Duck', for others, 'Dead Duck', but the motion had passed, and the francophone Committee now demanded that it be implemented. Through the summer, the anglophones resisted, growing more and more embittered by the ongoing financial and political wrangles they thought Leger's departure had ended; they finally agreed among themselves that a split was inevitable.

"By September," said Murray Thomson, "I had come to the conclusion that it probably wasn't going to work, and it would probably be best if we separated. I made a somewhat impassioned speech to the Board to that effect."

At a stormy meeting that month, the anglophone members sat across the table from their francophone counterparts and presented their proposal for a complete divorce. Yvan Labelle, the new SUCO Executive Director, refused to entertain the motion on the grounds that it violated the approval given to DAPDUC at the previous annual meeting. The anglophones persisted in calling the question, but before the vote could be counted, the francophone members stood in a body and once again left the room. The anglophones, somewhat bewildered, but resolute in their newfound unity, went ahead and passed the resolution which would be carried forward to the 1974 Annual General Meeting ten weeks later.

In the ten weeks leading up to the Annual General Meeting, there was a frenzy of political activity within CUSO. Local committees across the country saw the faltering CUSO/SUCO relationship as a portent of Canada's future; they lobbied Board members, wrote papers and signed petitions on the need for cooperation. SUCO, suddenly cast in the unaccustomed role of wounded federalist, was alarmed by a cut in the CIDA allocation for the coming year, a warning — if any was needed — that alone they could not survive.

Juanita Poole, a British Columbia Board member who would become CUSO's Chairperson in 1984, attended the francophone meeting in Montreal, and came away with some clear impressions:

> Autonomy is no longer the real issue for the francophones as it was last year . . . SUCO's openly declared aims are 'socialism versus capitalism as necessary to development (i.e. liberation) — be it in Canada or in the Third World' . . . SUCO realizes the confrontation it is causing with CIDA and feels this is a necessary

step in revealing some of the wrong approaches to development
and then pursuing the more desirable socialistic ones.

"My own feeling." she added, "is that CUSO is not ready for this."[27]
It was not that CUSO didn't have its own share of 'verbaux'; it did,
and would continue to. But despite some terrible battles in the later 1970s
regarding 'wrong approaches to development', there tended to be a more
pragmatic attitude to differences of opinion, and a willingness — sometimes uneasy, but nevertheless there — to live within a pluralistic environment. This pluralistic approach tended to stress people rather than
governments, and allowed for CUSO efforts in countries with practically
every permutation of free enterprise and socialism, as well as countries
which moved in and out of parliamentary democracy, one-party systems
and military rule.

The 1974 Annual Meeting finally arrived; it was held during the first
weekend of December, in a crowded, stuffy amphitheatre at the University
of Ottawa. The freezing rain, black ice and gusting winds outside matched
the mood of the two factions inside as the debate opened. It went on
through Friday night and all day Saturday; most speakers regardless of
their viewpoints, delivered long, dramatic pleas for cooperation and denounced fiscal mismanagement and political brinkmanship. There were
repeated emotional outbursts and angry recriminations over past misinterpretations and insincerity. Dozens of would-be parliamentarians waved
their proxies and raised points of order over technical rulings. At one
point, the business was halted by a twenty-minute argument over whether
debate on an amendment should be restricted to fifteen minutes. When
the result of that vote was announced, one of the delegates called out,
"Mr. Chairman, that's not fair; I didn't know what we were voting for!"[28]
So a recount was taken. But throughout it all there was none of the
'socialism versus capitalism' discussion that Juanita Poole had heard in
Montreal.

Just before the meeting began, Murray Thomson and Yvan Labelle
met for two hours to try to come to an understanding. It was an exceed-
ingly difficult time for Thomson, on whose shoulders now rested, or
seemed to rest, not only an important symbol of Canadian unity, but all
the progressive notions he held about the future of CUSO. Sensing com-

mitment on SUCO's part to a renewed effort at partnership, he had an eleventh-hour change of heart, and to the astonishment of many, announced his support for DAPDUC. Enraging some ("most of my staff," he said), and confusing others, he changed the mood of the meeting entirely, giving credence to the SUCO charge that the whole thing was an effort to expel them from the organization because they were French, and because they identified more strongly and more honestly with the oppressed.

Just before the final vote was called, a Toronto Board Member, Michael Sinclair, stood and announced that many of the anglophone Board Members also had changed their minds after reading some of the written pleas for unity. He was most impressed, he said, with the paper written by Thomson and Labelle suggesting that a team of outsiders examine the situation: "fresh minds, unencumbered by the mistakes, frustrations and failures of the past." It was a call for national unity in microcosm.

When the vote was taken, fifty delegates cast their ballot for separation; one hundred and thirty-two opposed it. More than half the opposition came from anglophone delegates.

David Beer, who had recently returned to Ottawa to manage CUSO's own development education, felt that the vote reflected growing CUSO confidence in SUCO's "ideology of solidarity." "There is no question that SUCO has influenced CUSO," he said. "They set a precedent with their development education program and did the groundwork for evolving a rationale for development assistance."[29]

Jacques Fournier, who described Beer as "one of the really progressive people in CUSO," said that the vote demonstrated that there were now more progressive anglophones who shared SUCO's analysis of development than non-progressives who did not.[30] Fournier had neatly divided the world into two parts: there were only 'progressives' — those who agreed with SUCO's analysis — and 'non-progressives'.

In the following months, a new constitution was accepted which ensured equal francophone and anglophone representation on the Board. In practice, the anglophone committee restricted its interests to CUSO affairs, while the francophone Committee concentrated on SUCO; the full board met infrequently and briefly, and then only to argue about the division of the CIDA budget. SUCO experiments in collegial management overseas all but abolished field staff, leaving administration in the hands of committees of volunteers, under whose aegis programs withered and closed. Placement targets, agreed upon when the annual budget was being divided, were seldom met; and a CIDA penalty clause was avoided on several occasions only because of CUSO over-placements, squeezed out of a proportionately smaller share of the budget.

Moving on to higher planes of analysis, SUCO produced an even more refined policy approach to development as outlined in a 1978 Board submission:

> We advocate a type of cooperation that will assist people in counterbalancing western modernization which is capitalistic and imperialistic . . . our role should be to prepare the political struggle or foster the emerging of the partisan political struggle of popular movements . . . and in Quebec and in Canada (sic) . . . to analyze mechanisms of exploitation and domination, and explain the resistance process of affected populations.[31]

The final showdown occurred at the 1978 Annual Meeting, at which proxy-carrying SUCO delegates proposed resolutions equating Zionism with racism, and supporting every liberation movement from the Mediterranean to the Cape of Good Hope; they professed "commitment towards Vietnam," denounced the Chilean dictatorship and demanded the release of political prisoners in Quebec. A month later, CUSO's own management was in disarray, its Executive Director had been fired and a devastating million-dollar reduction in the CIDA allocation had been announced: the CUSO Board finally took charge of itself and resolved that separation was the only salvation. SUCO, also badly hit by the CIDA reduction and having survived its many scandals over the years, forgot about the protection CUSO had provided, and agreed. In December 1980, proposals for a split and the creation of two separate corporations went before the last Annual Meeting of Canadian University Service Overseas/ Service Universitaire Outre Mer. Ironically, after so much debate and passion, the motion to separate was read to the assembly, and the vote, taken without debate, was unanimous.

The old corporation was left behind as an empty shell, an umbrella under which the two new bodies could meet if they so desired; the new organizations — 'CUSO' and 'SUCO,' no longer acronyms — were incorporated under new federal charters with new bylaws, new tax-deductible numbers from Revenue Canada, and separate funding arrangements with CIDA.

In the summer of 1982, SUCO appointed a new Executive Director, Jacques Jobin, who had been a volunteer in Uganda in the 1960s, and had subsequently worked in the Ottawa SUCO office. He had been Executive Director of Oxfam Canada in the 1970s, and had extensive experience as a social worker in Quebec when he returned to SUCO. Level-headed and politically astute, he seemed to offer the experience, the stability and the political know-how that the organization badly needed. But Jobin was shocked by what he found. A collective agreement had been signed which not only guaranteed what he felt were unjustified and overly generous wage increments, but which basically shackled the Executive Director to a management system almost totally dependent upon the directives of the Annual General Meeting and unwieldly staff committees. The organization had fifty staff but barely one hundred volunteers overseas, and was immersed in a private world of cant and political sloganeering; furthermore, it was running a severe deficit.

For a year, Jobin worked within the system, and then offered his solutions to the SUCO Annual General Meeting in the summer of 1983. Much greater emphasis would have to be placed on meeting the recruitment targets which had been contracted with CIDA, and it would have to be done with fewer staff. In order to deal with the accumulated deficit, now running at $625,000, a dozen jobs would have to be cut. The organization would have to adopt a less strident political stance, and the collective agreement would have to be amended. Not surprisingly, the Annual Meeting rejected his proposals, and on June 22, he resigned. Seven other staff went out with him through the revolving door and more would follow.

The matter reached the media in the form of an open letter, (published in La Presse), to the Chairperson of the SUCO Board from Andre Guindon, the volunteer who had gone to Madagascar in 1965 and had questioned the westernizing process he was involved in as a twenty-two year old school teacher. Now, almost twenty years later, six of which he had spent as a volunteer, he asked what had become of the organization. He questioned the election procedures which regulated the organization's much vaunted 'democracy' and said that the previous annual meeting had confirmed his suspicions that delegates were influenced by organizations all having the same "leftist ideology and Marxist analysis."

"How many potential volunteers or employees have these people forced out because they don't conform to this ideology?" he asked.[32] A week later, the media was having a field day. Jobin, and the others who had resigned, issued a widely published statement, saying there had been an "unacceptable gap between the theory and the practice of using human resources overseas, in the financing of projects and in public education." There had been "an inability to discuss fundamental issues," a "perpetual power struggle," and despite years of claims to the contrary, "democratic and open leadership has not been possible."[33] It was almost an exact replay of what happened nine-and-a-half years earlier, right down to the amount of money in question. And the SUCO Board responded much as it had a decade earlier, castigating Jobin for his autocratic style, his inability to deal with the deficit 'collegially', and accusing him of being "a man whose ambitions are certainly not those of international solidarity."[34]

This time, however, the outcome was different. In a simple letter, CIDA informed SUCO that there would be no further federal funding for the organization beyond March 31, 1984. SUCO managed to whip up a little concern in the Quebec media about dreadful anglophones and the meddlesome federal government, but it did not last. *Le Devoir* recognized that "the financial and ideological crises that surround SUCO are not new"[35] and the *Globe and Mail* editorialized, "The organization's Marxist view of development and its $625,000 deficit left its benefactor with no alternative, especially once the new management team which had been trying to salvage SUCO resigned in frustration with staff militancy."[36]

SUCO cranked up a feeble letter-writing campaign, urging all its supporters to join the final struggle by writing to the government. Most of the letters were sent by volunteers serving overseas, some nervous about their own standing should the organization slip beneath the waves. The Minister for External Relations, Jean-Luc Pepin, addressed their concerns in an open reply, reaffirming the government's determination to cease funding in 1984. He cited the growing deficit, a thirty percent shortfall in placements in 1982 and 1983, and a breakdown in financial control and reporting since the departure of the finance director in 1982. He also noted, parenthetically, that a replacement finance director had been "rejected by SUCO employees, as permitted by their collective agreement."[37] Avoiding reference to the plague of ideological debate that had assailed the organization for fifteen years, he limited his comments to the catalogue of demonstrable deficiencies, pointing out that the staff resignations had now risen to a dozen. "The government decision to cease funding SUCO is an isolated case. This is the first time in fifteen years of working with NGOs that the government has taken such a step," added Pepin. He assured anyone currently serving overseas that they would be assisted with the completion of their contract and with passage home. For SUCO, totally dependent on government grants for its survival, it was the final curtain.

As Frank Bogdasavich had understood years before, the dynamics within SUCO were neither static nor monolithic. Sometimes the forces were complementary; other times they worked against each other in ways that CUSO never understood. The separatist tendencies were often sunk in murky ideological imagery that both concealed and justified an ongoing struggle for power. Nationalistic imagery, in turn, was used to veil the ideological currents which eventually inundated the organization. Had SUCO been able to evolve pragmatic and demonstrably sound programs overseas, little of this might have mattered, but these, too, declined and were drowned in ideological debate and inaction. Its public education programs had been so unsuccessful, even among its own carefully selected volunteers, that, by 1982, only one hundred of the two thousand who had served were actually making personal donations to the organization.[38]

More concerned with appearance than reality; gesture than action, SUCO had survived for years by riding on the coattails of CUSO's paternalism, its anglophone fear of rejection and its guilt, until finally, independent at last, it simply collapsed under the weight of its own rhetoric.

Shortly before the SUCO staff moved away from Ottawa to Montreal in 1974, they erected a barricade between the anglophone and francophone sections of the office. Colin Freebury arrived at work on the morning and was amazed at what had happened: "I remember the day they put that curtain up and rearranged the filing cabinets so they were blocked off totally and the CUSO staff couldn't walk through the SUCO area . . . suddenly it was sealed off. The CUSO staff reaction was 'Jesus, we better not tread into this'.''

In fact, they never had. SUCO was something that the French-Canadians within the organization had to create themselves, more against anglophone reaction and apathy, than in consort with anglophone assistance and understanding. The division was an integral part of the Canadian condition, woven into the fabric of the organization as surely as if the participants had sat down at a loom and crafted the fabric that would eventually hang across the corridor in the Slater Street office.

Chapter 24

Bolivia: The Tin Men

Everything in Bolivia is immense; everything except man.
— Alcides Arguedas

The setting is Bolivia: treacherous, unkempt soldiers open fire, tragically ending the lives of those two loveable soldiers of fortune,
Butch Cassidy and the Sundance Kid — and the film named after them.
It was 1969, and Director George Roy Hill was following the time-
honoured Hollywood tradition in which Canadians pretend to be Americans, Americans portray Mounties, and all Latinos are either 'greaseballs'
or dark slinky sénoritas. Another film released the same year, (one of
the few Bolivian movies ever made), painted a far more realistic picture
of the country; it dealt with the depressing plight of the impoverished
Quechua Indians — dehumanized and exploited by whites, *mestizos* and
even a thinly disguised Peace Corps. *Blood of the Condor* was banned
in Bolivia; it occasionally turns up on the late show, but when viewers
see anything that purports to be set in Latin America, they are far more
likely to be dragged through the ketchup-splattered carnage of the 'spa-
ghetti westerns' which were solid gold at the box office for almost a
decade.

Apart from the fantasy created by Hollywood, the Canadian experience of Latin America can be divided into three periods. Before the Second World War, Canadian private sector investments flew down to Rio, Havana and Caracas on the coattails of British and American entrepreneurs: there were railways in Cuba, Guatemala, Mexico and Brazil; there was electric power in Bolivia, Brazil, Ecuador, Mexico and Venezuela. Sun Life, Montreal Engineering, Massey Ferguson, Brazilian Traction — later Brascan — Canadian banks, and others, developed lucrative and sometimes large interests in the region; although in most cases actual field operations were carried out by American, Scots and English surrogates instead of Canadians.

When the war began, Canada started taking a greater interest in pan-American affairs, due in part to pressure from Washington.

"As you know," President Roosevelt wrote to Mackenzie King, "I have 'hunches' — not always good, but sometimes accurate . . . my present 'hunch' is that it would help if Canada could take a greater part in the struggle between the forces of totalitarianism and the forces of democracy that is now being waged in Latin America . . . Canada can help."[1]

The American Government had run hot and cold on Canadian involvement in Latin America for forty years and would continue to do so for the next forty; Washington wanted another North American voice in the Organization of American States, but was ambivalent about growing Canadian commercial interests south of the Rio Grande.

In 1940, Canada opened its first two embassies in Latin America, (in Brazil and Argentina), followed in the next six years by missions in Mexico, Peru and Cuba; but the new era of sustained Canadian interest really began only in the 1960s, after the Cuban revolution had irrevocably changed the political balance of the region. The Canadian government debated at length the wisdom of joining the OAS; a tentative Canadian aid program to Latin America began in 1964 and was expanded when Pierre Trudeau became Prime Minister.

In his wide-reaching 1968 foreign policy review, Trudeau said:

> We have to take greater account of the ties which bind us to other nations in this hemisphere — in the Caribbean, Latin America — and of their economic needs. We have to explore new avenues of

increasing our political and economic relations with Latin America, where more than four hundred million people will live by the
turn of the century, and where we have substantial interests.[2]

Between 1970 and 1981, Canadian exports to Latin America and the
Caribbean increased from $443 million to almost $4 billion; although this
represented only five percent of Canada's total exports, it accounted,
directly and indirectly, for a sizeable and growing number of Canadian
jobs.

For CUSO, Latin America was one of the most difficult regions in
which to establish aid programs. Undoubtedly, there were needs the
organization could address, but the history and culture of this vast area
was more alien to Canadian experience than parts of Asia and Africa,
which shared the Commonwealth connection. Even the designation 'Latin
America' belies the diversity of a region peopled by Indians, 'mestizos',
(people of mixed race), blacks, and whites of Iberian and other stock.
The histories and economies of the nineteen republics are as diverse as
their geography. There is Mexico, Central America, and the Hispanic
Islands of the Caribbean. There is the continent of South America: the
modern cities, rapid industrialization, and rich culture of Chile, Colombia,
Venezuela, Argentina and Brazil, seemed to act as a beacon for the many
'newly emerging' nations of the Third World in the 1960s. Some could
boast impressive literacy rates, low infant mortality and all the indicators
of rapid economic development. But away from the bright lights of Buenos Aires, Lima and Rio, in the squalor of the *barrios* and the depression
of countless up-country Indian villages, a deep-seated poverty gnawed
at the statistical averages and mocked the brave development façade.

Undoubtedly, there were needs which CUSO could address in Latin
America, but potential entry points were limited, not only by language
problems, but by cultural and political barriers in countries which, un-
tempered as in Africa and Asia by the Commonwealth connection, were
alien to the Canadian experience. By 1965, there were still only four
volunteers posted throughout all of Latin America, while their numbers
were mounting in Africa, the Caribbean and Asia. The CUSO board
decided that a full-time staff person was required if the organization were
to be taken seriously in the region. It chose as its representative Raya

Pearlman, who had worked as a volunteer in a *barrio* in the slums of Caracas. She set about the difficult task of trying to 'sell' CUSO to Latin America: travelling back and forth across the continent, meeting with government officials, development agencies and Canadian embassies; talking to missionaries, teachers, doctors, professors. Through her efforts, thirteen new postings were made in 1965, mostly teachers and nurses in Peru, Colombia, Ecuador and Bolivia; further assignments in these countries and in Chile were developed for 1966. Raya Pearlman continued her travels to build on this beginning, but fate intervened — suddenly and tragically. While she was on yet another CUSO mission, in March 1966, her aircraft crashed in Peru, killing all on board.

Through the 1960s and much of the '70s, CUSO's work in Bolivia had neither the coherence nor the consistency of a planned program. This small, remote and 'inscrutable' country was to CUSO what it had been to much of the world for centuries — a poverty-stricken backwater of minor importance.

It had not always been that way, however. In 1538, (six years after his murderous conquest of the Incas in Peru, and only forty-six years after Columbus had first set sail for the New World), the strutting *conquistador*, Francisco Pizarro founded the city of Sucre, high in the Bolivian Andes. Permanent settlements were established in Potosi in 1545 and at La Paz in 1548, in order to serve the Spanish trade route between Lima and Buenos Aires. The lure of gold brought the Spanish to South America, but it was the discovery of an entire mountain of silver at Potosi that made Bolivia prominent in the Viceroyalty of Peru. The mine yielded a quarter-of-a-million kilograms a year, on average,[3] and Potosi became the largest city in the hemisphere. In Europe, such wealth contributed to inflation; the Indian miners who secured it suffered slave labour and poverty. The conquest ravaged their civilization and brought pestilence.

The humble potato was a second and less costly Bolivian contribution to Europe. First cultivated by the Indians in the rocky soil of the wind-swept, treeless altiplano, potatoes became a staple in Ireland by the 17th century; by 1800, the potato was established across Europe as a cheap substitute for wheat and corn; and stored in the ground, potatoes were less susceptible to marauding armies.

Independence came to the altiplano, as to most of Latin America, in

the 1820s; the hopeful new republic named itself after the great Vene-
zuelan liberator, Simon Bolivar. But for the Indian population, independence only meant greater hardship and oppression; although the
government was constantly being replaced, power and land remained in
the firm grasp of a tiny white elite. There was no great improvement in
the Indians' lot even after 1952 when the tin miners of Cochabamba
successfully launched a revolution, then carried out land reforms and the
nationalization of mines previously held by absentee owners.

Despite these reforms, the Bolivia of today is second only to Haiti as
the poorest country in the Americas; illiteracy is widespread, and the
infant mortality rate is almost double that of any other country on the
continent. The average annual per capital income in 1983 was $600.[4]
Most of the country's six million people are crowded onto the high
altiplano, in the midst of the Andes. This arid, cold plateau is one of the
most densely populated areas of the world.

Seventy percent of Bolivia's people are Indian, twenty-five percent
are *mestizos*, and the remainder are of European extraction. Most of the
population depend on farming for their livelihood, although mining —
predominantly of tin — accounts for half the country's foreign exchange
earnings. In 1975, a ton of tin, much of it hacked by hand from Bolivia's
dust-choked mines, or sifted laboriously from old tailings, could purchase
about six hundred and forty barrels of oil. But such are the fortunes of
primary producers that by 1985 the same ton could purchase fewer than
450 barrels.[5] Inflation, fuelled by this devaluation of its major export,
and by the political vagaries of successive juntas and governments, doubled between 1983 and 1984, reaching 800 percent and making the peso
virtually worthless, both in Bolivia and abroad.

Until 1978, CUSO's work in Bolivia was treated as an adjunct to its
larger program in Peru, and was administered from Lima by a Field Staff
Officer who paid only occasional visits. Raya Pearlman had decided early
that postings would have to be made outside normal government structures, simply because of the transitory nature of most Bolivian administrations.

Since 1825, there have been almost as many Bolivian presidents as
there have been years; between 1978 and 1983, there were thirteen presidents; and there were three in one day in October, 1970. Most CUSO

postings, therefore, were to mission schools, hospitals and the private sector, rather than government institutions.

The first four volunteers posted to Bolivia, in 1965, were two nurses, a secondary school teacher and a twenty-seven-year-old commerce graduate, André Desjardins, who spent two years working in church-sponsored radio broadcasting. Desjardins established a CUSO involvement with Radio Pio XXII that continued in one form or another for two decades — broadcasting literacy programs, farmer education, cooperative management, popular theatre, health and nutrition programs. Four more volunteers arrived in Bolivia in 1966, including Tim and Sherry Thomson (who had missed the first day of orientation in Canada because they were getting married). Their postings were typical of many that followed over the next decade; Tim, who had told CUSO he would do anything except teach, was posted to a private secondary school where he taught math and physics; Sherry's job was to transform a mission closet full of sample drugs into a hospital. Based at Calacoto, a town at the end of the paved road on the outskirts of La Paz, and sheltered from much of Bolivia's grinding poverty by their mission environment, they had a challenging but straightforward experience. They heard of French Canadian priests up in Oruro, where André Desjardins worked, "doing political work with the peasants," but it seemed distant from their lives.

At about the same time, Ché Guevara slipped into Bolivia, which he hoped could become the vanguard for a continental revolution: for months, he led a guerilla war in the lowlands, trying to inflame the peasantry against a populist military régime. Although his uprising failed, it had caused great unrest in Washington and in the corridors of power in La Paz. But to the Thomsons, Ché Guevara seemed as remote as other realities outside their town. "There was some student unrest; the odd truckload of police," said Tim.

And one day, Sherry was teargassed while travelling on a bus. "I was just riding along minding my own business. No one paid much attention to it; we just waited until it went away and then we carried on."[6] The Thomsons didn't realize until they returned to Canada that a 'revolution' had been going on, and that Ché Guevara had become a martyred icon of the left — only 300 miles from where they had worked.

Up in Oruro, however, and in the nearby mining centre of Siglo XX, André Desjardins could see more clearly what it was all about.

"The causes of underdevelopment are all interrelated to such an extent," he wrote, "that it is extremely difficult to distinguish them."[7] It was obvious, however, that a "large proportion of the Indian population had moved out of the interior regions of the country into the urban centres with the aim of increasing their incomes." The surplus of 'cheap labour' tended to decrease wage levels; families were often crowded into one or two rooms, surviving on an income of a few hundred dollars a year. Desjardins saw women standing in line at eleven in the evening, waiting for water; and he watched malnourished, listless children trying to pay attention in school. Incest, alcoholism, disease, family violence and early death were constants in mining communities.

"The men who extract the ore work under pitiful conditions," Desjardins observed. "Almost all the miners suffer from silicosis (a disease caused by absorption in the lungs of mineral dust) after ten years on the job. After spending his whole day in this thick dust, the miner finds that he has lost his appetite. To make up for his undernourishment, he chews coca leaves (from which cocaine is derived) all day long. This deadens his hunger and stimulates him with enough energy to get through the day. For his eight hours of heavy labour, he earns ninety cents a day."

During this period, the Government of Bolivia suffered one of its periodic financial crises and decreed a "rationalization" of all state owned mining operations; this meant lower wages and mass layoffs for miners. For their families, it was a disaster. Unemployment insurance was unheard of; village life and farming were a thing of previous generations. Uneducated, unskilled, facing an airtight job market, the miners turned back to the only thing they knew — mining. Because of the abundance of tin in Bolivia in the 1920s and 1930s, the large mills had been designed only for high-grade feed. The recovery rate then had been unimportant, and as much as 50 percent had escaped into the tailings. In addition, many mines had been abandoned early, and still contained a great deal of unmined (if low-grade) ore, considered unprofitable by the large private firms and the state-owned *Corporatión Minera de Bolivia* — COMIBOL.

Perhaps concerned that cutbacks might provoke one of the uprisings for which mining areas were famous, and grateful for a potential solution to the layoff problem, the government granted the miners permission to work the tailings and abandoned mines. The sole condition was that they form cooperatives. By 1968, six regional cooperative federations had been formed, united at the national level under the *Federación Nacional de Cooperativas Mineras* — FENCOMIN. Eventually, FENCOMIN comprised ninety-six cooperatives with more than twenty-one thousand members — a third of Bolivia's miners — digging not only for tin, but also silver, lead, sulphur, salt, gold and limestone.

While these changes were taking place in the Bolivian mining towns, CUSO's approach to Latin America had also begun to change. CUSO programs had previously responded to the tremendous shortage of Latin American nurses. Colombia and Peru had requested thirty or forty CUSO nurses at a time; now there were more locally trained nurses. By 1974, Peru didn't request any nurses, whereas only a decade before, CUSO couldn't find enough Canadian recruits to fill the postings. CUSO's attention began to turn towards preventative medicine. In Bolivia, a volunteer who had been posted to a public health cooperative in 1971, redirected the nature of CUSO's work in that country, identifying it more and more with the cooperative miners.

Father Jacques Laneuville, a young priest from Ville Marie, Quebec, went to Bolivia in 1966, as part of the wave of missionaries who heeded Pope John XXIII's call for help in Latin America. The Pontiff said that the Church there was identified with repressive oligarchies and elites; so there were not enough recruits into the priesthood. In response to his call, the number of Canadian Catholic missionaries in Latin America doubled between 1961 and 1970; many, like Father Laneuville, who went to Bolivia to offer spiritual assistance, became involved instead, in social action.

Father Jacques Laneuville quickly became known as 'Diego'. "When you go as a priest," he said, "normally they try to translate your name into Spanish. The problem was that there was no similar translation for 'Jacques'; it had to be either 'Jaime' or 'Diego' or 'Santiago', and since a few of the priests already had Jaime and Santiago, they decided to call me 'Diego'."[8]

Diego it would remain, even after he had left Bolivia and the priesthood (having married a Bolivian along the way). But Canada could not contain him for long, and when an opportunity to return to Bolivia as a CUSO volunteer arose in 1971, he jumped at it. For two-and-a-half years, he and his wife lived in a small tin-mining community, working among

1,300 families who were members of the local cooperative. Along with another CUSO volunteer, Dr. Susanne Labelle — a nun from Hull, Quebec — they organized health training programs, a health insurance scheme, health care broadcasts on Radio Pio XXII, and an extensive public health network. Their little health cooperative in Llallagua — not far from Siglo XX, where André Desjardins had worked several years before — was the first one in Bolivia. The culmination of Laneuville's work with Dr. Labelle was the planning, financing, and construction of a thirty-six-bed hospital.

Looking at the mining cooperatives to which their patients belonged, however, Laneuville could see that organization had brought few improvements to their lives. Most members had joined only to gain legal access to the marginal mineshafts and the tailings; they were far from cooperatively minded. Most miners worked as individuals, occasionally hiring one or two employees to work a small corner of a mine or a river bed. The technology was crude and productivity low; while the cooperatives accounted for one-third of the Bolivian mineforce, they produced less than fifteen percent of the country's mineral output. Their small incomes were heavily dependent upon fluctuating world prices which fell further and further behind inflation in the wake of the international oil crisis. Loans — essential for upgrading the primitive technology — were difficult or impossible to obtain, and in a desperate attempt to fend off starvation, the workday was increased from eight to twelve hours, seven days a week.

Bolivian miners work at some of the highest altitudes on earth: many of the surrounding mountains are twice as far above sea level as the Canadian Rockies. Twenty-five of Bolivia's largest mines are more than 11,500 feet; and the town of Potosi is several thousand feet higher than Lhasa in Tibet.

A delegation from the British National Union of Mineworkers visited Bolivia in the late 1970s and issued a shocking report on the conditions of the miners:

> Although no statistics are available, it is estimated that an underground worker contracts first degree silicosis within five years. At the age of 30 he will have second degree silicosis and by the age

of 35 it will have progressed to the stage where he cannot be saved. The average life expectancy for an underground driller in the block system is 30 years . . . While conditions are bad in most mines throughout the world, the situation of the Bolivian miner and his family is doubly oppressive due to grossly inadequate living conditions . . . a collection of dismal shacks overshadowed by bleak mountain ranges . . . where there is no drinking water and sanitary conditions are grossly inadequate.[9]

In 1974, Diego Laneuville was appointed CUSO Field Staff Officer for Peru and Bolivia, based in Lima, the capital of Peru. Unable to devote the attention he would have liked to Bolivia, and to the peasant groups and cooperatives he had come to know, he persuaded the volunteers to form a CUSO local committee. Through his own contacts, he was able to involve peasant leaders in a committee of four Bolivians and two volunteers, who themselves would establish the direction of CUSO's future in Bolivia. "International agencies are always faced with the danger of judging from outside and imposing their own view, and often false solutions, on the problems of Latin America," Laneuville wrote at the time, insisting that Bolivians rather than Canadians should set the priorities for CUSO.[10]

In 1976, the committee made its first direct contact with the central cooperative body, FENCOMIN, which subsequently requested CUSO assistance in setting up an Education Department. A CUSO grant of $17,000 established courses in co-op mining, accountancy, industrial safety, mechanization, exploring, prospecting and extraction. It was a difficult undertaking, for ninety percent of the miners were illiterate and most were unable to even add and subtract.

During the period of the first CUSO project, a significant achievement was accomplished by a Bolivian lawyer, hired by FENCOMIN with CUSO funds. A major obstacle to efficient cooperative mining was the five-year leases government granted to the cooperatives; the lawyer was able to negotiate a new arrangement with the government, extending leases to fifteen years. By 1978, Laneuville was excited enough about the growing potential among the mining cooperatives to recommend a full-time CUSO Field Staff Officer for Bolivia; later that year, he took the position himself. Unlike most other aid officials who set up their headquarters in the relative comfort of La Paz, he established the CUSO office in Cochabamba, which was more accessible to the country's mining industry — and the country's poor.

Having seen what a small grant could do in developing FENCOMIN's Education Department, Laneuville now helped establish a Technical Assistance Department, arranging in 1979 for two CUSO engineers to be posted to Bolivia. He would later admit that he, FENCOMIN and the two engineers went into the project with different but equally fanciful notions about what might be achieved. The cooperatives thought that their problems were mainly technical and that a good dose of transferred technology would herald a brighter day. Laneuville, somewhat beguiled by the success of the Education Department, and aware that simple technical problems impeded even the most basic progress at the mines, hoped that Canadian engineers would be able to help. The volunteers — Darrell Martindale, a young mining engineer and Ron Wensel, a thirty-four year old applied-development engineer on leave from The Chalk River Atomic Energy plant — arrived with standard CUSO enthusiasm.

Martindale, Wensel, and Wensel's wife Diane travelled the country for two years, seldom settling in any location for long and living in whatever crude accommodation the cooperatives could provide, usually without electricity and often without water. Martindale's first exposure to Bolivian mining was the country's largest cooperative, 'El Progresso', at Kami. He developed a soft spot for the place, but often thought that the softness was in his head.

"The grand expectations I brought with me caused great illusions of what I could do at this mine," he later wrote. "However it was here that I learned the basics in Bolivian reality, not only with respect to cooperative mines, but also in regards to politics and injustice."[11] For the cooperative to get its fifteen-year lease, it was necessary to have a resident engineer as mine manager, and Martindale was surprised when he arrived to be addressed by many workers as "Manager." He found that most of the directors of the cooperative were miners who had made a success of their operations; and with *peones* now working their claims, they had become a kind of elite, using the cooperative for their own benefit, wholeheartedly supporting their autocratic president who occasionally visited from La Paz, and fully expected Martindale to get drunk with him. The arrangement in the mines was anything but cooperative: each individual had to seek out his own digging area, and pay any development costs himself.

"So when mineral is found," Martindale discovered, "in essence it belongs to the man who found it. He then exploits the mineral in the way he sees fit. There is no preparation work in order to exploit the vein rationally. Needless to say, this leads to a very chaotic and dangerous situation when you have a mine full of individuals all trying to take mineral out how they please. It strikes me as very ironic that the people who have worked so hard to find their mineral, out of greed and haste to get it out before the next guy steals it, lose half of it.''

Ron and Diane Wensel faced their first experiences of Bolivia at the Bolsa Negra mine, three hours' drive northeast of La Paz and 4,000 metres high in the mountains. Bolsa Negra, one of the largest and richest of the cooperatives, had 300 adult members and a total mine population of about two thousand — half of them children. Although there was electricity, only four of the houses had water and toilets. Diane had to invent her own job, as a social worker; she visited as many of the community's 500 women as possible during the day, and worked with the co-op's six women directors to form an active women's group, in which about one hundred women eventually became involved.

"Two nights a week," Diane wrote from Bolivia, "we met for discussions or classes on nutrition, hygiene, cooperativism and the women's role in it, health and child care. We also talked a great deal about their future workshop. Three nights a week they spent teaching each other how to knit, embroider, spin wool and crochet . . . the provincial federation is now arranging to construct a workshop for the women: two sewing and knitting teachers will instruct the women for a year.''[12]

Diane's husband, Ron, was having more success than Martindale with some of the cooperative's mechanical problems. The Bolsa Negra was one of the more mechanized mines, having rented a generator to operate crushers, a concentrator, and compressed air rock-drills; but much of the equipment was out of order when he arrived, because of poor maintenance.

"I concentrated my work on improving the capacity of the mine to maintain its own equipment, developing repair procedures, fabricating replacement parts and modifying existing designs," he said. "During my two-and-a-half months at the mine, we developed a repair technique for worn rock-drills, enlarged the workshop, fabricated a hydraulic press for the disassembly of rock-drills using discarded materials and components, and assessed the needs for additional workshop tools.''[13]

After their experiences at El Progresso and Bolsa Negra, Martindale and Wensel joined forces to work on problems at the '16 de Octubre' cooperative near La Paz. Their first job was building a new hydro-electric plant to increase the productive power of the mine equipment; later they drew up plans for installing an aqueduct to carry water to the concentrating plant during the dry season. They tried to act as consultants rather than as supervisors, and were touched when the cooperative invited them to become *socios* in their mine. They could begin to see a difference not only in their own work at '16 de Octubre', but in the attitude of the miners. The most striking difference between this mine and others was that at '16 de Octubre', the cooperative actually owned the mine, and the members knew that any improvements they made were for their own benefit.

One of the cooperative's proudest moments was the completion of the road from La Paz. Although only navigable by jeep and truck, it was a vast improvement on the slow, torturous mule transport that had previously serviced the remote mine. Martindale noted that the road had to cross a pass of 5,100 metres: government engineers said that it couldn't be done, but the cooperative, working weekends, finished the project in four years — doing all the work by hand.

Wensel and Martindale were, in Diego Laneuville's words, "real pioneers." Sometimes their job seemed hopeless: technology could not improve the lot of the miners without access to credit, a commitment to cooperativism, better guarantees of security from the government and from COMIBOL, and real wage equity for the miners.

"There were days when everything was going wrong," said Martindale, "and naturally the conclusion was that there is nothing that can be done for this poverty stricken country." But they both knew that many things could be done; along with Diego Laneuville and FENCOMIN, they began in 1980 and 1981 to lay out plans that would require a much larger CUSO contribution to the cooperatives.

One of the many things Martindale had in mind was a simple ventilator scheme for the mines, which were often abandoned — not for lack of minerals, but for lack of air.

"After a few hundred metres," Martindale reported, "the circulation of air is so bad that the miners cannot enter the mine. After blasting, you cannot enter the mine for two days or more until the gases dissipate. This wastes a lot of time if you can only drill and blast once or twice a week. Another disadvantage of not having good ventilation is the dust in the air when drilling. This is why a lot of the miners suffer from silicosis and other lung diseases. The simplest solution . . . is running a ventilator by an electric motor off the air compressor. The ventilator would be very easy to make and very portable, which in the mines is important.''

Laneuville was hopeful of extra funding from the Canadian government, for this and other programs, because of CIDA's initial enthusiasm, and its stated aim to increase its work at the 'grass roots' level through additional funding support for good NGO projects. Similar projects in Bangladesh, Thailand and Jamaica, as well as positive discussions with CIDA officers in the Canadian embassy in Lima and Ottawa, gave further reason for optimism when the tentative outline for a three-year program was presented to CIDA in 1981. In addition, Canada imported almost $100 million worth of primary tin metal annually, most of it from Third World countries, and the metal's fortunes had a direct impact both on Canadian jobs and the Canadian consumer.[14]

Tin was the subject of an international agreement for years among major non-communist producing countries, of which Malaysia, Indonesia, Bolivia and Thailand are the most important. Originally intended as a guarantor of minimum prices and as a hedge against inflation, in post-war years the agreement also included consuming nations and came to be seen as a model for the more widespread commodity agreements envisaged by UNCTAD as part of a "New International Economic Order." Commodity agreements would help stabilize the international economy, and ensure that the economies of developing nations like Bolivia, so heavily dependent upon a single export, would be protected against diverse industrial exports from consuming nations. An UNCTAD commodity agreement for tin would also include a fund for technological improvement and marketing assistance to developing-nation producers. Such a fund would be of most benefit to Bolivia, where outdated equipment, and extra costs due to its geography, have weakened its international competitiveness, and depressed its economy.

In a comprehensive study of the international economy of tin, William Robertson made a compelling case for assistance to Third World producers — most particularly, Bolivia:

The potential of a modernized industry would be a better source of revenue than an industry continually on the margin of bankruptcy. Where the tin importing countries could help, would be through a major investment program which paid off in more efficiently produced tin.[15]

As a result of such investments, there would be less pressure for higher international tin prices, and less need for consuming nations to develop technological innovations and substitutes for tin. As well, the living standards of those in the tin mining industry would rise to levels commensurate with other mining industries; this would, as Robertson says, "accord with the general policy of helping the poorest in developing countries in a constructive way."

But as far as most industrialized countries are concerned, the long-term international benefits of commodity agreements and investment in primary producers are outweighed by short-term political and economic considerations. Some tin-producing countries continued to seek protection through the International Tin Council. Others, like Bolivia, took their chances on the open market.

Canada, bedazzled by an array of glittering trade and business prospects with economic giants such as Brazil, Venezuela and Colombia, saw Bolivia as a 'minimal interest' country. In the end, the work required to reallocate funds, reorganize internal approvals and make the necessary arrangements with Bolivia to fund the CUSO project, simply wasn't worth the effort in CIDA headquarters.

Despite various drafts and revisions, CIDA finally declined CUSO's request for financial support of the tin mining project. Undeterred, Laneuville rewrote the project again, presenting a bare-bones plan which could be supported from core CUSO funds by slightly reducing other budgets in Latin America, and by applying for a larger allocation from CUSO's central project pool in Ottawa. What emerged for 1982–83 was a plan derived from the work of Ron Wensel, Darrell Martindale and other volunteers; the budget was $128,000, of which FENCOMIN itself would contribute over $55,000.

CUSO was able to help the national Technical Assistance Unit, and six newly established regional centres as well.

Darrell Martindale had already outlined some of the criteria; he observed that travelling engineers were simply not effective enough:

"The miners are impressed with engineers who like to be with them. "Engineers that come from the city, look around, give a few orders, get drunk and return to the city a day later don't impress anyone. I'm not saying that you have to impress anyone, but to gain the confidence necessary to do good work is more important."

He felt that even two years in one spot was insufficient:

"Two years is not enough time to get anything done, let alone to get to know the people. In Bolivia this is even more true, as to gain the trust of the Aymara and Quechua peoples of the altiplano takes a long time. I won't begin to try to explain why, as reasons vary from the cold hard life of the altiplano to over 450 years of oppression."

He said that any technical changes had to be coordinated with social changes:

"Just increasing production or concentration methods is relatively easy when compared with the problems the volunteer will have when he attempts to teach cooperativism at the same time . . . but if no social changes occur with the technical changes, then the existing system just exaggerates itself. This feudalistic system was brought by the Spanish and continues to exist in the laws and the attitudes of the people. If the cooperatives wish to operate as real cooperatives, then this attitude has to change."

The CUSO program, which began in 1982 and was scheduled to run until 1986, would eventually provide FEMCOMIN with eight engineers — two Bolivians, and six Canadians.

At the national level, they would concentrate on coordinating the regional efforts and providing a central resource bank for cooperatives with specific problems. They would establish a small mobile laboratory to analyze ore content, and to train miners in this process. They would prepare a plan for a central workshop, and organize a minimum of four training programs a year on specific production, processing and marketing problems.

At the regional levels, the engineers would work more closely with specific co-ops and their problems; as well, they would set up training programs to help cooperatives solve their technical difficulties, and demonstrate the benefits of applying collective talents and labour to the task at hand.

Diego Laneuville was gratified, not only by the growth of the project and its successes, but by the response of other organizations which offered further financial support to the project: the Catholic Church in Canada; a Canadian Embassy fund in Lima; the Irish organization, Trocaire; Christian Aid and Oxfam in Britain (which assisted with the establishment of a revolving loan fund for technical projects). The international recognition was a small sign that CUSO's work in Bolivia had come of age.

CUSO continued to work in other sectors in Bolivia, as it always had; with *campesinos*, women's groups, and other Bolivian organizations. In 1982, a CUSO electronics engineer, Wayne Cousineau, completed a technical reorganization of Radio Pio XXII so that its educational programs — assisted almost two decades earlier by André Desjardins — could continue. In 1983, Dr. Susanne Labelle returned to Bolivia as a volunteer to work on rural health projects with remote Indian communities, and to work again with Diego Laneuville, whose enthusiasm for Bolivia had not diminished after fifteen years.

But it was in the mining sector (CIDA's minimal interest notwithstanding) that CUSO's work was probably most germane to Bolivia's long-term problems. It was the lure of the mines that first brought the conquistadors to Bolivia; it is the mines that provide the country with what modicum of development exists today. And it is undoubtedly the mines that will determine what the future holds for Bolivia and its six million people. The mining towns have always been the crucible of Bolivian politics; their people will ultimately decide the fate of the nation.

Chapter 25

Kampuchean Refugees: Sorrow in the Land of Smiles

Bright red blood which covers towns and plains of Kampuchea,
our motherland,
Sublime Blood of Workers and peasants.
Sublime Blood of revolutionary men and women fighters!

Official translation of the National
Anthem of Democratic Kampuchea

In the late 1960s Cambodia* was a peaceful island of tranquility in the midst of the upheaval and chaos of the Vietnamese War. *Sunday Times* reporter William Shawcross, called it "an idyllic, antique land, unsullied by the brutalities of modern war . . . a conservative, religious country where most land is owned by the tiller, where even the most relaxed

---

*Cambodia is a synonym for Khmer, which refers to the Khmer Empire of the 13th century. 'Cambodia' was derived from the French, 'Cambodge', which was a corruption of 'Kambuja', a name used to describe descendants of Kambu, the Aryan king whose dynasty founded the country two thousand years ago. In 1975, The Pol Pot regime changed the name of the country from Cambodia to Democratic Kampuchea; in 1979, the Vietnamese-backed regime of Heng Samrin renamed it People's Republic of Kampuchea.

could usually be assured enough rice, and where fish were to be had for the drop of a net."[1] To another British journalist, John Pilger, "it seemed the most inoffensive and graceful land, where people cherished their obscurity and never held out a begging bowl and never knew hunger."[2]

Like most flattering portraits, the bucolic serenity portrayed by foreign journalists in Phnom Penh during those turbulent years was a simplification, if not an illusion. Cambodia's history of ancient enlightenment, centuries-old irrigation systems, and fabled temples of Angkor Wat, was also one of war, invasion and bondage — either to its western neighbours, the Siamese,* or the Vietnamese, to the east. It was in an effort to halt the invasions and prevent the destruction of his country that King Ang Duong solicited French assistance, signing a protectorate treaty with France in 1863. Ninety years later, King Norodom Sihanouk negotiated an end to the protectorate, abdicating in his father's favour and making himself the princely head of government.

Sihanouk furthered the economic development that had begun between the wars; he vastly increased the number of primary and secondary schools, and built a university and a seaport at Kompong Som. Politically, he sought an independent role for Cambodia, while maintaining a friendly relationship with China. In the late 1960s, as the Vietnam war began to boil over into Cambodia, he allowed the North Vietnamese more frequent use of Cambodian territory for supply routes to the south; this led to a series of cross-border raids by South Vietnamese and American troops, and then, in 1969, the first covert bombing of Cambodia by the American Air Force. In 1970, Sihanouk was deposed by one of his generals, Lon Nol, who lost no time in shifting to the American position. The bombing increased, American military aid was stepped up and Cambodia slipped inexorably into the grip of war. Over the next few years, the economy disintegrated as the American Air Force dropped on Cambodia the equivalent of four times the tonnage of bombs used during the entire Korean War.

Huge numbers of people were uprooted: the population of Phnom Penh swelled from six hundred thousand to three million as the destitute and the homeless surged into the city. The Khmer Rouge, once a ragtag collection of Marxist guerilla factions with little support among the pop-

---

** Siam changed its name to Thailand in 1939

ulace, began to gain importance. "They had no popular base among the Khmer people, who preferred the tradition of Buddhist harmony to upheaval," wrote John Pilger, " . . . and their 'revolution' lacked an external catalyst. The inferno of the Kissinger bombing provided that catalyst."[3]

When the Americans finally left Indo-China, it was only a matter of time before the inevitable happened: in the spring of 1975, the Lon Nol government fell to advancing Khmer Rouge troops, and Pol Pot, Secretary of the Kampuchean Communist Party, took power. What happened in the following four years may remain obscure; the basic facts, however, are known: The new government's first act was the total evacuation of Phnom Penh and other large centres. Thousands of people perished in forced marches; tens of thousands more died in rural camps under conditions of extreme hardship and brutality. In an attempt to create an entirely new society, the government nullified anything with a western taint: money was simply abolished; schools and libraries were obliterated; anyone associated with previous regimes or with Vietnam, was killed — as were countless others who evinced the slightest sign of western education. Possession of a pair of glasses — evidence of bourgeois links — was enough to single a person out for execution. Terrible tales of mutilation, dismemberment and torture began to emerge; and of widespread starvation, as harvests failed. The death toll during those years can only be estimated at something between one and three million; probably one-fifth of all Cambodians died during those cataclysmic forty-eight months between 1975 and 1979.

Border skirmishes between Kampuchean and Vietnamese troops escalated an increasingly hostile war of words between the erstwhile allies; finally, in December 1978, in the name of humanity (but doubtless also in the interest of its age-old designs on Kampuchea), Vietnam invaded the crippled nation. As Phnom Penh fell, Pol Pot's troops retreated to what they knew best — guerilla warfare — based in the Cardamom Mountains against the Thai border. The invasion, and the subsequent disruption of an already weakened population, effectively ensured that the 1979 planting season was lost; by summer, starvation again stalked the land. Thousands of hungry Kampucheans began to walk towards Thailand.

Thailand was already a country of refugees — four hundred thousand since 1950 — when the Kampucheans began to arrive. There were Chinese, the remnants of Chiang Kai-Shek's defeated armies; Vietnamese, fleeing north after Dien Bien Phu in 1954; and Burmese, following the 1959 Ne Win takeover. A much larger wave of refugees arrived between 1975 and 1979, some fleeing the new Communist regimes in Vietnam and Kampuchea, but most of them from Laos. But in 1979, with a major Vietnamese offensive in September, and alarming food shortages later, the movement of refugees across the border suddenly became a tidal wave, as more than one hundred thousand people massed on the highway that runs between the Kampuchean town of Battambang and Arany-aprathet in Thailand. Thousands were on the verge of death from starvation and disease, and, as the first horrifying pictures emerged, the world's relief agencies began to gear up for a response. Within a matter of weeks, the number of refugees mounted to almost a million.

CUSO's involvement with the Kampuchean refugees began almost by accident, as had its involvement in Thailand during the 1960s; as in other countries, too, CUSO's work in the 'Land of Smiles' originated with one of the men involved in the founding of CUSO: Dr. Cyril Belshaw. Director of the Regional Training Centre for United Nations Fellows at the University of British Columbia in 1960, Belshaw was actively involved in the President's Committee for a Canadian Overseas Student Service. Through contacts with Lewis Perinbam and Francis Leddy, he attended the first planning meeting in March 1961 to discuss the idea of a national organization. The following June, at the founding meeting in Montreal, Belshaw seconded the motion which led to the first draft constitution of CUSO. Four years later, Belshaw was in Thailand, working with the United Nations Technical Assistance Board in Bangkok. Belshaw, a noted anthropologist, would later be accused and acquitted of murdering his wife in Switzerland, and would go on to write the 1985 'Complete Good Dining Guide to Greater Vancouver Restaurants' along with a dozen scholarly works. In 1965, however, he was in Thailand, working with the United Nations Technical Assistance Board in Bangkok. Seeing British and American volunteers at work, and aware of the country's manpower gaps, he wrote to Ottawa, suggesting that CUSO investigate program possibilities.

In May 1967, Bob Pim, a former CVCS volunteer in Jamaica and now the CUSO coordinator in India, was sent to Thailand on an exploratory mission; three months later, the first five CUSO volunteers stepped off the aircraft at Don Muang Airport to a welcome from officials and a small horde of reporters and cameramen.

The first volunteers — and many to follow — were teachers, either at the university level, or at teacher training colleges.

Most of them came to love Thailand, and many would maintain their bonds of friendship long after leaving the country. For those who stayed on — and the CUSO extension rate in Thailand was very high, especially among men — many would marry Thais and seek a career in the region. Most of the Field Staff Officers in Thailand over the years were men, and all but two married Thai women. (Both of the exceptions were already married when they arrived, the second — Murray Thomson — to a Thai.)

Murray Thomson's experience, knowledge of Thailand and approach to development quickly altered the direction of CUSO's work in the country. A 'local Committee' to help with program planning and direction included government officials, and helped them to understand Thomson's interest in fostering Thai development groups as well as providing Canadian teachers and medical personnel. With the assistance of his deputy, Jim McFetridge, Thomson began to look at programming possibilities in community organizations, credit unions and cooperatives, not least because they tended towards the collegial processes which he felt were essential to any effective development. He encouraged two volunteers to work with the racially and culturally distinct Hill Tribes who had been isolated for generations from mainstream life in Thailand: what emerged was a marketing cooperative for some of their colourful and distinctive handicrafts. The Thai Hill Crafts Foundation, controlled and managed by the Tribe, made an important and lasting contribution to the area. Small grants were made to the Chiang Mai YMCA for community projects identified by CUSO volunteers working there, and workshops were conducted on diverse development topics with a variety of organizations.

Jim McFetridge became involved in a scholarship program for 'third country training' which gave Thais access to special training programs within Asia. McFetridge felt this training would prove more effective than the traditional aid-agency scholarships to Europe and North America; as well, it would give Thais a broader understanding of their own region, and help loosen some of the rigid parochial attitudes prevalent in Asia at the time. The first scholarships sent seven instructors from the Department of Teacher Training to an intensive upgrading course at the Regional Language Centre In Singapore, and at a similar centre in Bangkok. The experiment was well-received by the government, and one official, speaking with unaccustomed Thai candor, said that "sometimes a scholarship is more helpful than a volunteer."[4]

On Christmas Eve, 1970, 62-year-old Harry Durance, one of the most respected CUSO volunteers in Thailand, was electrocuted while working on a poultry incubator at Khon Kaen University. Volunteers established a memorial scholarship fund in his name; with support from the Durance family and CUSO, and a matching grant from CIDA, the fund swelled from sixteen scholarships in 1971 to sixty-three just a year later. By 1980, the Harry Durance Foundation had become an autonomous Thai organization, providing a variety of community development projects, as well as training programs.

In the fall of 1973, Murray Thomson left Thailand to become Executive Director of CUSO; a year later, McFetridge left as well. Raymond Cournoyer, elevated to the position of Regional Director for Asia, had little time for what he felt was an over-emphasis on CUSO's 'process' and 'democracy'. Cournoyer's 'See; Judge; Act' philosophy was firmly rooted in an innate understanding of Asia and a strong commitment to the development of institutions which suited Asian needs. He rarely moved on an issue without careful consultation across his widespread network of Asian contacts, and his work in India and with *Proshika* in Bangladesh stood as testimony to the success of his approach. But to some CUSO people, especially those in Thailand who were imbued with the more subtle, indirect Thai approach and Murray Thomson's highly participatory style, Cournoyer was a bull in a china shop. Before he left Thailand, Jim McFetridge sensed Cournoyer's disdain for the Thailand local committee, and watched him play Ayatollah to Murray Thomson's Mahatma.

"In 1974, at my last Asia Regional Meeting, at Chainat," recalled McFetridge, "the Ayatollah made it very clear that the democratic, consultative structure built by the Mahatma was not to his liking."[5] Over the following two years, CUSO's work in Thailand was essentially in a holding pattern: twenty-five volunteers served in medical, teaching and engineering positions, and a few small projects were maintained.

Then, when the Thailand FSO terminated unexpectedly, late in 1976,

Cournoyer asked Paul Turcot if he would consider taking the job. Turcot, a lanky, fair-haired Quebecois, was a volunteer in Thailand between 1974 and 1976; he loved the country, but decided to return to Canada to add a masters degree to the two he already held in arts and engineering — hoping to upgrade his qualifications and return to start a career in international development. Turcot accepted the offer on the condition that he could finish his studies at Carleton University, leaving Cournoyer to cover the program in Thailand for the next six months. Having felt for some time that the scattered volunteer placements in miscellaneous disciplines were both directionless and diffuse, Cournoyer now set out on an extensive tour, travelling for weeks through the remote north and northeast. And there were other, even more compelling reasons for his journey; he was also responding to a study which revealed that for all the apparent wealth and development of the urban and southern parts of Thailand, there were eleven million people estimated to have inadequate nutrition, clothing and shelter. The majority of the poor lived in the rural northeast, where primary health care and education were in short supply, and where bad weather, poor soil and government indifference had conspired to reduce farmers to single crops, low yields and endemic poverty.

As a result of his travels, Cournoyer began to redirect CUSO's efforts towards the rural northeast: engineers, agriculturalists and health workers were assigned to small irrigation projects, agricultural extension work and a village health worker scheme concentrated in this region. But when Paul Turcot returned to Thailand as FSO that summer of 1977, neither he nor Cournoyer would know how demanding the northeast would become to CUSO just two short years later.

By late autumn, 1979, it was clear that the refugees flowing across the border from Kampuchea into northeast Thailand were not a temporary phenomenon, and that a catastrophe of major proportions was underway. At first, Cournoyer discussed the possibility of CUSO involvement inside Kampuchea with Oxfam/UK representatives in Singapore, but he rejected the idea for political considerations. The Oxfam consortium of agencies had been able to make contact with the new regime in Phnom Penh and was beginning to establish a supply line for relief goods — but there was a cost. In order to address the Kampuchean government's charge that the refugees in Thailand were all genocidal Khmer Rouge, Oxfam had agreed unconditionally to the demand that no Oxfam relief would go to the refugees on the border;[6] in addition, all relief goods would be handed over to government for distribution. Although Oxfam, and its supporting consortium of NGOs, did an important and essential job inside Kampuchea, Cournoyer decided against CUSO participation because he saw it as a short-term operation concentrating on relief, and having none of the components or opportunities for further development work that he felt should characterize a CUSO program. He also felt that since CUSO's budget for Asia would be tight in 1979, any efforts with the refugees in Thailand would be vastly inferior to the need: CUSO should stick to what it knew best.

As the situation worsened, however, there were hints from CIDA that extra funding might be available should CUSO develop a plan; after several telephone discussions between CUSO's Ottawa Headquarters and Cournoyer's Singapore office, he agreed to fly to Thailand to investigate the situation at first hand. He arrived as the first camps were being constructed by the United Nations High Commission for Refugees (UNHCR). In a matter of days, a camp for thirty-two thousand people was constructed at Sa Keo, forty miles from the border, on barren riceland that quickly became a quagmire. As the first refugees started to arrive on government buses, the camp still lacked wells, sewage and drainage facilities; only a crude collection of shanties and tents had been set up at the perimeter.

Two American relief workers, Linda Mason and Roger Brown, wrote of the shocking condition of many of the refugees:

> In the first two weeks, about 400 of the Khmer died. Every day, more sick and starving refugees came to the camp. The dying Khmer could not be bussed from the border fast enough. Many of the refugees died during the short one and a half hour trip from the border to the holding centre. At first, more Khmer died outside the hospital than within, as the relief workers struggled to care for the sick and starving and get a hospital built at the same time."[7]

That was in October, 1979. In November, the UNHCR had ten days to construct a new camp at Kao I Dang before the refugees started to arrive; by January, it held more than one hundred fifty thousand people, making it the largest resident community of Kampucheans in the world.

It was inevitable that there would be confusion, duplication and mistakes. "What struck me," said Cournoyer, "was the same thing that had struck me in the camps in India in 1971. In Kao I Dang you had all those dispensaries — one CRS, one International Red Cross, one Thai Red Cross, one Quaker, one Mennonite . . . all separate. And the refugees had nothing to do apart from eating, sleeping and gossiping; they were kept in an unproductive refugee situation."[8]

He was bemused by the ineffectual attempts to impose some form of order on the food handouts when a truck arrived, loaded with sweetened milk, vegetables, and two foreigners. Heads of families in that section of the camp were called together and made to sit on their haunches in a straight line while one of the foreigners explained the distribution procedure to them. In English. "It was the same farce I had seen so many times in the camps in Calcutta. After the careful explanation, the two foreigners were surrounded by people, all pushing and shoving, and in the end, they simply gave up and walked away and left the damned stuff there for people to fight over."

By December, UNICEF and the Red Cross were distributing rations for seven hundred thousand people, and the numbers were still growing. Apart from the understandable chaos of the camps, there were other elements to contend with. Corruption was rampant, both within the Thai military and amongst the refugees; often, the neediest were denied their rations. Duplication of effort was common; at times there were more than five hundred foreigners working in Kao I Dang, while at other camps almost as large, a handful of workers struggled with bigger problems. Cultural differences were a major handicap; few of the relief workers spoke Thai, much less Kampuchean.

"Translations were garbled," wrote relief workers Mason and Brown of their experience: "fish unloaded instead of rice, tickets given instead of withheld, the wrong medicine administered." Because of a fear that the Vietnamese might invade, few of the camps had any specialized medical equipment; and even such simple tools as sewing machines, pottery wheels, looms — which might have better occupied the refugees' time — were denied them for fear that they would be lost in an attack. In addition, the relief workers compounded the problem through their own distorted view of the refugees and of the relief operations. Because donors want to help the neediest, and expect that corruption will be minimized, agencies attempt to conform to the image expected of them. "As a result," Mason and Brown observed, "relief workers tended to perceive the refugee camps as the donors and they themselves wanted them to be: filled with hungry and helpless people in desparate need of aid. Relief workers rewarded helplessness with compassion, self-reliance with suspicion."[9]

Raymond Cournoyer was not surprised by what he saw, nor by what he observed at a meeting of relief agencies in Bangkok: of more than one hundred officials, only five were Thai. The local people, as had happened after the Biafran War in Bangladesh, were simply excluded from the operation, as though they had nothing to say on the subject, and nothing to offer. With Paul Turcot, Cournoyer began to develop an idea based on his experience of the Calcutta camps. Together they discussed various approaches with a number of Thai organizations with which CUSO had contacts. Knowing that the government intended to reduce the size of the larger camps and construct a series of smaller ones, they went with their ideas to the Director of UNHCR, which had been given overall coordinating responsibility for the foreign relief effort.

CUSO would take on a single camp of about ten thousand people, Cournoyer proposed, but it would be the sole foreign agency involved. The camp would be operated exclusively by Thais, rather than by Canadians, and they would work towards a level of self-sufficiency among the refugees within the shortest space of time possible. Furthermore, camp activities would not be exclusively devoted to the refugees, but would in some cases be opened to Thais in the surrounding villages, in order that the camp should not become a ghetto. It was a simple enough idea, but it was so far removed from what other agencies were doing that Cournoyer expected a chilly response from the UNHCR Director. Instead, his first question was "When can you start?"

Cournoyer was not a little anxious, as the project would cost hundreds of thousands of dollars, and had not yet even been outlined to Ottawa. Within a matter of days, he was in Canada for discussions in the secretariat and with CIDA's NGO Division Director, Romeo Maione. Maione, who had just returned from a visit to Southeast Asia, seemed positive; but he said he had no funds for the refugees, despite External Affairs Minister Flora MacDonald's recent commitment of an extra $10 million to refugee support.

Maione's reaction was disappointing, but a meeting was finally arranged between the Minister and several CUSO staff, including Cournoyer and David Beer, who had just returned from Southern Africa. It was the twilight period of the Clark government, and Flora MacDonald was now almost exclusively working her Kingston riding as the election drew near. The meeting (squeezed in between party functions) took place on a cold January night in a highway motel near Cornwall.

Cournoyer outlined his plan to the Minister, making it clear that the CUSO effort would be the only strictly Canadian activity among the refugees, and pointing out that without additional CIDA support, CUSO could simply not proceed. The Minister was sympathetic, and, making notes on the back of an envelope, she asked a number of pointed questions about the political situation in Thailand and the state of the refugees in the camps. Finally, she asked: "How much do you need?"[10]

Only the most preliminary of estimates had been made, but it seemed a six-month effort with ten thousand refugees would cost something in excess of a million dollars: "One point two million," Cournoyer said, without blinking.

"Send me as much information as you have," the Minister replied. "During the election campaign, we're having our cabinet meetings on Fridays. I'll try to have the question addressed this Friday; if it's positive, the fastest way for you to find out would be to attend the afternoon press conference." And with that, she hastened off into the night for her next meeting.

The Public Affairs Department sent an observer to the Friday Press Conference, but nothing was mentioned. Nor was anything mentioned the following Friday. Then, in the middle of the third week, a small item in the Toronto *Globe and Mail* announced that funds had been released to assist refugees both in Kampuchea and in Thailand, and that $1.2 million had been reserved for Canadian NGOs.

The jubilation at the CUSO secretariat that morning was short-lived, however, when it was discovered that CIDA had already divided the funds equally between the Catholic Church, World Vision and the Mennonites — who had apparently not even made a request to CIDA.[11] When it was pointed out to Romeo Maione that the money had been released in response to a specific CUSO request — after he himself had suggested the political route — he replied: "Well, if you're so friendly with the-politicians, why don't you get my decision changed?"[12] A call to the Minister's office confirmed that CUSO had been expected to receive some of the money (the total of which coincided exactly with the amount mentioned to the Minister). It was a particularly difficult afternoon, as calls flashed back and forth between the Minister's office on Sussex Drive and CIDA Headquarters in Hull, but the decision finally came: CUSO would only receive one-quarter of the total, since the other agencies had already been informed that they would each receive grants. And the CIDA contribution of only $300,000 was totally inadequate for the task Cournoyer envisaged.

However, a tentative plan was set in motion, and Cournoyer insisted on the involvement of Suteera Thomson, a microbiologist with degrees from Thai, Canadian and U.S. universities, and impeccable qualifications for helping to set up the project. As Murray Thomson's wife, she knew CUSO well; as a former lecturer at the prestigious Medical School of Mahidol University in Bangkok, she had excellent contacts at both governmental and non-governmental levels in Thailand; and as a consultant at the Science Council of Canada, she had concentrated her most recent efforts on a critical study of Canadian aid entitled, "Food for the Poor." Suteera agreed to undertake the mission, and was given a month of paid leave by the Science Council as its contribution to the project.

In Ottawa, several CUSO departments began to address the problem of additional funding; they sounded out provincial governments, foundations, current donors and returned volunteers from Thailand. One day, Public Affairs Director Sharon Capeling noticed a clipping from a Vancouver paper: Iona Campagnolo, the former Minister of Fitness and Amateur Sport, was giving up politics, and thought she might like to go overseas with CUSO. It was an offhand remark in a flippant article, but on the slim chance that she might be serious, the Ottawa office contacted Campagnolo and asked if she would be prepared to help raise funds. She agreed without hesitation, and CBC's investigative news program, *the fifth estate* agreed to divert Eric Malling and a crew to look at the CUSO effort in Thailand on their way home from an assignment in Japan. It was a hopeful beginning for CUSO's publicity and fund-raising campaign.

In Thailand, Suteera Thomson and Paul Turcot wasted little time;

although the financial details were far from settled, they informed the UNHCR that CUSO was making a commitment in principle. They began to make arrangements to involve several Thai agencies, including the Community Based Emergency Relief Services (CBERS), Mahidol University, Chulalongkorn University, and the Thai Committee for Refugees. In a call to Ottawa on March 27, Suteera reported on some of the details: "The camp is at Kab Cherng, about 400 kilometers from Bangkok along the Thai-Kampuchean border. Half the 45-acre campsite will be living space, and half will be open. UNHCR has just completed the layout and construction will begin on April 15th. The refugees, presently at Kao I Dang, will be moved in some time before the middle of June."[13]

"The proposal we are dealing with basically covers two phases," Turcot reported. "The first will be for a period of about two months and the second for four months. The overall cost is estimated at two million (dollars), of which CUSO's share is estimated at about seven hundred thousand dollars . . . You can work out what the per-person cost would be from that, but by our figures it amounts to thirty-eight cents per day."

CUSO committed itself to quickly raising $400,000 more than its fund-raising target of $500,000 that year. Fund-raising had never been CUSO's forte: in 1963, a study predicted a maximum of $250,000 from private sources — one of the reasons that by 1964, CIDA support had become so critical. CUSO fund-raisers had hoped to improve the performance — volunteers returning from the field would assist with the task. Although they did help, their fund-raising efforts, by 1970, seemed limited to about five hundred thousand dollars a year. When the overall budget was small, such an amount was not unimpressive, but as the budget grew — along with CIDA's contribution to it — private contributions declined, both proportionately and absolutely. There were many explanations, most suggesting that CUSO lacked appeal to donors. Public perception linked CUSO to 'university students', and occasionally to political controversy: the image was not nearly as compelling as that of organizations which boasted of saving lives and feeding children for only pennies a day. So an additional $400,000 during a period of high interest rates and growing Canadian unemployment would be far from easy.

Sharon Capeling was banking on the impact of a positive *fifth estate* program: "I understand that the Canadian ambassador has been quite supportive of your efforts," she told Turcot over the phone. "It might be good, just as a courtesy, to let him know that the *fifth estate* is coming. Embassies tend to be very nervous about the press, but I feel he should know. One thing I must warn you about, though, is that they will be looking for some dirt . . . all I can say is that you should let any criticism of the relief effort so far come from the Thai people and not from CUSO . . . Don't let them draw you out . . . they are sympathetic to us, and I think this could be what we need in order to get our fund-raising off the ground.''

As it turned out, the *fifth estate* program was a phenomenal success. Cournoyer and Turcot rose to the occasion and host Eric Malling discussed some of the themes with which Cournoyer had been preoccupied for months: the costly duplication and mismanagement in some of the larger camps, where dependency was perpetuated and a fundamental resource — the Thai people — ignored. The morning after the show was aired, the head of the Nichol Family Foundation of Calgary dispatched a cheque for $10,000 to CUSO: the fund-raising was on.

There never was an undertaking of any significance in CUSO that did not have its detractors within the organization; the Kampuchean refugee operation was no exception. Initial concern focussed on the origins and political affiliations of the refugees.

Many of those driven across the border in the first wave had been bedraggled — but unrepentant — Khmer Rouge troops. But they could never have represented more than six or seven percent of all refugees, even if every Khmer Rouge soldier, (an estimated fifty thousand to seventy-five thousand) survived the Vietnamese attack, the famine, and jungle marches of four hundred miles or more. Other Kampucheans, fleeing both the Pol Pot regime and the Vietnamese invaders, organized a right-wing military force known as the Khmer Serei. But most refugees were simply fleeing for their lives.

For many of the foreign relief workers, the presence of Khmer Rouge among the refugees presented a terrible moral dilemma: how could assistance be justified for people who had murdered so many? Should relief agencies help military or paramilitary refugees to grow strong and train in the safe asylum of the camps? When the alternative was starvation, the answers were by no means simple for the larger agencies; for CUSO, with its limited resources and its relatively minor mandate, a safe course would have been to remain uninvolved.

Cournoyer and Turcot did go to great pains to avoid political refugees: at its peak, Kab Cherng would house 8,500 people, families drawn mainly from the huge Kao I Dang centre. The Thai military, eager to identify and isolate the Khmer Route and Khmer Serei, held the militants in separate camps and away from relief agencies as much as possible. Those who went to Kab Cherng were civilians, mainly third-and-fourth-generation Chinese-Kampuchean; of the 8,500, 56% were women and 35% were children under fourteen.

Despite these assurances, however, criticism of the project continued to simmer. In a flourish of convoluted logic, CUSO's Edmonton coordinator, Lily Mah Sen, claimed that the project would somehow damage CUSO's 'regular' funding base at the University of Edmonton; a base, she noted, which declined from $9,454 in 1978, to $4,859 in 1979, and to only $462 in the first quarter of 1980. Unable to "answer questions on whether we were supporting Pol Pot and the Khmer Rouge," she submitted a resolution from eight members of her committee stating that "because there is a possibility that some of the refugees may be members of the Khmer Rouge; (because) the amount of money is out of proportion with past CUSO projects; (because) a project of this magnitude is outside the scope of CUSO . . . (and) furthermore questions the role of CUSO in government aid programs (sic), it was moved that (the fund raising department) be asked to submit another project in place of the Cambodian refugee camps for ads in Edmonton papers."[14]

What really bothered hard-core critics was that aid for refugees in Thailand might be seen as support for the enemies of Vietnam, a country which had suffered so badly at the hands of the American military. This attitude, dubious in its relevance to CUSO and to the issue at hand, was perhaps best expressed by the noted development writer, Susan George. At the height of the influx, with almost a million hungry destitutes jammed into small pockets of desperation along the border, she asked, from her home in Paris: "How can we learn the truth about Cambodia today when well-intentioned people are about to undertake an ill-advised action which may only help the murderers of the Cambodian people and the new Sino-American alliance?"[15]

The "new Sino-American alliance" was the key to unhappiness about

CUSO's work with the refugees — and, in fact, about CUSO's work in capitalist Thailand, a country which had often allied itself with American policy in Southeast Asia. No doubt the continued tension along the border did serve American interests; Washington had little desire to see a successful Vietnamese occupation of Kampuchea. But to simply shun so many refugees, because of what Washington might or might not want, seemed a brutally specious approach to world events, even for purists far from the fray.

Iona Campagnolo's arrival on the scene helped to shift the fund-raising effort into overdrive. The Ottawa secretariat was at first nervous that the elegant 'Iron Lady' might become something of a burden, especially during her trip to the refugee camps to see the situation at first hand. There was also concern in some quarters that the outspoken former minister might be too politically partisan for CUSO's own good. In the end, however, the fears turned out to have been unjustified. Iona, as everyone called her, *was* tough — of that there would be ample demonstration — but throughout her months of work on the refugee program and later in the Caribbean, she became a fierce advocate for the refugees and for international development.

In June, she and Paul Turcot toured the camps and spent time at the Kab Cherng centre, now rapidly taking shape. They required special military passes to travel in some areas because of a Vietnamese military incursion near Aranyaprathet; and at one point, on a deserted highway, they stopped the CUSO car to listen to the whump of field artillery in the distance. On her return to Canada, a cross-country schedule of speaking engagements, media interviews and letter-writing campaigns was set up, and the indefatigable Iona set out with a vengeance.

The press, skeptical of her 'abandonment' of politics, nevertheless loved her. Dan Turner, formerly of CUSO in Nigeria and now writing for FP Publications, called her "a mix of Dragon Lady and Mary Tyler Moore," and wrote: "You do know one thing about this glamorous version of Lotta Hitschmanova. She will raise the $400,000." In his nationally syndicated column, Richard Gwyn said: "If we don't cough up the $400,000 she wants and CUSO needs, we deserve to get stomped on."

In fact, the $400,000 was surpassed, allowing the camp to go on for more than a year after the initial six-months period. The Tibetan Refugee Aid Society in Vancouver gave more than one hundred thousand dollars, and the Government of British Columbia also made a generous contribution. But most of the money came in the form of small donations, and through the work of CUSO local committees and individuals. A Toronto woman, Shelly Nacimento, set the record by singlehandedly raising almost eighteen thousand dollars from her friends and neighbours.

When Iona Campagnolo returned from the camps in Thailand, she brought a few gifts. For Lewis Perinbam, Vice-President of CIDA's Special Programs Branch, she had a pair of sandals fashioned from truck tires. For Senior Vice President Maggie Catley-Carlson, later President of CIDA, a selection of the multi-coloured condoms that some of the aid agencies were passing out among the refugees. And for Canadians, a message:

> "When I ask for funds for the Kab Cherng project, I am often
> politely refused by those who say that charity begins at home.
> *Home does not begin where it used to*; McLuhan's global village
> is here, today, and that mass migration of humanity called refu-
> gees and immigrants is an indication of the ever-shrinking size of
> our common living space . . . we cannot sit idly by and rational-
> ize reasons for not taking action."[16]

CUSO had taken primary responsibility for the camp, signing a formal agreement with UNHCR and the Government of Thailand; sub-contracts were made between CUSO and the Thai agencies it had brought together. Logistically, the operation of Kab Cherng was a massive undertaking, not unlike the administration of a very complicated small town. CUSO and the Thais had to organize the purchase, storage and distribution of almost all the daily necessities of the camp, from medical supplies to cooking fuels. Nutritionists, doctors, teacher trainers, literacy workers and vocational teachers had to be found; CUSO had undertaken to provide public health education, training for community health organizers and a paramedical training scheme. Garbage and human waste had to be collected and disposed of; latrines pumped, garbage burned. Spraying for airborne diseases had to be arranged; and the maintenance of facilities provided — including the camp generator and trucks, camp roads, drains and buildings. Schools had to be organized for the thousands of children and for adults in literacy and vocational training programs. Social workers had to be found to handle the anticipated social and family problems.

Initially, some of CUSO's volunteers already in Thailand, especially the engineers, assisted with preliminary arrangements; one, Peter Van Adrichem, extended his contract to act as CUSO coordinator in the first months of the camp's operation. Then, in mid-August, with camp construction completed, the first refugees began to arrive from Kao I Dang; within days, there were more than eight thousand five hundred people.

The Thai organizations were ready and waiting. CBERS became the lead agency, handling food distribution, repair and maintenance of camp facilities, and sanitation. Basic education was organized by the Chao Surin Association, while the Harry Durance Foundation managed non-formal education and vocational training programs. Recreation, cultural events and under-five programs were the responsibility of the Friends for All Children Foundation, and Mahidol University organized medical and nutritional programs.

Kab Cherng could hardly be described as a nice place to live, but unlike other centres, it was clean and orderly; and the refugees were not the wizened, staring automatons that characterized so many camps. The houses were semi-permanent constructions, raised slightly off the ground on concrete pillars to avoid problems of monsoon flooding. A basic plywood floor, asbestos-cement walls and corrugated tin roofs formed the basic shell, to which each family would add its own features, making partitions with the bamboo and reed matting they were given. The houses were built in groups of six, and set in rectangular quadrants around small concrete tanks, which supplied water for bathing or watering the families' small vegetable plots. With only forty-five acres for the entire camp, land was at a premium; every square foot counted. Water proved a constant problem and during the worst of the dry season, it had to be trucked in. During the monsoon, however, it was collected from the roofs of the houses in huge clay cisterns made by the refugees in one of the workshops.

In addition to the houses, administration buildings had been constructed, along with eight schools, two handicraft and recreational centres, a small food distribution centre and a 25-bed hospital and dispensary. As soon as teachers, or potential teachers, could be identified among the refugees, classes conducted in Khmer were organized; two sessions a day for children, and one in the evening for adults. Within a matter of days, there were thirty-two classes of Grade One pupils — some of them ten or twelve years of age and attending school for the first time — and twenty classes of students between Grade Two and Grade Four. In all, almost two thousand six hundred children were in classes, providing jobs for fifty-five Kampuchean teachers and two dozen support staff. Another five hundred children benefitted from under-five programs, and five hundred adults enrolled in sewing, knitting, carpentry, agriculture and adult literacy programs, which also provided employment for camp members. But it was the health program which probably had the greatest long-term impact. Many of the new arrivals suffered from respiratory infections, pneumonia, malaria, tuberculosis and diarrhoea; although most of the problems could be cured or at least treated, there remained ongoing problems of public health and sanitation. Dr. Kawee, the Thai physician in charge, supervised the hospital and the out-patient clinic — which treated as many as four hundred people a day — and established training programs for twenty-two medical trainees, seventy primary health care workers, and three hundred sixty-seven 'health communicators' to tell residents about basic sanitation and nutrition; this information, it was hoped, would remain with Kampucheans after they returned to their homeland. As well, Dr. Kawee helped establish a traditional medicine clinic, operated by traditional Khmer homeopaths he identified among the refugees.

Although the Kab Cherng camp was situated in one of the poorest areas of Thailand, it became clear that the refugees were, in some ways, better off than the Thais in surrounding villages. Outpatient and hospital facilities in the camp were extended to Thai villagers; and at one point — perhaps encouraged by Dr. Kawee's award as Rural Doctor of the Year in 1980 — as many as a thousand people were journeying to the camp daily, from as far away as one hundred kilometres. CUSO encouraged local food purchases for the camp and avoided the standard UNHCR practice of buying centrally in Bangkok: local villages got a better price for their produce, and Kab Cherng usually got cheaper food than other camps, because the middle-man system was eliminated. Kab Cherng also meant jobs for local people in road repair and the construction of reservoirs. And, for the first time, there was cheap fertilizer — a by-product of the anerobic waste and sewage treatment established in the camp by a Thai agency.

These developments encouraged Cournoyer's hope: that the camp ex
tend its services into the surrounding Thai community, providing a demonstration of Thai NGO capabilities, and a kind of training ground for
further CUSO activities in the area. "I thought that even though it would
do something for the refugees," he said, "the program should have a
long term perspective; it should help us to redefine ourselves to the Thai
Government; and it should help us to reinforce some of the Thai NGOs
and assist them to work together; the refugee program should lay the
foundation for longer-term programs in development."

By the spring of 1981 — while the Kab Cherng camp was going into
a second extension — Cournoyer, Paul Turcot and Suteera Thomson were
already contemplating a program to maintain some of the services in Thai
villages after the camp closed. In 1981, exhaustive discussions, with the
local NGOs, the Government of Thailand and CIDA officials in Bangkok
and Ottawa, paved the way for the North East Thailand Project – NET.
Launched in October 1981, its aim was to continue the cooperation among
Thai NGOs in a major self-help project for fifty-three villages in the
vicinity of Kab Cherng. Specifically, the NET project initiated the provision of basic health care, primary and adult education; improved agricultural production; introduced income-generation activities, and
strengthened planning and management links between the villages and
the Thai NGOs. Once again, CUSO acted as the coordinator, but with
nine Thai NGOs — many with the vitally important experience of Kab
Cherng behind them — CUSO's role would eventually diminish.

Iona Campagnolo had seen the germ of the NET project in a small
village months before. The Thai houses were less sturdy than those at
Kab Cherng, and medical facilities were simply non-existent. "The children I shared my lunch with at the tiny kindergarten in Koke Samakhi,
receive their rice ration from diverted military convoys on their way to
the giant camps. CUSO has built a village well here, putting the local
money lender, whose loans were given at 125% interest, out of business.
The well cost Canada $260, and in addition, CUSO has taught the children
to grow their own vegetables at school, which are used in their daily
noon lunches which are, for some, their only meal."[17]

In October 1980, former External Affairs Minister Flora MacDonald
toured Asia, and stopped for a few days in Thailand, specifically to see

the camp at Kab Cherng which she had helped to bring into existence months before. Although MacDonald and Iona Campagnolo would return to their vigorous partisan conflict in Canadian politics, Kab Cherng had united them, along with thousands of donors, in an attitude that transcended the parochialism of daily Canadian life. Long after the camp had been closed, the trenchant Progressive Conservative foreign affairs critic and the President of the Liberal Party of Canada would co-sign a CUSO fund-raising letter:

> Both of us have seen at first hand the good work that CUSO is
> doing in Asia and elsewhere . . . We have both volunteered our
> time and money for CUSO because we have seen its ability to
> support and encourage good grass roots development work . . .
> Our funds — and yours if you will join us — support programs
> targetted at those most in need of assistance.[18]

When Flora MacDonald visited Kab Cherng, conditions were already beginning to improve. "The situation is better than it was a year ago," she said, "but for the thousands still living in makeshift quarters in camps beset by monsoon rain and floods, the living isn't easy."[19] Nevertheless, the numbers were declining. Many had left for Europe and North America — Canada agreed to take sixty thousand people in 1980 — and as the military situation eased in 1981, twenty-thousand refugees returned voluntarily to Kampuchea. In December 1981, the Thai government merged smaller camps into larger holding centres, from which repatriation or third-country emigration could be more easily arranged. On Dec. 27, 1981, the last full bus of Kampucheans pulled away from the administration building of Kab Cherng.

The impact of the Kab Cherng project was considerable. To begin with, eight thousand five hundred people were helped to survive and to improve their lives over a seventeen-month period. Martin Barber, the UNHCR Director, said that there were fewer problems at Kab Cherng than at almost any other camp.[20] Barber mentioned the cultural understanding that Thai agencies brought to the problem: the agencies had certainly helped minimize the violence and corruption; for example, when a senior Thai military officer demanded kickbacks on food deliveries at the camp, the Thai agencies quietly went to work in Bangkok, and the man was replaced within 48 hours.

An independent evaluation of the project spoke highly of the administration, educational facilities and medical services, and noted that the total cost averaged thirty-seven cents per refugee per day — slightly less than Raymond Cournoyer had predicted almost two years before. Seen in the context of benefits to thousands of Thai villagers — farm produce sales, jobs, and health care at the camp clinic and hospital — the cost was even lower.

But the major impact of the project was its indirect and longer-term effects: Kab Cherng, despite its great challenge to CUSO, was only one of many camps; its numbers pale in significance beside the total. It was the unity created among Thai NGOs that was probably the most important long-term benefit of the project: they realized that they could do as well — if not better — than the foreign organizations; and they discovered the effectiveness of joint action.

"All participating NGOs agreed that the experiences gained and the lessons learned from the project were very useful," the formal evaluation stated, "particularly in strengthening their staff capabilities. All . . . expressed confidence in coping with the difficult problems of rural underdevelopment — by participating in the NET project, which could never have occurred without the positive experience of Kab Cherng." That the NGOs had been successful was also a salient lesson for the Government of Thailand. At first, there was tangible official reluctance regarding their involvement; composed mainly of young social activists, the NGOs were not entirely welcome around tables dominated by representatives of a conservative (if benevolent) military regime. But Kab Cherng proved a leavening experience, both for the government — which could hardly deny the effectiveness of the approach — and for the agencies, which were able to conduct their programs unhampered, and even found unexpected responsiveness from the government on thorny issues. That they could come together in the subsequent NET project testified to the growing maturity of all the parties concerned.

For CUSO, Kab Cherng was a watershed: it proved that the organization could once again rise to an emergency while maintaining the unique insight of an organization with a priority of development — not relief. CUSO was able to transcend some of the traditional approaches that hamper larger relief agencies, and provided a service — to refugees, Thai residents, and the Thai development community. From the internal perspective, CUSO proved to itself that there also remained a Canadian responsiveness — a remarkable team spirit in the Ottawa office and across Canada, despite the occasional political difficulty. The fund-raising target had been surpassed, making 1980–81 the most successful year in the organization's fund-raising history; and the project had also helped to reestablish CUSO's credentials with CIDA and the Canadian public.

With the confidence generated by the Kab Cherng project, it was a small matter to convince CIDA that the larger North East Thailand project was viable; and the special funding arrangement worked out for NET paved the way for other Canadian NGOs to approach CIDA with similar large rural-development projects in other countries, on significantly liberalized terms and conditions.

But what eventually transpired in Kampuchea dampened these positive conclusions. In an effort to isolate the Vietnamese, most Western nations — including Canada — refused to recognize the Heng Samrin regime in Phnom Penh; a Pol Pot–Sihanouk coalition continued to receive a form of recognition through the UN, long after every shred of legitimacy had fallen from Khmer Rouge claims. Through the first half of the 1980s, the Khmer Rouge and the Vietnamese played a bloody cat-and-mouse game while thousands of Kampuchean victims were pushed and pulled relentlessly back and forth across the Thai-Kampuchea border each dry season. In the summer of 1985, Khao-i-Dang held 55,000 people — the highest number in years — while the Vietnamese-backed Phnom Penh government began constructing a 760-kilometre 'security fence' along the entire length of the border. That the international fiction which 'recognized' Pol Pot should have continued longer than his rule in Kampuchea was both a cruel irony, and an ineffective means of pressuring the Vietnamese to withdraw. On the contrary, it helped reinforce the Vietnamese position and made life in Kampuchea — effectively cut off from all but a trickle of foreign aid — a continuing tragedy.

It was politics that created the Kampuchean disaster, and it was politics that prolonged it, years after the refugee crisis and the attendant media excitement had passed. International politics had defaced this ''inoffensive and graceful land,'' and would sustain the affliction for years, denying the Khmer people the international assistance to which many other countries, with far more dubious regimes, had full access. The Kampucheans, reluctant latecomers to the Indo-Chinese conflict would continue to pay — long after the major players had left.

Chapter 26

The Jumblies

They went to sea in a sieve, they did;
In a sieve they went to sea;
In spite of all their friends could say . . . .
And in twenty years they all came back -
In twenty years or more;
And everyone said, "how tall they've grown"!
For they've been to the Lakes and the Terrible Zone,
And the Hills of the Chankly Bore

— Edward Lear

I n their scholarly study, *Canada as a Principal Power*, David Dewitt and John Kirton place most theorists on the subject of Canadian foreign policy in one of two camps. The 'liberal-internationalist' school sees Canada as a middle power: active, responsible and influential, "a committed internationalist nation, distinguished by its diligent pursuit of values largely shared by the world community."[1] Critics of this vision generally embrace the theory of 'peripheral dependence', characterizing Canada as a "penetrated, semi-peripheral power" dominated by and supportive of an imperial America and the "world capitalist system that it largely controls and from which it derives disproportionate benefit."[2] It is a kind of Pollyanna-versus-the-Radicals categorization which Dewitt

351

and Kirton feel obscures a more complicated reality, one in which a post-Mackenzie King Canada begins to mature — in a state of 'complex neo-realism' into a self-respecting principal power. This approach and categorization is, perhaps coincidentally, relevant to the way CUSO has viewed itself, and to the way it has been viewed by both its supporters and its critics. Although the terminology — internationalist, peripheralist, realist — is awkward, it is not inappropriate to CUSO, where once serviceable words — pragmatist, idealist, progressive — have lost all useful meaning.

Liberal-internationalism certainly dominated the thinking of CUSO's founders in the early 1960s, and has had strong adherents among the majority of its staff and board members ever since. The early motto, "to serve and learn," was the embodiment of this ethos: CUSO would help develop effective, harmonious links between Canada and the Third World, and would contribute to building a more just international order. The organization saw itself as a moderately independent, responsible contributor and participant, both in the development of positive Canadian attitudes towards the world, and in steady, gradual Third World advancement.

As a result, CUSO sought a preferential arrangement with the Canadian Government and a relationship with CIDA based on mutual respect and common goals — an approach which precluded support for immediate changes in the international order. As Development Education evolved, it reinforced the basic thrust: that the public could be persuaded, by factual evidence, that successful development activities were essential to the common good of both developing and industrialized countries. Despite the failures of two decades of concerted international development work, emphasis was placed on qualitative improvements to the aid establishment and on significantly increased levels of international assistance. Statistics on unrelieved poverty, malnutrition, child mortality and disease could be offset by equally compelling statistics on increased standards of living, improved life expectancy, greater literacy and the reduction of disease — including the worldwide eradication of smallpox — as examples of what would be possible with even more and better assistance.

"We are trusted," stated the 1980 Parliamentary Task Force on North-South Relations, venerating a long-standing tenet of Canadian faith. "Trusted by developing countries because we are not a colonial power and because we are not so powerful as to be tempted to force our will. Trusted by developed countries, by the United States and Europe, because we share political and cultural traditions and many of their concerns."[3] Canada was the inveterate bridge builder, and the NGOs, of which CUSO was the largest, were important players in what Lester Pearson called a partnership in development.

Seen in the perspective of the 'peripheral dependence' school however, CUSO was simply a 'para-statal agency' which was "almost totally dependent upon government financing," and which had been diverted "towards fighting poverty abroad instead of fighting and criticizing CIDA at home."[4] Because most of the CUSO budget was devoted to recruitment, administration and air fares, it was, like most Canadian aid, spent in Canada and, linked to the dispatch of Canadians, it was as much a form of tied aid as any official government program. Canada's aid programs and, by association, CUSO, were intimately linked with "the imperial strategies and structures of the largest western powers"; activities which conflicted with this approach, such as support for Southern African liberation movements or work in Cuba, would always be kept on a short leash.

Some adherents to this view of CUSO nevertheless joined the organization — to try to change it. They felt that CUSO should identify more strongly with the oppressed — to the extent that it was possible within the dependent relationship with CIDA; and that the organization had to become more independent, even at the expense of programs. In their critique of Canadian aid programs, *Perpetuating Poverty*, Robert Carty and Virginia Smith argued that effective development work would come about, "not by providing aid, but by educating Canadians and building solidarity"; by empowering organized groups in Canada and the Third World: "trade unions, peasants, non-governmental organizations, political movements, churches, in their struggle to gain power and make essential choices."[5] The peripheralists emphasized liberation, and progressive revolutionary regimes, such as Mozambique, Nicaragua and pre-invasion Grenada, where the struggle to gain power and make essential choices had in their opinion been successful.

Ironically, it was also the peripheralist view which most attracted the attention of CUSO's critics at the far right. "CUSO is part of the terrorist-support network," wrote Paul Fromm, Director of Citizens for Foreign Aid Reform Inc. (CFAR).[6] One of CFAR's researchers, Branca Lapajne, went into the subject at length, pointing out that CUSO was "very closely tied to CIDA's purse strings"; and had "almost unlimited access to the coffers of the Canadian government." CUSO managed to get away with its "socialist/communist ideology,"[7] such critics argued, because it had so many faithful aluminai strategically placed in key positions of government and Parliaments: Lewis Perinbam, Bill McWhinney and others had become vice presidents of CIDA; Walter McLean, MP ("on the left of the Conservative Party") 'Red' Tory, Flora MacDonald, and the uncategorized but presumably radical Iona Campagnolo.

Right-wing critics aside, it is fair to say that almost any CUSO activity could be used to support either a liberal-internationalist interpretation of the organization, or the peripheralist view. Neither approach, however, adequately describes the organization as a whole, nor the continuum of its work; nor does the notion that CUSO was simply an uneasy alliance between two opposing factions. In fact, it was the beguiling idea — put forward by both sets of proponents — that one side or the other *could* prevail, that turned an often creative political dynamic into the destructive semi-paralysis of the late 1970s.

There is an entirely different way of looking at CUSO — from a viewpoint similar to Dewitt and Kirton's 'complex neo-realism'. Such a view holds that CUSO has been managed by experienced, realistic staff who understand Third World needs, and are able to mount pragmatic responses to them. They did not pretend that CUSO could remain apolitical in a highly charged political forum, nor did they accept that it should pursue, uncritically, the chic causes and dramatic experiments that arose as alternatives to flawed liberal-internationalist thinking.

The 'realist' view of CUSO is supported mainly by the fact that the organization not only survived, but grew and thrived over twenty-five difficult years; became a multi-million dollar, professionally-run corporation; and achieved widespread respect, both in the Third World and in the international development communities of Europe and the United States. It did so despite violent, protracted, public and internecine attacks on its integrity from both right and left. Neither canny liberal-internationalism nor sheer simple-minded goodness could possibly have sustained it through the financial and management crises, the bloody warfare with SUCO, and the media attacks on its alleged support for terrorism and communism. Had CUSO been consumed by radicals, as some suggested, it could hardly have justified and continued to receive generous funding from a liberal government notoriously skittish about its own reputation — a government that chopped the CYC, SUCO and a dozen of its own do-gooder social service schemes in as many years. Nor could its survival be explained by its having lots of friends in high places. Many of the founding fathers, uncomprehending and despairing of the child — or perhaps more to the point, fearful of its critics — disowned CUSO during its most troubled times. Others came or returned to the organization late in its career; they lent their names, their times and their advice only after the darkest days had passed.

Most observers of CUSO failed to appreciate that the organization had somehow to convert its original good-Samaritan intentions into concrete programs that addressed real needs in Third World countries. And it had to do so within the context of the outdated liberal-internationalism of its backers and the media, and the mixed (and occasionally mixed-up) motives of its mother-funder, CIDA. At the same time, it had to deal with concerted internal assaults by its peripheralists, whose criticism, while often uncomfortably close to the mark, usually implied pulling the whole thing down and starting all over again.

CUSO guarded its independence from CIDA fiercely, despite being financially dependent on it; their frequent arguments often arose when CUSO resisted pressure to change policies of which CIDA disapproved. The two organizations generally maintained a cordial, professional relationship, however; one that was mutually supportive where interests coincided. But CUSO seldom hesitated to criticize, and consistently tried to influence government policy — informally, through its contacts with civil servants and politicians; and more formally, through its many apperances before the House of Commons Standing Committee on External Affairs and National Defence.

Overseas, CUSO went to great lengths to avoid being directly asociated with or compromised by Canadian embassies and high commissions. It made its own contacts with Third World governments and negotiated its own arrangements, working unassisted in dozens of newly independent countries where there was no Canadian representation. This was no easy matter, for CUSO, unlike church organizations, had no resident missionaries to build contacts and provide advice. Latter-day Canadian NGOs, gingerly following in CUSO's footsteps, found a well-blazed trail; in any case, many of their staff were former CUSO volunteers and field staff, as is much of CIDA's present-day senior and middle management. CUSO, however, still operates in many countries — Bolivia, Mozambique, Sierra Leone, much of Central American and the Caribbean and all of the Pacific — where there are no Canadian embassies, and little Canadian presence of any other kind.

While CUSO enjoyed the freedom of its independence, it also assumed responsibility for its own predicaments. When serious problems arose in the Caribbean in 1982, the CUSO Executive Director met privately with the Prime Ministers of Jamaica and Dominica to discuss solutions. The Canadian Department of External Affairs was kept informed, but didn't become involved. Most embassies kept their contact with CUSO to a minimum; outside the regular business of passports and visas, they were far removed from life 'up-country' and knew little about the work involved in placing and supporting volunteers, or about small project development, management and evaluation.

Cuba was a prime example of the realist approach in CUSO. It instituted a program there in response to a perceived need that it could help to satisfy; Cuba was treated like dozens of other countries, despite wide-spread North American fear of the Castro regime. Going to Cuba was both a practical continuation of CUSO's general mandate and a dem-onstration, to organizations and governments elsewhere, of CUSO's de-termined independence. The program continued even after government funding cuts — further evidence of CUSO's confidence in its own actions.

CUSO has generally responded to good programming opportunities rather than acting on internally-generated quests for righteousness. Proj-ects and volunteer placements are judged on their developmental merit and chances of success — not their politics. In 1983, for example, CUSO spent twice as much on volunteer programs in Papua New Guinea as it did in Mozambique, and three times more in Thailand then in Nicaragua. The decisions were based on practical considerations, not political rea-sons. The needs in Thailand and Papua New Guinea, among the people with whom CUSO worked, were as great or greater, and the coincidence of programming opportunities, attitudes and structures made work there as effective and as cost-efficient as anywhere else.

Frank Bogdasavich and — especially — David Catmur were sceptical of the placement of volunteers as the sole solution to the problems of the

Third World. When Jack Pierpoint, annoyed at CIDA's apathy towards post-war Nigeria, proposed the Schools Reconstruction Project, Catmur accepted the idea, and created a Projects Division in Ottawa to encourage similar projects elsewhere. When the Latin America program recommended short-term placements to handle specific, limited tasks, he agreed. When field staff in the Caribbean suggested hiring West Indians as volunteers, he developed the notion of 'host national' volunteers. When experienced Canadians were unavailable for the increasing number of field staff positions, the jobs were given to Asians, Africans, Latin Americans, Europeans, and even Americans — adding new talent to the organization's overseas planning and management.

It was during this period, too, that CUSO and SUCO began to drift apart, and a form of decentralized management gradually developed.

In all this, government remained uninvolved, except to acquiesce — through its annual contribution to the budget. It was only during the half-dozen years of CUSO's severe ideological division, between 1974 and 1979, that CIDA and other government departments became concerned about CUSO's ultimate direction; but even then, the government didn't exercise its influence in a very clear, straight forward manner. The occasional CIDA budget cuts were usually effected without explicit reasons or admonishments; so CUSO was left to draw its own inferences and to act accordingly.

This was the period of the most open and difficult splits between the organization's liberal-internationalists and those seeking to alter its peripheral dependence; the camps that Murray Thomson referred to as the 'pragmatists' and the 'socialist roaders'. While these struggles continued, volunteer numbers declined and little arose to replace them. The organization's development education efforts became characterized by ineffectual gestures of solidarity and inept verbal attacks on banks and multinational corporations. Distressed liberal-internationalists railed and plotted, and sometimes resigned in protest against what they saw as the destruction of CUSO's once splendid dream.

The relationship with CIDA finally became adversarial — and unpleasant.

This was the time of greatest danger for CUSO, a period during which the hard-learned realism appeared to be forgotten and the organization seemed determined to retreat into one or other of the two favoured dreamlands. There were power struggles among staff; costly to morale, to the organization's image, and to overseas programs. The Board of Directors became transfixed by the unrelieved hostility between the anglophone and the francophone sectors, and management drifted aimlessly from debate to paralyzing debate on the virtues of various approaches to administration.

The arguments culminated in senior staff changes in 1979, and a sobering CIDA reduction; in the period that followed, the Board of Directors was completely reshaped: changes included a wider membership base, greater emphasis on external fund-raising, and improved financial planning and control. The split from SUCO was finalized. The formation of a union ended much of the power struggle that had preoccupied staff for five years, and emphasis was placed on rebuilding the confidence of government.

The positive effects of these changes included a re-emphasis on the organization's professional capabilities overseas and a halt to the decline in volunteer numbers. Innovative proposals for programs in Asia, the Caribbean and Africa were enthusiastically accepted. The Kampuchean Refugee Project in Thailand, (a major effort), was initiated. CUSO not only consolidated its work, but opened new programs in Vanuatu in the Pacific, Togo in West Africa, and Zimbabwe.

The organization continued to have its difficulties, however. Chris Bryant, appointed Executive Director in 1983, explained the problems that accompanied the shift to more sophisticated postings. "In Papua New Guinea we have placed several senior people with provincial governments. Like senior public servants in Canada, no matter how neutral they try to be, they are identified with the government they serve. A change can leave them quite exposed." Bryant was not suggesting an avoidance of such placements. "But we must recognize," he said, "that they pose many more political problems for CUSO than their predecessors or colleagues in lower level jobs faced."[8]

Grenada was perhaps the most dramatic example of this dilemma. CUSO began to work on the island when Maurice Bishop was still a teenager. When Bishop became Prime Minister and introduced sweeping social and political changes, CUSO remained, providing volunteers and project support for government programs as it had been doing for years. Yet despite the uncritically enthusiastic support of many CUSO people for Bishop's policies, and their understandable dismay at his death and the subsequent American invasion, CUSO remained in Grenada, committed to working with Grenadians, as it had for two decades.

Another aspect of the dilemma arose from government, media and public perceptions — as well as CUSO participants' views — of the organization's motives. African liberation movements, for example, found some support in CUSO among those who believed they heralded a socialist millenium; for most CUSO workers, however, ideology was of secondary importance in a clear-cut moral struggle for human rights and justice.

The move away from placing teachers within the formal educational system in many countries was also seen by some as 'progressive', especially where, as former Zambia volunteer and later Field Staff Officer John Saxby put it, the "capitalist mode of production" was dominant. This was a poor base "from which to launch a drive for socialist reconstruction," he wrote in a lengthy thesis on the subject.[9] "The education system is implicated in political contradictions — class antagonisms of the society. These aspects of the role of education in the production of class relations in Zambia seriously qualify the extent to which it can effectively discharge a legitimizing role."[10]

Whether or not the education systems of Zambia and other countries were implicated in class antagonisms, there was stronger and less theoretical evidence on which to base a change in CUSO programming. Research had shown that the formal education system, especially where it was based on inherited colonial models, was expensive, largely irrelevant, and contributed significantly to problems of both urbanization and unemployment. It was estimated that in 1980, there were only enough jobs for 25% of the fifteen-year-old school leavers in Africa, and less than 50% in Latin America and India.[11]

The major example of CUSO's 'peripheral dependence', has been its source of income; yet here, too, there is clear evidence of a highly developed sense of independent realism. An analysis of two or three figures in the 1979 financial statements demonstrates that a disproportionate amount of CUSO's income — as much as 95%, — came in the form of direct grants from CIDA. By 1983, the figure was reduced to 83%, thanks to improved-fund raising and increased contributions from other organizations in Canada and Europe. But the statistic is misleading: most of the volunteer salaries were paid by overseas employers rather than by CUSO, and so did not appear in the financial statements; nor did the costs of housing, furniture and local transportation, which were also borne by the employer. Factored into the real cost of the program, these figures reduced the CIDA contribution significantly. Another important element missing from the financial statements was the voluntary contribution to CUSO of goods and services. Pharmaceutical companies donated the medical kits that went out with each volunteer; many universities provided office space, secretarial time, university telephones and accounting services for local committees across Canada; and returned volunteers did much of the recruitment, selection and interviews — entirely on a voluntary basis.

Even more significant, however, is the contribution made by the individual overseas volunteer. Few earn more than four or five thousand dollars annually, despite the fact that most could make many times that amount in Canada. The difference between what they earned and what they might have earned, represents a tangible contribution, which CUSO's critics conveniently forgot when they examined the balance sheet. As Geoff Andrew once told Lester Pearson, these voluntary contributions all have real value, and would cost real money if the government were to attempt to undertake them itself. Taken as whole in 1984, the private donations, voluntary contributions and the cash input from Third World employers, accounted for approximately sixty-five percent of the CUSO budget.

Ultimately, the real story of CUSO begins and ends with the volunteers. They, like the organization, are studied, dissected and analysed six ways to Sunday. They are costed: the social cost, the political cost, the financial and educational costs. They are studied in terms of what they bring back: self-knowledge, political awareness, new skills, a message for Canadians, a spouse, bilharzia. Even the volunteers themselves veer towards abstraction when they debate their role. This was not, however, the case with Mohan Srivastava who completed his two-year assignment in Nigeria in 1984.

"I was once a cog," he wrote, "on a wheel that churned out reserve estimates for a mining company that dug up uranium for a consortium that made profits for an industry that created jobs for a country that . . . It is a vast and necessary machine and inevitably, I'll return to some part of it. But when I do, it will be with a more complete view of myself and the world; and with a commitment to maintain a broader and more human perspective." But he was concerned about the number of CUSO volunteers. The decline of the mid-1970s had stopped in 1979, but by 1984, the numbers were on the way down again. "CUSO's strength is in people," Srivastava wrote, "not projects. CUSO as an organization seems to have lost faith in its original mandate . . . cooperant numbers decrease as CUSO moves more to project funding and administration." If the transition were ever completed, he said, someone would have to invent CUSO all over again because of the real need for the valuable service CUSO provides.

"Dissatisfied with its 'volunteers', CUSO changed them to 'cooperants' and now it appears that we may become 'development workers'. What was wrong with being volunteers? CUSO is always eager to provide evidence that the average age of its cooperant population is rising. What was wrong with being young? CUSO trumpets the fact that it is now recruiting people with specific development skills . . . What was wrong with being 'a keen idealist filled with romantic notions of saving the world?'

"I really don't know if Nigeria is a better place for my having been here. I know only that I am a better person for having been here. My idealism was scuffed a little and lost some of its shine, but that makes it more valuable. Experience tempers idealism . . . It bothers me that CUSO is always struggling to prove that it is not some sort of Third World Outward Bound. I wish that CUSO would take pride in apprenticing development workers; in showing Canadians first-hand the Third World, its injustices, its frustrations and its joys; in returning more aware, more thoughtful and more concerned citizens to Canada."[12]

In his own thoughtful and concerned eloquence penned from Africa, Srivastava could hardly have known that he echoed almost perfectly the words of Donald Faris, written in India thirty years earlier; the words that had given Keith Spicer the idea for CUSO: "Our youth possess a tremendous potential of energy, idealism, and enthusiasm, just waiting to be tapped. The reagent needed is the challenge that life's fullest expression is found in serving others." Visualize, he asked, thousands of young people combatting "the advancing enemy. . . . If, in addition to technical skills, these junior experts were equipped with humility and courage, with sincerity and wisdom, they would be able to transmit not only physical satisfaction to the needy, but also lasting values such as friendship, goodwill and understanding.''

In the end, it is possible to arrive at the last page of the CUSO photograph album having seen a series of interesting snapshots taken over the years; to have had a theoretical and occasionally emotional discussion about what it all means, and yet still miss the flavour of the CUSO experience. In fact, it cannot really be tasted without spending time with volunteers at their postings. There is, of course, no typical CUSO posting: they range from Judy Pullen doing deep knee-bends with Tibetan monks; to Bruce Edwards in his Cessna, high over the Peruvian jungle. More CUSO volunteers have been teachers than anything else, however; and more served in Nigeria than in any other country. And although they were all individuals with highly individualistic experiences, Jennifer Harold could have been almost any one of them, at almost any time in CUSO's history.

Jennifer Harold inherited more than twenty years of CUSO history in Nigeria and four hundred years of Nigerian contact with the white man — explorers, traders, missionaries, slavers, colonizers and development experts. She became part of the devalued idea that volunteers were a temporary phenomenon, filling short-term, middle-level manpower gaps. She went to a Nigeria that had changed since the days of Walter McLean, Dan Turner and Keith Bezanson. The war and the optimistic period of reconstruction had passed; the oil boom was over. While it lasted, it expanded expectations vastly, but widened opportunity only slightly. In 1976, Nigeria introduced universal primary education, and in that one year, the number of grade one students doubled. In 1982, more than two million students were ready to enter secondary school; by 1985, there were more Nigerian children registered in primary school than there were people in Ontario and Quebec combined. Exceptional achievement of the collective will; reckless gamble; whatever it was, the demand for schools and teachers burgeoned and standards declined. Jennifer Harold had to cope with all this, and she inherited the legacy of Margery Michelmore, legendary Peace Corps postcard writer, who more than anyone else crystallized and focussed Nigerian resentment towards outsiders who came to help.

Tundey Yusef expressed it best in an article that was spread lavishly across Nigerian newspapers more than twelve years before Jennifer Harold's arrival.[13] He seriously questioned

> . . . the contribution towards development that somebody who
> has just graduated with a BA in history or a BSc in biology or
> chemistry can offer . . . In fact (I) suggest that such a person has
> nothing to offer us. On the contrary, he has more to learn from
> us . . . You are modern day missionaries who wish to sacrifice
> two years of your lives to bring civilization to the underdeveloped
> people of Africa . . . missionaries are the last people we want
> back in Africa. You have caused enough problems already . . .
> How can you morally justify sending hundreds of people with
> BAs to places like India, Ghana and Nigeria where there are liter-
> ally hundreds of natives with exactly this qualification without
> jobs?

Virulent, proud, fuelled by generations of embittered contact with the white man, Yusuf denounced CUSO's volunteers as 'unwanted parasites': "We got rid of the Peace Corps," he wrote, "and we are none the worse for it. It is time we got rid of CUSO too. None of them has anything to contribute to our development. If we can deport Michelmore for saying some stupid things on the back of a post card, surely we can throw out these impudent snobs who think they know more about our own country that we do."

Jenny Harold, then, a happy, round-faced twenty-three-year-old science graduate from the University of Guelph, becomes, in her modest way, the CUSO prototype: we meet her in November 1983, the fifteenth month of her assignment, in the tiny Yoruba town of Ikaram-Akoko, fifteen kilometres of bad road north of Ikare in Nigeria's Ondo State.

The houses of Ikaram-Akoko, their corrugated tin roofs brown with dust, stretch out in the sun along the main road. Most of the inhabitants are farmers who walk to their fields during the day. Nothing much happens in Ikaram-Akoko; there are few shops of any sort. There is one 'chop house' where cooked food is sometimes available; otherwise there isn't even a vulcanizer to repair a bicycle tire. The main industry is education, a commodity prized above all else by the townfolk. There are three community high schools, two of which are three years old; the third, at which Jenny teaches, is in its seventh year. The community has paid to have the school built, bought the materials, hired the contractor, paid the masons, the carpenters, the labourers. They have bought the desks and equipment, and although the government was supposed to provide text-books, paper and teachers' salaries, the parents have ended up providing everything except the salaries — and even these do not arrive on time.

Before Jenny, there has been only one other white person in Ikaram-Akoko: a colonial-era British District Officer, who lived in a house on the hill. The ruins are still visible. He is remembered largely because of the water that had to be hauled up to him. "When I arrived, I was scared," Jenny said.

> At orientation, people were talking so much about all the prob-lems you could have, and I kept thinking all those things were going to happen to me in one day. I didn't know how to fit in; I didn't know about the people; the kids seemed scared of me . . . walking down the street everyone was looking at me and yelling, and I had to keep waving — both sides; like royalty. They were saying, 'Kabo — welcome, welcome.' In that situation, when I was feeling so nervous, little victories were sweet. I remember going to the market. I was so scared; I didn't know whether I could wear flip-flops because I thought worm eggs might be in the sand and get into my feet; crazy things. I bought a puff-puff — a deep-fried sugary doughnut — it was fresh out of the oil and I didn't know what was in it, but I thought I'd risk it, and I ate it, and it was such a victory. I thought, 'Hey, I can *do* it!'[14]

Not long after she arrived, Jenny bought a motorcycle (a Yamaha 125) so she could take weekend trips to visit other volunteers, and also do some of her shopping in Ikare. The Five Day Market at Ikaram-Akoko often falls on a school day, so she would miss it; at first, she also missed it sometimes because she couldn't calculate which day it was going to be held. "The market is every four days," she said, "but they call it a Five Day Market because they count one day twice." Jenny lives in the servant's quarters of a large house. She has three small rooms: a sitting room with two chairs, a table and a bookcase; a bedroom with a bed, a clothes rack and a shelf; and a kitchen. "Because I was the first CUSO volunteer, there was nothing when I came. There weren't even shelves, and I didn't get paid until January, so I didn't have any money to get shelves. Now I'm used to not having them."

The kitchen is where she spends most of her time, because night falls early and quickly in West Africa, and she has a small twelve-volt flourescent light there which she runs off her motorcycle battery. There is no electricity in Ikaram-Akoko, and although Jenny used a kerosene Tilley lamp in her first year, it gave off tremendous heat and was expensive to operate because she kept breaking the fragile mantle behind the glass.

"There's a well, which is fantastic," Jenny says. "And there's a water tank. It leaks, but if you fill it about one-fifth full, you can have running water if you pump it up." Unfortunately, however, the pump hasn't been working for five months, so Jenny takes bucket baths. The water is good; it doesn't require boiling, and last year, even at the height of the drought, when three-quarters of the yam crop was lost, her well was one of the few in town that didn't go dry.

In addition to her Nigerian colleagues, there are a dozen Ghanaian contract teachers. Jenny is the school's only biology teacher, and the work is tough. "There's not a lot of job satisfaction in teaching itself. Last year, I got really frustrated because I had this idea that I was going to educate these students and they were going to learn something. But it didn't seem to matter how much time I took in explaining something, how much I drilled them, only a third would understand. And then last year, at the end, we had the Akoko Common Assessment exam for classes 3 and 4 — which are like Grades Nine and Ten, and only three students passed out of 300. It was the same in math and English."

"It has a lot to do with the system," she explains. That year, there were only seventeen weeks in which to cover a thirty-four week syllabus. Because of financial difficulties, Ondo State opened the schools late and closed them early. When salaries were delayed, the other teachers downed chalk and refused to work. There were endless sports days and religious holidays and a strike. And the kids were often tired. Some worked on their parents' farms after school and on weekends, and because of the water shortage, many had to haul water from a well where they would often have to line up for four hours at a time; Jenny would see them returning home with their precious buckets as late as ten in the evening. Some were not well, and when one of the twenty-eight kids in her home class died, she was shocked. "I thought they were normal, happy, healthy kids. They would complain that they were hungry, and I thought they meant like all kids. But they *are* hungry, and they get tired."

Three others were seriously ill that year. "One of my students had some sort of fever. When he came back, he had scars all over his forehead. He had suffered from terrible headaches which the doctors couldn't cure, so he went to the Babalao — the juju doctor — who made the cuts and let the blood out." Guinea worm is endemic. "It comes from the water," Jenny explains, "and gets under the skin, and you have to wait until it comes to the surface; then you cut the skin and grab the tail of the Guinea worm and over a period of days wind it onto a matchstick . . . if you break it, the eggs inside the worm will get into your body and you will have thousands. It's quite sore . . . "

But it is the teaching that is most discouraging. For all the students, English — the medium of instruction — is a second and sometimes a third language. Cognitive skills, sacrificed to rote learning in overcrowded primary schools, are weak; cheating is commonplace. And most students have little knowledge of anything beyond Ikaram-Akoko. "I didn't know about Nigeria when I came," Jenny says, "but they don't even know what countries are on their border." So she bought a big world map and stuck it up on the dingy concrete wall of her classroom. Students visit her at home after school, to joke and talk and hear stories about Jenny's 'village'. "They ask me about other subjects — math and English — so I've made up a set of flash cards, and I've told them that the student who can get through all of the flash cards will get a biro. Ballpoints are now 50 kobo, so that makes it worth something. I have a little garden with green peppers and beans and carrots, and they're interested in that."

She is proud of the fact that she can control the students without beating them, as other teachers do. And her class is the only one that works on the school farm without creating trouble, perhaps because, if they work hard, she buys them each a puff-puff. At twenty-eight for a naira, it isn't a major financial outlay for her, and though she knows it smacks of bribery, she points out that most of the kids don't have any breakfast.

"How do you judge your success?" Jenny asks. "If I wasn't at my school, there would be no biology teacher, so that's something. And I don't think judging your work by whether kids pass or fail is necessarily valid."

When they all flunked the common assessment exam, she had to decide how she would approach her second year; whether she would unrealistically attempt again to get them all through it, despite the terrible impediments, or simply concentrate her efforts on the better students and abandon the rest. It was a difficult decision for a Canadian imbued with egalitarianism, and a driving ambition not only to succeed, but to make a contribution to this sleepy little backwater. She decided, in the end, to concentrate on the better kids in hopes of getting a few through the exam.

Instead of abandoning the rest, however, she feels that there are a few basics she can teach them. They won't pass the exam, but they can learn something that will be helpful. "The most important thing about the tapeworm, for example, isn't its life-cycle; all you really have to know is that if you cook your meat properly, you won't get it."

She has redoubled her efforts at helping students understand. "We have a microscope that is like a toy," she says, but she wanted the students to see the microscopic algae, Spirogyra. "It was fantastic, because they couldn't believe there was actually something inside that little green strand. Even though it took a whole double period to get everyone to see it, it was worth it."

She has no gas for a Bunsen burner, so experiments are highly restricted, and there is no glassware. Instead of beakers she uses lids from insecticide tins. There are almost no chemicals, but she did have some formaldehyde and another school had some Benedict's Solution, so she arranged a trade. "Now we can preserve a few tadpoles," she says, stoically.

Breaking down some of the myths about white people was an important contribution for Jenny. "White people are very, very rich. So the students and teachers were surprised to discover when the salaries were late, that I was in the same position as the Nigerian teachers. The teachers were pretty impressed that I was getting exactly the same pay as a Nigerian teacher with the same qualifications, and they said so. I wasn't here for the money and that seemed important to them." Some of the other teachers provided her with rice while they all waited for their salaries. "I know my parents thought it was a terrible thing to have to eat rice for three months," she recalled, "but it didn't seem so bad to me, because I knew there were others who didn't even have that."

Long-distance taxi trips over the terrible roads were always an ordeal, partly because of the sheer physical discomfort of the dusty, sweaty, crowded, bone-jarring journey, but also because it was a real novelty for Nigerians to find a white woman taking public transport. "They talk about me — 'Oyibo this and Oyibo that' — they're stunned: it's as though they're saying, 'What on *earth* are you doing in a taxi?' And they always touch my hair . . . "

She was impressed at how frank and guileless people seemed. "Here you don't have a lot of word games and mind games: a man will say, 'I love you', and you will say, 'Well I don't even *know* you, so forget it', and it's OK."

Despite Jenny's bravado, however, and her pragmatic 'make-do' approach to all the difficulties of her first year, she was profoundly discouraged when the kids failed the Akoko exam. "I really thought I was teaching them something," she said. "I really thought they were understanding, and I felt positive about what I was doing. And then, when they all failed, I thought I might as well go home; I wasn't doing anything here; I didn't want to stay. But I couldn't go home, because that would have been admitting defeat and I couldn't face that. Having been defeated as a teacher is one thing, but being defeated as a person would be worse."

Overweight, thanks to her starchy diet, sick four times with malaria, and as unhappy as she had ever been in her young life, Jennifer Harold parked her Yamaha 125 with a friend and crammed herself into a crowded Lagos-bound taxi. Her parents had sent a ticket to London, and she was going to join them for a short, restorative summer in Britain. But after the conveniences of London, Nigeria seemed worse. "I had grown so used to everything — the shortages, the dirt — that when I came back I was shocked," she said. "I didn't remember it like this. I went to Chellerams and there was nothing on the shelves. There was bean flour — bean flour! And tomato paste for 60 kobo a tin!"

"I didn't remember walking down the street and breathing the dust and getting it in my throat; I didn't remember the beggars that would come up to the taxi and harass me. I hated it. I didn't know how I was going to cope. I thought I was going to die."

"But then I got into this crowded taxi, heading for Dugbe, and everyone was yelling and making noise and the taxi driver was weaving in and out of the traffic and the crowds, and I remember the 'conductor', such a kindly little kid, hanging out of the window yelling to potential passengers, 'Dugbe! Dugbe! Dugbe!'. There was so much life. I suddenly felt I was back home again, and instead of being an observer, I felt a part of it. And I remembered the good things too.

And then, when I came home to Ikaram, where I had been suspicious of people cheating me, slipping me a bad tomato, it didn't matter any more. I realized that I had missed pounded yam when I was in England, and I really missed the market. I went into a supermarket in England and the checkout clerks didn't even say hello; I smiled at them and they didn't know what I was doing.''

She recalled standing atop Hadrian's Wall with her parents and 'greeting people' the way Nigerians do. There is nothing extraordinary in it, you just say hello. ''Good afternoon,'' she said to a couple walking along the wall. ''The woman turned round and almost ran away. She didn't say anything, and the man looked down at the ground and just mumbled.''

''So to come back here and have everybody say, 'Welcome; welcome; good morning', and to have all the kids wave and yell at you, making you feel that they are happy to see you, is good. You're *somebody*, you're not just nobody walking down the street — that changed my attitude entirely. Now I can say that I really like Nigeria. I just love it.''

Jennifer Harold completed her assignment in the summer of 1984. But regardless of what she does over the rest of her life — as a biologist, as a teacher, or anything else — what she learned in Ikaram-Akoko will always remain with her. ''I'm going to miss Nigeria a lot,'' she says wistfully. ''I'm going to miss driving my motorcycle, driving through the bush, dodging the potholes and the taxis. There's so much life and there's so much to do. I don't really know how to describe it, but it's good.''

References

Chapter I

1. All quotations taken from "The Way We Were" by Peter Hoffman; *CUSO Forum*, Vol 3, No 4, 1981, and from the author's interview with Peter Hoffman, July 2, 1983.

Chapter II

1. Unless otherwise noted, all Perinbam quotations are taken from the author's interview, Aug. 10, 1983.
2. "Canadian Volunteer Graduate Program," by Lewis Perinbam, June 1, 1959.
3. *To Plow With Hope*, Donald K. Faris, Harpers, New York, 1958, p. 202.
4. Unless otherwise noted, all Spicer quotations are taken from an interview with Barbara Hoffman, Oct. 31, 1980 or from Spicer's letter to the author, Dec. 10, 1984.
5. Fred Stinson, interviewed by Peter Hoffman, Autumn, 1980.
6. *Twenty Years of Peace Corps*, Gerald T. Rice, Peace Corps, 1981, p. 1.
7. In *One Million Volunteers*, Arthur Gillette, Pelican, 1968, the author quotes Nixon as criticizing the sending "as America's representatives young men he calls volunteers but who in truth in many instances would be trying to escape the draft" p. 176.
8. *The Making of an unAmerican*, Paul Cowan, Viking Press, New York, 1967, p. 48.
9. Unless otherwise noted, Leddy quotations are taken from "The Origins of CUSO," By Dr. J. F. Leddy, 1981, CUSO files.
10. "On Assignment to Help the World" by Michael Graham, *Globe Magazine*, Toronto, March 31, 1962.
11. *Ibid.*
12. *Ibid.*
13. James George to Keith Spicer, Feb. 21, 1961.
14. James George to Fred Stinson, Sep. 29, 1961.
15. "Report of a Tour of Southeast Asian Countries" by Lewis Perinbam, Sep. 25, 1961.
16. *Ibid.*

Chapter III

1. Report of Associate Executive Secretary, Terry Glavin, on trip to Jamaica, 1-9 September 1964.
2. Author's meeting with Edward Seaga, Kingston, Jamaica, 19 March 1982.
3. *Capitalism and Slavery*, Eric Williams, Capricorn Books, New York, 1966, p.52.
4. Author's interview with David Beer, 18 July 1983.
5. Author's interview with Guy Arnold, 29 November 1983.
6. Author's interview with Gordon Cressy, 17 August 1983.
7. *Man Deserves Man*, McWhinney and Godfrey, eds., Ryerson Press, Toronto, 1966, p.262.
8. *Ibid*, p.248.
9. Author's interview with Ray Clark, 6 September 1983.
10. *Man Deserves Man*, op cit, p.271.
11. *Ibid*, p.275.
12. Author's interview with Sharon Capeling-Alakija, 29 October 1983.
13. *The Computer Centre Party*, Dorothy Eber, Tundra Books, Montreal, 1969, p.53
14. *Jamaica: Struggle in the Periphery*, Michael Manley, Third World Media, London, 1982, p.44
15. Proceedings of the Senate Standing Committee on Foreign Affairs, 25 February 1970.
16. Author's interview with Jeanna Baty, 25 June 1983.
17. Clark interview, op cit.
18. "The Changing Face of CUSO in the Caribbean," *CUSO Forum*, Winter 1980.
19. Hugh Shearer to CUSO, 25 November 1981.
20. *Toronto Star*, 22 January 1982.
21. *Kingston Star*, 13 March 1982.
22. "Three CUSO Jamaica Projects, An Evaluation," September 1982: CUSO files.
23. *Kingston Star*, 9 January 1982.
24. Eugenia Charles to author, 25 March 1983.
25. All Green quotations from author's interview with Marlene Green, 24 June 1983.

Chapter IV

1. Author's interview with Guy Arnold.
2. *Portrait of India*, Ved Mehta, Penguin, 1970, p.297.

3. "Further Comments on Kangra," John Hayson, June 14, 1963.
4. Mehta, op cit, p.295.
5. Author's interview with Jean Carberry, Aug. 14, 1983.
6. Mehta, op cit. p.295.
7. *CUSO Forum*, Vol. 6, No 3, 1978.

Chapter V

1. All McLean quotations are taken from the author's interview with Walter Maclean, June 29, 1983.
2. Unless otherwise noted, all McNeill quotations are from the author's interview with Bill McNeill, July 25, 1983.
3. Ojukwu, C., Odumegwu; *Biafra: Selected Speeches and Random Thoughts*, Perennial Library, New York, 1969; Vol. 1 p.1.
4. *Ibid*; Vol. II, p.86.
5. All Turner quotations are taken from author's interview with Dan Turner, July 20, 1983.
6. Author's interview with Robert Sterling, July 25, 1983.
7. Forsyth, Frederick. *The Biafra Story*, Penguin, London, 1969, p.105.
8. Madiebo, Alexander. A. *The Nigerian Revolution and the Biafran War*, Fourth Dimension Publishing, Enugu, 1980; see p.272.
9. Forsyth, op cit, p.224.
10. Brewin, A. and MacDonald, D. *Canada and the Biafran Tragedy*, James Lewis and Samuel, 1970; p.154.
11. Lewis, Stephen. *Journey to Biafra*, Thistle, Don Mills, 1968; p.38.
12. Sterken, Jacob. *The Nigerian Civil War; The Role of the Humanitarians*, unpublished PhD thesis, University of Waterloo, 1973, p.139.
13. Edgell, A., writing in *Civil Wars and the Politics of International Relief*, David, M. (ed); Praeger, New York, 1975, p.67.
14. Akpan, N. U. *The Struggle for Secession, 1966-70*, Frank Cass, London, 1971; p.160.
15. Lloyd, Hugh G. et al; *The Nordchurchaid Airlift to Biafra, 1968-70, An Operations Report*, Folkekirkens Nodjaelp, Copenhagen, 1972, p.229.
16. Stremlau, John J. *The International Politics of the Nigerian Civil War*, Princeton University Press, Princeton, 1977; p.239.
17. Lloyd, op cit, p.240.
18. *Ibid*; the name of the agency was Diakoniches Werk.

19. *Ibid*; p.200.
20. Stremlau; op cit, p.241.
21. Lloyd, op cit, appendix 9.
22. Stremlau, op cit, quoting Bevery Carl, Deputy Chief of Nigeria/Biafra Relief and Rehabilitation program, USAID; p.242.
23. Susan Cronje puts the figure for Nigerian arms expenditures at US$40 million in her book, *The War and Nigeria*, Sidgewick and Jackson, London, 1972.
24. Stremlau, op cit, p.242. Okwechime was probably referring to a $24,000 grant from the Presbyterian Church of Canada to its counterpart in Biafra.
25. *Ibid*, p.120.
26. Tape from George Orick, Sep. 18, 1968; CUSO files.
27. Cable, Malone to External Affairs, Oct. 7, 1968.
28. "How to be a Global Villager," *Maclean's*, Feb. 1969.
29. Interview with Gayle Turner, nee Cooper, Aug. 15, 1981.
30. *Position Paper for CUSO Board*, David Cayley, Apr. 19, 1969.
31. Brodhead an author to Bogdasavich, Apr. 19, 1969.
32. Obasanjo, Olusegun. *My Command*, Heinemann, Ibadan, 1980, p.79. This version given by Obasanjo, who later became Nigerian Head of State, contradicts a popular version at the time which maintained that the incident had been carried out by one of the 'cowardly' white mercenary pilots who reputedly never effectively closed Uli because they wanted to keep their well-paying jobs.
33. Stremlau, op cit, p. 328.
34. *Toronto Star*. Jan. 2, 9 & 12, 1970.
35. *Ibid*, Jan. 26, 1970.
36. *Toronto Telegram*, Jan. 21, 1970.
37. *Coups and Earthquakes*, Mort Rosenblum, Harper Colophon Books, New York, 1981, p.27.
38. *Toronto Telegram*, Jan. 21, 1970.
39. *Toronto Star*, Jan. 21, 1970.
40. *Toronto Telegram*, Jan. 23, 1970.
41. *Montreal Star*, Aug. 15, 1970.
42. Toronto *Globe and Mail*, May 7, 1970.
43. Brewin and MacDonald, op cit, p.162.
44. Author's interview with Tim Brodhead, July 26, 1983.
45. All Pierpoint quotations taken from author's interview with Jack Pierpoint, Sep. 8, 1983, unless otherwise noted.
46. Pierpoint to Brodhead, Mar. 22, 1971.
47. Author's interview with Jean Pelletier, Aug. 15, 1983.

48. F. J. Chambers, CIDA Planning Division, to CUSO, May 26, 1971.
49. CUSO Finance Officer to CIDA, Nov. 8, 1972, and to CUSO/Nigeria, Jan. 5, 1973.

Chapter VII

1. The section dealing with Murray Thomson's pre-CUSO career is based largely on an unpublished Master's thesis by Paul McGinnis, who was a volunteer and later a Field Staff Officer in Thailand; "Murray Thomson: Prophetic Reformer in 'The Land of Smiles'," Paul St. Clair McGinnis, University of Saskatchewan, 1972.
2. *Ibid*, p.42.
3. Unless otherwise noted, all Thomson quotations are taken from the author's interview, June 4, 1983.
4. Minutes of the first CUSO Thailand Committee Meeting, cited in McGinnis, op cit.
5. Jim McFeteridge to author, Aug. 8, 1983.
6. Author's interview with Dave Beer, July 18 & 20, 1983.
7. Author's interview with Peter Hoffman, July 2, 1983.
8. Minutes of Asia Regional Meeting held at Kuala Lumpur, July 21-25, 1971, quoted in McGinnis, op cit p.63.
9. Catmur to Thomson, quoted in McGinnis, op cit.
10. All Gordon quotations taken from author's interview, Aug. 25, 1983.
11. Murray Thomson to author, Oct. 4, 1973.
12. All McNeill quotations taken from author's interview, July 25, 1983.
13. All Bryant quotations taken from author's interview, June 21, 1983.
14. "CUSO and the Development Process" by Rob Dumont, *The Green and White*, University of Saskatchewan, Spring, 1974.
15. Author's interview with Lewis Perinbam, Aug. 10, 1983.
16. All Freebury quotations taken from author's interview, July 20, 1983.
17. Author's interview with Ray Clark, Sep. 6, 1983.
18. Speech by Murray Thomson at the 44th Couchiching Conference, printed in *Canada and the Third World*, Canadian Institute on Public Affairs, Toronto, 1975, pp.156-7.
19. Author's interview with Jack Pierpoint, Sep. 8, 1983.
20. Jim McFeteridge to author, Aug. 8, 1983.
21. Thomson to author, Oct. 4, 1973.
22. Couchiching speech, op cit.

Chapter VIII

1. Minutes, ECSA Regional Meeting, Sept. 1980.
2. Author's interview with Peter Hoffman, July 2, 1983.
3. "Decentralization and the B.S. Debate," by Robin Wilson, May 9, 1977.
4. Author's interview with Stan Percival, June 21, 1983.
5. "Go Abroad Young Man, The Home Front's Hell," *Maclean's*, March 24, 1979.
6. Ann McRae to CUSO Board Chairman, Feb. 12, 1979.
7. *Maclean's*, op cit.
8. "Youth and Responsibility," by Gordon Fairweather, *Canadian Business*, Jan. 1969.

Chapter IX

1. "Major Personal Changes in a Group of Canadians Working in Nigeria," Glen Filson, unpublished PhD Thesis, University of Toronto, 1975, p.139.
2. "Major Personal Changes in 40 Returned CUSO volunteers," Paul McGinnis, unpublished PhD Thesis, Department of Educational Theory, University of Toronto, 1975, p.143.
3. Toronto *Globe and Mail*, Oct. 16, 1961.
4. *The Caribbean Connection*, Robert Chodos, James Lorimer, Toronto, 1977, p.185.
5. *World Development Report 1984*, O.U.P., New York, 1984, pp.178-9.
6. Author's interview with Rieky Stuart, July 18, 1983.
7. "Volunteers and Neo-Colonialism" by Glynn Roberts; quoted in *CUSO Forum*, No. 2, 1973.
8. "Smiling Faces Going Places," by Tim Brodhead, *CUSO Forum*, Vol. 3, No. 4, 1981.
9. *Newstatements*, Vol. 1, No. 1, 1971.
10. Stuart interview, op cit.
11. "Development Education in the Schools: A look at the Main Issues," G. Lacelle & J. Maxwell; Department of Adult Education, OISE, 1983.
12. "Reaching an Impasse: The North South Debate," by Brian Tomlinson. Published in *Ties That Bind; Canada and the Third World*, Between the Lines, Toronto, 1982, p.82.
13. *CUSO Forum*, July, 1976.
14. Ken Wyman, Oxfam fund raiser, quoted in *Maclean's*, Apr. 13, 1981.
15. All Shulman and Wilson quotation taken from "Transcript of Morton Shul-

man interview with Robin Wilson, CITY TV, July 12, 1977;'' CUSO files, unless otherwise noted.
16. Author's interview with Robin Wilson, Aug. 8, 1983.
17. See *Pressure Groups in the Global System*, Peter Willetts (ed.), Frances Pinter, London, 1982.
18. Kasper Pold to author, Nov. 3, 1980.
19. Speech at AQOCI Meeting, Feb. 15, 1982; quoted in ''Development Education in Canada,'' op cit.
20. ''A Report on Canadian Attitudes Towards Foreign Aid,'' prepared by Adcom Research Ltd., CIDA, May 1981.

Chapter XI

1. Latin American Working Group *Letter*, Toronto, Vol. IV, No. 3/4, March, 1977.
2. ''My Washington Years,'' Charles Ritchie, *Saturday Night*, Aug. 1983.
6. LAWG Letter, op cit.
4. All trade statistics taken from records of Statistics Canada and Department of Industry, Trade and Commerce figures.
5. Fidel Castro; English Language *Granma*, March 24, 1968.
6. All Bogdasavich quotations taken from author's interview, July 27, 1983.
7. Author's interview with Chris Bryant, June 21, 1983.
8. Joe Vise to Richard Ingram, March 24, 1971; CUSO files.
9. ''Collaboration between the University of British Columbia and two Latin American Universities in Post Graduate Engineering Education,'' paper presented by Dr. A. Neisen to UNESCO Symposium, Paris, Dec. 11-14, 1979.
10. Recounted in *Globe and Mail* editorial, Jan. 22, 1981.
11. LAWG letter, op cit.
12. ''Cuba, The Soviet Union and Africa,'' by E. Gonzales, published in *Africa and International Communism*, D. E. Albright, ed., Indiana Press, 1980, p.153.
13. *Men in the Shadows*, John Sawatsky, Doubleday, 1980.
14. Author's interview with John Gordon, Aug. 25, 1983.
16. Recounted in *The Canadian Caper*, Pelletier and Adams, MacMillan, 1981.
17. ''Statement on East West Relations and Detente, Distributed on Behalf of the Secty. of State for External Affairs, Flora MacDonald, to Delegates and Members of the Press at the North Atlantic Assembly Ministerial Meeting, Brussels, Dec. 13, 1979.''

18. R. Maione, Director General, NGO Division, CIDA, to CUSO Executive Director, Jan. 8, 1980.

Chapter XII

1. Quotations are taken from Bezanson letter to author, Feb. 13, 1984.

Chapter XIII

1. Author's interview with Jean Pelletier, Aug. 15, 1983.
2. "Village Technical Training Program:" A Proposal; 1972, CUSO Files.
3. "Bangladesh Task Force Report," Oct. 1974, CUSO files.
4. Quotations relating to Raymond Cournoyer's early life are taken from a letter from Cournoyer to M. Yahiya and Siddiqur Rahman, Mar. 1, 1979.
5. Unless otherwise noted, quotations relating to Cournoyer's work in Calcutta and with CUSO are taken from author's interview with R. Cournoyer, June 15, 1983.
6. Cournoyer letter, op cit.
7. Statistics are taken from "Canadian Development Assistance to Bangladesh," Roger Ehrhardt, North South Institute, 1983. Ehrhardt states: "For the greater part of the 1960s, the major food donors in Bangladesh (including Canada) chose to concentrate their efforts on . . . . program food aid, and thus on balance of payments and domestic revenue problems. But there has been some dissatisfaction with this approach, mainly in terms of distribution of benefits and the potential effects on Bangladesh's food policy. Although program food aid has indirectly benefitted food consumers in the urban and rural areas (including deficit and marginal farmers), the most direct benefit has gone to urban residents and government employees, who are relatively well off compared to these poorer groups. Food aid has thus been an inequitable way of easing the food burden of the poorest groups in Bangladesh." p.106.
8. *Common Crisis*, Willy Brandt et al, Pan Books, London, 1983.
9. *The Agrarian Structure of Rural Bangladesh*, F. T. Januzzi & J. T. Peach, Westview Press, Boulder Colo., 1980, p.33.
10. *Ibid*, p.41.
11. *CUSO Forum*, Vol. 6, No. 3, 1978.
12. "Foreign Aid That Really Works," article by Douglas Roche, M.P., in *Reader's Digest*, Feb. 1978, p.51.

13. *What Development is All About*, Douglas Roche, M.P., NC Press, Toronto, 1979, p.125.
14. *Reader's Digest*, op cit.
15. "Studies of the Small Development Activities of the NGOs," Ministry of Agriculture and Forests, Government of Bangladesh, Dhaka, May, 1979.
16. "A Study into the Proshika Process," S. Dasgupta et al, Vol. 1, July, 1981; CUSO files, Ottawa.
17. *CUSO Forum*, op cit.

Chapter XIV

1. *Royal Service*, Stephen P. Barry, Avon, New York, 1983, p.175.
2. Author's interview with Raymond Clark, Sep. 6, 1983.

Chapter XV

1. "Report of Visits to Six Countries in East and Central Africa," Duncan Edmonds, July/Aug., 1962, CUSO files.
2. Unless otherwise noted, all Beer quotations are from the author's interview, July 18, 1983.
3. *Man Deserves Man*, McWhinney and Godfrey (eds.), Ryerson Press, Toronto, 1968, p.342.
4. *Ibid*, pp.316-17.
5. *Ibid*, p. 321.
6. Author's interview with Colin Freebury, July 20, 1983.

Chapter XVI

1. *Portugal in Africa*, James Duffy, Penguin, 1961, p.111.
2. *In the Eye of the Storm: Angola's People*, Basil Davison, Doubleday Anchor, New York, 1973, p.153.
3. *Autobiography of Kwame Nkrumah*, K. Nkrumah, Nelson, New York, 1957, p.14.
4. *Guerilla Struggle in Africa; An Analysis and Preview*, K. W. Grundy, Grossman, New York, 1971, p.133.
5. *Words and Deeds: Canada, Portugal and Africa*, TCLSAC, Toronto, 1976, p.8.

6. *Portuguese Africa and the West*, William Minter, Penguin, 1972, p.71.
7. *Ibid*, p.103.
8. Minutes of Proceedings and Evidence of the Standing Committee on External Affairs and National Defence, June 1, 1971.
9. "The Situation in Southern Africa," Excerpts from a Press Conference by Hon. P. E. Trudeau, Singapore, Jan. 20, 1971.
10. *Globe and Mail*, Toronto, March 10, 1971.
11. *Ibid*, March 12, 1971.
12. Beer interview, July 18, 1983.
13. *Globe and Mail*, Mar. 19, 1971.
14. "Minutes" op cit. pg 30:66.
15. *Ibid*, pg 30:102.
16. "Canadian Humanitarian Aid for Southern Africa," by Paul Ladouceur, printed in *Canada, Scandinavia and Southern Africa*, D. Anglin et al (eds.), Scandinavian Institute of Foreign Studies, Uppsala, 1978.
17. "Canadian Humanitarian Aid for Southern Africa," Statement by External Affairs Minister Mitchell Sharp, Feb. 21, 1974.
18. Memo, Dave Beer to CUSO Board of Directors, Feb. 28, 1974.
19. "Common Statements," endorsed by several NGOs for transmission to Mitchell Sharp following a meeting in Toronto, Mar. 6, 1974.
20. Ladouceur, op cit.
21. Author's interview with Jean Pelletier, Aug. 15, 1983.
22. Ladouceur, op cit.
23. Author's interview with Brian Rowe, July 1, 1984.

Chapter XVII

1. *The Struggle for Zimbabwe*, David Martin & Phillis Johnson, Zimbabwe Publishing House, Salisbury, 1981, p.1.
2. "Report of Visits to Six Countries in East and Central Africa," Duncan Edmonds, July/August, 1962; CUSO files.
3. Martin and Johnson, op cit, p.51.
4. *Ibid*, p.55.
5. *Under the Skin; The Death of White Rhodesia*, David Caute, Penguin, 1983, p.56.
6. Martin and Johnson, op cit. p.58.
7. *Ibid*, p.93.
8. *Ibid*, p.61.
9. *Ibid*, p.63

10. Caute, op cit, p.40.
11. *Ibid*, p.369.
12. *Guerilla Struggle in Africa, An Analysis and Preview*, K. W. Grundy, Grossman, New York, 1971. p.44.
13. Martin and Johnson, op cit, p.212.
14. Interview with Saul Ndlovu, Victoria Monday Magazine, Victoria, B.C., June 22, 1979.
15. *CUSO and Radicalism*, B. Lapajne, C-FAR, Toronto, 1983, Introduction.
16. "How Far Can They See?", Chris Bryant, *CUSO Forum*, Jan. 1984.
17. "Canadian Bank Loans to South Africa," John Saul, printed in *Canada, Scandinavia and Southern Africa*, D. Anglin et al (eds.), Scandinavian Institute of African Studies, Uppsala, 1978, p.29.
18. *Words and Deeds: Canada, Portugal and Africa*, TCLSAC, Toronto, 1976, p.21.
19. *Winnipeg Free Press*, Aug. 18, 1979.
20. David Beer to David Humphries of the *Globe and Mail*, July 5, 1979.
21. Aide Memoire: "Briefing With Doug Roche: July 13, 1979," CUSO files, Ottawa.
22. *Globe and Mail*, Aug. 4, 1979.
23. *Globe and Mail*, Aug. 9, 1979.
24. Toronto *Sun*, Aug. 9, 1979.
25. Toronto *Sun*, Aug. 10, 1979.
26. Toronto *Sun*, Aug. 19, 1979.
27. Webster to Beer, Nov. 12, 1979.
28. Roche to Dupuy, Aug. 31, 1979.
29. *Man Deserves Man*, McWhinney and Godfrey (eds.) Ryerson Press, Toronto, 1968, p.326.
30. Caute, op cit. p.427.
31. Author's interview with David Beer, July 18, 1983.
32. Letter from CUSO et al, to Robert Mugabe, Feb. 17, 1983; CUSO files.
33. Minutes of meeting between R. Mugabe and M. Behr et al, Harare, Mar. 2. 1983.

Chapter XVIII

1. Quotations form *CUSO Forum*, Vol. 6, No. 2, 1978.

Chapter XIX

1. *Profile South Africa*, Australian Catholic Relief, Sydney, 1983.
2. *South Africa in the 1980s*, CIIR, London, 1981, p.14.
3. *Biko*, Donald Woods, Vintage, New York, 1979, p.31.
4. *Southern Africa; The New Politics of Revolution*, Davidson, Slovo & Wilkinson, Pelican, 1976, pp.139-141.
5. *Living in the Interregnum*, Nadine Gordimer, New York Review of Books, Jan. 1983.
6 United Church Observer, June, 1981
7. *Minutes of Proceedings and Evidence* of the Standing Committee on External Affairs and National Defence, House of Commons, June 1, 1971.
8. "Canadian Humanitarian Aid to Southern Africa," Paul Ladouceur, published in: *Canada, Scandinavia and Southern Africa*, Anglin, Shaw & Widstrand (eds.). Scandinavian Institute of African Studies, Uppsala, 1978, p.87.
9. *Report of the Commission of Enquiry* into the Espionage Activities of the South African Government in the International University Exchange Fund, 1980, CUSO files.
10. Woods, op cit, p.146.
11. *The Observer*, London, Jan. 6, 1980.
12. 'Report . . . . ' op cit, p.38.
13. *Sunday Times*, London, circa Jan. 1981.
14. Author's interview with Tim Brodhead, July 26, 1983.
15. 'Report . . . . ' op cit, p.5.
16. *Ibid*, p.24.
17. *Black Trade Unions in South Africa*, M. Plaut & D. Ward, Spokesmen for the Bertrand Russell Peace Foundation, Nottingham, 1982.
18. *Kaunda on Violence*, Kenneth Kaunda, Sphere Books, London, 1982, p. 178.

Chapter XX

Quotations from *FORUM* Vol. 2. No. 4 1980.

Chapter XXI

1. All quotations from Lewis Perinbam are taken from author's interview, Aug. 10, 1983.
2. House of Commons Debates, Mar. 24, 1961.
3. Quoted in CUSO Bulletin, Apr. 1962.
4. Author's interview with Bill McWhinney, July 6, 1983.
5. All quotations from Dr. G. C. Andrew are taken from an interview with Barbara Hoffman, Oct. 29, 1980, or "Personal Recollections of the Origins of the Early Days of CUSO" (transcribed), by G. C. Andrew, Jan. 19, 1982.
6. Author's interview with Duncan Edmonds, Aug. 3, 1983.
7. Quotations from Dr. F. Leddy are taken from an interview with Peter Hoffman, Autumn 1980, and from "The Origins of CUSO" by Dr. F. Leddy, May 16, 1981.
8. Chester Ronning to Under Secretary of State for External Affairs, Mar. 15, 1964.
9. Speech by Hon. Paul Martin to National Conference of Canadian Universities and Colleges, Ottawa, Apr. 20, 1964.
10. For a discussion of the early days of The Company of Young Canadians, see *The Children's Crusade*, Ian Hamilton, Toronto, 1971; and *The Revolution Game*, Margaret Daly, New Press; Toronto, 1970.
11. "Statement by the Prime Minister; Canadian University Service Overseas," Press Release, Feb. 7, 1966.
12. *A Samaritan State?*, Keith Spicer, University of Toronto Press, 1966, p.103.
13. *Ibid*, p.215.
14. *Half a Loaf*, Clyde Sanger, p.128.
15. Author's interview with Frank Bogdasavich, Jul. 27, 1983.
16. Author's interview with Murray Thomson, June 4, 1983.
17. *Strategy for International Development Cooperation*, Information Canada, 1975, p.23.
18. Author's interview with Peter Hoffman, July 2, 1983.
19. Author's interview with Robin Wilson, Aug. 8, 1983.

Chapter XXII

1. Quotations are taken from Ray Clark's letter to CUSO/Ottawa, Oct. 3, 1982, or from the author's interview with Clark, Sep. 6, 1983.

Chapter XXIII

1. "Report — Trip to Africa," Louis Berubé, Apr. 1965.
2. *Man Deserves Man*, McWhinney and Godfrey (eds.) Ryerson Press, Toronto, 1968, pp.138-39.
3. Letter, Paul Hitschfield to author, October 10, 1984.
4. All Guindon and Tellier quotes are from McWhinney and Godfrey, op. cit. pp 117-123
5. Unless otherwise noted, all Bogdasavich quotations are from the author's interview, July 27, 1983.
6. "CUSO and Canada," F. Bogdasavich, circa 1968, CUSO files, Ottawa.
7. "Options of Legislative Reform," Henri Sire, July 4, 1973, CUSO files.
8. Unless otherwise noted, all Pelletier quotations are from the author's interview, Aug. 15, 1983.
9. Unless otherwise noted, all Gordon quotations are from the author's interview, Aug. 25, 1983.
10. Unless otherwise noted, all Leger quotations are from the author's interview, July 13, 1983.
11. *"CUSO: What Price Unity?,"* Roxanna Spicer, Journalism Honours Paper, Carleton University, 1975, p.18.
12. CUSO/SUCO Board Minutes, July 7, 1973.
13. "The SUCO Crisis," letter from returned volunteers and staff, circa Aug. 28, 1974: CUSO files, Ottawa (translation).
14. Letter, John Gordon to David Beer, Nov. 2, 1973; CUSO files Ottawa.
15. Spicer, op cit. p.16.
16. Unless otherwise noted, all Thomson quotations are from the author's interview, June 4, 1983.
17. "CUSO Trends in 1974," Murray Thomson, *CUSO Forum*, Jan. 1974.
18. "A Position Paper," Kasper Pold, Apr. 18. 1975; CUSO files, Ottawa.
19. Spicer, op cit, p.28.
20. *Ibid*.
21. "The Constitutional Issue: The New Pattern of Our Relations with CUSO" SUCO Regional Meeting Document No. 10, 1974 (translation); CUSO files.
22. Spicer, op cit, p.32.
23. "Anglophones Provoke Crisis in SUCO," SUCO Press Release Board Document No. 51, Mar. 7, 1974; CUSO files (translation).
24. Letter, R. Leger to Board, Mar. 5, 1974.

25. Minutes of CUSO/SUCO Board Executive Committee telephone call, Mar. 20, 1974; CUSO files, Ottawa.
26. "The SUCO Crisis," letter from returned volunteers and staff, circa Aug. 28, 1974: CUSO files, Ottawa (translation).
27. "Visit to Francophone Regional Meeting," Juanita Poole, Nov. 16, 1974; CUSO files, Ottawa.
28. CUSO Forum, Jan. 1975.
29. Spicer, op cit. p.21.
30. *Ibid*, p.35.
31. "New Horizon For Cooperation," A. Ambrosi et al., CUSO/SUCO Board Document No. 44, 1978 (translation).
32. *La Presse*, Montreal, July 8, 1983 (translation).
33. "Why We Are Leaving SUCO,"J. Jobin et al., Le Devoir, July 14, 1983 (translation).
34. Telegram to French language media from Chairperson, SUCO Board of Directors, July 14, 1983 (translation).
35. *Le Devoir*, July 18, 1983.
36. *Globe and Mail*, July 22, 1983.
37. Letter from Jean Luc Pepin to SUCO volunteers, Oct. 1983, (translation).
38. "New Horizon For Cooperation," A. Ambrosi et al., CUSO/SUCO Board Document No. 44, 1978 (translation).

Chapter XXIV

1. "Canada and Latin America." J. C. M. Ogelsby, in *Canada and the Third World*, Peyton V. Lyon and Tareq Y. Ismael eds., Macmillan, Toronto, 1976, p.169.
2. *Ibid*, p.181.
3. *Land and Power in South America*, Sven Lindqvist, Penguin, 1979, p.108.
4. *South* magazine, July 1985.
5. *Ibid*.
6. Author's interview with Tim and Sherry Thomson, Nov. 7, 1983.
7. *Man Deserves Man*, McWhinney and Godfrey eds., Ryerson Press, Toronto, 1966, p.299.
8. Author's interview with Diego Laneuville, July 5, 1983.
9. "CUSO and Workers Unite," *CUSO Forum*, Vol. 6, No. 2, 1978.
10. CUSO Country Plan, Peru/Bolivia 1976-77; Oct. 1975; CUSO files.
11. "Work in Bolivian Mining Cooperatives: Final Report," Darrell Martindale, July 1981; CUSO files.

12. *CUSO Forum*, op cit.
13. "Mining with Little Machinery," *CUSO Forum*, Winter, 1980.
14. *Tin: Its Production and Marketing*, William Robertson, Croom Helm, London, 1982, p.188.
15. Calculated on the basis of 1979 import levels and 1983 prices; Robertson, op cit, and *South* (magazine), Jan. 1984.

Chapter XXV

1. *Sideshow*, William Shawcross, Pocket books, New York. 1979; pp.36-37.
2. *Letting a Nation Die*, John Pilger, *CUSO Forum*, Summer, 1980.
3. *Ibid*.
4. "Murray Thomson: Prophetic Reformer in the Land of Smiles," Paul McGinnis, unpublished PhD thesis, University of Saskatchewan, 1972, p.81.
5. McFetridge to author, Oct. 25, 1983.
6. An example of the official Kampuchean attitude is quoted from the Hanoi daily newspaper, Nhan Dan, in *Rice, Rivalry and Politics*, Linda Mason and Roger Brown, University of Notre Dame Press, 1983, p.23:

> The imperialists and international reactionaries have been resorting to a new calumnating trick against the PRK charging the latter with refusing or hampering humanitarian assistance to the Kampuchean people. Trying to show off themselves as humane, they put out the so-called 'assistance to both sides.' . . . But all these allegations are in fact nothing but a smoke screen to cover up their dark design of making a picture of the existence of the Pol Pot-Ieng Sary genocidal administration, the lackeys of Peking, overthrown by the Kampuchean people — and then deceiving world public opinion at large . . . The ugly calumny resorted to by the imperialists and the international reactionaries only lays bare their trick of using humanitarianism for interfering in the internal affairs of Kampuchea, and trying to reanimate the Pol Pot corpse.

For a detailed discussion of the Oxfam position and the overall relief effort, see *The Quality of Mercy*, William Shawcross, Deutsch, London, 1984.
7. Mason and Brown, op cit, p.38.

8. Author's interview with Raymond Cournoyer, Nov. 25, 1983; all other Cournoyer quotations are from this interview unless otherwise noted.
9. Mason and Brown, op cit, p.172.
10. Meeting took place in author's presence.
11. Reported to CUSO Ottawa by Raymond Cournoyer in a memo dated April 14, 1980 after a meeting with MCC representative in Bangkok.
12. Maione discussion with author, Feb. 1980.
13. Transcript of telephone conversation; Thomson/Turcot to Ottawa, March 27, 1980; CUSO files, Ottawa.
14. Memo from Lily Mah Sen to Barbara Brown, April 11, 1980; CUSO files, Ottawa.
15. "Cambodian Relief is Being Used to Bolster Pol Pot" by Susan George, *Le Monde*, Jan 31, 1980.
16. "They're Not Our Brothers, They're Us;" Notes for an Address to Vancouver Kiwanis Club, Iona Campagnolo, Vancouver, July 31, 1980; files.
17. *Ibid*.
18. CUSO fund raising letter signed by Hon. Iona Campagnolo and Hon. Flora MacDonald, Aug. 1983; CUSO files.
19. *Kingston Whig Standard*, Nov. 3, 1980.
20. "Report of the Project Evaluation," Malee Sundhagul et al, CUSO Bangkok, February, 1982; CUSO files.

Chapter XXVI

1. *Canada as a Principal Power*, D. B. Dewitt and J. J. Kirton, John Wiley & Sons, Toronto, 1983, p.81.
2. *Ibid*.
3. *Parliamentary Task Force on North-South Relations; Report to the House of Commons on the Relations Between Developed and Developing Countries*, Canadian Government Publishing Centre, 1980, p.18.
4. *Ties That Bind*, Robert Clarke and Richard Swift (Eds.) Between the Lines, Toronto, 1982, p.162.
5. *Perpetuating Poverty*, Robert Carty and Virginia Smith, Between the Lines, Toronto, 1981, p.178.
6. *CUSO and Radicalism*, Branka Lapajne, Citizens For Foreign Aid Reform Inc., Toronto, 1983.
7. *Ibid*.
8. "Additional Notes on C-FAR," Chris Bryant, Jan. 1984; CUSO files.

9. "The Politics of Education in Zambia," J. C. Saxby, unpublished PhD Thesis, University of Toronto, 1980, p. 651.
10. *Ibid*, p.683.
11. *Universal Primary Education in Nigeria*, Mark Bray, Routledge & Kegan Paul, London, 1981, p.4.
12. *CUSO Forum*, Vol. 3, No. 3, May 1985.
13. *New Nigeria*, Kaduna, June 17, 1971.
14. All Harold quotations are taken from the author's interview with Jennifer Harold, Nov. 5, 1983.

UNCTAD	United Nations Commisson for Trade and Development
UNICEF	United Nations Childrens Fund
UNDP	United Nations Development Program
UNESCO	United Nations Educational and Scientific Organization
UNHCR	United Nations High Commission for Refugees
USAID	United States Agency for International Development
UWI	University of the West Indies
VSO	Voluntary Service Overseas
WUS	World University Service
WUSC	World University Service of Canada

Following their independence a number of former colonies changed their names. The colonial name has been used in the text of this book when referring to events which occurred before independence.

New Name	Former Name
Bangladesh	East Pakistan
East Pakistan	East Bengal
Ghana	Gold Coast
Guyana	British Guiana
Harare (capital of Zimbabwe)	Salisbury
Maputo (Capital of Mozambique)	Lourenzo Marques
Malawi	Nyasaland
Malaysia	Malaya
Rhodesia	Southern Rhodesia
Sri Lanka	Ceylon
Tanzania	Tanganyika
Vanuatu	New Hebrides
Zambia	Northern Rhodesia
Zimbabwe	Rhodesia

AGM	Annual General Meeting (CUSO)
ANC	African National Congress (South Africa)
AUCC	Association of Universities and Colleges of Canada
BCM	Black Consciousness Movement (South Africa)
BOSS	Bureau of State Security (South Africa)
C-FAR Inc.	Canadians for Foreign Aid Reform Inc.
CIDA	Canadian International Development Agency
COV	Canadian Overseas Volunteers
CUSO	Canadian Univeristy Service Overseas; after 1981 there was a legal name change; although it was no longer an acronym, it was still printed 'CUSO'
CVCS	Canadian Voluntary Commonwealth Service
CYC	Company of Young Canadians
EAO	External Aid Office; forerunner to CIDA
FNLA	National Front for the Liberation of Angola
FRELIMO	Front for the Liberation of Mozambique
FSO	Field Staff Officer (CUSO)
IRM	Inter-Regional Meeting (CUSO)
IUEF	International University Exchange Fund
JBC	Jamaica Broadcasting Corporation
LSE	London School of Economics
MPLA	Popular Movement for the Liberation of Angola
NGO	Non Governmental Organization
NUSAS	National Union of South African Students
OAS	Organization of African States
OAU	Organization of African Unity
Oxfam/Canada	Oxfam/UK started during World War II and is today
Oxfam/UK	One of Britain's largest charitable
Oxfam Quebec	organizations. The Canadian branch became independent in the mid-1970s, and Oxfam Quebec separated from the Canadian operation at the same time. There are also Oxfam organizations in Belgium and the US
PAC	Pan Africàn Congress (South Africa)
PAIGC	African Party for the Independence of Guinea and Cape Verde
RV	Returned Volunteer
SACTU	South African Congress of Trades Unions
SCI	Service Civil International
SUCO	Service Universitaire Canadien Outre-mer; after 1981 there was a legal name change; although it was no longer a translation of CUSO, nor an acronym, it was still printed 'SUCO'
TESL	Teaching English as a second language

UNCTAD	United Nations Commisson for Trade and Development
UNICEF	United Nations Childrens Fund
UNDP	United Nations Development Program
UNESCO	United Nations Educational and Scientific Organization
UNHCR	United Nations High Commission for Refugees
USAID	United States Agency for International Development
UWI	University of the West Indies
VSO	Voluntary Service Overseas
WUS	World University Service
WUSC	World University Service of Canada

Following their independence a number of former colonies changed their names. The colonial name has been used in the text of this book when referring to events which occurred before independence.

New Name	Former Name
Bangladesh	East Pakistan
East Pakistan	East Bengal
Ghana	Gold Coast
Guyana	British Guiana
Harare (capital of Zimbabwe)	Salisbury
Maputo (Capital of Mozambique)	Lourenzo Marques
Malawi	Nyasaland
Malaysia	Malaya
Rhodesia	Southern Rhodesia
Sri Lanka	Ceylon
Tanzania	Tanganyika
Vanuatu	New Hebrides
Zambia	Northern Rhodesia
Zimbabwe	Rhodesia

Index

Dalai Lama, the 54-6
Demarara Bauxite Company ('Demba') 27-9, 39
Desjardins, Andre 315-6, 318-326
development, definition of iii-iv, 181
development education 88, 99, 103, 112, 122-138, 207, 298, 304
Dewitt, David 351, 354
Diefenbaker, Elmer 10-11
Diefenbaker, John 10-12, 27, 144, 255-7
Dominica 43-5, 49-50, 356
Dupuy, Michel 221-223, 225, 272
Durance, Harry 332

Ecuador 313
Edmonds, Duncan v, 193-4, 212-213, 256-63, 269, 275
Edwards, Bruce 249-53, 362
Enang, Felix 81
Eriksson, Lars-Gunnar 241-46
Esmonde, Phil 47
Essien, Udo 160-162
Ethiopia 150, 193
Evoy, Lance 105
External Affairs, Department of 50, 73, 146, 155-7, 233, 267, 293, 297, 356
External Aid Office (EAO) 109, 256, 258-9, 264

FENCOMIN (Federacion Nacional de Cooperativas Mineras) 317, 319, 322, 324
FRELIMO (Front for the Liberation of Mozambique) 201, 207
Fairweather, Gordon 121
Falke, Herman v
Faris, Donald K. 9-10, 361
'Fifth Estate, The' 338, 341
Filson, Glen v, 123
Filson, Vivian 123
Forsythe, Frederick 66-7
Ford, Robert 10
Forum (CUSO) 228

Williamson, Craig 241-6
Wilson, Harold 197
Wilson, Robin v, 113-117, 119, 132-3, 272
Wings of Hope 250-3
Winsor, Hugh 196, 205
Wise, Susanne vi
Wood, John 95-7, 288
Woolcombe, Steve v
World Council of Churches 69-70, 208, 241
World University Service (WUS) 6, 8
World University Service of Canada (WUSC) 6-9, 12, 15-16, 101, 255
Worthington, Peter 78-9

YMCA 30-32, 331
Yusuf, Tundey 363

ZANU (Zimbabwe African National Union) 215-217, 320-322, 226
ZAPU (Zimbabwe African People's Union) 214-217, 219, 221, 226, 230
Zaire (Congo-Kinshasa) 206, 281, 285
Zambia 71, 105, 194, 197, 205, 212, 215, 220, 225, 238-9, 248, 359
Zimbabwe, see also Rhodesia 153, 212-230, 358
Zink, Ria 220
Zukowski, Helena vi